WITHDRAWN

Brown Was the Danube

Brown Was the Danube

HELEN HILSENRAD

With an Introduction
by Harry Golden

New York · Thomas Yoseloff · London

Library of Congress Catalogue Card Number: 65–17828

Thomas Yoseloff, Publisher

South Brunswick, New Jersey

Thomas Yoseloff Ltd

18 Charing Cross Road

London W.C.2, England

6292

Printed in the United States of America

Acknowledgments

I want to express my heart-felt gratitude to Leslie Winter Strom, Harry Golden, and Roger Klein, without whose help and encouragement this book would not have been possible.

Introduction
by Harry Golden

Ah, the Danube and Johann Strauss, and the *"Tales From The Vienna Woods,"* and *shnitzel,* and the kaiser roll with poppy seeds yet, all of which helped camouflage some of the most pathological anti-Semites in the world. Adolph Hitler, let us remember, was an Austrian too.

And the Jews themselves were not immune to the romance. Most of us from the Galician province of this Austrian remnant of the Holy Roman Empire always answered "Vienna" when the teacher asked us where we came from. *"Aus Wien!"* And how we all loved to say that *Aus Wien,* "from Vienna."

Brown Was the Danube is a sad book, sad not only because of the story Helen Hilsenrad tells us about the life of the Jews in Austria after the Nazis took over the country, but sad because between the lines you can sense Helen's terrible chagrin and sorrow that all of this could have happened in Vienna, Vienna, Vienna! Ah, Vienna!

Part of the romance too was old Emperor Franz-Josef. My own father, as did most of the Jews, spoke of him as *Froyem-Yussell,* a Yiddish translation of the name, and they spoke of him with stars in their eyes and often with a tear or two. But the benevolent monarch was getting old and Austrian anti-Semitism asserted itself at every possible opening. Way back

9

in the 1890's, when the Christian-Socialist Party gained power under the leadership of Herr Lueger, the legal restrictions against the Jews were passed into law, which made them second-class citizens. This came to pass only a few years after the Jewish Rothschilds had built the railroads of Austria, and the Jewish-owned Witkowitz steel plants built the armaments for the Austrian armies. It's what I tell my Jewish audiences— *gurnisht helffen,* nothing helps.

With the coming of Hitler the anti-Semites came out of the woodwork in droves and Helen Hilsenrad tells a moving story of what happened to the Viennese Jews, the elite of European Jewry. There are no horrors in this book, as we have come to learn of Dachau and Auschwitz horrors, but Mrs. Hilsenrad tells us what a steady process of dehumanization is like. And precisely because Helen Hilsenrad is not a professional writer this autobiographical sketch, of one of the most critical moments of world history, is not only a moving story but one of great value to students and scholars of the future.

Listen to Mrs. Hilsenrad as she tells us how this process of dehumanization worked : as an example, the Nazis had confiscated the wealth of the Jewish community. Then they sent warrants ordering the Jews to leave Austria within five days or be sent to a concentration camp. The order contained one qualification. All the back taxes had to be paid in full. Since the Gestapo knew full well that they possessed all the available funds belonging to the Jews, there was no way in which anyone could pay these back taxes. We all know the rest of the story.

Maybe Austria regrets it now. Because if the anti-Semites inflicted a terror upon the Jews, they inflicted as great a terror upon themselves and upon the world. They believed for a moment in history, you could make barbarism a policy of state. They inspired brutishness not only in their beaurocrats but in a people who for years had sat in pleasant coffeehouses listening to the strains of the "Blue Danube Waltz."

But Helen Hilsenrad reminds them that it was really *The Brown Danube*—and I am grateful to her for putting it in such good writing.

Foreword

IN THE YEAR 1795, POLAND WAS PARTITIONED AMONG ITS neighbors—Prussia, Russia, and Austria. Galicia was the part which came under Austrian domination and remained so until the end of the First World War. The three largest cities in Galicia were the capital, Lwow, Cracow—once a place of residence for Polish kings—and Przemysl, which was a fortress. There were also towns, but most of them were *shteitls* (little towns) and were inhabited by many Jews.

When in the twelfth century Jews were dispersed from Germany, Boleslow the Pious, ruler of Great Poland, encouraged Jews to come to Poland and gave privileges to them. Again in the thirteenth century, the noble King Casimir the Great invited more Jews to enter Poland and added more regulations to safeguard the Jewish population. They brought to the country western civilization and low German, which compounded with Hebrew and a little Polish emerged as a dialect known as Yiddish.

Although the Jews suffered many persecutions under later kings, who were anti-Semitic, as was the Polish population, they remained true to their religion and traditions. This was especially true in the *shteitls*, of which the best known was

13

Belz, because of a dynasty of wonder *Rebbes* who lived there. Most of the Jews were Hassidim, followers of the founder, Baal Shem Tov. They grew beards and earlocks. Their traditional clothes were long black coats and black round hats.

On the Sabbath they wore long black heavy silk coats and fur-trimmed hats called *shtramel*. Generally, they lived in poor conditions, but on Sabbath every Jew was a king. Each *shteitl* had its own *Rebby*. In the morning the men went to *shul* and in the afternoon, at the *Rebby's* house, they rejoiced and hallowed the holy Sabbath.

When boys reached the age of three, they were sent to *heder* where the *melamed* (teacher) instructed them in the *alev baith* (the Hebrew alphabet). By the age of five, a boy could chant parts of Genesis.

There were also more progressive Jews in those *shteitls* and in the larger towns, where parents sent their children to public schools. Generally, the Jewish people lived in Galicia and were no different, under the laws of nature, from others who lived there. They sought a peaceful existence and the freedom to pursue their own way of life. Then came the holocaust. The Nazis destroyed them, young and old, in a barbarism unprecedented in human history. Only the old broken houses in those *shteitls* and towns remained as witnesses that there was once Jewish life there.

Contents

Illustrations

Brown Was the Danube

PART I
Childhood: The Ingrown Years

I

In 1895, I was born in the town of Przemysl in Galicia, which was under Austrian domination. Because this city was a fortress, there were several military camps where many soldiers and officers were stationed. There was also a coffeehouse, frequented by officers and prosperous townspeople. In addition to the public school, which covered the first eight grades, there was also a gymnasium in Przemysl, as there were in large European cities. This was a school which offered higher academic education. The gymnasium was a source of great pride in my town, raising its importance over other towns of its size, and implied the presence of a vigorous and intelligent population in Przemysl. The main street, Franciskanka, was a wide one with large stores on the main floors of two- and three-story houses.

My parents had come to Przemysl from a *shteitl* called Ulanow. They were second cousins, which was not uncommon in marriages at that time.

My father enjoyed telling us children of his first impressions of my mother as a young woman, and of falling in love with her.

"The first time I saw her, she was a baby on her mother's lap. My father had taken me—a boy of seven—to visit her family. Her mother drew me close and showed me the little girl. Then she said 'You see, this is your future wife.' Of

21

course, I didn't understand what she meant, but I never forgot it." He told us that later she had become a very beautiful girl. As the years progressed, my mother never ceased to appear beautiful to me, although in fact her looks faded early from the difficulties of her life. She had large and splendid blue eyes, a broad, high forehead, a stright attractive nose, and a proud bearing. Being a pious woman, she wore a *scheitel* (wig) which was black, the color of her own hair. The purpose behind this custom of wearing wigs was to reduce a woman's attractiveness once she was married. In a *scheitel*, she would (theoretically) appear less attractive to other men.

My father was good looking, also. Dapper in his young married years, he had a full head of brown wavy hair and the same blue eyes and high forehead as my mother, who was his cousin as well as his wife. Although he was a religious Jew, he was not a Hassid. Therefore, he wore no earlocks, but only a square beard and whiskers, both of which added no little dash to his appearance. Only on Sabbath did he don the traditional black robe and the fur-trimmed *shtramel*. He had studied Talmud, as a boy, but did not pursue this learning too much as an adult. Since it was necessary to earn a living, he became a baker. Good-natured though occasionally excitable, he was fundamentally carefree and left all the worries and troubles to my mother, who in contrast took them to her soul. She used to say to my father : "With your nature, you will live a long time." (He died at the age of 99.)

My pious little mother in her *scheitel* lived a very simple life, completely absorbed in her husband and children. She seemed always to be either carrying or nursing a child; yet she still found time to assist my father in running the bakery and selling bread. My mother bore nine children. There were five girls— Hanna, the oldest, I, Helena, Olga, the middle one, and, much later, Mela and Stela, the youngest. The four boys were

Abram, the first born, Leon, the second son, and Saul and Bernatz, the youngest.

Unlike her children, my mother had not attended a public school in her youth. Instead, it was usual in those days to have Hebrew teachers come to the homes of young girls. She had studied the *Tze'enah u-Re'enah* a basic text for women, an ethical commentary on the Five Books of Moses, printed in Yiddish. She knew and understood every word of this difficult book, as well as the Bible and other holy books, and brought us up according to their teaching. A religious person, she believed that the destiny of a woman was to bring children into this world.

I was intensely pious as a child. I feared and loved God, dreading to commit a sin.

But with her piety, my mother had basic wisdom and good-heartedness. We were not rich, but had enough to eat and to wear. There were poorer people who needed help and they could invariably count on getting it from my mother. Her response to need was spontaneous and uncomplicated. But she always helped in a way which did not embarrass the person involved. And to me she often said, "Never refuse help when somebody asks you for it."

As was traditional, the boys went to *heder* when they were three years old, whereas the girls took private lessons in Hebrew. All children were expected to participate in the study of Jewish life. When each child made progress in this area, my mother was filled with pleasure, for these things, together with the healthy development of her children, were all she seemed to ask of life. She was happy when each baby started to smile, walk, talk, and go to school. But not everything went on as smoothly as she might have wished. Thus, she used to remark : "Little children, little worries; big children, bigger worries."

When we were very young—even the eldest of us—my

grandmother lived with us. She was a tiny old woman who wore a kerchief over her head. I can see her now, rocking the baby's cradle, singing a lullabye generations old :

"In the fireplace a fire is glowing and the room is warm. The *rebbe* is teaching the little pupils the *alev baith*. He says, 'learn my children, what I am teaching you. Only when you grow up will you understand the tears and suffering that lie in the Hebrew alphabet.'"

None of us understood the meaning of that song as children. Its plaintive quality grew dear to us, however, through my grandmother's gentle voice. Her presence, in those early years, was an immense relief to my mother. She taught us our daily prayers and helped with the feeding and bathing of my mother's ever-growing brood.

But my grandmother could not stay forever. While we were still small, before some of us were even born, she decided to live with my aunt in the country, leaving us before we were old enough to get to know her properly. I was never to see her again.

After my grandmother left, an orphaned cousin of ours came to live with us. Her name was Rifka, and she was several years older than I. She was a great help to my mother, as my grandmother had been.

Rifka and Abram did not go to public school, but my mother hired a private teacher who came to our house and taught them to read and write Polish. Meanwhile, the family was growing. During those years Mela and Stela were born.

As I grew older, my little world started to enlarge. Besides our home, I knew the house, the garden in front, and the courtyard in back of the house. It was a small one-story and main-floor house that had been whitewashed. We lived in the basement, which had large windows. A major of the Kaiser and King's Regiment lived on the main floor with his

wife and two children. A judge, who was our landlord, lived
on the first floor. The garden in front belonged to the major
and only his children were allowed to play there. We used to
play in the courtyard, which was a large one. There was space
enough for a covered wagon and a stable for our horse, which
my father needed for distributing bread to his customers. He
sometimes took me with him on such trips.

When I was six years old, I started to go to school. By then,
I already knew my address. It was 11 Garden Street. (It was
called Garden Street because it was composed of villas with
gardens enclosed by iron grill fences.) I remember my first
school day.

The children walked into a new school building. A priest
came into our classroom and sprinkled it with Holy water.
The children whispered stories about ghosts walking around
the rooms. I was very much afraid.

The school was situated far away from our home. We
children had to cross a bridge over the San River to reach it.
This was strange and unpleasant in the winter, because it was
still dark in the mornings and despite heavy clothing we grew
bitterly cold. We crossed this bridge silently, our breath freezing. We never quite grew used to that trip in the winter season.

But this same river San was a pleasant thing when the
summer came. My father used to take us swimming there. On
one bank there were little cabins for changing in and out of
swim clothes. At the edge, the water was sufficiently shallow
for children. My father, who was an excellent swimmer, went
out deep one day and swam across to the other bank. Abram,
who was eleven, swam after him. I did not notice that Leon,
my younger brother, had disappeared from the cabin. Suddenly, I heard a scream for help. I looked out of the cabin and
saw Leon, his head nearly submerged in the water, struggling
frantically. I ran into the water, which quickly grew too deep.
I had to walk on tip-toe to keep my head above it, until I

reached Leon, who threw his arms around my neck and clutched me tightly. Somehow, I don't know how, I carried him back to the cabin. I was seven years old at that time. For years, the family told of this rescue, as though describing a miracle.

The river divided the city of Przemysl into two parts: The one we lived in was Zasanie. The other was the city. There was a large park on a hill called Zamek, on top of which stood the fortress. Father once took us children to the citadel and explained to us: "If there should be a war, our soldiers would shoot through those holes in the wall to prevent our enemies from taking the city." I was horrified at the prospect. The image of killing made me shrink away from the place.

The first time in my childhood I realized that men shed blood was when I learned about the pogroms in Kishenew, then belonging to Russia under the Czarist domination. I understood all the horrible things people talked about. Russian hordes attacked Jewish homes, cut off the breasts of women, slashed the stomachs of men, and cut children apart. Many of the Jews saved themselves by escaping to other countries, and so some of them came to our city and told all these stories. Our people helped them with food and clothing. Then they left for America.

I also became aware for the first time that there existed a country such as Russia, where people were so horribly cruel and inhuman, and another country like the United States, which opened the doors to the poor and oppressed and gave them freedom and security.

We Jews were fortunate to live under Kaiser Franz Josef I, who was a humanitarian and would not permit any form of persecution to exist in a country over which he reigned. He was the Emperor of several smaller states of different nationalities. He granted freedom of religion and culture to all his

people, whether Polish, Hungarian, Czech, Ukrainian, Yugoslavian, or Jewish. They were all allowed to have their own
schools where their own history and other subjects were taught
in their own language. The Kaiser was popular among his
subjects. They used to say: "As long as Kaiser Franz Josef
lives, the Monarchy will remain united. But as soon as he dies,
it will fall apart. Every state will fight for its independence."

There was a little bridge near our home, over which trains
passed on their way to the railway station. I remember once
seeing the Kaiser on a visit to our city looking out of the train
window and waving his hand. The train moved slowly and all
the people watching cheered him.

While the people had rights as a minority under a foreign
power, they did not live as peaceful neighbors with each other.
In our city there lived Polish, Ukrainian, and Jewish people.
The Polish people claimed that the city and this part of the
state was Polish; the Ukrainians claimed this part of Galicia
was Ukrainian. But on one point they did agree, and that was
on their dislike of the Jews. I learned about anti-Semitism for
the first time when I witnessed two big Polish boys whipping
Leon and calling him "dirty Jew." I ran crying to my mother
and asked her, "Why did they do it?" She answered, "They
don't like us." "Why?" "You see, their parents don't like us
and the boys learn this hatred from them." "Don't they believe
in God?" "Yes, they have their religion which also teaches
them to love their neighbor as themselves, as it is written in the
Old Testament. They probably don't want to understand that
'neighbor' means every human being. Maybe they think it
means only their fellow nationals."

Later, I learned more about anti-Semitism. There was the
case of Hilsner in Czechoslovakia. He was accused of killing
a Christian boy for a ritual purpose. This proved to be an
infamous lie. The anti-Semites wanted to stir up the people

against the Jews in order to follow the Russian pattern of making pogroms.

These were the times of mass emigration to America. Some left because of anti-Semitism; others wanted to try their luck in this almost mythical land of opportunity. And, in time, the magnetic lure of this great and distant country was to touch certain members of our family, too.

My Uncle Henoch was the first to go. He was my father's brother and was fourteen years younger than he. Up to now, he had worked in the bakery. We children regarded uncle Henoch as a permanent fixture there, and probably he would have remained so had not a bizarre twist of fate propelled him away. He won some money in a sweepstakes. It was not a great deal of money, for the prizes were in proportion to the amount risked, but it did cover his passage to the United States. As the time for his departure came, great excitement stirred us all. It was as if my uncle were leaving for another planet, and indeed he might well have been, as far as the likelihood of our seeing him again. His mother, that little kerchiefed grandmother of mine, was kept in ignorance of his plans until the last minute. He knew she wouldn't want him to go. For when would she see him again? Thus it was with mothers and sons who sought self-realization in the New World.

My Aunt Sarah was the second to go. A younger sister of my mother, Sarah knew tragedy early in her married life. Her husband was a staff sergeant in the cavalry of the Austro-Hungarian Army. One day he was thrown from his horse and was killed instantly, leaving Sarah a young widow with a baby daughter. Shortly thereafter, Sarah was sent passage to America by relatives of her deceased husband. It was typical, in those days, for relations, however slightly established, to help their kin to emigrate.

The next to go was Rosa, youngest of my mother's sisters, with her new husband. Her wedding, which was given by my parents, made a great impression on me. It was a traditional Jewish wedding and it was the first celebration I had ever attended.

Two rooms were crowded with guests. In one room, the bride was seated on a high chair, wearing a long satin dress with a veil on her head. All the women and girls were in the same room. In the other room sat the bridegroom with all the men. Music played in the room of the bride, and girls danced only with girls. Then came the exciting moment for the bride. They put her on a chair in the middle of the room and covered her face with the veil. All the women gathered around the bride. A man called "little marshal" took his place behind her chair and in a singing voice talked and talked, chanting to the bride. He reminded her that with this day all her carefreeness was ended. Now she would enter a new life, with responsibilities, hard work, worries, bearing children, and so on. He surely pictured her future in far from rosy colors, because she cried bitterly and all the other women shed tears, too. After the man finished, the bride got up and two women, one of them my mother, put their hands under the bride's arm and walked into the other room. Everyone else followed. There, four young men held the canopy. The rabbi was standing under the canopy to which two men were leading the bridegroom. The women walked the bride seven times around the bridegroom and left her by his side. The rabbi performed the usual ceremony with the groom breaking the glass with his shoe. After everybody had wished the couple *"mazeltov"* (which means Good Luck), the music started to play again. A woman with a large *chalah* (twisted bread) in her hand danced a *kozak,* a Russian dance, in front of the bride and groom, and led them to the table. They sat at the head of a large table, around which were seated all their relatives and friends. Soon the food was served. First the bride and groom got their so-called golden soup. They were hungry, because they had fasted all day. After the dinner, there was more dancing. One dance particularly amused me : a man and a woman pretended not to be on speaking terms. She acted like the offended one and he begged for her forgiveness. Women formed a circle where she tried to hide with her face covered in her hands. He rushed to her with hands folded and singing to her "Don't be mad at me, please. Let's be friends again." She only shrugged her shoulders, indicating that she did not want to talk to him. At last she gave in, they danced together, and everyone was happy.

The men remained sitting in the other room, eating and drinking beer and singing songs. The words of one of the songs remain in my memory : "Brother, hitch the horses to the wagon and run after the younger years. When you reach them, ask them to come back. They reached them on the high mountains, but the years refused to return. They said : 'You should have treated us more wisely when we were with you.'"

I was nine years old when we moved to the city. Our house was a large one-story building. You entered from the street through a gate and then walked down a long passageway which led to a large courtyard. Here, steps led to the rear house which had a large balcony extending along the whole length of the building. From this balcony you entered each apartment, which consisted of no more than one or two rooms. You entered the flats on the main floor from the courtyard. At the far end of the courtyard was our bakery. Across the court from the bakery there was the stable for our horse and a place for our wagon. Next to the bakery, there was a one-room flat, occupied by a tailor who lived there with his wife and also used this room for his workshop. Next door to him, a shoe-

maker put his small flat to similar use. Finally, there was our
two-room flat. Another neighbor was a Jewish scholar. Often
a priest visited him. His daughter told me that her father
studied *Kabbala* with the priest. Across the court from our flat
was a large workshop where trunks were produced. The owner
of the shop put this large place at our disposal when my third
brother, Saul, was born. You can imagine that there was quite
a celebration when a boy followed the birth of three girls in a
row. The workshop was nicely decorated, tables were set with
drinks and food. Many friends and relatives came to this
circumcision party and brought honey and other kinds of
cakes.

Rifka, my orphaned cousin, had become an important part
of our household. Being nineteen, it was natural that she
assume the role of mother's helper. The work of caring for the
young in our home was ceaseless, as were the chores of cooking
and cleaning. Rifka had a deep sense of obligation to my
parents, who had taken her into their home, and she gave of
herself generously. This domestic life, however, automatically
cut her off from many outside pleasures which a girl of her
age should have been finding. As a result, Rifka found her
pleasure inside, in the world of books. Her inclination for
romance sublimated itself in the reading of ballads and lyrical
books. In these she found herself, and through her enthusiasm
for Adam Micklewich and Slowacky, I gradually became infected with the same literary fervor and began to memorize
with her poems like "Granada." So it was through Rifka that
the world of books became a part of life for me. Rifka even
started her own book in those days, part of which I read. It
described two little children whose parents had died. They had
gone to heaven. There was not even a soul to pity the children.
Only, from the walls water dripped down, as if shedding tears
for the plight of the orphans.

Rifka also assumed the role of moral teacher to me. Charity was one of her favorite subjects. "When a beggar asks you for a piece of bread, never refuse," she advised. "God will reward you."

One day I was crying from a toothache when a beggar knocked at the door. I rose spontaneously and gave a piece of bread to the poor man. Suddenly, like a miracle, the toothache was gone. Rifka seemed to me a prophetic friend.

It was therefore with great heartache that I discovered that she was to leave us. Relatives had arranged for Rifka to go to America and find her life there. I was twelve years old when I saw her off. She looked out of the train compartment and said, "Helena, this is the last time I will breathe the air of this city." Such was the finality of departure.

That was in the year 1907. Around this time, the Social Democratic Party was in its early stages of existence. I remember a riot on election day, when police shot at the people. There was terrible excitement. A few people lost their lives. Dr. Liberman, a lawyer, was the first Social Democrat elected as a representative of our city to the Parliament. The workers demanded more wages and better working hours and conditions. When the bakery owners refused to comply, the Social Democrats opened their own bakery. They placed a stand next to ours in the market and sold their bread for a lower price than we were able to offer. All our customers naturally wanted to save money by buying cheaper bread. This resulted in a tremendous loss of income to our family. My parents decided to leave. With their eight children, they went to a larger city, Lwow, which was the capital of Galicia.

2

AT FIRST MY FATHER FOUND A PLACE IN A SECTION OF LWOW where Jews lived in a self-imposed ghetto. There he rented a bakery and a flat to live in. Most of the Jews living there were poor and had to struggle to make a living. But they complained little; they did not even know about the existence of a better standard of living. They worked hard during the week, earning so little that they brought home scarcely enough to feed their families. On Sabbath or holidays, however, they forgot their daily plight. As was commanded in the Ten Commandments, this seventh day was kept holy, bringing a pervading solemnity into the homes and streets every Saturday. Stores were closed; men went to synagogue with their sons. The Sabbath Torah study, providing spiritual enrichment, punctuated their lives with something joyous and seemed, indeed, their only real sustenance.

After a short time, we moved to another section of Lwow, on one of the main streets, Ulica Grodecka. Here I saw my first horse trolley car, which ran down our street from the railroad station to the center of the city. In this section there lived a mixed population of Poles, Ukrainians, and Jews, and thus it contrasted sharply with the ingrown and intensely Jewish community from which we had come.

Coming from a smaller town, I was very much impressed by Lwow. It was the largest city I had ever seen and I was thrilled

33

with its main street, its large stores and coffeehouse. This street was, at least to my mind, vastly broader than the one in Przemysl. On Karola Ludwika street people promenaded up and down, greeting acquaintances. It was customary for men to lift their hats to ladies, and for the ladies to nod discreetly in response.

Lwow was proud of its beautiful city theater, in which operas, operettas, ballets, and classical dramas were enacted by the most outstanding Polish performers of the day. There were also a few primitive movie houses, most of them firetraps, which were always crowded with young people.

To add to the prominence of the city, Lwow had a university and a commercial academy, several gymnasiums, and a *realshule,* where engineering was taught. All of this, of course, was in addition to the public and high schools.

The houses were larger here than in Przemysl, some even boasting four stories. Our new home was a large, two-storey one, with a grocery in front. A large courtyard led to another two-storey house in back, where we had our flat on the second floor. Here, in the basement, was our large, light bakery. And behind this, there was another large, pleasant courtyard with trees. A fence separated this courtyard from a large garden in which stood a building occupied by Jesuit priests. A narrow street led uphill to their cloister. Across from the cloister, there was a city park for public use, called the Jesuit Park. I used to go there often.

Abram, my eldest brother, was now old enough to assist my father. Every day, with the help of a Polish boy, he used to drive our horse and wagon to deliver bread to customers in various parts of the city.

Hanna also, being the eldest daughter, was now automatically designated as assistant. In her fourteenth year, she appeared mature, because she was tall for her age, and appeared heavy, because of her well-developed bust. Too young, she was forced to assume a daily round of child care and housekeeping. Her education was halted early so that she might be constantly at home. In those days, parents took that kind of sacrifice for granted, just as they accepted the idea that children were conceived without too much deliberation.

But Hanna never really accepted this lot, although she honestly tried. Trapped in this role, her resentment mounted with the years, expressing itself often in impatience and anger. She slapped the younger children, to my mother's distress, alienating them when she might have elicited devotion. I think my parents were blind to Hanna's resentment.

Hanna was a robust girl, while I, the second eldest daughter, was not. Accordingly, heavy duties were freely assigned to her, while my mother often sighed sympathetically over a chore that I assumed. Thus, Hanna grew jealous of me, thinking I had the better of my mother's love.

But my mother was too busy to take notice of the dissatisfaction of one or another of her children. There was simply no time for reflection. Each morning she had to sell bread in an open market not far from our house. This she did on freezing winter days and through weeks of sweltering summer. I used to come to help her after school sometimes. But she always sent me home, unless the weather was mild. For her own welfare she showed little concern. She did not mind suffering. She did not know any other kind of life than to work hard, worry about others, and forget herself completely.

The Sabbath alone was her relief from labor and it was a relief enforced by piety, which forbade work of any kind. On this day, my mother renewed her strength, resting in that holy atmosphere, at peace with her home and family. For us children, it was as if our mother changed into another person one day a week. She wore her good dress; her hair was combed with care; above all, she relaxed in our presence, elevating all of us by her pose of leisure. And a picture of her, lighting the Sabbath candles combined itself with the sound of my father chanting the *Kiddush*. Our identities seemed to change once a week, uniting us with a serenity which eluded us on all other days.

On Thursday we already started to prepare for the Sabbath, for there was much work to be done in advance. On Thursday night, my mother helped to twist the *chalah* in the bakery. I made the noodles and helped Hanna prepare the gefilte fish and other dishes. On Friday, there was general cleaning in the apartment. Thus, by evening, everything, children included, was shining. My father went to the synagogue with the boys. Meanwhile, we set the table with a clean, white cloth on which four large candlesticks were placed. Next came two large *chalah* loaves, covered with an embroidered cloth, beside a bottle of wine and a silver cup. My mother in her Sabbath dress, a nice half apron, and a silk kerchief on her head, lit the candles. She covered her face with her hands and said the blessing. Then she prayed for the health and welfare of her family and for the peace and happiness of all mankind. We children stood around the table and looked on. The atmosphere was solemn indeed, engraving the scene permanently in our hearts and minds.

When my father came home from the synagogue, he always brought a poor man with him to eat dinner with us. This was an old Jewish custom. Sabbath meals, after all, were prepared as feasts. And since there were many poor people who were not able to buy much food for every day, it was the duty and privilege of more fortunate Jews to invite them to a Sabbath table.

Upon entering the room and saying *"Gut Shabbes,"* the men sang *"Shalom Alaychem"* (Peace be unto you). Then, standing at the head of the table, my father chanted the *Kiddush* (the blessing over the wine). When he finished, we all said "Amen." At this point, we all sat down and enjoyed the feast of fish, soup, and chicken, which my mother served with Hanna's help. And this glowing Sabbath scene sustained each of us from week to week, particularly my mother.

In my thirteenth year, something occurred which drew me closer to my mother and clarified my whole idea of her plight. For I, too, had begun to mature. When I first was told that she was expecting another baby, her ninth, I accepted the fact without dismay. I had always assumed that children were born to families in a seemingly endless cycle and did not see fit to question it. But my mother's pregnancy was not accepted so nonchalantly by Abram and Hanna.

"You simply don't understand," Hanna said impatiently to me. "My whole life is already tied up with small children, Helena. Another one to care for will leave me no time to myself at all!"

"Not to mention the embarrassment," Abram grumbled. "I'm seventeen years old! How is it my mother is still having babies?"

But this particular baby was to have more effect on me than either Hanna or Abram. In the last month of Mother's pregnancy she came to school to talk with my teacher. She wanted to take me out of school, because she needed me to take care of the baby she expected. So this is how it was to be! I had never thought my education, like Hanna's, would be halted in favor of domestic services.

She came into my classroom. The children whispered and laughed at her. I was so ashamed and unhappy that I burst into tears. They had ridiculed my mother, whom I loved so much. After that I was glad enough to leave the place. A few weeks later, Bernatz, my youngest brother, was born.

His birth took place in September, on a mild day. The younger children were sent out to play. My father nervously occupied himself in the bakery. Only Hanna and I remained indoors, staying close to the door behind which our mother labored with only a midwife in attendance. I was tense, and full of fear for my mother. And even Hanna, who at first had so resented the idea of the baby, was terribly excited. The labor, being her ninth, was probably a short one; but to Hanna and me it seemed endless.

As our mother's contractions came close to each other, a series of piercing screams rent the atmosphere, cutting me with pity for her. At last the midwife appeared, announcing to our tearful relief : "It's a boy."

Later, we all grew to love this baby very much. Although Bernatz was the ninth child, he was a strong boy, and was undeniably the best looking of the entire family. He was an irresistably beautiful infant, with golden curls and large blue eyes.

But this last little boy had taken his toll of my mother. For the first time, she was forced to hire a wet nurse to breast-feed him, for the birth had left her very weak. Gradually, her strength returned.

In contrast to our big family was a family on another floor called Schwartz. Mrs. Schwartz used to laugh goodnaturedly at my mother for having so many children. She was a progressive woman and had only two girls and one boy. Her way of life was very different from that of my mother. She went to theaters and other entertainments, and entertained friends frequently at home. Her teenage daughters were likewise socially inclined and held gatherings. Helka, the older daughter, was my age, and included me often in these affairs. The Schwartz family considered themselves Polish and were ashamed of their Jewish birth. The atmosphere in their house

was intensely Polish. They often arranged amateur performances of Polish plays and poetry recitations, which I found
terribly intellectual. Soon I found myself participating in their
activities.

Helka was my first outside influence, both political and
personal. She was very mature for her age, physically and
intellectually. She was short, with dark curly hair, dark flashy
eyes, and an olive complexion. Helka knew how to talk to
the boys and she liked to flirt. I, on the other hand, was shy
and often was afraid to open my mouth in their presence.
Certainly, I felt inferior to her in company, and looked up to
her. This, however, did not prevent me from enjoying her.
Indeed, Helka tried to console me about my shyness, assuring
me that poise would come with time.

"Wait till you get older. You'll learn how to treat boys. You
can learn much from me."

I was thankful for those lessons, although I never followed
through on her methods.

Being an assimilated Jew, Helka belonged to an organization called Goldmanowka. This was a group of Jewish boys
and girls who considered themselves Polish, rather than
Jewish. They went as far to see themselves as Polish patriots.
Helka brought me to these meetings and at first I was interested, for I was curious to see what these ideas were all about.
Besides the political part of the meetings, there was sociability
afterward to attract us; food was served and there was
dancing. So for a while I was a willing companion to Helka.
At that time, there was much discussion and argument among
the Jewish youth. I wondered if it was right to consider myself
a Polish patriot. The Poles themselves, with their anti-
Semitic attitudes, reminded me that I was Jewish and did not
belong to them.

Actually, Poland did not even exist as a nation at that time.
Polish people lived as a minority under Austrian domination.

Therefore, it was more realistic for me to think of myself as an Austrian Jewess. As time went on, it became clear to me that I could not really identify myself with the sympathies expressed by the Goldmanowka group and eventually, I dropped out.

The Schwartz family moved from their apartment shortly thereafter and, as a result, I was able to see Helka only occasionally.

3

THERE WAS ANOTHER FORCE WHICH DROVE ME AWAY FROM Goldmanowka. I had learned, through one of Hanna's friends, of another movement, whose aims were vastly more convincing to me. This was the Zionist Organization. It was in its early stages then, and young people, ardently involved, tried to attract more and more of their fellow Jews to join.

The founder of the Zionist idea was, of course, Theodor Herzl. Originally an assimilated Jew himself, Herzl had gradually formed the conviction that the only solution to the Jewish problem would be the creation of a national homeland. This conviction came as a result of the anti-Semitism he had witnessed over the years and was confirmed by the shattering conclusion of the Dreyfus Case, which, in 1894, he had covered as a journalist for a Vienna newspaper.

As for me, I now read the *Jewish History* of Heinrich Graetz, which convinced me where I belonged — sharing the sufferings of my people, helping the Zionist idea become a reality. This idea was, of course, a future dream. None of us knew when it would come true, if even it could come true. Thus, in addition to this involvement, there were many other interesting things for a girl of sixteen to do.

Hanna took me to dancing school with her, as was considered proper for a girl at that time. Here I became popular, more popular than Hanna was. This was unfortunate, for the jealousy she felt for me at home now found reason in a new situation. Yet with it all, she did not hate me. My sister's love for me persisted and she took me along wherever she went.

One of the most exciting events of my girlhood in Lwow was a ball. I still remember the large, illuminated ballroom, the dazzling row of girls in bright gowns and the boys in frock coats. I wore a long white full dress, drawn at the waist by a sash and a big bow in the back. Hanna's gown was similar, but blue. My mother had accompanied us, her two eldest daughters, according to etiquette. As we entered the ballroom, she took her place on a bench along with the other chaperones.

Now the girls received little dancing books, where boys put their names under the dance number they wished to claim. I loved dancing the quadrille, lancers, and popular waltzes. That night my book was rapidly filled with boys' names. But Hanna, for once, was not jealous. Indeed, there was a serenity about her, a nonchalance which was new and, therefore, quite baffling to me. I observed her expression over the shoulders of my dancing partners, mystified.

What I did not know that night was that our mother had had an ulterior motive for bringing us to this ball. Hanna, who was dancing close to me, happy and detached, had developed an infatuation for the boy next door, a youth not considered desirable by my parents. Thus, this strange and wonderful treat, this ball had been lavished upon us in the hope that here Hanna might find a new beau to distract her. But all in vain.

At eighteen, Hanna had become very attractive. Taller now, she was still plump, but altogether fashionably buxom. She had bright, deep-set blue eyes, black hair, and a dazzling smile that emphasized her high cheekbones. She had fallen in love with Nathan, a frail boy, who was our neighbor. I was rather surprised, for, as one does with neighbors who seem not exceptional, I had taken Nathan's presence for granted, never dreaming he would attract my sister.

He had dark hair, a long nose, and large ears. He looked consumptive. But Hanna did not see him this way. He was an educated boy who studied at a teacher's academy. And Hanna had fallen in love with his learning and his desire to impart some of it to her. I would see him reading to her now, sitting on the steps of the corridor. Or, as he left for school each day, I discovered that he made his way up the hill, then stopped abruptly at a certain spot to wave to Hanna. She, in turn, was always at her window, transfixed.

It must have been his desire to elevate her through learning, to take her out of herself, which had caused her to love him so much. For Hanna up to this time had been truly starved for an opportunity to realize herself properly. His very frailty, which might have been distasteful to some, probably strengthened the intellectual image she had of him. In contrast, he adored the robustness of Hanna, the abundance of health and vigor she had.

My mother, in her ceaseless daily rounds, had been too busy to see at first that a romance was developing. By the time she had perceived it, Hanna was hopelessly in love and told her so.

Now this match which had developed was genuinely alarming to my mother. Ordinarily, she would have been delighted if the eldest of her five daughters were to find a mate. But the idea of Nathan was terrifying to her. First of all, he had tuberculosis. With the diagnostician's eye of a wise family woman, she knew this with certainty. She believed that his years, if not his days, were numbered. In addition, he was preparing to become a teacher, a profession in those days which yielded starvation wages. It was a terrible dilemma.

Here was Hanna, the resentful, the dissatisfied, suddenly transformed into a lovely, glowing creature. And the object of this exquisite change was a diseased boy, who could only ruin her future.

My heart was broken for Hanna. My mother would never consent to a marriage with Nathan. It was for Hanna's own good, I knew. And yet this new happiness of hers! How was one to live in such a world of contradictions? The arguments now ensued, often becoming violent, full of tears. Hanna, in her anguish, recalled all the years in which she felt our mother had not loved her enough, and now threw this up to her, blaming her disapproval of Nathan on this lack. It grew worse and worse. Hanna became inconsolable; Mother was heart-sick, but reason forbade her consent.

Ultimately, a desperate solution had to be worked out. Mother arranged for Hanna to take a trip to Berlin to visit cousins of ours. The visit was to last for a year, in which time it was hoped that Hanna's grief would lessen. By the time she agreed to go, Hanna had begun to perceive the gravity of Nathan's illness herself, and with resignation she finally agreed.

No sooner than Hanna was gone, Nathan and his family moved out, abruptly, from their apartment. It was a sad business.

4

When Hanna left for Germany, I was seventeen years old. I missed her terribly, but hoped she would return cured of heartache, with Nathan completely forgotten. Since it was impossible for me to take over all of Hanna's duties in addition to my own, my mother took a country girl, who helped with the household. Mother refused to take Olga out of school, as she had with Hanna and me. And Olga accepted this difference as a matter of course — an attitude which Hanna had always resented. But Olga had always shied away from domestic chores, preferring to retreat to the couch with a book. Books became her shield against the onslaught of dishes, baby care, cleaning, and laundry. Our parents intuitively respected this absorption in books and shrank from disturbing Olga's privacy with them. In addition, Olga, by her fourteenth year, had become an above-average student. At this time she began to change physically, turning slowly into womanhood, becoming slightly plump, which then was fashionable. And Olga had a pretty face, framed with brown wavy hair, and had the same high forehead that we all had. She had a small nose and mouth, but her eyes were her most arresting feature. They were blue eyes with a dreaming quality which made her look different, as if she were expecting something unusual in her destiny. People predicted that she would achieve something

45

special with her life. Personally, I felt this way, too, and was proud of her.

My brother Leon, in contrast to Olga, was having difficulty at school. His imagination was not captured by academic subjects and he did poorly with them. As time went on, however, Leon began to show an aptitude for mathematics and physics. It was therefore decided that he should be sent to a *realschule*.

Abram, as before, continued to help my father with the bakery business, while Mela and Stela, the two youngest girls, now started to attend public school, where they made average progress.

But my brothers and sisters did not have the only claim to my attention in those days. I met a girl whose family had just moved into our building. Her name was Dorka Hersches. Shortly after they moved in, tragedy struck the family : both her father and her eldest brother died within a few months. Her poor mother was left with three daughters and had to struggle to survive. We felt terribly sorry for them, but my sympathy went most to Dorka, who was about my age. She was not good-looking but had a very pleasant disposition.

Her sister Tonka, in contrast, was a beautiful girl with black hair and enormous blue eyes, a straight nose and a heart-shaped mouth. Tonka was well aware of her beauty and, indeed, engrossed in it. This was apparent to anyone who spent time with her. She frequently bit her lips to keep them looking red. Her nature, which was moody, also seemed shallow. She was more than anything a flirt, and was already, in a community such as ours, a little too fond of kissing boys.

Dorka was nothing like Tonka. Dorka appealed to me more because of the steadiness and warmth of her disposition. Dorka was always in good spirits, even when under mental stress. She had a good voice and was eager to sing on any occasion. Invariably, her songs were of love, of being forsaken, of heartbreak. In point of fact, Dorka was heartbroken, and the cause was my own brother Abram. She had fallen in love with him; he, in turn, was totally indifferent to her.

Abram was already in love with a girl of entirely different background and nature—a fragile, slender little creature called Sala Brand. She was very petite, and Abram looked large and protective beside her. More intelligent than Dorka, she was very serious and distinguished in her manner. Sala came from a large, patriarchal Jewish family which was at once rich and orthodox. The refinement of her background seemed ingrained in her small, chiseled features, in the gentleness and young wisdom they expressed.

It was easy to see why Abram loved this girl. And she, in her turn, was deeply in love with him.

Well bred, she would not go out with Abram unless an escort or chaperone accompanied them. Thus, at first, they took Pepa, Sala's sister, along with them. But her presence proved a slight encumbrance to Abram's courting. Soon my brother hit upon the idea of taking me along, too. This would give Pepa someone to talk to, and would take the pressure of her presence off the two sweethearts.

This dual chaperoning led instantly to a friendship between Pepa and myself. We understood each other at once and felt that we had much in common. During our walks with Abram and Sala, we were perfectly happy to fall considerably behind the lovers in order to create privacy for our own intimate observations. For example, we began to discuss the meaning of life and happiness. Pepa, like Sala, was intelligent and a reader. In general, I found her conversation most stimulating.

"With your beautiful blue eyes, Helena, you must attract the boys," Pepa observed.

I blushed, uncertain of how to respond to this.

"Yes," she continued, "You are really such a good-looking girl. Aren't you interested in boys?"

"No," I answered. "I am not. I simply don't believe that the only interest for a girl is to think of boys, or to wait till one asks you to marry him."

"But Helena," Pepa protested, "it is every woman's destiny to marry, build a family, and to be supported by her husband."

"I don't agree with you, Pepa," I answered. "A woman can just as well learn a trade and support herself."

But Pepa just smiled at this. "You will change your mind, Helena," she assured me.

When I came home, I reviewed my conversation with Pepa. She had told me that I was good-looking; this idea was one which I hardly considered before. When had I had time to think of my looks? In those days, a girl looked natural. Powder and lipstick and other makeup to improve one's appearance were used only by stage actresses or indecent women.

Now, inspired by the conversation with Pepa, I was moved to go to the mirror and examine myself thoroughly for the first time. I had that much inherent vanity.

The face? A nice oval, I supposed, framed by brown hair with a great black bow in back. The forehead high, a family characteristic. . . . Pepa had spoken of my eyes. . . . Yes, they seemed pretty. They were large and sky-blue. . . . Was my mouth nicely shaped? Eh! Who cared! Looks were not the most important thing in my life.

Nevertheless, I now studied my figure. It was a normally developed picture of an eighteen-year-old figure, the bust young and full. I felt a little ashamed of having observed myself so conciously.

5

ABOUT THIS TIME, ABRAM HAD A FRIEND WHO WAS A STUDENT at a commercial academy. His scholastic achievements were high, and he tutored his own classmates. Abram brought this friend home one evening and introduced him to Mother. It was thereupon arranged that this young man would give me lessons in bookkeeping twice a week.

His name was Jim Hilsen. He was 18 — my age exactly, which made it seem strange that he should teach me. Tall and slim, with reddish-blonde hair, he had stunning good looks, though still a boy. A dimple in his chin connected radiantly with his smile. Yet he was a serious fellow, too serious perhaps for his age.

At first, Jim Hilsen came only to give me lessons and left as soon as we finished. Later, he began to stay longer, and we discussed things of an academic nature. He, too, had been exposed to the influences of the two movements, Assimilants and Zionists. Like me, he recognized that our place was on the side of the Zionists, that our duty was clearly to work for its ideals. He had heard about pogroms in Russia, which had made a deep impression on him. At fifteen, he had written a drama in three acts entitled "Pogrom." Now he belonged to the Zionist Organization. As our acquaintanceship extended, I went out with him sometimes with a box to collect money for the Jewish National Fund. The money was to be used in the purchase of land from the Arabs in Palestine. The land, now neglected, was to be turned into fruitful settlements by Jews who fled from Russia. Thus our acquaintanceship was, at first, forged by common sympathies.

He was an avid reader, too. Before long, he brought me books to read. One of them was *His Goddess* by Emile Mataja. In this book there was a diary, which gave me the idea to write one of my own.

The Diary

January 8, 1913

I have decided to write a diary. Although my life seems monotonous to me, and I don't have much to write about, I suspect I will be glad to read it in the future. It will recall my youth, its joys and anguish; the way I think and act now.

Today nothing special to report, my diary. The morning was usual. I helped the maid to wash and dress the children, gave them breakfast, and sent them to school. Like Hanna, I am busy at home all day long now, and begin to understand what she has given of herself these past few years. Evenings, I enjoy reading. I try hard to understand what the author wishes to say. During the day, while working, my mind is preoccupied with all kinds of thoughts. I think how soon life passes by and wonder what makes a human being worthy of life and what makes one happy. My girlfriend, Dorka, who lives upstairs, and with whom I often discuss such questions, said to me once: "You have no reason to trouble yourself with thoughts of this kind. You're a lucky girl, Helena. You have whatever you need, you are not in love, and therefore don't have to suffer. I, as you know, am in love with your brother, who cares nothing for me. He loves another girl. This brings me constant suffering. To add to my misery, both my father and brother are dead now and we have to struggle to make a living." I have mulled over Dorka's problems and I am truly sorry for her. But luckily for her, she doesn't take things too seriously, is generally gay, and gets easily over her troubles.

January 9, 1913

Maybe it is ridiculous to write in this diary, because the days are all alike and not interesting at all. But at least I can pin down the thoughts that whirl around in my head all day long. I have thought about what Dorka said to me. She is right. I have every reason to be content with my life, but still, I am not. Something is missing. I am trying to find out what this is. A woman has to have a goal, but I refuse to admit this is marriage only. I do not care much about men, and I would like to keep it so. It is terrible to watch a woman all torn up with love, as Hanna with Nathan, or even Dorka. When I think about it, I'm sure I have too much pride to be devastated like that. Instead, I would like to have a goal to strive for. Perhaps if there were a Jewish convent, it would satisfy me to be there. I could exchange a material life for a spiritual one, serve God only, and help needy people.

January 10, 1913

Another day of housework and thinking. Today I asked myself : "Why do I waste my time with this brooding for what is not present? Why don't I live like other girls of my age, instead of troubling myself with such thinking? Am I not unrealistic to scorn love? Yet since it has been unknown to me I view it from afar, a trap with curved teeth that close about one. What would become of me in the grips of it? Of my desire to do something useful for society? No! Not I, but the others waste their time with senseless living." But I can't write anymore. I am exhausted from all this thinking.

January 11, 1913

Today I went to the city with Dorka. I haven't been there for a long time. I enjoyed strolling through the streets. We had a good time. Dorka is good company. I can talk freely with her about everything. I really don't care much for the company of men. In the evening, we played chess.

January 12, 1913

This morning I went to the clinic with Stela, my youngest sister. She had an infection of the gum, which had to be lanced. While I waited outside in the hall during Stela's ordeal, I observed the scene at the clinic. Doctors and nurses rushed from room to room to accommodate the sick. "The most pitiable people," I thought, "are the sick ones, while those who help them are the most noble." What awe I felt, what admiration for those doctors and the patient nuns who assisted them. Surely they must be happy, with lives dedicated to relieve the sufferings of their fellow creatures. Something in me seemed to reach out to them. Spiritually, I joined them spontaneously, finding the joy, the untold relief of their selflessness. But as the time came for little Stela to emerge from her cell of pain, I was my true self again. I could never be a doctor or nurse; I am queasy and soft-hearted; my nerves are poor. My destiny will take a different direction. I wonder what it will bring me.

January 13, 1913

Today I went to school to talk to Olga's teacher. More and more, my life becomes like Hanna's—a mother's assistant. But on the way home, I met Mr. H., my tutor. (This reminded me that my education had not come to a complete halt.) He asked if he could accompany me. I told him that Olga's teacher had said that the child was a brilliant pupil. This led us to a discussion of character. I asked what he thought of me, then trembled while I waited for the answer. He told me my

character was good, that I was a dreamer, and that I seemed
not to care much about men. But a "perfect" man, he guessed,
could win my heart. How surprised I was that he judged me
this way. So clear and accurate was his picture of me that I
was pleased, yet troubled, as we walked along. Our conversation was so engrossing that I did not notice when we arrived
at my house. It was just time for our lesson.

February 15, 1913

I return to you, my diary, after having abandoned you for
a few weeks. I have been busy. Mr. Hilsen comes twice a
week, as usual to give me lessons. The subject, I admit, does
not interest me much. But the discussion about books and
people, after the lesson, does. He brings me many books to
read. In addition to Polish writers, like Mickiewicz Slowatcki,
I am now being introduced to works by de Maupassant, Zola,
Hugo, Proust, Mariot, D'Annunzio, Dumas, Tolstoy, Dos-
toyevski, and others. What an expanse of world! And it is
Mr. H., my tutor, who leads me quietly to these new land-
scapes. For this I am most grateful.

March 1, 1913

Today was a day of days, and you, my diary, must know of
it. Mr. H. met me in the park after school and took me to
lunch in a little pastry shop. We have been meeting in the park
quite often. But today, he presented me with a gift—a set of
twenty beautiful cards illustrating *Quo Vadis*. Still more
excitement was to follow. Mr. H. has been taking me out lately
to the city theater (where Nathan used to take Hanna). There
we have been seeing operas, dramas, and ballets. Tonight,
Mr. H. got tickets for *Peer Gynt*—a thoughtful idea, for he
knows I have recently read the book by Ibsen. The performance, dear diary, surpassed all the others we have seen of late.
It was a radiant and beautiful rendition. Grieg's music so

strengthened Ibsen's story that the total effect was overwhelming.

March 3, 1913

After today's lesson, Mr. H. asked me to go for a walk with him. In the park, we talked about the performance of *Peer Gynt* which we had both so enjoyed. I told him that I especially loved Solveig's Song. He told me that this was his favorite, too. This subject led us to a discussion about music. It had always attracted him deeply. Mr. H. then began.

As a boy, he liked to sing and had a good tenor voice. He would have liked to study music, but his parents could not afford to finance him in such a pursuit. Nevertheless, he sought an outlet for his love of music. At the age of eight, he began to sing in the temple choir. By a stroke of luck, the temple choir director happened also to be the director of the chorus at the Lwow city opera. This man noticed Mr. H.'s voice and helped him to obtain a position in the city opera's chorus. There, as a boy member of the chorus for several years, Mr. H. had sung in such operas as Faust and Carmen. At thirteen, he had been given a leading role in a Polish operetta. It is all such a revelation! This quiet young man—who would have guessed that he has a taste for the dramatic, even the flamboyant? I enjoy his company more and more. . . . It is still only as a good friend and teacher, however.

July 17, 1913

Apologies again, dear diary! This time I've neglected you for several months. But I have been absorbed in reading, and what a place it is—this world of books! The last two I read were *The Brothers Karamazov* and Zola's *J'Accuse*. You can see what heavy literature I take on these days. But I am eager for this reading, for afterward I have the pleasure of discussing the books with Mr. H., who understands them so well. To tell you the truth, my diary, I am flattered that he seeks my company.

August 1, 1913

I could hardly wait to be undisturbed, to tell you my diary, what happened today. I'm trembling with excitement now, although maybe someday in the future when I read this, I will laugh out loud.

Pepa sent me a note, asking me to meet her at two in our usual spot in the Jesuit Park. It was beautiful there. We had a marvelous stroll, all the time talking about Sala and Abram, the sweethearts.

"It must be wonderful to be in love, don't you think, Helena?" Pepa asked me.

"How would I know? I've never experienced the feeling. Frankly, I doubt if I'd like to fall in love," I stated.

"But why not?"

"Love can make you unhappy."

"Yet look at Sala and Abram!" she pointed out. "They seem radiant with happiness."

Love and boys are Pepa's favorite subjects. Soon she was asking me, "What about Mr. Hilsen? Aren't you attracted to him?"

"He's my teacher, Pepa!" I replied impatiently. "And we are friends, that's all."

After we parted, I was very surprised to see Mr. H. coming toward me. He lifted his hat as usual, and asked if he might take me home. I agreed. While we were talking of many usual things, he suddenly asked me how I would act if he touched my face. The question came as a shock. Never before had there been a hint of the physical in our relationship. Immediately, I was confused and angry.

"I warn you not to do it," I advised, my face flaming. "If you do, I will never speak to you again."

After an embarrassed silence, normalcy set in again. By evening, I was composed enough to take my lesson with him and he seemed much as always. We decided to go to Dorka's house. And our visit was gay. We all laughted, were all in a good mood. Then, abruptly, Mr. H. reminded me of our conversation in the park and asked me if my answer still stood. I said "yes."

But he only smiled, reached out, and touched my face.

Anger made my eyes burn with tears. I struggled to hold them back. It had really been a small thing, but my pride reared at his defiance, and I felt, unreasonably, hurt.

His face now expressed regret, but he would not admit it. Meanwhile Dorka, perceiving all, begged me to forgive him. I refused to do so. When he left, I shook hands with him coldly, regarding him as my teacher.

With a pained expression, he confessed, "This is the first time in my life I have been defeated."

This information, I confess, was rather satisfying, since I had learned that he was popular with girls. I was trembling with confusion from the whole business. Frankly, I doubted whether I would be firm enough to refrain from speaking to him as I had threatened. I resented this new thing he had brought out between the two of us — resented it because it brought my desire into conflict, demanding definition for which I felt unready. And what of my dreams of a life of social dedication? What implications for these lay in the touch of his hand on my face?

I was human enough to like the excitement of it, the change it made in my daily life. But the excitement was not completely pleasant.

August 5, 1913

I am so grateful to have you, my diary, a place where I can freely unburden my feelings. I am already amused, thinking of rereading you at some future time, with so many years gone between that I'll be like another person. Today is my eighteenth birthday. My brother, Abram, surprised me with a "Memory Book." Hanna sent me a blouse from Germany. I also received a few birthday cards. One of them, from Mr. H., read as follows: "I know it will be unpleasant for you to receive a card from me, but please forget your anger with me for a moment and let me express my sincere good wishes for a happy birthday. Now that this blissful moment is over for me, you may continue to resent me, till our friendship ceases." He then quoted from *Quo Vadis*: "As you caja, as I cajus" — As you are, I am. It was signed, "Your friend H."

I felt badly when I read this. So when he came for our lesson, I handed him a note saying, "I don't dislike you. I, too, feel friendship toward you and forgive you."

He later responded with a letter which said: "I am surprised that you have at last overcome your anger and forgiven me. You can't remain firm against someone just as firm as you."

Indeed, dear diary, what was there to forgive? I have been taught a lesson. I should not have written my note. I did it only because I felt sorry for him and wanted to make him feel better. Now I realize it was a matter of small importance and feel little anger. I don't care about him anyway. I feel indifferent toward everything.

August 6, 1913

Today I had my picture taken. I am very curious to see how it will turn out. I asked Dorka to ask Mr. H. to return the note I had written to him yesterday, which I had done in good faith. But he disregarded my attempt to be on good terms with him again. He had become offended, believing that my intention was to hurt him by not trusting him to keep this note from me. That was not true because I still like him and consider him my friend whom I wouldn't like to lose.

August 8, 1913

All day I had a most unpleasant feeling because of an unexpected letter I received from Mr. H. Two days ago, he became offended because I asked that my note be returned to me. I did not suspect that he was so terribly hurt. Moreover, I thought he cared much less about me after that incident. But he still seems convinced that it was my purpose to punish him. For now he writes: "You are worthy of your deed." How can he think I could be deliberately cruel? His charge made me cry because I don't deserve it. I would like to prove to him how wrong he is. . . . But how? He writes that he does not want an answer. Otherwise, I might give him this diary to read (rash thought!) from which he could find out his mistake in judging me. His letter to me is not finished. Did he start to hate me toward the end of it? But I still like him, really, and he does sign it, "I will always remain your friend. H."

This situation could continue till the time comes for my lessons to be at an end and he no longer comes to the house. Then our paths will separate. I'll ask him to write in my Memory Book. I can even imagine him writing: "Someday in a future, happy moment"—as if there will ever be any!— "you will accidentally open this page and ponder over the name written here . . . briefly, of course. And then you'll forget it." (Perhaps I will!) . . . I may also give him my diary to read. He may find it ridiculous, but I don't care.

I could write more, my diary, but it is Friday. I have to prepare for Sabbath so I must stop now.

August 10, 1913

Oh my God! How blue I feel today. Such an endless emptiness in my heart. I really don't know why. In the morning I went to the Jesuit Park, in the hope of meeting Pepa there. But, instead, Mr. H. was sitting on a bench. At first, I thought it would be as before. He would rise, walk toward me, and ask if I cared to go for a walk with him.

But he ignored me, not even lifting his hat. I did not care. I preferred to be alone with my thoughts. In the afternoon, Dorka and I went to the second courtyard where we spent a pleasant time. Dorka cheered me up with her singing and joking. It is impossible to feel depressed in her company. But suddenly Mr. H. appeared and I lost my composure, feeling as if somebody had tied me with a rope. I wanted to free myself and run far away from him, but felt strangely bound to the earth. In the past, I used to feel so free in his company. Now it is just the reverse. During my lessons, I always felt at ease because we concentrated on the subject only. But after today's lesson, I was tense and sad and was relieved when he left. I wandered out to the courtyard again and was surprised to see him coming back. Dorka asked me to talk to him, which I refused to do. I do not care about him and I am sure he feels the same way. I sat there in the courtyard, alone, my mind dreaming and wandering, a stranger to itself, and I found that I was crying.

August 12, 1913

Today is the anniversary of the destruction of the Temple in Jerusalem. Everybody is fasting, and so am I. When I got up this morning, I felt queer because of a peculiar dream I had during the night : it was winter. Dorka lived somewhere else. I could see the place from my window. She had just left my house when Mr. H. entered the room.

Although I was aware that we are not on speaking terms, I asked him to look out of the window, pointing at Dorka's house. Strangely, we then had a gentle, sympathetic discussion. He asked me to forget our antagonisms, and I agreed. Then we shook hands and he left. I went out into the street, as if swept there. Two men and a woman passed me. One, who was clean-shaven, stared at me. I became frightened and rushed home. He pursued me. I could feel my heart beating faster and faster. Inside, I locked the door, which he opened by force. He asked me to marry him. When I refused, he struck me in the leg with a large pin. I felt great pain. I did not want to be hurt again, so I agreed to marry him. He said he was rich and he left. Soon after, I felt relieved. Then Dorka came in and I babbled forth my experience, telling her that I would also confide it to Mr. H. Most expediently, he appeared that instant. I gave him my hand, which he pressed. As I began to tell him my dream, I woke up.

I looked at the clock and saw that it was five o'clock. Too shaken to go back to sleep, I rose, dressed, and waited until six, when I crept out of the house and went to the park. It was beautiful there, just past dawn. I breathed in the fresh air and felt easier. But this was short-lived. My dream came back to me, spreading fear over me like a cloak. I was afraid that such a man would appear and molest me while I was alone in the park. Tensely, I sat on a bench, the scene distorted by my dream. Soon men passed, on the way to work. Everyone terrified me. Now I consciously wished that Mr. H. would appear to protect me, but this seemed wildly improbable at such an hour.

Thus, when he approached in reality, my joy was such that it, too, was like a hallucination. While I confusedly fumbled for the right words, and wondered whether to speak at all, he greeted me, saying, "At last, I have the courage to speak up. Please, let's forget everything." I was delirious with relief, now. Suddenly, we were free with each other again. I told him my dream and we both laughed over it. Going home, we both admitted that it was silly to get into arguments.

August 13, 1913
I had not intended to go to the park today, but my father

asked me to do an errand for him. On the way, I had another
encounter with Mr. H., whom I now call Jim. He accompanied me on the errand, then saw me home. In the afternoon,
I went to the photographer to pick up my picture, which I
had taken a week ago there. It was not ready. At the house,
Jim was waiting for me. He had brought the Memory Book,
in which he had written a little story. I was deeply touched
when I read it. The moral of his tale was that beauty may
fade, wealth may dissipate, but virtue perseveres. In addition,
he had written a beautiful poem. Now I was moved to do the
thing which I had (as you know) been tempted for days to do.
It is hard to explain how I, so withholding of myself, had been
at the same time yearning to present the one document which
would expose my inner life, with all its absurdities, limitations,
and dreams. Yes, I wished clearly to give my diary to Jim
to read. And I did so. He disappeared with the diary for some
time. When he returned, he told me he was very sorry that
he had made me suffer. He wanted to write something in it,
but said he would wait for a significant time—his departure
for Vienna the following year. He is going there to continue
his studies. . . . Altogether, this has been a happy day. I like
Jim Hilsen. I cannot deny that.

August 14, 1913

I would not have written in you, today, my diary, but I
am unable to sleep, although it is half past two in the morning.
I have just finished a letter to Hanna, which left me still wide
awake. Now I turn to you. Jim came this morning to give me
my lesson. For the first time, I consciously became aware of
my family in relation to the two of us. Have they perceived a
note of something more than academic? Have they guessed
that our evenings at the theater have had motives beyond
that of cultural expansion? I wondered little before about the
others, for I had admitted nothing to myself. Now, my merry

carefree father seems to glance at me with still an added twinkle in his eye. What complicity is there? Hanna asked in her letters how much I liked Jim. At that time, I was hasty to answer her that I admired his Zionistic zeal, his learning, and his patience, but certainly nothing more. But Hanna, with her new maturity born of loss, has sensed for some time the complexity of my feelings. It is a credit to her sensitivity that she hesitates to question me further. I almost feel that she is hoping for a liason between Jim and me. Can she be vicariously living her love for Nathan again in reading my letters? Is it possible that she equates the scholarly but consumptive Nathan with Jim, who is also erudite? Only Mother, forever absorbed with the young ones, the bakery, and Father, seems to notice nothing. She is always the last to know. It was so with Hanna.

August 20, 1913

Today, I gave Jim still another section of my diary to read. He said that nothing he read surprised him, because he knew me better than I realized. In the afternoon, we went to get my picture, which was ready. There were a few copies. I sent one to Hanna and gave one to Jim. The latter was presented in front of Abram, so that no one should think I was making a secret of it. I think it is quite proper to give him my picture, because he is my friend. He has promised me one of himself.

* * *

Here I stopped writing my diary, but the romance continued. Jim came over daily now, and remained for longer periods. We used to sit on the corridor steps near a large window. Jim did not speak to me of love. Knowing that I was uncommitted, within myself, he feared my response. He constantly observed my attitude toward him, however. When he was hurt, sometimes he said nothing. But at home he wrote down all his feelings and handed a piece of paper to me next day.

Then a new incident brought things to a head once more. Abruptly, as we sat in the corridor one day, he tried to kiss my hand. Alarmed, I pulled it back. When he left, he seemed disconsolate. Later, I received the following letter :

"I am now in a state in which I am afraid. I want to end my young life. I have not yet experienced or accomplished anything beyond the recognition of this feeling in my heart, which is called love. Yes! I do love her above everything in the world. . . . And she? She only likes me. No! She is not able to love. And should this satisfy me? Three days have passed, and I can't forget the hurt (that withdrawal!) when I tried to kiss her hand. No, I can't force her to love me. It is her nature not to be able to fall in love."

Shortly after this missive, there followed another. This new one he called "The Truth." He wrote : "I write this to you because despair torments me. It is still the same. When I am near you, I feel happy because I imagine that you love me. But soon your attitude destroys my belief and causes me great suffering. Tonight I had a dream which showed me the whole truth. I have never believed in dreams, but this one was too convincing. You probably remember my colleague, Benek Grunbaum, who committed suicide last summer because of an unhappy love affair. In the dream, it was he who came to me, saying : 'I know everything about your love for Helena. I want to tell you that she does not love you. You know this well, but won't admit it to yourself. You are a dreamer, just as I was when I was alive. Now you are a living corpse. Watch yourself, I warn you, or you will end as I did. If you don't believe me, a cat will prove it !' When I arose in the morning, I forgot the dream completely. I dressed and ate breakfast. It was six A.M. But when I went to open the door, the dream suddenly came back to my mind. A cat was standing in front of me and gazing at me. He wouldn't move when I tried to chase him away. Now I believed in this dream and felt like the "living corpse" described by my phantom friend. I wanted to laugh but was suddenly plagued with tears instead. For not only the dream but the experience in your home last evening undermined me, made the dream somehow valid instead of absurd. I had an urge to kiss your face, but did not dare. And when I tried only to kiss your hand, you pulled back, and dismissed me saying, 'Good night.' And while I am certain now that you are not in love with me, I love you more passionately than ever. I can't live without seeing you, being near you, although I know the truth. Now that I have told you this, I feel relieved. The dream torments me less."

This letter sent me into a turmoil of emotion. I, myself, did not know for certain whether I loved him. I knew I liked his company, but there was something about the kissing that disturbed me, made me shrink away. Heaven knew he was attractive enough! What was it, then? Perhaps I wanted to suppress my feeling for him. Perhaps I was worried because kissing between couples who were not engaged was not considered nice. On the other hand, you don't consider such rules when you are in love. . . . And so it went. He still came every day to see me, and gave me lessons twice a week.

By now there could be no doubt that members of my family were aware of the growing relationship between Jim Hilsen and me. There could be no more guessing about my father's devilish winks, the nudges that Abram gave Olga when they passed the corridor.

It was about this time that Hanna returned from Germany. I began to confide my plight to her, baring my unrest and confusion at once. Hanna had matured vastly during her year in Germany. It was not really that her grief over Nathan had vanished; rather, although it had ended as an active yearning, it had become part of her, in some way. Hanna seemed softer now, and quite resigned. She no longer seemed to think of falling in love. She had had that experience and it was set apart for her, like a luxury to know only once. Now, for example, she could imagine marrying without love, an idea unpalatable to the younger Hanna. The subject of my romance with Jim was quite another thing. Hanna was charmed with it, encouraged it in every way. She tried to soothe my confusion, to explain me to myself. Wide-eyed, I listened to her telling me how wonderful it all was. She even went so far as to foresee the time of my engagement and worried on my behalf lest her own unmarried state deter me. It was customary that sisters wait for the eldest to be engaged first.

I saw that Hanna was getting carried away with the idea of my marriage to Jim. It was almost as if she would do anything to promote it.

Jim, meanwhile, was relentless in his emotion, going into excesses which were really out of character for one so reserved. For example, he wrote another story in my Memory Book. This one was entitled "The Hell of Love and Death," and it was a grisly, symbolic tale, similar to his dream of suicide provoked by unrequited love. Severe as this story was, I failed to suspect the depth of his anguish. Then, several days later, a friend of his, Mr. Grinfeld, wrote me a letter which excited me very much.

Jim had asked him to lend him his gun. He said that he knew very well that Jim was not in difficulty at school, nor did he believe there were any problems at home. His only reason for violence could be his love for me (of which the friend was aware). Therefore, he had written to advise me of the situation.

I was frightened now and talked with Jim earnestly. He agreed readily not to kill himself; indeed, he languished happily in my terrified concern.

How young we were then! No gesture seemed too bold, too rich to express the aching heart.

6

I HAD BEEN STUDYING BOOKKEEPING WITH JIM FOR SOME TIME
now, and despite the emotional complications which had been
ribboned in with this study, I thought myself somewhat pro-
ficient at it. Soon the time came when I was to take my
examination. Jim was to accompany me to the commercial
school where it was given.

I went into the classroom with the other students and
worked a long time on my paper. The atmosphere was tense
with hope and doubt. Nevertheless, I was relatively certain
of success.

When we discovered, the next day, that I had failed, the
news struck me like a thunderbolt. I flung myself on my bed
and cried bitterly. Looking back, I can see that this defeat
assumed proportions which were not justified. No doubt I was
embarrassed in front of my parents, and Jim, too. The latter
took the blame upon himself. This was not fair either. But I
was soon consoled, for more interesting things were to follow.

Jim's own studies had been progressing, and now, in
September of 1913, the long-awaited study trip to Vienna
was to be taken. He would travel with his class and the
instructor.

A brief but glorious correspondence joined us during his
absence. Stunning colored postcards and long letters arrived

at my door daily, in which he described each day's impression of this metropolis so unlike Lwow.

In one letter he wrote: "Vienna is a beautiful city with large houses. The city itself is like an eternal castle of the goddess Vindobona, and the god Danubius, to whom her soul belongs." He described the places they visited—the Hofburg; the residence of the kaiser; the museums; the stock exchange; the Adriatic Exhibition.

"All this," he wrote, "is splendid. But it is only half enjoyed, because my thoughts are constantly with you."

I would take his letters off to a quiet corner where I could enjoy them, undisturbed. The time passed with wretched slowness until Jim returned to Lwow.

At last I received a card announcing his homecoming. As I put on my best clothes I was extremely nervous. I envisioned the encounter. . . . Would he reach out to kiss me? And, if so, what response was in order? My feelings about him were still touched with ambivalence.

What actually happened when we met was an extension of our hands to each other. We kept holding them, and I did not think of pulling back. Yet even then I had no clear realization of my feelings for him. But a few incidents stand out in my memory.

I had received a card from Pepa, asking me to meet her in the park. Jim accompanied me there. It was a large park on a hill called Zamek. The Ukrainians predicted that when the time came, they would bombard Lwow from there. It began to rain, so Pepa did not show up. Jim and I were all alone there. We walked down the hill, which was slippery, and I took his arm. And there was a new ecstasy for me in this closeness. The rain on us was pleasant, not annoying, and we were radiant from within.

About a week later, we were sitting by the window in the corridor. Following a whim, I asked him to sing "Sorrento," which I liked so much. His voice, singing that song, was beautiful. I suddenly felt a desire to kiss him. But stubbornly, I held back.

Soon afterward, a friend of Hanna invited us all to the movies. Afterward, she asked Jim to see her home. I, in turn, went home with Hanna and felt miserable. I was wildly jealous. I had thought that for everyone he was implicitly, mine. Retreating to our corridor hideout, I wept furiously. When Jim returned, he found me still crying and asked me the reason. I babbled forth my true emotions. He took me in his arms and kissed me. Throwing my arms about his neck, I returned the kiss, much in love with him. Nobody in the world could shake that conviction now.

With this confirmation of our love, we had new things to talk of and to dream about together. But there were a number of obstacles to overthrow and we both knew this well. Jim had completed his studies at the University of Commerce and had received a two-year scholarship to a more advanced school in Vienna called Export Academie. If he finished this course, it would be possible to receive a Doctor of Commerce degree. That, of course, would be a great help when he went to seek a position in the commercial world. But all of this meant a two-year separation. I hated to think of it, but realized the plan was necessary to his future. For now, we wished to become engaged, and made this known to our two families.

My father, to whom we talked first, gave his consent right away. But it was not so easy with my mother. She had several objections: Hanna was not yet engaged and this made it not quite seemly. But more to the point, she objected to Jim's age. Like me, he was nineteen. While a girl of nineteen was considered mature enough for marriage, she wondered whether a boy of the same age could be serious enough. Then too, was it so wise to marry a man who was not older than you? Might he not seek a younger woman as the years progressed? Furthermore, this two-year stay in Vienna alarmed my mother. In these two years, he could easily find another girl and forget me. Perhaps that very tender regard which my mother always had for me, and which Hanna used to resent, showed itself here; for she could not bear to think of me being hurt by such a possibility. But all of Mother's arguments were fruitless. Jim assured her that his love could not be altered or challenged in the two years. He swore he would never leave me. I told my mother that I loved him, believed him, and would never give him up. It soon became obvious that no amount of opposition would dissuade us, and mother finally gave us her blessing.

Jim's father's opposition, however, was harder to overcome. He was a strict man. He had served in the Kaiser and King's Regiment as a staff sergeant for twelve years. His rule with his subordinates was obedience to discipline. His military position had given him a strong feeling of authority and he transferred it to his family, demanding absolute obedience from his children. Following his term of military service, he had a job with the post office. This provided a meager salary on which he had to support a wife and five children. Jim, being the eldest son, not only maintained himself by giving private lessons, but also contributed to the support of the family. Doubtless, his father had hoped that this subsidy would be continued.

At that time, it was customary all over Europe for a girl to bring a dowry to her husband when she was married. The bigger the position a man occupied, the larger the dowry he could command. Thus, rich girls married lawyers, doctors, and managers of big concerns or independent businessmen. Yet sometimes a man fell in love and money did not matter.

Jim knew very well that my dowry would be a modest one, but he didn't care. His father, on the other hand, regarded a match with a poor girl as highly inexpedient. He had put all his hopes into Jim, and the news of his involvement with me was a letdown. He refused to consent to the marriage.

But now he had to contend with Jim's emotion, which he had failed to measure in advance. A quarrel ensued between father and son of such violence that the father acquiesced finally. He gave Jim his consent, at last, out of fear that the boy would commit suicide if he did not. This was not uncommon in Europe, at that time. Love thwarted or unrequited was frequently sufficient motive to end a life.

Joyous at having the consent of our four parents, Jim and I now decided to be gracious and wait for Hanna to become engaged before making our announcement.

Hanna only weeks before had met Josef Selinger through the connivance of my mother. A friend of Mother's had a nephew who seemed both to his aunt and my mother an ideal possibility for Hanna. Josef, from the first, was attracted to Hanna, and let it be known that he wished to marry her. My sister had been willing to cultivate him, but certainly showed no signs of being in love. Josef was tall, strapping, athletic-looking, but he was not highly educated and really had not too much in common with Hanna. I suspect she took his appearance into account when making her appraisals. But she was very matter-of-fact about him, never giddy. My mother watched hopefully for signs of interest from Hanna, for the shadow of Nathan still hovered over our memories. But for a while Hanna gave no indication that she could regard Josef as anything more than a friend.

One day, Hanna came home from shopping and retreated wordlessly to a chair. After a few minutes, when she had failed to greet me, I walked over to her and saw with alarm that she was deathly pale. Her hand, on the arm of the chair, was trembling.

"What is it Hanna?" I whispered, frightened. "Are you ill?"

She shook her head, and tears formed silently in her eyes.

"Tell me, then," I begged. "What has happened?"

"I saw him," she stated bluntly.

I looked at her with confusion.

"Nathan," she clarified. "And he was with another girl. Helena, I thought I had overcome so much of my feeling for him. But when I saw him today, and with his arm linked to that girl's, my heart just about broke. It was agony. I felt that he still belonged to me. I was outraged to see someone else in that possessive way with him!"

"How did he look?" I asked, not knowing what comment to make.

"Terrible," she admitted, wiping her eyes. "Yes, Helena, he was half a block away, but I could see he was paler than ever. He is worse. Mother was right. He must be ill."

"You know, Hanna," I began timidly, "I wonder if you could forget Nathan, altogether, and try to concentrate on someone who is whole and healthy, like Josef. . . . Do you think you could grow to love him. He *is* rather attractive."

"Yes," Hanna conceded. "He has a certain sex appeal."

It was probably this sex appeal of Josef's that caused Hanna to see him with a heightened interest. In the following days, a note of finality about him had struck her. She now saw Josef constantly.

My mother was delighted, because she liked Josef very much. He had a great deal of warmth, and always had something apt to say to people. I do not really know the complexities of thought which Hanna experienced during those weeks, but gradually a decision formed within her. It came as no great surprise to any of us when she finally gave her consent.

I had secret misgivings, of course, when she told me she had decided. I was afraid that the fear of spinsterhood had pressured her, that even her desire to smooth out the path for my marriage might be prompting her.

Still, it was a gay time when her engagement was announced, the same month as ours, June of 1914.

7

Now a happy time followed for Jim and me. The ordeal of his courtship with me had won him my love. For me, it had resulted in a revelation. The joy that I now experienced in the excitement of being in love, with the attendant certainty that it was returned, exceeded any youthful dreams or ambitions. Now my earlier speculations about a woman's destiny succumbed to the commonplace, which in the living of it seemed more rare than anything. In our case it was even more intense than usual because of the year of conflict and struggle which had preceded our engagement. It was clear to me now that a mutual love brought a happiness not approached by any other in life.

So I began to live permanently with a consciousness of Jim. Everything about him pleased me in those days of constant discovery. I found his manners distinctive, was constantly aware of his intelligence, which seemed so finely graded. His style of writing struck my fancy. And then his face, his whole person, was wildly attractive.

He, too, existed in a radiance of conquest and gratification at my response. People around us seemed always to be smiling, indulging us in our mood.

Abram had known about us for a long time, and was delighted that the long, vacillating months had culminated in romance. After all, it was he who had first brought his friend, Jim, to the house. Hanna was immensely relieved when I became engaged, feeling that at least I had achieved the situation which had eluded her — a union with a loved person.

The younger children, of course, understood little of the nature of betrothals and what went into them. But Olga, now fifteen years old, had known for months about the mounting tension and love that was building between Jim and me. And she rejoiced with the idea of it. She was an avid reader of books and poems dealing with the subject of love. Now she chose to regard Jim and me as heroes of a love story.

Thus wrapped in our new status and in the glowing confirmation of our happiness by relatives and friends, we felt that nothing could interfere with us.

But there are forces against which one is powerless and which may choose to intervene just when one has achieved a goal of years' standing. We, for example, could not stop the war, which finally broke out in August, 1914. Our dreams now had to be altered, and we felt that dark clouds, dreary ones, had appeared in the sky. We knew that war meant only destruction and death. Yet at the beginning of the war, people were enthusiastic and shouted : "Long live the war!"

Automatically, Jim and I were drawn into this mass response, found ourselves caught up in gatherings and in groups marching down the streets. We must have forgotten ourselves completely. It was as though we became a part of the people with whom we shared a mutual destiny. Nobody knew who would survive the war.

There were many heartbreaking scenes. Fathers, sons, brothers, and fiancés joined the army and abruptly were gone. Our family was no exception. My poor mother had to relinquish Abram, her eldest son. All her crying and lamenting could not hold him back. And now Josef, Hanna's fiancé, was also called for duty. I was lucky Jim was too young to be drafted.

Still, we lived near the battle front and the war was perilously close, always. At any time, any one of us could have lost his life. Shortly after the war broke out our soldiers had to retreat. We saw them marching down our street. They walked slowly, their uniforms dirty from dust and blood. They were hungry and thirsty. We brought out bread and water and distributed them among those pitiable men.

Naturally, escape was rife. People were fleeing from Lwow. Families everywhere were lining up valises in front of their homes, dashing about to make quick arrangements to leave, if they were lucky enough.

I had noticed, in the chaos, that my mother seemed unwell. She had been extremely pale since Abram had left for the army and now suffered attacks of queasiness at the table, often pushing away her food altogether. I supposed that the scene of flight and unrest all around us had upset her rather severely.

But one day her illness came to a crisis. Hanna and I had noticed that she had gone to lie down right after breakfast. This was highly unusual for mother. Later, Father had gone into the room to see how she was feeling. A few minutes after that, he burst out of the room and ran to Hanna.

"Go to your mother, right away, Hanna. She's ill. She will tell you!"

Hanna ran into Mother's bedroom, leaving the door open. I heard my mother groan.

"Hanna, it's not so well with me. . . . I'm pregnant. . . . I didn't tell you. This morning I felt faint. . . . I had cramps, violent ones. Now I'm losing the baby."

I heard Hanna mumble something and then she ran from the room.

"I'm going for the doctor now," she said to my father.

I went into Mother's room, and sat down on the bed beside her.

"Why didn't you tell us before about the baby, Mother? We could have helped you more, made things easier. Why did you keep it a secret?"

She closed her eyes as a wave of pain went through her.

"I was embarrassed, Helena. At my age, another baby? I have a son in the army and two engaged daughters! I really couldn't bring myself to mention. . . . And I haven't felt well for weeks. Since Abram left, I've been faint and weak. . . ." She broke off, moaning again.

I sat talking with her for about half an hour. Father kept looking in and then pacing around by the front door. Why hadn't Hanna returned with the doctor? Mother's condition was growing worse.

Hanna came in then, annoyed and frightened.

"But where is the doctor?" I gasped.

"What doctor?" she retorted. "I don't think there's one to be had in all of Lwow! Our doctor was gone—fled. I asked around and got two more names. When I went to their offices, one had just left with the army and the other had several emergencies waiting for him. At the hospital, they were under-staffed, they couldn't let anyone go!" She tiptoed to the door-way of Mother's room.

My father, as Hanna had spoken, had emptied both his pockets and part of the contents of a small box.

"Here, Hanna," he said, and he pressed a considerable amount of money into her hands.

"But Father. . . ." she began to protest.

"She's very bad, Hanna, and somewhere, find a doctor. Give it all to him, but bring one," my father pleaded. "Your mother's got to have a doctor, that's all."

Hanna raced out of the door again like one possessed. I wanted to go with her but one of us had to stay here with Father, to help Mother if possible.

Mother had now grown very faint in her agony. I held her

hand and her pulse seemed very slight to my unpracticed fingers. She tried not to cry out, but occasionally a tear or two escaped from her lowered lids. I kept imagining that I heard Hanna returning.

After half an hour, Hanna entered the apartment breathlessly, with a man in tow. She had found a doctor.

The doctor examined my mother briefly and began to act quickly. He asked Hanna to cover the dining room table with sheets, to boil water, and to assist him.

After that, the two of them worked over mother behind closed doors. Father and I waited miserably outside. The doctor's expression had shown clearly that her case was urgent.

Once we heard Mother scream terribly. In less than an hour, he had operated without any anesthesia.

"She is out of danger," he informed us, as he emerged from the bedroom with Hanna, who looked pale and faint, herself.

"Thank God!" my father said, sinking into a chair.

When the doctor was gone, I talked with Hanna a long time about the strangeness of the incident, our ignorance of the expected baby, Mother's feeling about it, and the miscarriage.

"It may have been for the best, in some way," I said. "If we flee with the others, she would have lost the baby en route, which would have been worse."

The next day, Jim rushed into the house excitedly and said, "Helena, my father just got an order from the Postal Office to leave Lwow. We are going to Vienna! Now what about your family?"

I sighed, pausing in my labors. I was preparing lunch for Mother.

"Oh, my father tried to get us accommodation a while back, but all the trains had been taken by the army. Now we can thank God we didn't leave. Mother had a miscarriage yesterday, Jim," I confided. "Had we been travelling, I doubt she would have lived through it."

"A miscarriage?" Jim said, astonished. "In this town at this time. Thank God it's over, you are right!"

"I am still a bit shaken from the whole business," I confessed.

Jim was pacing back and forth nervously, biting his lip and thinking. He turned to me intensely.

"So as of now, you have no way out of Lwow?"

"None."

"Helena, whatever happens, I won't leave you. From this point on, I stay where you stay. I'm going now to talk with my father and ask him to do everything he can to help your family get out of Lwow. He's a government worker, after all. There must be some way he can manage accommodations for all of you!"

Jim rushed home. In the afternoon he returned with the news that his father had managed to get permission for our family to leave on the same train that they were taking—the next evening at nine. It was a special train which the government had put at the disposal of its employees. So we were really going to flee Lwow with the others. How unreal this seemed even in its urgency! Hanna and I frantically prepared the essentials, insisting that Mother rest until we left the house. We packed the necessary clothing, a flour bag with bread, and a large milk can containing homemade preserves.

We somehow found a carriage to take Mother and the children to the station. The rest of us had to walk, for the trolleys were not running.

It was late in the evening when our train started to move slowly out of the Lwow station. Jim and I looked out of the window. We heard detonations from a distance. The sounds did not seem far away. In the darkness of night, we saw the fire-red sky. It seemed to me a mixture of fire and the blood of fallen soldiers, which had risen so high, covering the sky. I have never forgotten the sight of that sky.

The next morning, we stopped at the station of Tarnow, a small town. There we saw trains standing, crowded with refugees like ourselves from other cities. Some asked whether we had bread to give them. They and their children were very hungry. My mother did not hesitate. Readily, as was her way, she dipped into our supply and handed them bread through the train windows.

Later we got off the train in another small city, Rzeszow. Here we remained for a brief time. My father rented rooms and also a bakery, where he baked bread. It was the only thing people wanted now. But we were soon forced to flee from Rzeszow, also, because the enemy was moving nearer and nearer. Everywhere we saw the pitiful picture of our retreating soldiers.

Our two families packed again. This time we were put into cattle wagons, which were to take us to a town in the Carpathian Mountains. The journey was arduous with noise, discomfort, and fear. Children cried and could not be consoled. I watched my mother comfort Mela, Stela, and Bernatz. Her face was controlled, but somewhere within that ample frame I knew her heart must be breaking. Who could have foreseen this broken exile of ours, months ago, when a betrothal took precedence over all other news? Now all her years in Lwow were uprooted, jouncing in a cattle wagon. The wagon lurched suddenly, and I was thrown against Hanna. But she hardly seemed to notice. Her head was bent, her mouth fixed with depression. She must have been thinking of Josef. Where was he now? On what battlefield? Or was she perhaps even wondering where Nathan was, if he survived now.

I, in contrast to the misery of my mother and sister, felt almost happy. For Jim sat next to me, a strange refugee in this cattle wagon. My love, my newfound joy, had come along with us, and I now felt almost ashamed as I studied the others. My happiness was a terrible incongruity in the midst of this flight.

We arrived in the mountains very early in the morning. The large waiting hall of the railway station was crowded with refugees. Children and adults were lying asleep on the floor.

We did not mind sleeping there also, although it was a hard stone floor. We were very tired. The next day, we acquired two empty rooms, with only straw on the floor to sleep on. Half an hour's walk from there was a larger city where the Austrian High Command had its headquarters. There, Jim and I saw Crown Prince Karl and his generals on the street. We stayed in this little town over the High Holy Days. Then we continued our journey. This time, our goal was Vienna.

In Vienna, the government authorities were anti-Semitic and wanted to refuse to admit Jewish refugees. They were forced to yield, however, at the command of the Kaiser, who ordered them to admit his Jewish subjects to Vienna.

En route to Vienna, our train stopped at a very small station. Looking out of the window, I read the Polish name *Oswiecim*. This was a very obscure place. We never dreamed that twenty-six years hence this unknown little spot would become the most infamous crematorium of all time — *Auschwitz*.

Now we neared Vienna. From the bridge over the Danube, we saw the lights of the city. Never before had I seen such a dazzle of lights! Its beauty was before us, emboldening our hopes. And seeing it for the first time, I recalled the words that Jim had written to me from Vienna, when he had come here as a student.

"This is the eternal city of the goddess Vindobona, and of the god Danubius, to whom her soul belongs." I felt happy and grateful to be together with my family and Jim.

This was our first escape from war.

PART II
Vienna

8

On a late September night in 1914, we arrived in Vienna, forlorn and anxious in the immense railroad station. My father could barely conceal his relief when Jim, the only one of us who could speak German, took over, finding a taxi for us on the mobbed street. In the car, we were packed three deep. Jim asked the driver to take us to an inexpensive hotel. As we rode, we forgot our discomfort because the lights and broad streets of Vienna excited us so. Except for Jim, who had been here last year, none of us had ever ridden in a taxi before.

Arriving at the hotel, I counted six flights to the building. Hanna and I were terribly impressed. At the desk, we heard Jim asking the clerk for two rooms, one for the males, one for the females. We poured into those rooms gratefully, hardly caring which of us lay on beds, which on the floor, so great was our exhaustion from the journey.

In the morning we awoke feeling rested and, somehow, happy. We were also famished. Hanna, Leon, and I were utterly enthralled with the hotel dining room where we were served breakfast. The little ones murmured with delight, sensing a certain relaxation in their elders. Bernatz, only five, kept leaving his chair and running around the room. It was difficult to restrain him. Our gaiety was such that it all began to seem like a party, until my father sobered us with his remarks.

"We won't be able to live in a hotel very long, children. Our money would soon run out. Remember, this money we've saved is all we have in the world and there won't be anymore till I find a way to make a living." He paused to smile briefly at my mother. I glanced around self-consciously. Were the other hotel guests staring at us because we spoke in Yiddish?

My mother sighed. "You are right. It won't be easy in this large city, with no relatives, no friends to help us." A familiar anxiety gripped her expression.

"Never mind!" my father said with sudden vigor. "There are Jews here who surely won't let us down. I'll go out and I'll find one. Don't worry! Someone will be able to advise us. Now, my first concern is to find a place for us to live."

Fifteen minutes later, I watched my father leave the hotel. Despite his courageous expression, he looked a little pathetic in his shabby suit, worn out on the journey from Lwow. I blinked once or twice, then turned my attention back to Jim and the others. Mother stood up and began to herd the little ones back to the room. I was about to follow her when Jim caught my arm and said, "Helena, let's go out, for a little while at least. I can show you the immediate neighbourhood."

Gladly, I followed him outside. Our hotel was situated a block away from Praterstrasse. This wide street was lined on either side with city dwellings, coffee houses, and stores. Jim, who saw how impressed I was, began to laugh at me.

"This isn't the main street of Vienna, Helena! Only a street in Leopoldstadt. Most Viennese Jews live in this district."

We walked down the Praterstrasse to the Praterhauptallee, a long boulevard lined with chestnut trees. It was a beautiful autumn day, still warm and highly colored from the turning leaves. On the ground, ripe chestnuts had fallen in their open green shells. Benches were placed on either side of the road and these were occupied largely by children and their nurses. People promenaded on the road itself, but I was most fascinated by the luxurious coaches conveying noblemen and ladies in brilliantly colored dresses. On a high seat in the rear, a footman in livery was perched. How beautiful this scene was! I had dreamed of visiting this city, which, in my imagination appeared as a fairyland of castles and kings. I had never imagined that my longing to see the place would be realized so soon, or under such circumstances.

We turned then and walked to a side alley which led to an extraordinary place called the Prater. This was a glowing amusement park, the first I had ever seen. Its main attraction was a huge wheel called *Riesenrad* which conveyed its laughing riders to great heights overlooking Vienna.

It seemed a paradox that the horror of World War I had propelled us to this magnificent place, which I, as a young girl, could not help loving. The war, itself young, had not yet touched Vienna, so that all its beauties were intact to beguile us.

Jim and I passed several hours, unaware of time. Hunger finally drove us back to the hotel, where my mother was waiting anxiously for us. Hanna and Olga had also ventured out, but had returned soon, afraid of getting lost. All of them bombarded us with questions.

"Where have you been all this time? What have you seen?"

With enthusiasm I described the Prater, the streets, and the people.

"You surely saw enough for the first day!" my mother exclaimed.

At this point my father entered and the attention of all was diverted to him.

Somewhat angrily, my mother addressed him. "What took you so long? Have you been sightseeing, too?"

"Sightseeing!" he retorted. "Pleasure is not on my mind

right now. I have other worries . . . you know, a home and a *parnuse*!"*

"So?" insisted Mother impatiently, "Where have you been and what have you accomplished?"

"Let me sit down and catch my breath, first. Then I'll tell you."

We waited patiently while he settled himself in a chair. Soon he began his story.

"When I left the hotel, I walked through the streets not knowing where to turn. It was impossible to distinguish a Jew, since everyone seems to dress alike here. How could I approach a gentile? He might be an anti-Semite, and anyway, I couldn't speak German. I was at quite a loss. Then, as if God had sent me a *sheliach*,** a Polish Jew with a beard came toward me. I asked him in Yiddish, 'Where are you from, Brother?'

"'From Rzeszov,' he answered.

"'How long do you live in Vienna?' I asked.

"'One month.'

"'Do you have *parnuse*?'

"'In such a short time, how can I?'

"'But what do you live on?'

"'I get relief,' he told me.

"Then he started to ask me questions—how long I was in Vienna. I told him I had only arrived last night with my family, that I was worried about using up all my money on hotels, that I didn't know what to do next.

"'Listen to me!' the Jew said. 'Go to Taborstrasse II. There is a refugee committee and they will give you relief.'

"'What does it mean, *refugee*?'

"'The Viennese Jews call us refugees. They don't like us Polish Jews. They think they're better than we are. Here

---

* Hebrew expression meaning "livelihood."
** Hebrew, "messenger of God."

they are at home and more cultured than we. They consider us inferior.'

"'Because we had to leave our homes and belongings escaping war, we are not worse than they!' I told him. After all, we also are Austrians. I refuse to be called a refugee!'"

"I agree!" Olga cried. "We don't want to be called refugees!"

"Don't interrupt Father!" I said. "We want to hear what happened."

Father continued his story. Not knowing any other course, he had gone to the refugee committee the man had spoken of. Before it, a long line of waiting men and women had formed, most of them more destitute than we. As he stood there, my father had become conscious that he was waiting in line for charity, and a terrible feeling of humiliation had seized him. Helplessly, he had begun to cry. A policeman, standing nearby had noticed him, come over, and asked the cause of his grief.

"I don't want relief!" my father told him. "I'm a good baker and I can work. If only I could get a bakery, I could support my family!" Miraculously, the policeman had smiled and told him, "I can help you. I know of a vacant bakery. Meet me here tomorrow at three and I'll take you to the place."

Suddenly, jubilation filled the room. The children started to dance and embrace my father. It was a happy prospect, indeed; he would have his own bakery again.

In October, my father took over the empty bakery. It was situated on the ground floor of a one-story house in Leopold-stadt. The bakery itself was a large, light place with windows facing a courtyard, and my father also rented a store in the front of the house for the purpose of selling his bread. There were only two apartments in the house, both of which were occupied. But in the rear of the bakery there was a large storeroom, and this was to become our temporary home. My father converted it into two rooms which, however primitive, we were grateful to have. They contained nothing except a few beds, a large iron stove for cooking, a table and chairs, and some nails on the wall for our clothes. At the beginning of winter we were residing in this place, our first home in Vienna. And it was nearly to cost the lives of my brothers, sisters, and me.

Autumn had passed, our first in the city. Then came the first cold winter day. The night before, snow had fallen and was now piled high in the courtyard. Our rooms were bare and terribly cold, lacking any form of heat except from the cooking stove. We went to bed that night in the usual manner, feeling cold as we undressed. Later I was awaked by a thin voice complaining, "Mommy, I'm cold." But I fell back to sleep.

When I opened my eyes, I was lying in snow in the courtyard, seeing people like ghosts rushing frantically back and forth. I closed my eyes, wanting only to go back to sleep. Never had sleep seemed so good, so sweetly persuasive, and I fought against all attempts to awaken me. Finally, the coldness on my face roused me slightly. I opened my eyes and discovered someone rubbing snow on my face and body, trying to revive me. Little by little I came to. Looking around, I recognized my father and mother in a very excited state; Hanna was beside them. Strangers had gathered in the courtyard to help or watch. When I sat up, I saw my little brothers and sisters, still lying in the snow, while people were working on them. Fortunately, we were all saved. At that point, however, I was not yet fully aware that we had all been victims of gas poisoning.

Later, I learned what had happened. When, deep in the night, my mother had heard Bernatz, her youngest, calling that he was cold, she had covered him with a coat she found nearby. After that, she was unable to fall back to sleep.

Worried that we might catch pneumonia, Mother rose earlier than usual, Hanna followed her in a little while. My father was already at work in the bakery, with Leon assisting him. By now the wood in the large oven was burned out, leaving little glowing coals. Therefore, Mother took a large tin plate filled with coals and, while we were still asleep, put them on top of the cooking stove in our room. Now she was happy; her children would be warm. My poor mother did not realize that this act of love might potentially result in the greatest tragedy.

About two hours later, she came in with a basket full of fresh rolls to make breakfast for us, calling "It's time to get up children!" No one moved. Incredulous, she again called out, "Helena, Olga, get up!"But there was no answer to her shouts. We lay unmoving before her eyes, deaf to her shouts. Terrified, she rushed to our beds and began to shake us, one by one. No one responded. Her piercing scream galvanized my father, Hanna, and Leon, who flew in from the bakery. Seeing our lifeless bodies, they, too, were terror-stricken. Hanna and Leon ran out of doors and began to shout for help. People came in from the street. One of them called a doctor. Others helped to lift us from our beds, carry us to the courtyard, and lay us in the deep snow, where we were ultimately revived.

This accident was reported not only in all the Vienna newspapers, but in certain American papers, too. By an extraordinary coincidence, a cousin of Father's, who had left Galicia some fifty years before to live in America, happened to read of the incident in a Philadelphia newspaper. From the article he learned my father's address and promptly wrote to him, enclosing a check for $1,000.

Not long after this incident, a large, four-room apartment on the first floor was vacated and after my father furnished it we moved in. We soon recovered from the shock of the accident. I, for one, was happy to be alive. Vienna, the beautiful city, enchanted me more and more. I gazed with wonder at the opera house, parliament, and other stately buildings. Jim had become familiar with Vienna when he had studied here and he liked to show me all of the places he had admired in a time of peace. But now, with the war on, he made a point of showing me the Ministry of War. It was a large, modern structure with high windows, a block long. Before both sides of the entrance, there were booths with guards standing in them.

"Can you read the inscription on the top?" Jim asked.

I read the following: "SI VIS PACEM PARA BELLUM," and shrugged my shoulders.

"This is Latin and it says, 'When you want peace, prepare for war,' Jim translated. "Here in this building generals hold conferences and discuss war strategies," he added.

Even as we stood there, many generals and high-ranking officers were going in and out of the building. They wore blue uniforms with gold-trimmed trousers and helmets with long green plumes. Their presence added to the pomp of the scene, suggesting more of story-books than war. But the posters nearby, bearing the latest war bulletins, reminded us of the war going on, of the shooting and killing in the territory we had left so recently. Our generation was fighting this war. We felt involved, worldly, changed.

Here, as in Lwow, my mother's world remained limited to the care of her family and the running of the store, where Father's bread was sold. He, in turn, was absorbed in his bakery. Only the children seemed to radiate with the expanse of our new metropolitan horizon. Possibilities undreamed of in Lwow shimmered in the very air we breathed in Vienna.

My mother seemed to understand how we felt, sensing our desire to feel adequate here, to gain a sense of belonging. Accordingly, she hired a tutor to come to the house to help

Hanna and me perfect our German, since this was the official language of Austria. In Lwow, the public schools had required the study of three languages—Polish, Ukrainian, and German. Consequently, our German needed more polish. Our tutor taught us better German by reading with us from German literature and mythology, thus broadening our knowledge of those subjects, too. Jim had no need to join us in this pursuit. His German was already perfect due to his years of study at the commercial academy, where language training had been on a very high level. He could hold his own with the most educated Viennese, a fact which I beheld with no little pride.

The younger children in the family now attended a public school and learned quickly, as children do. Olga, Mela, Stela, Saul, and Bernatz became small blossoming Viennese. Leon was now sent to an engineering school. But, of course, Abram, the eldest, was still missing from the family circle. We felt his absence keenly, and my mother worried about him constantly.

Hanna's Josef was lucky. Having advanced to the position of sergeant, he was transferred to a post on the outskirts of Vienna, where he was to train the newly enlisted boys. This placement expedited his courtship of Hanna, which delighted my mother. We were all grateful that Josef had been spared from combat duty.

My brother Abram was not to be as fortunate. Mother was stricken by the news that he had just been transferred to the front for combat duty. A shadow was cast over the family's spirit. But Sala Brand, his fiancée, was in a dreadful state. She, with her family, had also fled from Lwow to Vienna for the duration of the war and we maintained close contact with her. When Jim and I visited her, she wept, and it was clear that she lived in fear of losing Abram in battle. We tried to be reassuring, but what could one say when Abram's letters became less and less frequent, with great gaps of time between them?

As for Hanna, she was certainly pleased that Josef was safe and in a position to see her often. I cannot say that she was ecstatic, however. Her affection for Josef continued to be rather too mild, considering that they were engaged. Her loyalty to him, however, was unfailing. She would occasionally be invited out by some extremely eligible youths, here in Vienna, but, in the light of her engaged status, she did not dream of accepting. Technically, I saw now, her union with Josef was a *fait accompli*. She conceded that Josef was a striking figure in military uniform.

Jim was still in civilian clothes. In Lwow, he had hoped to attend the Export Academy in Vienna through the scholarship he had won. But the war had rendered his scholarship invalid, so he now had to find an occupation for himself. When we had first arrived in Vienna, Jim's family had settled in the outskirts of town, miles away from us because the rent was cheap. His father's pension was so small that it would have been impossible for him to support Jim as well as his younger children. Thus Jim, as a future son-in-law, came along with our family. He rented a room close to our place, which my father paid for. This was possible because the bakery, from the start, did not lack for customers. Jim, however, wished to become economically independent as soon as possible. He did not like to have my parents support him.

At the time, the only job he could find was in a war plant, and this was on the night shift. The work was very strenuous and the night hours difficult to adjust to. Frequently, he was unable to sleep in the daytime to catch up. Being unused to manual labor, and suffering from lack of sleep, he collapsed after a short time, and became ill. I became very alarmed about him. Jim was forced to stay in bed for a week, slowly recuperating. When he was able to be up, he looked pale and exhausted. Just at this time, the army notified him to report for duty. The medical division then promptly rejected him because of his physical condition.

Subsequently, he found a job with a government department especially created to meet the needs of wartime. This department's function was to confiscate grain, to control the distribution of flour to bakers, and to manage bread rationing.

Jim was pleased with his new job, happy to be self-sufficient. He proved himself capable in no time and was soon promoted to a department head. On Saturdays, I picked him up at his office and we would spend the afternoon enjoying Vienna. This actually constituted a departure from tradition, for on *Shabbas* in the old days, I was in the habit of remaining pretty much at home. At one time, particularly in Przemysl, it would have been unthinkable for any member of our family to spend money on Saturday. Even in Lwow, where the atmosphere was a little freer, we would have hesitated before patronizing a movie or a coffeehouse. Now there was a general inclination to spread out, to fail to differentiate ourselves as distinctly as before. Even my mother, who had left her *sheitel* behind in the flight from Lwow, had not bothered to get another one in Vienna. Now her beautiful black hair had grown full again and was worn neatly combed. She of course maintained the Sabbath strictly, as before. But I, wandering through Vienna with Jim, began to feel more progressive about things, and began to regard Saturday as Jim's day off — a day meant for enjoyment.

His office was located on Herrengasse, which was near the Hofburg. We had only to pass Ballhouse Square and enter from the inner part of the city to the Kaiser's castle. Here there was a large courtyard next to the castle where the Kaiser's guard was stationed. At twelve noon, the changing of the guard was enacted. This was a stirring spectacle, replete with music and marching.

On this particular Saturday, Jim and I decided to take a

guided tour through the interior of the Hofburg. The halls were full of splendor, glittering with crystal chandeliers, elegant with furnishings of the decadent Louis XIV era. The walls were hung with perfectly executed Gobelins and with portraits of all the Hapsburg dynasty. We were shown the halls where the Kaiser received his subjects, giving them audience behind a massive desk.

Saturday alone was set aside for Hofburg visitors. Suddenly, wandering through the Hofburg mobs, I was confronted with a face—was it possible? The dark, mischievous eyes roving, the olive skin and black hair—

"Helka!" I called. "Helka Schwartz!"

She whirled about, her face blossoming into a smile of recognition.

I pushed toward her, pulling Jim along with me.

"I can't believe it!" she said, genuinely delighted. "You, in Vienna, Helena!"

The three of us found a corner where we could speak. I kept staring at my old friend, the "Polish nationalist"! The world was not so big, after all. She related her move from Lwow. Her family had fled right after the war broke out, had come to Vienna. Now her father was well established here. He was making uniforms for the army. I told her about our exodus from Lwow, with all its uncertainty, and how my father had found the empty bakery from which our new survival stemmed. While I spoke, Helka kept looking at Jim.

"But what's the matter with me!" I exclaimed. "I haven't introduced you to my fiancé! Helka, this is Jim Hilsen."

"Oh," she said, appraising him well, "I didn't know you had found yourself such a good-looking boy!"

"I followed your advice," I answered glibly, and we all laughed, feeling close somehow.

Before we parted, I gave Helka my address and asked her to come and see me.

9

IN THE COURSE OF A YEAR, OUR LIVES HAD DEVELOPED A
certain pattern in Vienna. It was much different from the life
we had known in Lwow. Life had become much easier for my
mother and father. There was no need to keep horses and
wagons to distribute bread to the stores. Here, people came to
our store, which mother, with Hanna's help and mine, tended.
The need to solicit customers, so strenuous a chore for my
mother, had vanished. There was no lack of customers here;
instead, my father was faced with a lack of flour. He struck
upon the idea of importing grain from outside of Austria and
subsequently made a trip to Hungary where he bought some.
He had it processed by Austrian millers and thus was supplied
with enough flour to make the bread his customers needed.
This clever idea on his part was the beginning of prosperity
for our family. Things began to change. Suddenly, we could
afford to have a maid, so badly needed with so many children
in the house. As a result, Hanna and I were needed less and
enjoyed more free time.

But life began to change for Imperial Vienna, too. In the
summer of 1916, Kaiser Franz Josef I passed away at the
venerable age of 86. His death had a profound effect upon
the population. A benevolent leader, he had been almost
universally adored, so that his passing seemed to mark the end
of an era. On the day of his funeral, Jim and I watched the

funeral procession move from the Hofburg to St. Stefansdom, where the Hapsburgs were entombed in catacombs. Guards in black livery carried the casket and on all sides crowds, grief-stricken, pushed gently against the soldiers who formed its guard. These stood in rigid military formation, anonymous under their plumed helmets, their grief unread. Walking behind the casket was Crown Prince Karl and his wife, Zita, dressed in mourning black. Between them walked their three-year-old son, Otto, next pretender to the throne of Austria. Following the family, in slow steps, were the German Kaiser Wilhelm and the royalty of other friendly nations. After them came the nobles, the government dignitaries, and the high army staff. Every eye seemed hurt by the sight of the ornate casket. The loss was genuine and I was not alone in shedding tears for this good kaiser.

After the death of Franz Josef, his successor, Karl, was proclaimed Kaiser of the Austro-Hungarian Monarchy. It was just at this time that World War I was entering its second year. Now the gay picture of Vienna started to fade. In the streets, the number of soldiers in khaki uniforms increased. There was sadness in the city with their presence and their departure for the frontier. Later, the sight became more depressing when many of them returned, wounded and crippled.

Not only the street scenes became oppressive, but a food shortage began to be felt. Bread, dairy products, and other groceries were now rationed. The longer the war continued, the smaller the rations grew. On cold winter days, a long line of people stood before our bakery. My mother made tea and distributed it to the people while they waited suffering with cold.

In those gloomy days, Jim and I were happy not to be separated. Being young and in love, we had the power to detach ourselves from the misery of war, despite the fact that it surrounded us. We pictured our future in a peaceful world.

In Jim's spare time we continued to explore the city, seeking this time the section known as Old Vienna. There, narrow, romantic streets still existed. Its charming little one-storey houses were well preserved, with their small square windows and little balconies. Jim and I were particularly curious to see the inside of one of these houses. We entered one through a gate and walked onto a corridor. This led to a stone, plastered courtyard. From the courtyard, stairs led to a balcony which went all around the first floor. From various points of this balcony were the entrances to individual apartments. People were still living in them. In one of these houses, Schubert had lived and composed his music.

The other section of Old Vienna, significantly for us, was the Old Ghetto. It, too, was well-preserved, but in contrast to the section we had just visited, its one-storey houses were primitive. Nevertheless, Jews still lived in them and some ran stores in the fronts of these dwellings.

Now the *Israelitische Kultusgemeinde* was functioning there. This was a large, legal community house, adjoined to the oldest synagogue in Vienna, and it took charge of all Jewish affairs—religious, cultural, charitable, and funereal. Since there was no separation of church and state, each Jew was required by law to pay taxes to cover those expenses.

By 1917, with the war in its third year, the situation with food and clothing had worsened. The blackmarket was flourishing. There was no prospect of a speedy end to the war and its misery. Widows, orphans, and cripples were abundant. We followed the current events and walked daily to the Ministry of War, where a bulletin was posted with the news. Almost invariably, we read of a victory on our side. Yet we knew that all this news could not be true, and that we were losing the war. We seemed almost not to care—if only the war would come to an end.

That same year, news of great significance was heard by Jews all over the world. The Balfour Declaration, a document which declared Palestine, then controlled by the British, a Jewish national homeland, was proclaimed. Lord Balfour had made this proclamation as a sort of reward to Chaim Weizmann, a Jew who had done much for the British war effort. In addition, Lord Balfour was himself a great sympathizer with the age-old need for such a homeland.

There was much talk of this even in my father's bakery that spring. Before Passover, he had employed some young boys and girls to help in the baking of matzohs. Many of these young people, like us, had escaped from Galicia with their parents. Now, with the news of Palestine, there was constant talk among them of an organization, *Hashomer,* which most of them joined. This was a group which had formed and grown in Eastern Europe, comprised of young people who were willing and even yearning to toss aside their past lives and to endure any struggle, if they could go to Palestine and work the land as their own.

Many of this group from our bakery actually did go to Palestine. We had word of them through relatives in Vienna, who were close friends. They were called *Chalutzim* (pioneers) and they worked under the burning sun, building roads, with little food and water to sustain them. Many were to develop malaria there. Few were to live to see the later establishment of Israel. No one could deny that the conditions to which these *Chalutzim* were exposed were full of disease and danger.

Thus it came as a great shock to my family when Leon, the second oldest boy, announced that he would join them. Always a Zionist, Leon had been fired with enthusiasm by the discussions in the bakery. Among other subjects, it had frequently been mentioned that engineers and other scientific men were desperately needed in Palestine. Leon's idealism needed no other word. His study of electrical engineering in Vienna had equipped him to make a real contribution. And there was no dissuading him, once he had made up his mind.

My mother was disconsolate. It was not that she, herself, did not love the idea of Palestine. But her maternal instincts were stronger than anything. With Abram away at the front, how could she bear to have Leon leave for a country so far away, so full of peril? She implored Hanna and me to talk him out of it. But Leon would not be swayed. He tried to console my mother with the thought that engineers had better living conditions than some, that he would not stay indefinitely. When the group was to leave, Leon joined them.

We now regarded my sister Olga with a fearful eye. She, too, was an ardent member of *Hashomer*. She attended all their gatherings, and many of her friends had left with Leon's group. Although we were afraid to mention it out loud, we were afraid that her intellectual ardor might propel her to the Promised Land.

But we could have spared ourselves the worry. Fortunately for us, Olga was too fond of the soft life in Vienna. She was only too well aware of the rigors and disease which would await her as a *chalutz,* and, with admirable frankness, she disqualified herself.

Instead, she remained in Vienna, finishing the eighth grade, after which she enrolled in a private gymnasium. This particular gymnasium graduated certain of its talented students with a *matura*—a certificate of some esteem in Europe—and Olga was to be one of them.

10

At last the war came to an end. Immediately, Jim's family left Vienna. His father, with other government employees, was called back to Poland by the Polish government to resume the job he had left behind.

At this time, the misery in Austria had reached its peak. There was starvation and, in addition, Spanish Influenza, which claimed many victims. Our family was not spared. First the two youngest girls, Mela and Stela, were stricken. I sat up nights with them, watching their little faces fearfully, applying cool towels to their foreheads, and waiting for the fever to break. On the third day, a chill gripped me as I helped Mother prepare the food. By evening, it was clear that I, too, had the disease. The three weeks that followed put terror into the entire family. But fortunately we all survived.

This epidemic was compounded by the scene of soldiers returning from the front in pitiful condition. So much misery prevailed that it was difficult to realize that its basic cause was ended.

Among the ceaseless throngs of returning soldiers, my brother Abram returned to us. But our rejoicing was tainted by the picture of him, for he was altered by the war. He looked pale and sick. My mother could not help but be disturbed. Still he was here with us again. We had much to be grateful for.

And there was Sala Brand, waiting for him, rushing to embrace him, and uttering little cries over his pallor. Their reunion was rather heartbreaking. So long separated by the war, these two were again to be driven apart by circumstances. The Brands were moving back to Lwow, now that the war was ended.

"I'll marry her now!" Abram swore to me. "They can't take her away."

"But her parents, Abram!" I murmured, cautioning him. "Would they ever agree?"

It was indeed doubtful that they would agree. The Brands were, after all, a solid and well-to-do family who would be careful with a daughter and her fate. Here was Abram, a boy who looked ill and devastated from the war, whose economic future was in no way determined. Abram spoke to them, and Sala, so much in love with him, pleaded to remain. But the Brands insisted that she wait for a more normal time, for Abram to get established.

When Sala left Vienna, she promised to return to Abram in two years, when they would marry. Each vowed fidelity, and the parting seemed to me a cruel one.

Unlike the Brands, my parents did not object to Hanna marrying Josef at this time, although he had not yet been discharged from the army. As the time for the wedding approached, Hanna had assumed a very positive attitude toward Josef, I noticed. She had been reconciled for some time to the idea that she would certainly marry him; she had never fallen in love with him. Yet she seemed pleased about marrying him. And I was relieved to find it so. By the time they were to approach the altar, Josef seemed to appeal to her more than ever before.

The wedding itself had a wartime flavor. Many of the men were still in uniform, as was Josef himself. Hanna simply wore a navy-blue silk dress and a white hat with a brim and a veil.

She carried a bouquet of white flowers. I thought I had never seen her look so beautiful.

The ceremony was held in the Leopoldstadter Synagogue. I held back tears while the rabbi spoke the words to Josef and Hanna. I prayed that she might love him and be happy with him.

Later, the reception was held at our home. Among the guests, many of whom were old friends from Lwow, was Helka Schwartz, now boasting a fiancé of her own. Proudly she introduced him to us, for not only was he a lieutenant in the army but a doctor of philosophy as well. Although he was not a good-looking man, his intelligence and manners gave him an engaging quality. Helka invited us to her own wedding, which was to take place in the near future. Other officers, Josef's army friends, were among the guests at the reception and, considering the time, it was quite a gay affair. But later one of the officers sang a Jewish folk song, which lent us a note of sadness.

> "The wheels are turning,
> The years are speeding,
> Now I am old and gray . . . ."

How quickly indeed the time had passed since we left Lwow! And how everything had changed! Austria was now a defeated country. Beside all her economic problems, there was also a very tense political situation. Kaiser Karl was still the emperor of the monarchy, which was falling apart. Hungary, Czechoslovakia, and Poland declared themselves independent republics. The Austrian people were divided into four different parties: The Social Democrats, Communists, Christian Socials, and Monarchists.

There were still people who wanted Austria to remain a monarchy, particularly aristocrats and officers of high rank.

Also, many Jews were mindful of Kaiser Franz Josef's friendly attitude toward them, and remained loyal to his memory, and, therefore, to the monarchy. A Jewish general whose name was Sommer founded an organization called *Juedische Front-kaempfer* (Jewish War Veterans). They had a meeting-place where lectures and social gatherings were held.

Josef, who had just been discharged from the army as a sergeant, was one of the first to join this club, with Hanna. Abram, too, became a member. The members were free to invite anyone whose political sympathies were with the monarchists. Thus Jim and I began to attend the meetings. Looking back, it seems strange that we were monarchists and not allied to something with a more progressive sound. But we were in favor of anyone who let us survive.

The monarchists were in a very weak position and could not prevent the abdication of Kaiser Karl, which was forced on him by the Social Democrats, the strongest party at that time. He and his wife and their children went into exile and found refuge on the Island of Madeira, where Karl died in 1922.

There was not a bloody revolution when the Social Democrats proclaimed the Austrian Republic. But certain Austrian factions who were anti-Semitic, took advantage of the disorder which still prevailed in the city and began to riot against the Jews.

One Saturday, I picked Jim up at the office and we walked through the Ringstrasse. As we passed two men, we heard one of them say :

"Did you know there's a riot against the Jews going on right now?"

"Where?"

"On the Steubenring."

"Good for them, I say!" said the second man with a grin.

I felt an almost paralytic fear creep up my back. So it had

finally come to us! An outbreak of this horror which had filled the myths of our youth. This hate, which seemed never to have anything to do with us, was now exploding here in Vienna, blocks away from us.

If Jim had not gripped my arm and pulled me along with him, I would never have made it to the trolley.

"It will be all right, Helena," he said, "if we just get home fast."

I could not stop trembling on the trolley car. A priest sat next to me. His long beard nearly covered his white collar, making his appearance almost rabbinical.

Now the trolley had reached Franz Josef's Kai. We noticed through the window a mob gathering. They were shouting angrily and pushing pedestrians brutally. Suddenly, they stopped the trolley and ordered "All out!"

The priest climbed down just before me. A hand grabbed him by the shoulder and someone shouted:

"Here is another Jew!"

While I climbed down, they had begun to pull his beard and were beating him mercilessly.

Behind me, Jim had descended and grasped my hand. I trembled so violently, I thought I would lose control and collapse.

Suddenly one of the passengers broke loose from the crowd and began to run. At once, the mob went at him.

"There is another Jew!"

They began to beat him until blood ran down his face. All around us men shouted: "*Juden Heraus*!" (Out with the Jews!)

My knees began to buckle, but Jim kept gripping my arm.

"Whatever happens, Helena," he mumbled, "don't run!"

Other victims were plucked from the crowd, right at our elbows. The attackers made no effort to ascertain whether or not they were Jews. Slowly, we began to move forward with the crowd. We had not been recognized as Jews. Some had been allowed to move away from the scene. And among these fortunate ones were Jim and I.

Bit by bit, fearing to hurry at any point, we crawled away from them. Finally, we reached Marien Bridge, about two blocks away, and with consummate relief spotted Jewish war veterans reinforced by policemen. They were stationed there to prevent the spread of riots to Leopoldstadt.

Now I could give vent to my feelings. I burst into tears, while Jim kept pulling me along, now quickening his pace to get home.

"Why do they hate us?" I cried.

"Because they are beasts, Helena, and not men."

"That priest! My God, in their blindness they attack their own people. They're worse than beasts, Jim. They don't even make certain of their prey."

We had now reached the Taborstrasse, getting closer to home.

"Those bloody faces!" I murmured, weeping again. "How will we ever get them out of our minds? They might have been ours."

"We are almost home now, Helena. Try to calm yourself. Your mother will be so alarmed."

Slowly I regained control of myself as we walked along. When I was quieter, a thought came to me and I turned to Jim.

"You know, Jim, the scene we saw today makes me think of a verse from Schiller's poem, 'The Song of the Bell.'

> "It is dangerous to wake up a lion,
> And the bite of a tiger is malignant,
> But the greatest terror of all,
> Is a man in his madness!"

These anti-Semitic outbreaks did not cause serious damage

to the Jews of Austria because Karl Seitz, the new Social Democrat president, quickly halted them and restored order in the country.

Stories reached us through friends from Lwow who lived in Vienna that things were different in Poland. The Poles had lived for 123 years as a minority under foreign domination. In World War I they had formed an army under General Josef Haller and fought with the Allies. After the war, Poland was reunited again and was recognized as an independent country. General Haller and his well-organized soldiers occupied Poland. And they began to celebrate their independence with Jewish blood. In every city they entered, pogroms broke out.

In Lwow, Polish soldiers invaded the Jewish section, where the poor and pious lived. This was the section where we had first lived when we had moved from Przemysl. They forced the inhabitants of old, crumbling houses to stay inside at gun-point, while they set fire to the houses and burned these Jews alive.

In the midst of these burnings, a boy ran out of his house to a nearby synagogue to rescue a Torah. A few minutes later, he was shot down in the street, clutching it. Later, the boy was buried together with the Torah. Polish soldiers also killed Jews in other sections of the city.

We were, of course, terribly worried about Jim's family. Months later, we received a letter from them. In it, we learned that the anti-Semitic outbreaks had come to a halt under the leadership of Paderewski, the Polish-American composer who had come over from the United States to head the new republic. In the same letter, they also told us how lucky they had been, and how they had come to escape the fate of other Jews in Lwow. A group of soldiers had invaded their home and, indeed, had been about to shoot them. By chance, one of the soldiers looked at the wall and saw there a portrait of my fiancé's father in uniform. The soldier recognized this man as the staff sergeant of his company in the Austro-Hungarian Army. Thus my fiancé's parents had been spared.

I I

LITTLE BY LITTLE, VIENNA BEGAN TO RECOVER FROM THE ravages of wartime. Food arrived from America, people went back to work.

In 1919, the League of Nations came into being. It was hoped that all future disputes could be negotiated at a table.

For me, that year was memorable for another reason, too. Jim and I were at last to be married. We awaited the event with a certain gratitude; we had remained together through so much chaos and change. The love which had begun so painfully in Lwow had become perfected with struggle and suffering shared. Now we were genuinely at ease with each other, and this harmony gave meaning to both our lives.

We were married on August 10th. The wedding was a bigger one than Hanna's, which had been kept simple because of war conditions. Things were easing up now, so that it was possible once more for a bride to go to the altar in traditional pomp. Accordingly, I wore a white silk bridal gown and a long veil and carried a large bouquet. Jim stood beside me under the canopy in a tuxedo and top hat. The ceremony was held in Leopoldstadter Synagogue, which was packed for the occasion. Two rabbis officiated. One was the chief rabbi from the *Kultusgemeinde*, who had married Hanna and Josef. The other one was a relative of Father's who was an orthodox rabbi.

The reception was held at home and the rooms were bursting with friends and relatives. My father was in rare form, receiving congratulations and serving drinks to everyone. He embraced Jim's father, who had come all the way from Lwow for the event.

At one point, during the reception, my mother drew me aside and kissed me.

"I'm so glad now that you've married Jim," she said warmly. "As I have come to know him, Helena, I have no doubt that you will be very happy as his wife."

My eyes filled as she spoke and I embraced her quickly.

In the midst of the merriment, Jim and I quietly slipped out and left for our honeymoon retreat. We stayed at a hotel in Hinterbruel, a summer resort near Vienna. There we spent one idyllic week. But our return to the city brought us quickly back to the problems of daily existence.

Jim's first concern was to make a living. At this time, people were just starting to recover from suffering and had a desire to enjoy life. It was a period of inflation. People speculated to earn quick money. They bought merchandise which they sold at great profits. The next day, however, when they wanted to buy more of the same merchandise, they found it cost twice as much as they had sold it. It was a time of economic adventures.

Jim recognized the situation for what it was, and came up with the idea of buying a movie theater. He and Josef had each received a small dowry from my parents. Jim invested all of his share into this venture, while Josef invested only a fraction of his, since he had other speculations, of which we were aware but knew little about. Because the dowries had been small, Jim was only able to select a very old movie theater—the oldest in Vienna—with their funds. The name of the theater was Schuman-Kino, and it was decided that Jim would run it by himself, as Josef was involved in his other enterprises.

The Schuman-Kino was in the ninth district, and it was situated in an old house on a main street. In order to enter this movie house, one had to pass a long back-yard. The audience capacity was only two hundred. Yet this small theater was to start Jim upon a very successful future. Although very young, only twenty-four, he assumed a great deal of responsibility. I admired his confidence and nerve in running a business which was utterly new to him. But Jim was deeply aware of his new married status and seemed to function from some inner commitment to do well for both of us.

My own life had changed completely. As a married woman, I had left the protected atmosphere of my parents' home, and was responsible for running my own. And how happy I was to share this home with Jim! After all, we had waited five years to have it.

Months before, when we had set the date for our wedding, we had made all preparations for finding and furnishing a place in which to live. Apartments were very difficult to find, but my father, asking here and there, discovered one for us. It was a three-room apartment in a building constructed just before the war, within walking distance of my parents' home. It was ideal for a newly married couple. Then we set about furnishing it. Since very little furniture had been manufactured during the war, and what little there was, was of shoddy wartime materials, we decided to look for older pieces, made in a more graceful era. It was also cheaper, a point which we had to consider. My parents were to buy what we chose as a wedding gift, but we had to be prudent. Therefore, we decided to seek things at the Doroteum, a huge market, controlled by the government, in which items were pawned, later to be auctioned or sold. Many things sold there came

from the estates of aristocrats, sold after the fall of the
monarchy. Jim and I acquired a seven-piece mahogany bedroom suite which had once belonged to Count Sturgkl, a
former secretary of state who had been assassinated in 1916
by a fanatical Social-Democrat. It was somewhat ancient but
pleasantly elaborate. The second room, a living room, was
furnished with the possessions of a couple we knew who were
leaving for Palestine. They sold us a large ebony breakfront
containing a closet, and book shelves, a desk and chair, a
round table and a little settee, and two other chairs. We
also purchased a good carpet from them. In addition, they
presented us with all the books on the breakfront shelves,
including twenty-one volumes of Mayer's Encyclopedia, all
the works of Bjornson, Ibsen, Schiller, and Goethe. Two
Gobelin pictures which I embroidered at home adorned the
walls. Drapes and curtains were not missing. We were very
fond, I must say, of these, our first joint possessions. Our home
was cozy and seemed to us beautiful. Unfortunately, Jim was
not able to enjoy this home very much, so absorbed was he
in his new enterprise. In the mornings, after breakfast, he
would go to the Neubaugasse, the section of Vienna for film
distributors : American ones, such as Metro-Goldwyn Mayer,
Twentieth Century Fox, Universal, and Paramount, and also
the German Ufa. There were also coffeehouses in this district
where movie owners and distributors met and talked shop. To
make a go of a theater, a manager had to secure the best films
he could. In the mornings, the film distributors offered trade
showings of their pictures in movie theaters or in their own
projection rooms. Jim attended these showings faithfully. But
it was not easy to get the best films for such a little theater
as ours, to compete against the prices which larger theaters
offered. Jim became immersed in the challenge of the new
business. In the afternoon, he would return for lunch and a
brief rest, after which he would return to the theater, where

he remained until the last show was over, quite late at night. This routine of Jim's left me alone much of the time. It was not quite the life I had imagined and it began to disturb me a little. I found myself waiting with a certain desperation for his noon meal with me, for his exhausted return late each night. Between these hours, time hung heavily upon me. My household duties could not absorb all of it, and women in those days did not hold jobs. What really bothered me was the sense of dependence upon Jim, upon his nearness, which I had begun to have. Some instinct within me felt that dependency as a potential threat both to him and myself; I would become a burden, even a bore. Therefore, I became determined to find interests of my own, to spend my free time with some kind of independence in order to match the individuality and energy of the husband who, in fact, I was only beginning to know.

I began, first of all, to read some of the books which we had inherited, and discovered that literature could add a pleasant dimension to my life. Three evenings a week I visited our theater and saw whatever picture was playing there. These of course were the silent ones, with Rudolf Valentino, Buster Keaton, Mack Senet. A pianist accompanied the picture with appropriate music. I enjoyed these evenings very much. Occasionally, Jim arranged to take an evening off so that we might go out together. Usually he bought tickets for the opera or theater. We also frequented coffeehouses, where Jim introduced me to friends of his from the film industry.

These activities pretty much formed the patterns in our first two married years, At this time, we did not have many special friends, relying heavily upon family sociability. Each day I visited my mother, who lived close to us. And frequently I called on Hanna at her home. She had become pregnant already and was unhappy about it. Hanna had not wanted children so soon, and now she complained constantly, affecting moodiness. I was particularly disappointed when she confided to me that her feeling for Josef had decreased. It was during one of my visits to Hanna that I met an old acquaintance from Lwow, a young woman called Fanny Steiger. At one time, she had lived with her brother's family in the same building as we, but in those days she was most friendly with Hanna, whom she had rediscovered in Vienna. At first, in Hanna's living room, I had not recognized her and was therefore bewildered when she said, "Why Helena! You have changed so much. You are far more beautiful than when we lived in Lwow!" It took me only a minute more to place her from the past. And after this initial meeting, Fanny and I became close friends. She was now married and, like me, had quite a bit of free time to spend as she chose. Fanny was interested in crafts and she taught me how to make lampshades, which, as it happened, I needed for the apartment. Together, she and I also worked on Gobelin pictures, while she told me the most fantastic stories about her life. Since we had not seen each other for years, with a war in between, there was a lot of ground to cover. Fanny confided that she had had to leave Lwow quite suddenly. A gentile fellow had fallen in love with her when she was sixteen and had wanted to marry her. Fanny, though touched, was not in love with this man, and since, in addition, she came from an orthodox family, she could not seriously consider his proposal. Nevertheless, he had persisted with great ardor, had even offered to become Jewish, so great was his love for Fanny. She in turn felt pity and confusion. In her extreme youth how could she evaluate her own feelings? In time, the man threatened to commit suicide if Fanny continued to refuse him and this disturbed her terribly, although she did not believe he would actually do it. About this time, Fanny's brother, who was aware of the situation and its dangers, sent her to Vienna. She assumed her departure would be the end of it. But shortly after her arrival here,

Fanny learned that the man who loved her had in fact killed himself. The news was devastating. For several years, Fanny carried an enormous sense of guilt for this man's death. She had never taken his threat seriously. I doubt if she believed she could be so necessary to anyone. But she found it impossible to forget him for a long time. After several years in Vienna, Fanny finally fell in love. It happened just before the war broke out. She had not been engaged long when her fiancé was called to the army for combat duty. Fortunately, he survived. Then, in 1918, when the war was over, she went back to Lwow where she was reunited with her fiancé, and there they were married. But she was far from achieving serenity. In that same year in Lwow, she and her husband were victimized by the pogrom instigated by the Haller army. Later, she had been fortunate enough to escape with her husband and the two had returned to Vienna.

It was during the first days of our new friendship that Fanny was to experience still another drama concerning her family. One afternoon, we read together in the newspaper of a certain Mundyk Steiger who was accused of attempting to assassinate the president of Poland. His trial was already in session and was attracting international interest. As we pored over the article, Fanny turned pale and I realized that we were reading about Mundyk, her brother's son in Lwow.

"But it's not possible!" I gasped. "It can't be. Not Mundyk!"

"It's incredible," Fanny muttered.

"He was such a fine, intelligent boy," I reasoned. "Whenever I've thought of him over the years it is with the picture of Mundyk with a book in his hand."

Fanny kept shaking her head with disbelief. "He must be innocent! He simply couldn't have done it. You remember him as a little boy, Helena. As he grew older, he truly became a scholar. Why he's been studying law at the university in Lwow!"

We couldn't get over it! Mundyk, an assassin? It was just inconceivable that this innocent boy could have attempted the murder.

After that first article, there were succeeding ones in the newspapers each day. The defense attorney was ardently pleading Mundyk's innocence, in which he apparently believed. He was stressing the fact that there had been only one witness who claimed to have seen Mundyk try to shoot the president. Mundyk, himself, we read, as a student of law, also spoke at the trial in his own defense. Yet nothing we read in the papers cleared up the mystery of Mundyk's involvement. Then, a few days later, while the trial was progressing badly for Mundyk, Fanny received a letter from Lwow from her brother, Mundyk's father, which explained how it had all taken place. Mundyk happened to be standing among a crowd of people who were watching and cheering the Polish president and his staff as they paraded down the main street of Lwow. Suddenly, a shot was fired at the president which missed. A man standing next to Mundyk shouted: "Here is the assassin! I saw him shoot!" He grabbed Mundyk's arm with the words, "Here is the Jew who wants to kill our president!" Immediately, chaos and screaming ensued. Shouts of "Kill the Jew!" could be heard. But the police had seized Mundyk immediately and jailed him. The trial had followed.

Several days later, Fanny and I learned from the newspapers that Mundyk had been convicted and sentenced to death. My friend was disconsolate but still held a thin hope. The boy's lawyer, still convinced of his innocence, had asked for a postponement of the execution, in order to find more witnesses. This was not granted. The date of Mundyk's execution was set and grief settled over Fanny and her relatives in Poland. Then, almost at the last minute, the actual assassin, a Ukranian patriot, gave himself up and saved Mundyk. It was like a miracle.

Clearly, in Lwow the Jews still lived in danger even though the war was over. Time did not seem to diminish Polish anti-Semitism. And because the Polish state was still young and unsettled the problem was strong. We were lucky to be living in Vienna where we were not singled out, where we could lead normal lives like everyone else.

12

As time progressed, Jim made a success out of his small movie theater. Fate finally seemed to include us in her more benevolent times. As a result of his initial success, Jim encouraged my parents, now better off than in the old days, to invest their money in a larger movie house — Stadt-Kino — in the first district of Vienna. They purchased this property with the understanding that Jim would manage it completely and that they would derive a regular monthly income from the rent he would pay them. This turned out to be a mutually beneficial arrangement. My father, having been a baker all his life, had no idea of how to run a movie house, but was able to make money on his property investment. Jim, by contrast, took to this enterprise with great capability and resourcefulness.

At Stadt-Kino, Jim first introduced to the Viennese public American pictures — western and gangster movies. These movies were immensely popular and were frequented by all classes of society, including the loftiest intellectuals and former aristocrats. The house was always crowded. Jim and I began to prosper.

For my parents, things were also working out favorably. Their financial status was greatly improved. Their two eldest daughters had married to their satisfaction. The younger children were growing up in health. Good news came from Leon in Palestine. He was working as an engineer for the

117

British Government at the Telephone & Telegraph Company, and was provided with every comfort.

Abram had recovered from his post-war sickness by now, seemed himself again, and was active in helping my father run the bakery. The two years since his beloved Sala's departure for Lwow were over and, as they had hoped, circumstances had improved appreciably. Her parents, the Brands, were slowly convinced that Abram's situation was now sufficiently stable for Sala. Many letters were exchanged between Lwow and Vienna, asking her to come to Vienna now and marry him. At last, her parents consented.

Sala Brand arrived in Vienna accompanied by her two eldest brothers and a married sister. She was a delicate girl, flanked by so many chaperones. Sala was only five feet tall and very slender. Our Abram, though not really a tall man, looked large beside his bride-to-be.

Their wedding took place in December of 1920. Again, the same synagogue was crowded with people. I gazed at Abram and Sala as they stood under the canopy.

"No wonder the Brands were reluctant to let her go!" I thought, watching Sala's small face, its tiny features turned to the rabbi. She looked so small and helpless to me. Yet never had she looked so happy. Her dream had at last materialized.

Abram, on the other hand, had a strange expression on his face. I glanced at him again, to make sure. But there was no denying it. Something new was at play on Abram's features; something not altogether pleasant. A fleeting, lovely memory of the long lovers' walks in Lwow crossed my mind as the ceremony progressed. Abram and Sala walked on air in front, holding hands, Pepa and I, giggling with our own secrets, "chaperoning" from behind. Now my brother's expression baffled and worried me.

After the ceremony, I embraced Abram.

"I wish you every happiness in the world, Abram," I told him.

"Thank you, Helena," he said, smiling. But that expression again! I looked quickly at Sala to see if she had noticed anything foreign in his face, but to her apparently he looked as happy as she felt.

An ancient Greek philosopher once said: "Gods envy people who are too happy, and make them pay for this with disaster."

For Sala Brand, the Gods waited only a few weeks to seize upon her happiness and turn it to disaster. After four weeks of marriage Abram became ill and was confined to bed immediately. After making an examination, the doctor told us that Abram had an acute lung disease. The news felled my mother and Sala. Who would have imagined that a twenty-nine-year old boy would have a serious disease?

Probably he had caught this disease during the war. It had lain dormant for a while, flaring up so mildly, in so many common disguises, that a true diagnosis had never been made.

He suffered the first lung hemorrhage, from which he recovered slightly. We prayed for his full recovery. And one day during his convalescence I went to see him.

"On my wedding day, Helena," he confided, "a weakness filled my chest, even as I stood under the canopy with Sala. It terrified me. It was so unnatural, like a warning of a bad fate."

"Don't excite yourself now," I begged, stroking his forehead. "You must rest and get better, Abram."

"But that hemorrhage! Good God, Helena, can I be dying?"

To Abram it seemed most incredible, this affliction. His youth was a protest against it. It could not be so. None of us permitted ourselves to consider anything but his recovery.

Then the second hemorrhage came. Hanna and my father

rushed to Abram's bedside. Sala sat beside her husband with bowed head while the doctor administered to him as best he could. But Abram was beyond the reach of the doctor's skill. His death came violently as they sat there with him, choking off his youth. He died in Sala's arms.

This was a death we had never expected to suffer. I did not know how either Sala or my mother would endure it. There were heartbreaking scenes at the funeral. The same people who had packed the synagogue six weeks before, at the wedding, were now present at the cemetery. Sala and Mother were beyond consolation; it was terrible to see them. Both were prostrate after the funeral; neither was able to sit *shiva*.

"All the physical pain I had in bearing the nine," my mother said, "is as nothing compared to the heart pain of losing one of them."

And Sala lamented over and over, "Why me? Why have I been singled out like this? I loved him so much and had him so short a time!"

She was already pregnant with Abram's child. And now she was a widow. Sala's brother, who was still in Vienna, removed her at once from the scene of her loss and took her back home to Lwow.

Now Abram's death began to take its toll of me. I walked about the streets and everything appeared to me as if covered with a dark veil. My brother, my Abram, was gone. I no longer believed that happiness could exist. Slowly, my nerves grew raw; one actually became inflamed. And I became sick.

Jim was very worried about my health and consulted with the doctor about my condition. At the doctor's suggestion, Jim sent me that summer, with Hanna, to a resort called Bad Hall. There I slowly began to improve.

Hanna, who was now the mother of a 2½-year-old girl and a year-old boy, had brought the children with us. Esther, the girl, had been born exactly nine months after Hanna and Josef were married. For Hanna, this motherhood had come too soon. She had been upset with the idea as soon as she had discovered she was pregnant. She would have liked to avoid this encumbrance for a while. Her own plight as an eldest daughter, helping to raise her brothers and sisters, had left her with a conditioned distaste for the endless rounds of child care. And it was a pity, for her resentment of those early years could not help but rub off now on her own children.

To make matters worse, Esther was a rather whiny child and a finicky eater. Hanna lost patience with her too soon and slapped her frequently, and the child would run sobbing from the room, her own alienation beginning. These scenes were terribly disturbing to me. I saw a cycle of dissatisfaction begin to perpetuate itself. I begged Hanna to have more patience with Esther but it soon became apparent that a pattern had begun here which was to continue.

Esther, whom I loved dearly from the first, was a sweet little girl with curly black hair, brown eyes, and a longish nose. She resembled Josef. George, the baby, was a plump, contented little creature who ate well and was easily pacified. Hanna showed a marked preference for her little son, which fired jealousy in Esther.

During our stay at Bad Hall, I tried to relieve Hanna's tension by entertaining Esther. I read children's stories to her and taught her poems. She seemed to be very happy spending time with me. Afternoons, all of us would stroll by the concert stand, listening to music and sipping mineral water. We managed to have a fairly pleasant stay.

When we returned to Vienna my parents were overjoyed to see us. They were happy to see me well again, and they had missed Hanna's children, who were as yet their only grandchildren. My mother's face lit up when Esther ran to kiss her.

My mother still continued her duties, but the loss of Abram, her first born, left her with a wound which was never to heal.

Abram had died in January of 1921; Sala expected his baby in September. The birth was a frequent topic among us, and my mother thought that one of us should go to Lwow to be with Sala during her confinement. One of Abram's own kin, she felt, should be there to sustain the fragile Sala, even though her own family was with her there. Olga was eventually the unanimous choice for the trip, since Hanna and I were married.

At the beginning of September, Olga left Vienna with Mother's blessing and a few things for the baby — but only a few. According to Jewish thought, it was bad luck to buy an entire layette before an infant was actually born. So Mother had given Olga money instead, to buy the layette in Lwow after the baby was born. The child of her beloved first-born son, so young deceased, had to be well provided for. The baby was a boy. At the circumcision he was named Abram, after his father.

Back home again, Olga described the event in much detail to all of us. Mother was so gratified that one of us had gone to Lwow to represent the family. The thought of Abram's new son brought her combined joy and heartache, reawakening her sense of loss. We all tried to comfort her during this sensitive period.

I spent as much time with her as I could spare, and Jim encouraged me to do so. He was very sympathetic to all my family. We lived within walking distance of my parents' home, so I visited with them, and with Mother especially, every day. Her noble, good heart was full of pain which my visits seemed to ease a little. She was a woman of considerable wisdom and I, at least, found her philosophies an inspiration.

"Helena," she said once, "the life of a human being consists only of the present. The past is never to return and the future is unknown to you."

We would spend hours reminiscing about the old days at home when all the children were together. I would remind her of funny incidents and sometimes was able to make her smile. As for me, she marveled at my leisure; as a married woman, she had never possessed so many hours with which to do as she pleased. I had no children and I filled my time with Jim, Mother, and a little self-development, which I felt I needed.

Three evenings a week, I began to attend adult education courses in the nearby college. It was just at this time that the theories of Freud and Adler were being hotly discussed and disputed. Accordingly, I took a course for laymen on the subject of psychoanalysis. I became engrossed in this new academic life and branched out into English and German. One of my professors was Esti Freud, daughter-in-law of Sigmund Freud. I began to take private tutoring lessons with her.

But now my days and those of my family were colored with a bright anticipation. A letter from Leon had come from Palestine, announcing his homecoming. Hanna and I were overjoyed for our mother. Mother, in turn, could hardly believe the good news that her second son was really returning. I am sure that she had often believed that Leon was permanently gone. How much all of us prayed that Leon would help to fill up the terrible void created by Abram's death.

The day before his expected return, I was at my parents' house, helping Mother to plan the large family dinner at which we would celebrate. I happened, as we were talking, to glance briefly out the front window, and I gasped. But even before the word, "Leon!" had escaped my lips, my mother was tearing down the front steps and out into the street to embrace him.

It was strange to see Leon so changed. He had been away

for three years and had returned taller, bronzed from the sun, and radiantly healthy.

Now it was Leon's wish to re-establish himself in the heart of the family. He was eager to ease my mother's pain, and expressed his wish now to replace Abram in the bakery. Little did we imagine what wonders he would work there.

Being a capable engineer, Leon converted the old-fashioned matzoh bakery into a modern factory. He invented and constructed electrical machines and ovens for baking the matzohs, sparing hours of human labor. Before, matzohs had to be flattened with a hand roller.

By the next season, the factory had become the largest of its kind in Vienna and, in fact, in Austria.

All of this was deeply gratifying to my parents, not because their fortunes increased but because Leon had shown himself to be so dedicated a son. Although he had loved Palestine and might happily have remained there, he had chosen to respond to my mother's need before anything.

He had helped her a great deal, of course. But not one of us was ever fooled into believing that she would ever quite get over Abram's death.

13

THE SOCIAL DEMOCRATS, WHO HAD HALTED THE ANTI-
Semitic riots some time before, were now in control of Austria,
and the economic situation improved greatly. Their leaders,
Karl Seitz, Karl Renner, Dr. Julius Deutsch, and Otto Bauer,
were sincere and progressive democrats. Their goal was to
bring order into the country and to work for the betterment
of the people.

They built hospitals, kindergartens, and parks, and eased
the housing problem by building modern projects for the
workers. All this was made possible by the high taxes imposed
on industrialists by Hugo Breitner, and by the taxes gleaned
from luxury items and entertainment.

In our movies, the luxury taxes were highly increased, but
this did not harm our profit. Workers were earning more
money these days and the movies were always crowded.

Breitner's tax policy, as well as the Social Democratic
regime, was opposed by the second largest party, the Christian
Socials. This party was largely comprised of industrialists,
clergymen, and peasantry. Their leaders, Ernst von Starhelmberg, Emil Fey, the priest Ignatz Seipel, were anti-democratic,
anti-liberal, and their goal was to replace the Social Democratic regime with a fascist, autocratic state. This was an anti-
Semitic party.

Julius Deutsch saw the danger of being swept away by

these reactionaries and found it necessary to build up a people's militia called *Volkswehr*. The Christian Socialist, von Starhelmberg, founded an opposing army of his supporters, and this group was called *Heimwehr* (Home Defense). The Communists, at this time, were so obscure and weak a party that they constituted very little threat to anyone. And in spite of the political rivalries, life in Austria continued normally, and it looked as if peace and progress would continue.

Jim's movie business had proved a success and was even ready for expansion. He was now able to sell the Schuman-Kino and, together with Josef, purchased a larger movie, the Marian. Since Jim was already occupied with the Stadt-Kino, Josef became manager of the Marian, under Jim's supervision.

Jim was still busy mornings, selecting motion pictures which he would rent for his houses. At the Stadt-Kino, American films were shown exclusively. Thus Jim spent a great deal of time at the Vienna offices of Metro-Goldwyn-Mayer, Twentieth Century Fox, Universal, and Paramount.

During these first few years of our marriage, Jim had made the transition from youth to manhood. He had gained weight, which was becoming to him, and was now more strikingly handsome than ever.

My husband was now a well known personality in the movie business. Jim was liked and respected for his honesty and sincerity by movie owners and representatives of the film industry in Vienna.

As for my role, it represented the transformation of a girl from Lwow into a rather cosmopolitan young woman, immersed in the social life of a splendid city. Certainly, my life had become a broader, more secular one. On occasions when an important film was opening with great pomp at a large theater, and with press and celebrities attending, Jim always took me along.

Jim also took me out these days to the coffeehouses and

nightclubs of Vienna, where we frequently encountered friends of his. Once, while sitting with him in a coffeehouse, I noticed that he greeted a woman with a dazzling smile.

"She's quite attractive," I commented, "Where did you meet her?"

"She's a customer from Stadt-Kino. You know, Helena, in show business one comes across women as well as men. In the movie, I have to be friendly to everyone who is a customer."

"No doubt," I replied. "It would surprise me if several were not in love with you."

"What? You're jealous, Helena?" he teased, grinning at me. "I assure you there is no reason. You know I love you and would never make you suffer with that kind of thing."

Actually, I was not a bit jealous, for I trusted Jim. During our first few married years, I had come to know his character intimately. He was a very righteous man, conscientious to a fault. A perfectionist, his family meant everything to him. He was a terrible worrier, often, to my dismay, with little reason. Sometimes he was very excitable. When he thought he was right, nothing could sway him. In worldly affairs, he was hardworking, meticulous, and punctual. Everywhere, he was a little domineering. But he never spoke badly of anyone. For the most part, he kept to himself and his own affairs. I never knew Jim to ask for a favor, but he was eager to do favors for others.

At home with me, he was not demonstrative. His deep love made itself felt in other ways. He was considerate, generous, and deeply concerned with my well-being. As for his female admirers, they could not begin to guess at the puritan who existed behind the handsome face. I smiled complacently to myself at the thought. Even the love letters which he sometimes received from infatuated women failed to arouse my jealousy. I was rather sympathetic to these women when he showed me the letters. Who could fail to pity them? They loved without hope. But I was curious as to his reaction to these letters.

Turning to him now, I asked, "How do you feel when you receive one of these love letters, Jim?"

He flushed slightly. "I will admit that at first I found them flattering, Helena. I was that human. But when one or two of them took on a serious note, when I could actually see suffering between the lines, I called a quick halt. I told them to forget me and to find someone who was eligible."

Both Hanna and Olga were aware of Jim's appeal for women. A few days after the coffee shop incident, Hanna visited me and began to discuss it.

"You know, Helena," she began seriously, "I admire you. You know that women are wild about Jim, but you never seem to be jealous. I think I'm more jealous on your behalf than you are."

"I have no reason to be, Hanna," I responded.

Hanna shifted uneasily in her chair, pondering the question.

"But can you ever really trust a man? Shouldn't you be around him more? Maybe it isn't wise to have him away from you so much of the time."

I shrugged my shoulders and smiled at her. "That is first of all impossible. Second, it is pointless. Either it is not necessary to stand over one's husband, or else it does not help anyway," I told her.

Hanna sighed. "I suppose you're right, Helena. I can't be with Josef all the time, I just have to trust him."

Now the moment had come when I might legitimately bring up the subject which I had been wondering about for some time.

"And how is it, Hanna, with you and Josef now?"

Hanna's expression clouded briefly, but she quickly smiled and looked up at me. "You know, more or less, how things are between Josef and me. Nothing has changed, basically. I cannot truthfully say that I love Josef. We have so little in common!" She broke off, almost laughing, as if the thought were astonishing in the face of the facts. "He has," she continued, "always attracted me sexually. I was very candid with you about that, even before we were engaged." Hanna flushed briefly. "Naturally, as we live together, this has become even stronger. . . ."

"I know," I murmured, nodding.

"Sex had been the saving grace between us," she admitted.

"It's so remarkable!" I mused. "You say you aren't in love with him and yet this sensuality is possible? I can't see how it would work."

"Well, Helena," Hanna concluded, "we are not all as lucky as you. Actually, a woman who marries a man who pleases her in all respects is a rare one. I have to be satisfied with whatever pleases me in Josef, in any way."

Thus Hanna had made her peace with Josef, who was not educated, with whom she felt little in common except this physical bond.

Olga, too, was now destined to marry a man who was not the materialization of her dreams. As a young girl, she had been enchanted with my love affair with Jim. She had longed to experience the excitement of a similar romance, and I have no doubt that she cherished this hope for years. But her fate was to be entirely different.

At twenty-two, Olga was still unmarried. Not that she lacked suitors! There were boys madly in love with her. But none were good enough for my sister. To return the love or accept the proposal of any one of them was unthinkable for Olga.

For one thing, Olga was more a status-seeker than either Hanna or I had ever been. Since childhood she had nurtured a fairly lofty image of herself, which had, if anything, increased with the years. As far as I was concerned, she had a perfect right to think highly of herself. Her intelligence and good looks certainly seemed to imply a superior kind of husband. But

Olga had remained single up till now because she sought a man she could not only love but one who would inspire a kind of awe in her.

About this time, my parents' attorney, who was also a friend, suggested to Mother that Olga should meet a younger lawyer who practiced in his office. His name was Dr. Friedrich Landes. He was said to be a brilliant professional man and he stemmed from a famous rabbinical family. His character was reported to be of the highest caliber. His uncle was Chief Rabbi and a university professor in Johannesburg; his father taught religion and Hebrew in the higher schools of Wiener Neustadt. And the young man himself held a Doctor of Law degree. With such a list of distinctions Olga, who revered higher education, could not fail to be impressed. I believe she was predisposed to link herself with him before they actually met.

In person, Friedrich Landes was seventeen years her senior. He was short but had a fine and interesting face. Olga was inspired. Her ambition to become the wife of a distinguished attorney combined powerfully with her desire to be raised above her own intellectual level through marriage. Clearly, she did not bother to envision the day-to-day existence she would share with this man. And it was a pity she did not. For it appeared to both Hanna and me that sexually they would be ill-attuned. But Olga never considered this now—this, or the purely romantic aspects that were missing. When Friedrich proposed that autumn, she accepted him.

Again I had to reflect on my singular good luck in having Jim, whom I loved so. With Hanna joined to a man who was beneath her, sex alone compensated; with Olga, status would have to compensate for sex. I alone seemed to have a whole, marital relationship.

Nevertheless, my parents rejoiced as their third daughter came to the altar. As their lot had improved with the years,

Olga's dowry was much larger than either Hanna's or mine had been. And in January, 1923, Olga and Friedrich Landes were married.

14

AN ERA OF PROSPERITY NOW FLOURISHED. AND WE, TOO, enjoyed this state. My husband wanted to fix me in this new framework. Now he was presenting me with diamonds. Was it possible? Yet it was a matter of course, in those days, for a husband in Jim's position to make sure his wife wore diamonds.

In addition to these, he began to develop a keen interest in my wardrobe. I did not mind. Jim had excellent taste. And the spirit of the new, extravagant phase appealed to my most feminine self. One day, he suggested a shopping tour.

"Helena, you need some new dresses," he declared. "Let's go together and select a few."

We went to a first-rate shop where the merchandise was dazzling. The saleslady was very solicitous and helped me to try on a number of things. Of the items I modelled, Jim chose an expensive evening gown, two cocktail dresses, and a beautiful coat. Later, as he was paying the cashier, our saleslady grinned at me, winked coarsely, and remarked, "Just catch them spending like that on their wives! With them they are not so generous!"

"But I *am* his wife!" I protested in an astonished voice, not quite understanding. Did she think I was Jim's mistress? Embarrassed, the saleslady had turned away.

Out on the street, I described the incident to Jim, who

smiled at me somewhat indulgently. "Helena," he said, "these are times of pleasure and frivolity. Don't be so shocked! Mistresses are the order of the day. You have no idea of how common it has become for a man to keep one. Many men who make a lot of money want to spend it on pleasure. And some of them happen to be married," he explained casually.

"But how can they?" I protested, revolted by the idea of mass infidelity.

Jim laughed a little. "Don't get so excited, Helena. In many instances, their wives know about the mistress and accept the idea of sharing, as long as they get the same lavish treatment. Such a man also buys his wife jewelry and clothes. . . ."

"But not as expensive as the ones his mistress gets!" I said with annoyance, recalling the saleslady's words.

"Never mind. She finds her own compensations," Jim assured me.

I looked at him with some alarm. His attitude confused me.

"And you?" I screamed suddenly. "Have you a mistress, too?"

"Helena, Helena!" he said, soothing me. "Why should I have one? You know I love you, and it is not my nature. I take my life too seriously. Really, I don't have such frivolous desires. I'd rather save the money for the children we'll have in the future."

I believed him.

The time of the "Roaring Twenties" was an exciting one in Vienna. Post-war exuberance was everywhere, touching the movies, theaters, nightclubs and other entertainments. The dancing schools were crowded with people wanting to learn the latest dances—foxtrot, tango, Charleston. Nor was the traditional Vienna waltz neglected at this time.

In the spirit of things, Jim and I joined the others at dancing school. Jim, always too reserved to dance before, now discovered that he enjoyed it, and he became quite adept on the dance floor.

A highlight of the winter season was the masquerade balls at the time of Carnival. We attended the Caligari, Stage, Film and Artists Balls. They were held in the concert house, a huge building containing one very large hall, lined with boxes all around, and several smaller halls. An orchestra played music in the large hall. In the smaller halls, quartets played usually. There were also rooms where food was served from lavish buffets and all kinds of drinks were available.

It was customary for husbands and wives to attend these balls separately. They spent the early evening hours of the ball apart from one another, meeting at midnight, at an arranged spot. At this hour, the women demasked. The costuming procedure gave the women a definite advantage. While men wore only tuxedos to these balls and were not masked, the women wore evening gowns with masks, or else were disguised in beautiful costumes. Frequently, a husband had no idea of what his wife had worn to the ball. Each was on his own, and the consequences could be highly amusing. Always, these affairs seemed charged with a certain drama of the unknown.

Women, having the better of it, teased the men terribly. Mostly they toyed with men whom they knew, but who in turn could not recognize them.

"Oh, Mr. X., you look so lonely here! And your wife is having a wonderful time. . . ." went a frequent jibe.

And the answer, almost invariably, went: "Who are you, beautiful mask?" And then they would dance together. If a woman continued to conceal her identity successfully, and happened to know the man well, she could fairly devastate her partner with curiosity by telling him the wildest details of his own existence. Some of the women were positively devilish along these lines. Only at twelve o'clock could the

frantic fellow discover the face of the woman who knew so
much about him.

One time, Jim decided to take Hanna with us to a Caligari
Ball, since Josef never went to these affairs. My sister was
delighted with the opportunity to attend the ball, but when
we arrived she stayed in a box with Jim, preferring to watch
the spectacle, rather than to participate the first time.

I, on the other hand, was circulating on the dance floor.
My dress, this time, was well-known to Jim, because he had
bought it with me. It was a red and gold brocade evening
gown, and with it I carried a large fan of ostrich feathers.
For the first time, I wore real diamond drop earrings and
other gems, presented to me by Jim during the past year. I
felt very exuberant that night.

Jim did not usually approach other women at these affairs,
but many sought him out since he was well-known from his
movie theaters. And I was usually too diffident to make sport
of the men the way other women did. But on this particular
night, a very good-looking gentleman approached me and
said:

"Beautiful mask, so alone? Why not dance with me?"

"Yes," I replied. "I like the tango." And we engaged in a
round of this exotic dance with its dips and deep bends.

"Who are you, beautiful mask?" he murmured, tightening
his grip on my waist.

"Curiosity," I answered provocatively, "is supposed to be
a woman's quality, not a man's."

He stopped dancing suddenly and turned to me with a
smile.

"Let us walk a little and talk together. I might find out
more about you!"

He guided me to a room with a bar. Each table had
separate walls around it. We swept into the seats and he seized
hold of my hand.

"And now let us drink some champagne, eh?" he said meaningfully.

Instantly, I jumped to my feet. There was no mistaking his tone.

"Oh, no!" I cried, with embarrassment. "I don't want to disappoint you. I am really an older woman. I have a son who is your age. . . ."

Now the man rose gallantly, sensing my dilemma.

"You don't have to kid me," he said. "I don't know you, but I suspect you are a very decent woman and that your husband is somewhere around, watching you."

I could feel my face blushing under the mask. Glancing at my watch, I declared suddenly, "It's already twelve o'clock. I must leave you."

And with those words, I fled my first surreptitious encounter with a man.

By now, Jim was looking for me. It was such a relief to be back with him. Hanna joined us and on the side those two began to tease me about my exploits. I laughed heartily, while Jim observed, "You seem to have enjoyed yourself tonight, Helena."

Another incident which taught me a lesson occurred at the next ball, which was a Film Ball. This time I wore a pink silk dress, adorned with beads. It was knee-length, for this was a flapper dress. Jim knew this dress of mine well, but I had rented a domino to put on over it. This night I wanted to stay close to Jim and to play a trick on him.

Disguised in the domino, I spotted my husband standing alone. I approached him with a seductive gait. Disguising my voice, I grasped his hand with a pressure, and said, "How happy I am to find you here, Mr. Hilsen! Come, let us dance."

While whirling away on the floor, I pressed nearer to him, murmuring, "How good it is, at last, to be near you!"

"Who are you?" he demanded, his eyes narrowing.

"Never mind who I am," I stated, "Let yourself go. Have a good time, that's all!"

And without warning, I leaned and kissed him. Abruptly, he pulled back. I kissed him a second time, while he, with confusion, attempted to resist.

"Are you worrying about your wife?" I chided him. "Forget her tonight. She is having a good time with another fellow," I pointed out, desperately trying to keep a consistent voice.

Jim grabbed my hand suddenly and stared penetratingly into my eyes. For a second, I feared he had recognized me.

"You are right!" he declared, with abrupt relaxation. "Let's go into the bar and have some champagne."

Now I was tingling with amusement, for he hadn't guessed my game. I followed him into the bar with the same seductive air I had used to approach him.

Once concealed at our table, he reached for me ardently, put his arms about me, and kissed me passionately on the lips.

Anger started within me, and I thought. "So he is no better than all the other men!"

At this point, the waiter brought our champagne. I seized my glass and drank it down, all at once. Then I pushed away the glass and burst into tears.

"Now I see how indifferent you are to other women!" I murmured, and ripping off my mask, pushed my face forward. "Sorry to disappoint you! It's only your wife."

At this point laughter welled up in Jim, obviously suppressed until now, and it overcame him; he nearly wept with it.

"Good heavens, Helena! I knew it was you all along. I saw what you were driving at. And this, my suspicious one, is your revenge!"

Now we were both doubled up, thinking of my imagined betrayal. The fact was that I had a better time with Jim at these masked balls than with anyone else. And this was the last time I ever tried to fool him.

This Film Ball was mostly frequented by film stars and other people from the film industry. As usual at such affairs, motion picture photographers shot some film of celebrities after the unmasking. During the following week I was surprised, when watching the program in our movie, to see a picture of Jim and myself flash on the screen. The caption read: "Director and Mrs. Hilsen."

Jim and I were happy, perhaps singularly so, with each other. But as the years of our marriage progressed, the absence of a child began to increase my longing for one. During the first year or so of married life, I was happy not to conceive almost at once, as Hanna had done. I had enjoyed my new status as Jim's wife, had luxuriated in my progressing role of a Viennese lady. But I was soon enough satiated with freedom and began to hope for a baby. Jim shared in this hope for a child of our own. But three years had now passed fruitlessely. Hanna had two children, and now even our young Olga was the mother of a year-old boy, Eddie.

From time to time I grew anxious and slightly morose over my childlessness, although I tried not to let this lack color an otherwise happy existence. It would have been too ungrateful, I knew. Yet the anxiety of others about this condition inevitably mirrored and intensified my own.

My mother, for example, was worried about me being unable to produce a child. She advised me to consult with a physician to see if anything might be done about it.

Jim went with me to consult the best obstetrician in Vienna. After an intensive examination which revealed no defects which could preclude a pregnancy, this doctor advised me to go to a spa called Francensbad in Czechoslovakia, to take mud baths (a popular treatment, in those days, for promoting fertility and helping to cure female sicknesses).

Jim did not want me to wait and eagerly sent me, the same season, to Francensbad. Before I had actually left, however, he was very concerned about my going so far away all alone. Thus he was delighted to learn that the wife of a friend of his was already there, taking a cure for a mild malady.

This friend was Erich Schelman, and Jim had come to know him through business. He was the Vienna manager for Twentieth Century Fox, and the two men, having much in common, had formed a strong friendship. Somehow, we had never met his wife, Greta, so that Erich also was delighted that I was to join her. He asked Jim to give him a photograph of me, which he in turn would mail to his wife, asking her to meet me at the railroad station in Francensbad.

Accordingly, when I arrived there I disembarked expectantly, my eyes scanning the station, but no one greeted me. After a while, I took a taxi to the hotel where Greta Schelman was staying. I asked for her in the lobby and a porter showed me to her room.

"Come in," a voice responded to my knock.

When I opened the door, she jumped up from her chair. "Don't tell me!" she said breathlessly. "Are you Helena Hilsen?"

"Yes," I answered, smiling at her girlish excitement. "I was told to look for you at the station, but . . . ."

"But I was there!" she declared. "How could I have possibly known you, though?" She strode to the bureau, picking up my photograph. "Look! This is the picture Erich sent me of you!"

It was the photograph taken of me at the Caligari Ball. I was encased in brocade and diamonds.

"I tell you," Greta said, grinning, "I was expecting a a glamorous and sophisticated lady. To tell you the truth, I was not that anxious to meet you, after seeing that picture. After all, I came here to relax."

"Well," I offered, glancing down at my tweed suit and touching my plain hair-do.

Greta laughed. "It's such a relief! I like you so much better as you are!"

Both of us were laughing now. She was so delightfully candid. Greta's own appearance bore the forthright radiance of her personality, and was dominated by a broad smile of dazzling teeth. She was my height but a little heavier. Her beautiful brown hair was long, but it was bound in a knot in the old-fashioned style. We kissed one another, feeling at once an understanding and sense of absolute ease with each other.

That evening, Greta joined me for dinner, and later we spent hours in her room, talking as if we had known each other for years.

Greta told me all about her background, which I found fascinating. She was a product of a mixed marriage — Christian and Jewish. Her father had been a civil engineer, her mother a professional pianist. It was an unusually happy and successful marriage, and Greta had benefited by the warmth of it. She felt her childhood had been a happy and comfortable one. Through her mother, Greta, too, had become an accomplished, though not a professional, pianist.

While Greta's home atmosphere had been very congenial, her immediate outside environment had been rather bizarre. She had been born in Sarajevo, the capital of Bosnia, then connected to Austria and now under Yugoslavia. Sarajevo had a wildly mixed population composed of Orientals, Mohammedans, and Sephardic Jews. And Greta had grown up among them all, observing their customs, hearing all about their different ideologies.

She was schooled at a convent, where she was sent by her mother, a devout Christian. At home again, she knew the Jewish faith of her father who, although not really very observant, was still a Jew. Altogether, her background was charged with the flavor of variety and change. And her experience had been capped by one really extraordinary incident: Greta had actually witnessed the assassination of the Austrian Archduke, Francis Ferdinand, when watching the military parade from the window of her apartment. This historic event occurred in Sarajevo in 1914 and touched off World War I.

Her early life had made her very cosmopolitan and quite profound in character. The mixtures of customs and religions to which she had been exposed had not confused her. Rather she had compounded her own ideology from all of them. It was very broad. Greta believed in God, humanity, and righteousness.

Her parents, who had maintained their separate faiths for many years, worked a strange reversal as they grew old. Greta's mother became ill and felt her death slowly approaching. In this state of mind, the woman began to feel guilt because she had married a Jew. Her devoutness took this form as she grew weaker; her sense of having done wrong tortured her. Accordingly, she begged Greta's father to convert to Christianity. And so strong was his devotion to his wife, so acute did her suffering appear to him, that he agreed to convert. Thus, to the end of his days, Greta's father, who had retained his Jewishness for so long, was now a Christian, out of love for his dying wife.

I drew a breath, as Greta concluded.

"And Erich?" I asked. "Where does he fit into all of this?"

"I was visiting in Vienna, once," she said. "We met at the home of a friend. A whirlwind courtship followed — and before I knew it we were married."

I suppose I could merely claim that we had much in common, with our husbands both in the movie industry, with so many shared concerns and experiences. But actually it was something basic in both Greta and me, reaching out to communicate, as two women sometimes can. Although she was actually a little older than I, Greta maintained an enthusiasm which was almost girlish. Spontaneously, that free air of hers seemed to cut through my inherent shyness and reserve. In turn, I was liberated aud touched by her carefree attitude. Perhaps she felt her effect on me and was pleased by it. I only know that without preliminaries we became instant confidantes. And this first encounter with Greta in Francensbad was to be only the prelude to a long and significant friendship.

Francensbad was the smallest of three spas in Czechoslovakia. There was Karlsbad, a beautiful resort surrounded by mountains, which offered salt baths to cure gall stones and stomach diseases. Then there was Marienbad, frequented by people who had to lose weight.

Here in Francensbad, there was one large hotel and many smaller ones, as well as a number of guest houses. Greta and I enjoyed the main street, where we patronized the little coffee-houses and shopped at little specialty stores where wonderful small things, irresistible to women on vacation, were offered for sale. A park adjoined the main street and in it a band played during the day; people strolled or else sat and listened, peering through binoculars and sipping mineral water derived from the local fountain. Mornings were reserved for routine : We "*Kurguests*" went to take the mud baths which our doctors had prescribed for us and for which we had come to Francensbad.

Thus my days with Greta at the resort were compounded of this not unpleasant "cure" and outright leisure. Greta claimed an improvement of the female illness she had come for. Being the mother of a son, Kurt, she had not come, as I had, to promote fertility. It was of course impossible to assess any change in my state due to the mud baths until I was reunited with Jim.

Back in Vienna, we and our husbands were delightfully

occupied with our social lives. On Saturday evenings the four
of us went out to coffeehouses and nightclubs. We danced,
talked for hours, and enjoyed being together at any opportunity. Greta particularly was fond of this night life. Once,
when I teased her about it, she told me : "If there is ever a
choice between sleeping and going out, I always choose to
go out. I'll be sleeping long enough later on." Perhaps there
was a note of premonition in this urgency over good times. I
have never really known.

Not all of my friends were able to be as light-hearted as
Greta. There was Helka, for example, my old friend, the
"Polish Nationalist" from Lwow. Like us, she and her family
had escaped to Vienna during the First World War, but unlike
us she had never prospered. As a young woman, she had
married a young man who was a Doctor of Philosophy. But
the demand for this type of professional in the twenties was
dubious, and, despite his degree, her husband could not make
a living in Vienna. In time, he was forced to leave Vienna for
Warsaw, where he obtained a job.

This job paid very little — certainly not enough to keep a
wife and child. Helka and her daughter remained behind in
Vienna, where they were largely supported by her parents.
This was a great blow to Helka, and it was a turning point in
her life.

Helka was a very intelligent person, even one of some depth.
It had never occurred to me that one so analytic as she could
become so self-destructive. As time passed, Helka seemed to
lose interest in her absent husband. She might have led a
relatively happy life if she and her husband could have lived
together without poverty. But finding herself not only alone
but faced with constant money problems, she began to reach
out blindly, as if to find anywhere traces of the stability and
status which had eluded her. Thus a series of love affairs
followed for Helka. She was a woman clearly hungry for life

and she developed a philosophy to go with that hunger. This philosophy held that youth was brief and pleasure hard to come by. Helka dedicated herself to pleasure, however it might come to her, even if it caused her pride to break, or if it cost her self-respect. Her reasoning was a weapon against the avalanche of bad luck she faced; her lovers were a compensation. But she chose her men badly. Some exploited her blatantly. When she visited me, her unhappiness was expressed in these words: "Your life as compared to mine is as a zephyr to a hurricane."

I was fond of her and therefore pained to watch her become more dissolute with the years.

Helka visited me often and discussed her affairs in some detail. She lived in the neighborhood of one of Jim's movies and she stopped to visit with him from time to time, even confiding in him about her plight. He tried to dissuade her from following her way of life, spoke of the threat it held for her. But, like me, Jim held out small hope that Helka would change or her fate improve.

Yet which of us could, in those days, have fathomed the kind of fate that lay in store for either the Schelman's, the Hilsens, or Helka?

15

I WAS TO TRAVEL QUITE A BIT, ON AND OFF, DURING THE NEXT few years. Jim was so happy when I came back from Francensbad, for that month had been our first separation since we had met. No sooner had I returned than he announced that he wished to take me for a holiday in Semmering, a deluxe mountain resort fifty miles outside of Vienna. I prepared for this trip with the enthusiasm of a young bride.

This high-altitude retreat in the Austrian Alps was a spot of breathtaking natural beauty. It had an elevation of 1,000 feet and the air was different from any air we had breathed before. We registered in the fabulous Panhans Hotel. It looked like a castle ensconced in a mountain, edged with tall pines and thick gardens. Here we celebrated our second honeymoon. The hotel offered many activities to its visitors, including a nightclub where dancing and entertainment were held nightly. During the days, golden in that perfect air, hiking was of course a favorite pastime. But I took only short walks with Jim. In the back of my mind, I kept imagining that I had conceived and that too long or vigorous a hike would cause me to miscarry.

Our two weeks in Semmering were quickly over and we returned to Vienna. My hopes for some sign of a pregnancy were, as before, unrealized. I contented myself for the moment with city life, saw more and more of Greta, and visited my mother daily. By and large, the winter passed as others had, gaily surfaced but for me containing an underlying grief which seemed to grow with the weeks. My mother sensed my frustration and tried to console me.

"You can't keep worrying this way about a baby, Helena. Either it will be or not. No use devastating yourself about it."

But her philosophical approach simply made me feel that she was herself resigned to the thought that I might never have a child. By the time summer came, I had made up my mind to return to Francensbad for more treatment.

During those years I was to make four trips altogether to Francensbad. Jim was extremely generous to me each time I left for that place, providing me with more than enough to stay at the finest hotels and to patronize the most elegant restaurants.

Before leaving for Francensbad the second time, I became worried and preoccupied about Henney, a cousin of mine who lived in Galicia. When I visited Mother, we had long talks about Henney and her family. They were terribly poor and Mother was constantly sending them money whenever she could. But the family's poverty was now affecting Henney, the grownup daughter, for she was of the age to be married. Even in the poorest families in Europe, a dowry was essential before any kind of a match could be arranged. Mother and I were well aware of this but, knowing the economic strife of Henney's family, also realized that those people hadn't the faintest hope of scraping together a dowry for her. Thus, the vision of Henney, wasting into spinsterhood over the years, had troubled me for some time. My own life seemed one of such abundance by contrast. I did not wish to ask Jim for an amount like this for my relative, for he was already obliged to help support his parents, who were poor.

Soon, the subject of Henney became one of complicity

between my mother and me. We brooded over it, unable to see a way to help her, until it came time for me to leave for Francensbad. By this time I had found a way in my own mind, and Mother was the only one who ever knew of it: when I arrived in Francensbad, I did not go, as planned, to one of the luxury hotels. Instead, I found a room in an obscure and inexpensive boarding house on the outskirts of Francensbad. Instead of the lavish restaurants which Jim had assumed I would patronize, I cooked eggs up in my room for lunch and occasionally ate dinner in a very cheap cafe. The purpose was, of course, to send the money intended for this therapeutic holiday to my cousin Henney. Jim, meanwhile, had no way of knowing what I was up to, for the address I gave him would mean nothing to him. I suppose I derived a certain secretive glee from the whole business. My alarm and embarrassment could not be measured, however, when one day the landlady knocked on my door to advise me that two friends were waiting downstairs to see me. The identity of these two only augmented my discomfort— a VIP from the film industry and a leading actress of the day. Knowing my status, this gentleman did not hesitate to question my choice of lodging, for it was terribly humble.

"I have always had a weakness," I invented, "for the countryside. This little house by the woods just appealed to me."

My guests swallowed that story very well, Jim was never apprised of my location, and several weeks later Henney received her dowry money. In Vienna, Mother and I rejoiced.

Henny married soon after that and in subsequent years became the mother of five children.

As for me, my second trip to Francensbad proved as fruitless as the first.

I now returned to the obstetrician. Again he examined me and again he declared: "Go back to Francensbad. There is nothing wrong with you. Those mud baths are the only answer."

He swore by them, it seemed. And I, eager to seize hold of anything that held out promise, arranged a third trip the following summer.

After this third trip to Francensbad, I was thrown into a period of despair when I continued to be childless. Jim's longing for a child seemed to have increased with time, as had mine. And since we had now been married for five years, I began to feel almost guilty toward him.

One evening I approached him with absolute sincerity on the subject.

"I know how much you want a child, Jim," I said gently. "And it begins to appear that I may never be able to give you one. If you want your freedom, I'd give you a divorce without bitterness. After all, another woman could fulfill this desire. . . ."

"Don't be silly!" Jim scolded. "As if some other woman and a child would replace you! I'd never give you up for any reason in the world," he declared, ending that possibility for good.

But the extremes of my concern were now visible to him and he sought eagerly to distract me, to keep me from becoming morose. Accordingly, he planned for us to visit Lwow, our home town, from which we had been away for ten years. Also, we had not seen Jim's family, which had continued to live there, for five years.

This was a hauntingly nostalgic pilgrimage for Jim and me. Lwow was the scene of our youth, our ingrown years, and our early love. Almost every familiar sight brought a lump to my throat, while a surge of recognition rose in me. How we had dreamed in this town, what things we had imagined of our future!

And yet, as we walked through those unchanged streets, I

in all honesty had to realize how good the years had been to Jim and me. With what good fortune had we been dealt! But for the absence of a child. . . . Yet I was determined not to think of it here!

Jim's family was overjoyed to see us. The years had worked a terrible hardship on them. Jim's sister had died at seventeen from a kidney operation. His parents were altered with this grief, as my mother had been over Abram. Now our presence seemed to compensate a little. And they still had three other sons. The oldest, Lonek, worked in an office. The second, Wilhelm, had a good voice, like Jim. Slightly more aggressive than Jim, this brother, who had started as a boy to sing in coffee-houses, gained recognition and slowly worked himself into a position at the Lwow City Theater. He was in his late teens. The youngest boy, Fred, attended the Hebrew gymnasium.

It was exciting to rediscover Lwow with Jim. Every little tour, every encounter with someone from the past, was preceded with sharp anticipation. The city itself looked so small to us now. But that took nothing away from our enjoyment of it. Its value for us was contained in its dozens of memorable spots—the house where I had lived, the exact place where we had kissed the first time, the Jesuit Park (scene of countless meetings), and the streets we had walked on time and again. It awakened sensations within us, giving a rebirth to our youth and our love.

But during the decade of our absence, many changes had taken place in Lwow, most of them within the lives of those we knew.

One of our first missions there was to call on Sala Brand, who had fled from Vienna some three years before, when Abram died. The child that she had conceived before his death was a boy, now two and a half years old.

I trembled as we rang her bell, fearing to see some dreadful transformation which her loss had caused.

"You are probably too anxious, Helena," Jim murmured to me as we waited at the door. "She is remarried, after all. It is not so bad with her."

Sala came to the door, thinner to be sure and therefore seeming more fragile than ever, but she still looked young, and as a little boy stole up to her side it was clear that she had not lost her grip.

She embraced me with intensity.

"Helena, it is so good to see you. And Jim! How well you look. Come in, come in! This is my boy . . . yes, Abram, but we call him Addie."

As we were drinking tea, I studied my nephew. Unmistakably, he had some of my brother's features. The recognition was a little shocking, only because my brother was now dead and his son so very young.

Sala's new husband joined us. He was a highly personable man and treated young Addie with warmth. I was glad when he and Jim drew themselves into a male, business conversation, for I had a chance then to speak with Sala alone.

"I had little interest in remarrying after Abram," she confided. "But my parents insisted on it. You see, I was sick for a long time after I left Vienna, and after the baby was born I seemed to be wasting away in my thoughts of Abram. But I am grateful, of course. He is such a good man, Helena, and so good for the boy."

"It was right for you to remarry, Sala," I assured her. "You were so young to lose a husband. It is only natural that you should have a normal family life."

"Yes, but! . . ." Sala turned her head sharply to one side, and I could see she was weeping silently." "I'll never stop loving Abram, or suffering because he is gone!" she declared.

After she was calm, she told me about her sister, Pepa, my old friend and co-chaperone. Pepa was now married and was very well off. Hers at least was an easy story to hear.

We left Sala Brand relieved to know that her situation in life was protected and assured, whatever her heart might be missing.

Then we met Dorka on the street, just as Jim was looking in a store window. We had not, for some reason, planned to call on her. Yet now that we were face to face, so much of our old companionship was clear to me and I spoke to her eagerly. She insisted that Jim and I call on her the next day, and we agreed.

Dorka had never married, and looked old for her age now. At first I had attributed her worn appearance to the resignation of spinsterhood. But during our visit we were to hear of deeper tragedies than maidenhood. Tonka, her beautiful, raven-haired sister was the basic cause of Dorka's ravaged appearance. Their mother had died and during the war, when the Russians occupied Lwow, Tonka had given herself to the officers. At first I was thunderstruck at this information. But when I recalled the moody, exasperating, almost perverse expression on her face, even as a young girl, it all began to fall into place.

After this disgrace, Dorka explained, there was no fate left to Tonka except to become a prostitute. In this role, she had contracted syphilis and had died of it.

We left Dorka's house in a state of sadness. Tonka's fate seemed so far removed, yet Dorka's face was a living testimonial to its reality.

Jim and I spent most of our time in Lwow, of course, with his family. They were our most important reason for coming here. But one day there was a knock on my in-laws' door, and when I looked up, Jim had admitted Nathan's mother, our old neighbor.

"I live on this street, now," she said. "And when I heard you were in Lwow, Helena, I just had to see you again."

My heart acted absurdly, as a flash of Hanna's expression,

had she been here, appeared in mind's eye. But as I glanced at Nathan's mother, a kind of presentiment struck me, and kept me silent. I waited, glancing at Jim, and the woman began to talk.

Yes, Nathan had married, shortly before the war broke out. And, as he had planned, he became a teacher and had lived a scholarly life. But his wife became a widow after only a year. Nathan had died of tuberculosis.

So my mother had been right! It was as though she had read the very length of Nathan's days when she forbade Hanna to cast in her lot with him. She had never been so adamant about anything, it seemed in retrospect.

Now Jim and I had seen and heard enough of Lwow to tide us for a while. We decided to move on, to visit Berlin before returning to Vienna.

In Berlin we visited my cousin, with whom Hanna had stayed during the year of her forced separation from Nathan. But I shook my head clear of the past during our brief visit in this metropolis, determined to distract myself. Jim and I were impressed with the Brandenburg Gate, under the Linden, and with the other streets, too, the fine department stores, and the smart pedestrians. But we both agreed that we preferred Vienna.

Our brief stay in Berlin was quite luxurious. It so happened that Germany was in the throes of inflation at that time, and the value of the mark dropped from day to day. We, with our Austrian currency, seemed like millionaires.

Then it was time to go home. And we were glad to return. The trip had changed my perspective a little and before long I again began to think of having a child — not with a sense of futility, but again with hope.

Thus my fourth trip to Francensbad was arranged and that obstetrician who seemed to think more in terms of mudbaths than genes was as enthusiastic as ever.

This time I met a woman, childless like myself, who was there in Francensbad with a similar, quiet desperation. She was a very religious Jew, and even wore a *sheitel*. I suppose we were a strange pair. But our longing for motherhood drew us into long. conspiratorial conversations. And this religious lady had an idea.

"The answer," she announced to me, "lies in Karlsbad. The Beltzer Wonder Rabbi is staying there right now."

"Beltzer Rabbi?" I repeated, fascinated.

"Surely you know of the Beltzer Wonder Rabbi?" she asked.

"Of course, of course," I told her. "But do you really imagine? . . ."

"Why not?" she replied, shrugging philosophically, the way only a Jew can. "Others in distress have gone to him from all over Europe to receive his blessing. Extraordinary changes in their fate often followed a visit to him. And now he is so near — why not take advantage of being this close to Karlsbad."

"It seems . . ." I hesitated, fearing to offend her. "Well, frankly, it is just a little superstitious!"

Now the lady in the *sheitel* turned a severe eye on me. "And how many times did you say you have been to Francensbad, Mrs. Hilsen?"

"All right! You win. I'll go with you. My God, why not?"

Besides, I was eager to visit this resort, which was supposed to be very beautiful; it was just an hour's ride from Francensbad.

The reputation of Karlsbad for beauty was certainly justified. It was luxurious with natural wonders, hot springs of healing spa waters.

This was a more elegant place than Francensbad and it even attracted American tourists.

We went to the hotel where the Rabbi stayed. In an anteroom, a "Gabby," or Rabbi's assistant, approached us. One by one, he wrote down our names and then our problems.

I told him that I had been married for six years and was childless. That I was longing for a child.

The "Gabby" wrote this all down dispassionately and then left me. The room was filled with people waiting to see the Wonder Rabbi. It seemed hours that I sat there, waiting to be called.

Finally my turn came. I was ushered into a room which I don't remember at all. I can only recall the Wonder Rabbi. Never had I felt so insignificant as when I approached this holy man, with his long gray beard, black silk coat, and fur-trimmed hat. I wanted to shrink away.

But now the Rabbi studied the slip of paper which the "Gabby" had given him, containing my problem. Pressing an amulet in my palm, he stated abruptly and with certainty: "You will be blessed with a child in the coming year."

16

WHETHER THE RESULT OF THOSE MUD BATHS AT FRAN-
censbad, or an act of Divine Providence, I shall never know,
but I finally did conceive that year. At first, I could hardly
believe that it had really happened. Jim, too, cautioned me
against being too certain at the beginning. But when I was
three months pregnant, the fact could not be denied and,
feeling safe to acknowledge it, the two of us were overjoyed.
It is difficult to imagine two prospective parents more engrossed
in the subject of the coming child. Now our conversation was
only about this baby I carried. And why not? What could
have been more fascinating to either of us? Would it be a
boy or a girl? What would we name it? Whom would the
child resemble? We hoped this first baby would be a boy, but
agreed that a girl would be equally dear.

My mother's delight at my conception could not be
measured. She attributed this miracle to the Wonder Rabbi,
and I doubt that anyone could have swayed her from this
opinion. As for me, I cared little for theories now, or causes.
I carried a child. Let anyone explain it as he would!

Hanna was thrilled for me. But not for herself. For, at the
same time, she too became pregnant. And she did not want a
third child at this time. Basically, she did love her children.
She managed now to have a good relationship with little
George, her youngest, but Esther continued to be a difficult

child and the more impatient Hanna grew with her, the more recalcitrant she became. Then there was another reason why Hanna's third pregnancy seemed ill-timed.

Unlike Jim, Josef had been unlucky in some of his business affairs. At the present time, he and Hanna were not too well off.

Nevertheless, this picture of a family growing in all directions was immensely pleasing to my mother and father. Another member was to be added the same summer. Ellen joined us, to marry Leon.

Ellen was a beautiful girl with a round face and dimples in her red cheeks. She was endowed with dark hair and dark eyes and had a slightly superior air about her. Hanna had originally introduced this girl to Leon and he had been smitten with her from the start. In no time at all he had proposed and Ellen had accepted him.

Personally, I had misgivings about this union. There was something in Ellen's attitude toward Leon which was not quite right. It was as though in accepting him she had relinquished some other dream of a man quite different from Leon and now consciously made a compromise. She regarded herself as a woman of considerable intelligence and refinement. And I suspected that she felt our Leon to be a little beneath her, that she had accepted his proposal because he could offer her security. After all, Leon, in addition to his income from the matzoh factory, now owned 25 per cent of the Stadt-Kino, which rendered a good profit.

I hoped that I was wrong about Ellen, that I misjudged her. It hurt me to imagine that my brother could be marrying a woman who might be cold to him. As the day for their wedding approached, I tried to rid myself of such thoughts. I attended the affair in a maternity dress and was very proud of my state of pregnancy.

At just about this time, our finances took an upward turn,

as if fate itself smiled upon the enlargement of our family.
Jim had leased a third movie theater, the Turm Kino, not far
from Stadt-Kino, and offered on its screen *The Gold Rush*,
starring Charlie Chaplin. Since we had exclusive rights to it
in Vienna, the picture made our fortune.

My pregnancy advanced through the summer and into the
fall. By September, 1926, I was heavy with child, fascinated
with the movements it made within me. Knees and elbows
could be felt now, pushing forward, as though against a
confining wall. Already I felt a bond with the little creature,
a sympathy for it, straining for freedom.

On the evening of November 23rd, I felt my first labor
pains. At once, a feeling of happiness overcame me.

"The time," I thought, "is already here. I will soon hold
the baby in my arms—Jim's baby and mine!"

I phoned Jim at the movie and he soon arrived with a taxi
and took me to the private sanitorium, Loew. The maid
called my mother and when we arrived at the sanitorium
Mother and Olga were already there. Hanna, having delivered
a son, Robert, six weeks before, was unable to come.

My mother stayed in my room during most of the labor.
It was a great relief to have her sit next to me. Her presence
put everything in perspective; she confirmed my wonder that
it had finally come to pass, and she modified my fear as the
pain grew progressively stronger. She had a sedative effect
on me.

During this time, Jim was pacing in the lobby with a com-
pulsive excitement. Olga tried to calm him, but in vain.

Now the pain ripped down my back, announcing its importance. The real thing was close at hand. My mother's
expression changed as a contraction distorted my face.

Shortly thereafter, they came with a stretcher. I was carried
to the delivery room. En route I saw Jim. He was in a terrible

state. When I saw his devastated expression, I told him not to worry.

"I am all right, Jim," I murmured. "It is all going as it should."

In the delivery room, I lay on an operating table, and the pains were bad, worse than I could have imagined. But my mind still gripped the elation with which I had arrived at this place. I struggled with the pain, lest it blot out my joy with its violence. A baby was on its way, a child that would be my own.

A needle penetrated me and I began to sink into sleep.

"Press hard," the doctor said, and mingled sensations overtook me.

When I woke up, things were still unclear, hazy. Dimly, I saw two figures in white talking to each other. The obstetrician washed his hands, as did the woman doctor who had assisted him.

"It is a girl," they told me.

My head cleared and now the whole process of labor was sharply recalled. I was the mother of a baby girl and I had never felt so wonderful. The pain was forgotten at once as the doctor placed the small bundle next to me.

"Mine and Jim's!" I thought. It seemed incredible.

Clutching the little blanket, I struggled suddenly to stay awake. But weakness overtook me and I fell asleep.

When next I awakened, I was in my room again. The baby was in a cradle next to my bed, at arm's length. A nurse was there too, watching us both.

The most exciting moment was Jim's first visit to my room. His eyes quickly filled with tears as he took my hand.

"Until now, Helena," he said solemnly, "I didn't know how much I loved you."

The nurse picked up the baby to show her to us. How wonderful she seemed with her tiny white face and red cheeks!

I loved nursing her. The procedure was thrilling. Never before
had I felt so essential, so important in this world. I couldn't
take my eyes from the child.

Jim watched me nursing her. "The role suits you so well,
Helena," Jim remarked.

I answered only with a smile, intent on the infant.

Now my mother burst into the room, radiant. She had
been fitfully waiting to be called in. Her face was glowing.

"How much I was longing to live to see the moment when
you would have your baby, Helena. Life is good after all."

Not only our family rejoiced, but friends, too, responded
enthusiastically to the birth of our first child after a wait of
seven years. Jim proudly announced the birth of a daughter.
And baskets of flowers poured into my room from film per-
sonalities and other friends in Vienna. Relatives begged to
visit, messages of congratulations arrived, and by the time my
ten days had elapsed my room looked like a garden.

And then it was time to return home. I felt absolutely
triumphant. Jim hired a nurse to take care of the baby. Those
first weeks, I did not go out at all. I was too absorbed in
my daughter.

We called her Ingrid, And Jim thought her the most beautiful infant in existence. Each evening he came home and seated
himself next to her crib. It did not matter how tired he was.
He forgot himself, contemplating her, until I reminded him to
get up and have dinner.

With the birth of Ingrid, we had outgrown our three-room
apartment. Jim rented a magnificent seven-room suite, with
a huge foyer, and we set about furnishing it. We bought pieces
of furniture which, at one time, would have seemed forever
beyond our reach, and Jim chose oriental carpets for the floors.
We had Louis XVI furniture in our drawing room, and it was
truly a salon. The nursery, however, was our favorite room.
We employed both a nurse and a maid, and nothing was

spared that might bring comfort or delight to our small daughter.

Sometimes, I suppose, Jim went overboard with his enthusiasm. For example, he celebrated the first birthday of Ingrid by presenting her with a concert-size Steinway grand piano. As far as Jim was concerned, our mode of living seemed permanent and assured. He could not imagine it ever changing. However, this way of life was to last uninterrupted for only five years.

17

THE FOLLOWING SUMMER, 1927, JIM RENTED A LARGE COTTAGE for the entire season in Bad Voeslau, near Vienna. This was a lovely resort, especially suited to families with small children. Two swimming pools with constantly flowing mineral water from a spring provided delight for both parents and their off-spring. Afternoons, music was played in the park, and all around were woods where one could stroll and breathe the spicy scent of pine trees.

Hanna, with her three children, needed a change, too, and Jim invited them to stay with me. There was more than ample room for visitors. So Hanna joined us with her young, and I was delighted to have her near. We were both nursing our babies that summer — I, my Ingrid, and she, her Robert. Hanna seemed more relaxed with her children in that atmosphere of summer leisure, and when we nursed the babies together, all the closeness of shared experiences over the years became that much stronger in this new, common role. I, in fact, ran short of milk occasionally, and Hanna, being more abundantly supplied, would lovingly take over the feeding of Ingrid.

Ingrid was now eight months old, a beautiful fat baby. Her rosy-cheeked face was always smiling, and even in infancy she radiated happiness to others, so that all of us, and especially Hanna, called her our "sunshine." Hanna had developed a very special love for Ingrid, as I, in my turn, had a special place in my heart for her Esther. So we spent the days enjoying one another. Jim and Josef worked during the week but spent the weekends at the cottage. Josef had to miss a weekend sometimes, but Jim made a point of never doing so.

Since I had taken the maid and Ingrid's nurse, my round of guests was not overwhelming. Mother would come out and visit for a few days at a time, but always her old self, she was restless, certain that the family, the house, and the business were suffering because of her absence. Bernatz, my youngest brother, came with her and stayed longer.

Thus the summer began to progress with a happy family feeling. I especially loved the weekends, however. Every Friday evening, I waited at the entrance to the cottage to welcome Jim when he arrived from the city.

On the evening of July 15th, Jim did not come at the usual time. After the first hour of lateness passed, I became worried because of Jim's usual punctuality. He had always called me, in the past, if there was to be a delay.

At bedtime, he had still not arrived. Hanna coaxed me into undressing and getting into bed, but sleep was out of the question. Hanna, who sat in my room, tried to calm me, but by midnight, she, too, was alarmed and was unable to conceal it.

Then we heard the door slam and feet dash up the stairs. Jim burst into the room.

"Good Heavens, Helena! Am I glad to see you!"

With these words, he rushed to me and kissed me frantically.

"Jim! What's happened? We've been sick with worry!" I said.

He sat down and caught his breath.

"For once," he said, "you had good reason to worry. I was in danger of being killed tonight, Helena."

"What!" Hanna gasped.

I rose fearfully and pivoted all around Jim, searching for wounds.

"Are you all right now?" I asked, frightened, while still understanding nothing. Jim still panted for breath.

"Yes," he said. "Only still excited."

Hanna rose and moved toward the door.

"Now you try to relax with Helena, Jim. I'm going to make you some coffee and something to eat."

After she closed the door, Jim still said nothing. He got up and walked to the room where Ingrid was sleeping. As he peered down into her crib, he muttered, "Thank God for saving my life! How good it is to be with you and the child again."

Finally, when he was drinking his coffee, I begged him to tell me what had happened.

He took a long breath and began to speak.

"I was in a taxi, Helena, on my way to the railroad station. We had to pass the Ringstrasse. Here, suddenly, all cars were forced to stop. In the street, hundreds of people were running and screaming and shouting. It was some kind of demonstration, but nothing was clear. Policemen on horses chased some of the people. Another squad—foot police—were shooting at the demonstrators. Bullets were flying everywhere. And then some hit the taxi I was sitting in!"

Here Jim paused, mopping his face with a handkerchief.

"It was a miracle, Helena," he swore, "that I was not hit by one or more of those bullets. Then, from a distance, I saw a big fire rising. It was no less than the Palace of Justice in flames! Imagine! Ambulances screamed by to pick up the wounded and dead. Two *Schutzbund* Army men opened the taxi door and questioned me. Then they ordered the driver to turn back."

"And then?" I asked.

"And then it was over for me. I proceeded with my trip."

"But this chaos you describe, Jim! And in Vienna! What was it for?"

He rose and shrugged. "That is the remarkable thing. I still don't know the cause of the scene. Just that I was nearly killed in it!"

But the next day, everything was in the paper. The whole story of the mass demonstration was there, and the toll of its disaster. The Social Democrats blamed the Christian Socials for the bloody outburst and the Christian Socials, in turn, blamed them.

Actually, the demonstration had a history of events behind it. First of all, the tension between the two political parties had never ceased since the republic was first established. During these years, a group of extreme anti-Semites founded an organization and called themselves *Hackenkreuzler* — Swastika Men. The group was a forerunner of the Nazi Party in Austria. Since they were against both Jews and the Social Democrats, this group was tolerated by the Christian Socials.

On January 30, 1927, a tragedy had occurred in Schattendorf, near Vienna. The *Hackenkreuzler* killed a worker, a child, and wounded several other persons. Five months later, three men who confessed to firing the fatal shots were acquitted. This unjust verdict outraged the working people. The thought of it must have been festering in their minds all of those months, until now, in July, its venom burst in the Ringstrasse demonstration, where Jim had almost lost his life.

The Palace of Justice, where this gross injustice had prevailed, had been turned into a flaming symbol of the people's anger.

This date, July 15, 1927, marked the peak of the Social Democrats' power in Austria. An epoch of slow decline began for them. And with the descent of their power a new period of struggle against a rising tide of fascism began.

We were slow to acknowledge the presence of that tide.

Once Jim's brush with danger was forgotten, we were quick, as humans are, to dissociate the random rumblings of fascism from ourselves. As long as order prevailed, we somehow felt that it always would, that the good life we knew was as indestructible as our desire to maintain it.

18

THE PEOPLE OF VIENNA SOON FORGOT THE SCHATTENDORF trial and its attendant tragedy. As for the Jews, they regarded the *Hackenkreuzler* as an insignificant party. They were used, after all, to occasional, small outbreaks of anti-Semitism, and expected no worse consequences to evolve. Life went on and everyone made the best of it.

Jim and I continued to have every reason to be happy. Our desire for a child was fulfilled, we had a lovely apartment to live in, and all of our dear ones were free from want. The only thing left to desire now was another child. This time I had no difficulty in conceiving. Ingrid was just a year and a half old when I became pregnant again.

My friend Greta had been less fortunate than I during the past few years. Her marriage to Erich was rumored in shaky condition and, in addition, she had become quite ill. The female illness which she had pronounced "cured" at Francensbad several years back, had, in fact, grown progressively worse with time. The Saturday night foursomes we used to make with the Schelmans had become fewer and fewer due to Greta's illness, and soon I visited her at home instead. A tumor had developed in her reproductive organs and finally the doctor told her she would have to have a hysterectomy.

I had visited Greta the day after she received the news. Probably I was more shaken by the information than Greta

166

herself, for she was an exceptionally brave person.

"Greta," I murmured, "that you should have to suffer this!"

She shrugged and made a face. But I saw how pale she had become.

"If it will make me well, Helena, it will be worth going through. I have been feeling sick for so long that I would sacrifice anything to feel whole again and normal. I would prefer death to a lifetime of sickness."

"And Erich? Is he taking the news well?" I asked.

"He was upset, of course, Erich does feel for me. But as for not being able to have children after the operation, it actually doesn't matter, Helena. Erich and I had Kurt some time ago. We did not plan anymore."

"I see," I replied, not seeing at all.

"Sit down, Helena," Greta said. "Here, next to the bed. We may as well have a good talk while we're at it."

I seated myself, and she reached out and touched my hand for a moment.

"Somehow," she began, "I thought you had guessed how things stood between Erich and me. All those Saturday nights we spent with you and Jim. . . . In between the fun, didn't you feel the tension between us?"

"Tension?" I echoed. "No, not really. I guess it never occurred to me."

"And why would it?" she asked smiling, "Or should it? You have a marriage made in heaven. It's only natural that you tend to regard your friends as equally happy—until proven otherwise!"

"But how—when did it start, this trouble between you and Erich?"

Greta sighed. "A long time ago, when I first realized that Erich was seeing other women. That was shock enough! The deeper shock came later, though, when I realized it wasn't going to stop, that there would always be other women for Erich."

Here she paused and smiled.

"Don't feel sorry for me, Helena. Honestly! This is all so old to me that I'm quite used to it. I'm really very philosophical about it by now, and certainly resigned to it. And I'm not planning to do anything drastic about it for the present."

"Had you thought of separating from him, then?"

"From time to time it has occurred to me, of course. But look at me. I'm a sick woman, facing a major operation. And Erich still cares for me, however imperfectly. Right now, I couldn't be alone."

"No," I agreed. "You musn't even think of it."

Now Greta leaned forward and kissed me.

"Really, Helena. Why am I burdening you like this? Here you are so happy, expecting your new baby. When is it due?"

"Early in February," I told her.

"February!" she repeated, as though struck with some new idea.

"The first week in February, to be exact," I added.

"And where will you go for the confinement?"

"To the Loew Sanitorium, where I had Ingrid."

Greta's eyes glittered, dark in her pale face.

"Now I'll tell you what I'm thinking, Helena," she said eagerly, getting out of bed. "Why don't I arrange to have the operation at Loew Sanitorium the same week that you deliver. . . . It's a marvelous idea. . . . Just to know you were there, Helena! It would give me so much moral support."

"And I would love it, too, Greta! Do it, by all means. The whole idea of the hospital will be less austere with a friend right down the hall. I know just what you mean. It takes the edge off the anticipation, somehow."

Thus, our mutual date at the sanitorium was arranged. Within myself, I was still deeply concerned with Greta's physical plight. I knew, as she must, what a hysterectomy could, with bad luck, imply. I prayed that her operation would be successful, and naïvely I hoped that her trouble with Erich's infidelity would come to an end.

We were living through one of the coldest winters I could remember. As a result, I was not so eager to take the walks prescribed for expectant mothers. Ellen, Leon's new wife, was pregnant with her first child at this time. We visited one another and compared symptoms. I was growing to like the girl, despite what I continued to feel about her relations with Leon.

My labor started right on schedule. I arrived at the sanitorium, bundled in a fur coat against the cold, and was taken to the same room where I had stayed for Ingrid's birth. The labor was shorter this time, but before it became severe, I gave Jim instructions to phone Greta. She would arrange to come in a day or two. Her doctor had agreed to accommodate her plan, eager for anything that would help psychologically.

When I awoke, after my delivery, I was in my room and Jim was standing there.

"It is a girl, Helena. . . . Another little daughter for us," he said, kissing my face.

At first, Jim and I were a trifle disappointed that it was not a son. But in no time we were immensely grateful for this second little girl. She looked entirely different from Ingrid, who had been so round and rosy from the start. The new baby had a narrow, pointed face, which was rather pale.

We decided to call her Gerda.

Mother was standing over the cradle the first time Gerda opened her eyes. She took a long look at her and then pronounced: "This little Gerda will be a brainy one, Helena."

I laughed, lying in bed.

"Oh, come now, Mother! How can you possibly tell?"

"Wait," she told me sagely. "You will see."

I studied Gerda's little face, searching for signs of genius. "Who knows, Mother? Perhaps you are right."

Later in the day, I received the first report of Greta's condition. She had come through the operation with every apparent success. I gave the nurse a joyfully scribbled note to deliver to my friend, and thus communication between us two convalescents was begun. We kept the nurses busy exchanging notes in the next ten days. Neither of us was allowed to rise from bed. Greta wrote that she was grateful to be alive and, as the days progressed, began to say that she felt certain of a complete recovery. For my part, I mixed encouragement with little amusing anecdotes about Gerda. Erich, having come to visit her, stopped by to congratulate me. I kept thinking of the things Greta had told me about his other women, and then of Greta, lying so pitifully down the hall, and I had to control my voice so that it did not sound unnatural or hostile. Greta might be able to philosophize about such matters; I was not capable of doing so.

Eventually, my ten days of confinement were over. And once home again, my cup of joy indeed seemed full to overflowing, with Gerda in the cradle while Ingrid, now an active toddler, stared at her, calling, *"Bebele, bebele!"* with utter delight.

With the two of them, I was particularly grateful that we could afford the nurse and the maid. Caring for the babies was an endless and exacting job.

Ellen had given birth to a son, Henry, close to the time of my delivery. Since I had domestic help, I was free to visit her and Leon rather frequently.

These visits were sadly revealing. My original feelings about Ellen had been more accurate than even I suspected. Even with the pleasure she evidently found in her new little son, she failed to treat Leon, his father, with anything resembling warmth. The more I saw of them, the clearer it became that their entire married existence up to this point had been a cruel play between the passionate love he felt for her and the utter frigidity with which she received it.

I suppose I should have hated Ellen for depriving Leon of the fulfillment he should have found in married life. But a strange paradox was maintained in Ellen's relationship with me and with all of my family; Ellen was genuinely fond, and actively so, of all of us. And apart from Leon, she was somehow an appealing girl, offering a forthrightness, an honesty, that captured one. Even her shabby treatment of Leon could be called an extension of this honesty, for she did not have within her the duplicity to pretend in front of his family. Yet she showed such affection, individually, for the rest of us! The situation truly precipitated much inner conflict in me, as well as within my parents, sisters, and brothers. How was one to react?

In studying my brother and his wife, I tried to pin down for myself the things in Leon that must be offending Ellen, the characteristics that she could not reconcile herself to. Often, when in a group of people, especially a varied group, I would see Ellen stiffen slightly when Leon spoke. Clearly, she felt his delivery of ideas too ordinary, lacking a certain intellectual flair which she openly admired in others. That Leon was intelligent and gifted in his own special sphere, electrical engineering, was lost upon Ellen. Gradually, I came to see that her inability to accept him on a broad social level had affected her physical response to Leon. He was actually a good-looking boy and would have appealed to a number of women for that alone. But frigidity was all he could elicit from the wife he had chosen.

Leon, meanwhile, almost seemed goaded into loving her more. His love for Ellen, it seemed to me, had become nearly the most important thing in his life. After a while, it hardly seemed to matter what she did to him. She could have her way with Leon and it became understood between them, and to anyone else who cared, that even though his life was half a ruin, he was irrevocably bound in some special way to Ellen. This became so tacit, so certain, that after a while I, like the others in my family, became resigned to the idea that the relationship would endure, dismal as it might at times be. I became more concerned, for some reason, with the dilemma of Olga's marriage than with that of Leon's.

As all our families grew, the circle at my parents' table increased and at holidays everyone appeared. In addition to all the married ones and their children, there were also the unmarried ones at the table. These were jolly get-togethers for the most part and my parents felt their abundant good fortune in the size and health of the entire family. The High Holidays, however, were the most gratifying and significant of them all. What an atmosphere of subtle mystery and mounting tension was felt as Rosh Hashana, the Day of Judgement, approached! For the New Year, we all gathered at my parents' home. Then together we worshipped at a *shul* where my father was a board member. He secured tickets for the men in the family and for the married women, who sat with my mother (the unmarried girls did not attend services, except for Kol Nidre night). My mother, next to whom I sat, was well versed in every prayer and kept us in touch with the exact page and line to insure our following the service well. She particularly stressed the importance of a prayer called *Venusanu Tokef*, which commemorates the martyrdom of a 12th Century rabbi who permitted his hands and feet to be mutilated rather than renounce Judaism. Part of it goes: "On the first day of the year it is inscribed, and on the Day of Atonement the decree is sealed, how many shall pass away and how many shall be born, who shall live and who shall die. . . . But Penitence, Prayer, and Charity avert the severe decree."

Who could fail to be moved by such pronouncements? After services, we would collect the children, who had been playing in the courtyard, and go back to my parents' home for dinner.

The atmosphere which accompanied Yom Kippur was even stranger and more compelling than that of Rosh Hashana. We felt genuinely apprehensive as the Day of Atonement approached, for on this day God forgave sins committed against Him, but not those committed against one's fellow men, unless one asked the forgiveness of the wronged neighbor. On this occasion benevolence filled our hearts. We forgave each other for petty hostilities that had gnawed at us during the preceding year and all of us embraced.

About five o'clock on Kol Nidre night, which ushers in Yom Kippur, my mother served the dinner which was to sustain us through the next twenty-four hours of fasting. Then she lit a thick, long candle planted in a pot of earth on the table, to commemorate the dead. Afterward, she lit four candles in silver candlesticks, covering her face with her hands, and wept a little while praying for a good year to come. After this, my father put his hand on the head of every child and grandchild present, giving each individual the same blessing. Invariably, this elicited many tears.

Afterward, we went to *shul* together, my mother, Hanna, Olga, Ellen, and I, as well as Mela and Stela. The congregation sat in hushed austerity, waiting for the service to begin. Finally, the cantor's voice resounded with "Kol Nidre." We rose, chanting, "All vows, bonds, promises, obligations, penalties and oaths we did not keep, we repent."

Standing next to my mother, I felt a holiness exuding from this little lady, praying with all her heart and soul for her children. When she prayed one felt she was being elevated into higher spheres. Watching her, who could doubt it?

The next day, we all came to the *shul* early to fast and to pray. My mother stayed there all day, praying fervently. She

was worried that Olga, who was pregnant, might faint from
fasting, and finally said, "Go home and eat something, Olga.
I'll take your sins upon myself." I could distinguish my father's
rather loud voice chanting in the other room, which was
divided from ours by curtained windows. With him were Jim,
Leon, Josef, and Friedrich, along with the unmarried Saul
and Bernatz.

At sundown, we all went home and broke the fast with a
large and joyous dinner. Everyone was in a cheerful mood
then, and each wished the others that what he had prayed for
would come to pass. All felt relieved that this long, hard day
was over, and merriment prevailed.

The children, sensing the change, were exuberant. There
was Hanna's Esther, George, and Robert; Leon's Henry,
Olga's Eddie, and my own Ingrid and Gerda. My mother
never showed any favoritism, but I secretly suspected that she
was happiest with my two. After all, she had waited so long
for them, praying that I would become a mother. It could
certainly be said that all of these, her grandchildren, had
become now the greatest pleasure in her life, as her children
had been earlier. These, now grown, seemed destined to be the
living proof of Mother's proverb, "Little children, little worries,
big children, big worries." And my mother, unchanged by the
years, continued to be a worrier. She was concerned about
Mela and Stela, both of whom should have been married
by now, still living at home. She fretted over little conflicts
that Hanna, Olga, and Leon, had with their mates. She was
not a woman who could take life easy. Even though she now
had a maid, she seemed to work as ceaselessly as ever and
never to think of her own pleasure. My father, by contrast,
was ever ready to seize a bit of leisure wherever he could. Now
that he was getting older and a little richer, he could afford
to keep more help in the bakery. Then, too, Saul had become
a baker now and worked with him, relieving my father of

much responsibility. Thus, many an afternoon would find my father diverting himself in coffeehouses, playing cards with friends. My mother, far from resenting his inclination to do so, was only concerned that he should be well turned out before he left the house. She would examine his outfit critically, halt him, and call the maid to bring a brush.

"His sleeve," she would say, "has dust on the elbow. Give it a brush. And the collar. Turn it down, that's it!"

She was as selfless as ever in her love for my father. Her own desires remained as simple as they had ever been. I, for one, wished that she could worry less about all of us, since her worrying could do no good. That she had cause for worry, however, could not be denied.

For example, I noticed lately how poorly Friedrich was looking, watching him as he sat next to Olga at the family affairs. He had grown pale and a little haggard. Olga herself seemed more silent than usual, as if she were depressed. I decided to visit her alone and talk things over with her.

She smiled sadly when I broached the subject. "I seem depressed, Helena? What is the mystery? You know perfectly well that things have not gone well for Friedrich, here in Vienna. This city is teeming with attorneys. It's not easy to establish a significant clientele."

"But what about that little town where Friedrich was so well known?" I asked.

"Wiener Neustadt?" she asked. "It's too late for that. And it is my fault, Helena. Only mine. Friedrich wanted so much to move there, right after we were married . . . you remember?"

I nodded.

"He could have been a big man there. I know. He had so many contacts. But I refused to leave Vienna. I was so certain that he would do well here, Helena. I was selfish. I wanted Friedrich to be successful and I wanted Vienna, too!"

"Well," I murmured. "At least there is your income from the Stadt-Kino. Your dowry—it should help matters a little. . . ."

"Ah, yes, my 25 per cent of the Stadt-Kino!" she said bitterly. "Well, financially it does help. But it is poor balm to Friedrich's pride. A man is, after all, a man, Helena."

I left Olga's deeply discouraged. So it had all boomeranged for my younger sister. That intense longing for status which had motivated her marriage to Friedrich at the price of sexual compatibility and something of her own youth, had driven her so far that he had lost the status possible to him through the very extent of Olga's own ambition. At least, that was her interpretation of it.

And she may have been at least partly right. Friedrich, while quietly impressive, might have made his name and fortune in Wiener Neustadt. But he was perhaps not quite dynamic enough to shine out in the intense competition of Vienna.

I saw Olga a week later and we discussed the situation further.

"For myself, I care little at this point, Helena," she confided. "But Friedrich is so unhappy. His lack of success weighs upon him heavily. And I am to blame! If I can only make him happy, somehow. That is all I ask at this point. I'm afraid his health will fail if his mood does not lift."

I tried to comfort Olga as best I could. But what advice could I offer? Perhaps both she and Hanna should have been truer to instinct when making their choices. Yet what might have evolved from that? Marriage was so complicated. It made one's head spin to think of it.

Olga had another problem, too. Eddie, her little boy, worried her a great deal. He was unusually thin and refused to eat most of what was offered to him. Olga did everything to coax his appetite and keep him healthy. She even hired a dietary nurse to make him eat. At this time, Olga became more selfless than she had ever been in her life, devoting herself almost entirely to the child and to restoring to Friedrich whatever semblance of happiness was possible.

19

THE CONFLICTS WHICH WERE MAINTAINED BY MY MARRIED
sisters and brothers made me look to my parents' home for
relief. There, in the uncomplicated single state, I thought, were
my other four siblings, all of them in their twenties now.

But I was to be quickly swayed from this illusion. Trouble
was at hand with the two youngest girls, Mela and Stela.

When children are very young, they are still under their
parents' protection. They, in turn, usually do as much as they
can to make the children comfortable. But as children mature
and taste new, different environments outside the home, they
sometimes tend to adopt the opinions and manners of certain
influential friends.

With this new situation in my parents' home, Mother continued to assume her old role of worrier. Father as usual took
little seriously. Olga's current unhappiness was already a source
of concern to my mother, but even more severe shocks were
in store for her from her two youngest girls.

In high school, Mela and Stela had been average students.
After they completed it, neither sought out further formal
education or a trade. After all, it was not really usual in
Europe for a girl to learn a trade at that time.

They occupied themselves with *Hashomer,* the Zionist group
in which Leon and Olga had been so active in their unmarried
years. This was a new generation of *Hashomer* people. The

boys and girls met frequently, arranged many outings, and some prepared, as Leon had, to go to Palestine.

Mela and Stela were close in age and, consequently, were very close emotionally. Mela, who was now twenty-six, was slightly the elder. Physically she resembled me, having the same brown hair, blue eyes, and high forehead. But the intense, keen expression of her eyes and the determined set of her lips gave her appearance a quality quite different from mine. She had tremendous influence over Stela in every way. Always travelling in the same company, they had many mutual friends.

Among them was a certain young man called, simply, Schorr, with whom they had formed a close attachment. I had occasion to meet Schorr a few times when visiting my parents. He was good-looking and extremely talkative. He struck me as a bit presumptuous.

Later, I was to learn more about him. So young, he was already a perfected Talmudist. But he was fond of disputes with other learned people. He was inordinately fond of proving his prowess in the art of argument. And Schorr, despite his grounding in the Talmud, was actually a non-believer and enjoyed contradicting everything in the Talmud.

As he became a constantly more frequent visitor in my parents' home, it slowly became clear that of all his sharp interests, money was the strongest. He spoke of his transactions with a candor that was almost vulgar, and I was bored with him. He lived high and liked to spend freely.

Yet he had won over Mela and Stela completely. They could not have been more impressed. Thus, to my mother's slowly rising dismay, he insinuated himself more and more into the family circle, dropping in almost at will. He was certain of an enthusiastic reception from the girls. Not that he showed the slightest inclination to marry either one of them! But he acted as their advisor, worming his way into their confidence, bit by bit, until nothing of my parents' financial position remained unknown to him.

Mother, from the first, had sensed something distinctly unwholesome about Schorr, the nature of his interest in the girls, and the frequency of his visits to the house.

When she had spoken — as tactfully as she could — to Mela and Stela, her opinions had fallen upon deaf ears. The girls were offended by any poor thought concerning Schorr. With a kind of horror, my mother saw that her two youngest daughters had drifted completely away from the sphere of her influence, that she was helpless to protect them since they were too old to be forced.

Now Schorr had concerned himself with one particular aspect of the family finances: the dowries which Mela and Stela were to receive from my parents. Alone with the girls, he questioned them comprehensively on this subject. What did they know of their expectations? What had been the portions allotted to Hanna, to Olga, to me?

In a family of nine children, it is almost as if two families exist, so apart are some of the children in age. Sometimes, as was probably the case with Mela and Stela, the younger ones are too young to identify their childhood with that of a much older sibling who married and left the house before they were ten years of age. Too many experiences have gone unshared due to the difference which the years impose. It is only by this reasoning that I am able to explain how Schorr could have planted in the hearts of Mela and Stela such suspicion and design against their parents and against Hanna, Olga, Leon, and me.

Schorr adopted a theory about the family. He regarded Hanna, Olga, and myself as having been generously endowed at the time of our respective marriages. He kept telling Mela and Stela that our dowries had been lavish and he wondered if enough had been put aside for the poor younger sisters. He was doubtful that enough had. He suspected that my parents planned to give Mela and Stela less than we older girls had received.

Mother's manner grew increasingly cool toward Schorr. But Father characteristically was friendly to Schorr when he came for an evening. The two chatted warmly, and my father seemed to take the young man at face value.

On one such evening, I had also dropped in. Father and Schorr were having one of their friendly chats. Mother drew me into the kitchen to speak privately.

"Just look at your father, Helena!" she muttered. "How can he be so foolish? This fellow is so transparent. Anyone can see he's up to no good. Yet see how welcome he is made in this house! As if the blindness of Mela and Stela were not enough to bear!" she concluded furiously.

"I agree with you, Mother," I said, biting my lip. "This Schorr strikes me as a troublemaker and an egotist, unless he himself doesn't realize the consequences of his actions."

But neither Mother's feelings nor mine could halt Schorr's campaign, now in full swing, with Mela and Stela.

Dowries were given in proportion to the girl's parents' ability to be generous, as was customary all over Europe. But Schorr told Mela and Stela: "Your elder sisters and Leon are taking now much of what is rightfully yours. You will have to fight for your rights!"

And they did. But whom did they fight? My poor mother! What an undeserved suffering this was for her! But Mela and Stela were adamant, once they had begun. Now they began to treat Hanna, Olga, Leon, and me as if we had robbed them of their fortune. It was so absurd that we felt rather indifferent. But we were furious about the suffering they caused Mother, and we worried about her health now, which had not been too good since Abram's death.

The specific outrage which Mela and Stela finally perpetuated under Schorr's influence was to demand of my parents a cash settlement, then and there.

"What can you be thinking of?" my mother asked them, outraged. "Neither of you is getting married, now. When you marry, you will each receive a fair dowry, just as your sisters did."

"But will there be anything left?" Mela responded. "We doubt that there will, with Hanna, Helena, Olga, and Leon draining away everything. Who knows that they won't take even more than they have already. It isn't fair! Stela and I will end with nothing," she moaned.

"Foolish girl!" Mother retorted. "You create a fight for nothing. Nothing but love and good will has ever directed our feelings for both of you. And you turn against those who love you! For what?"

Thus, the argument was superficially ended. But an undercurrent of bitterness remained with both Mela and Stela. And they continued to see Schorr, whom the rest of us now despised. Mela and Stela were as impressed with him as ever.

Aside to me, Mother remarked: "You know, Helena, I forgive the girls. They are young and foolish and their understanding is incomplete. I only pray that God will be equally forgiving."

Still, the girls continued to live at home and in some respects a degree of normalcy was restored to their relationships there. Before the holidays, when there was much work at the matzoh factory, Mela and Stela helped a great deal. Mela was very capable and directed the selling and delivering of matzohs to stores. And this work was wholesome work for the girls, drawing them close to the family again, if even for a little while.

Saul, younger than Stela, had now finished high school and had decided to work full-time in the bread bakery. He wanted to become a baker. Saul had his circle of friends, both male and female. They were together constantly and enjoyed good

times. As for loyalties at home, Saul supported Mela and Stela
in their financial claims, since he was included in their protest
and thought himself to have been put at the same disadvantage
as they. But unlike Mela and Stela his attitude toward his
parents and toward us older sisters and brother remained
friendly.

Bernatz the youngest of all the nine children, grew up to
be the tallest and most handsome. A lover of sports, he had an
athlete's body and wide shoulders. He had tremendous blue
eyes, a broad forehead, and a radiant smile which revealed a
stunning set of teeth. In addition, therefore, to being the sole
family athlete, he was also the ladies' man. Since early adol-
escence, Bernatz was surrounded by admiring girls wherever
he went.

My mother took great pride in her youngest boy and wanted
him to become some kind of important man. She was determined that he continue his studies after finishing high school.
Accordingly, Bernatz chose to attend the Handels Academie
(the commercial academy of Vienna), which he completed
with average grades.

Upon completing his studies, Bernatz announced to the
family that he had decided to see all of Europe. Having next
to no money at all, he planned a hitch-hiking tour on which
he would stop and work in various spots to make enough for
food and lodging. My mother, of course, thought the idea
outrageous and fraught with danger. She begged Bernatz to
abandon the plan. But he had no idea of doing so. To him, the
tour was the most wonderful adventure imaginable. Bernatz
used to come over every Saturday to see my girls and to eat
my home-baked *Sachertorte,* which he enjoyed immensely.

This week, Bernatz came as usual, but this time took occasion to enlist my sympathy and aid for his project.

"Mother is so upset, Helena, and you have so much

influence with her. Can't you get her to calm down a little about my trip?"

"I'm not so sure it's a good idea myself," I told him.

"Look!" Bernatz said eagerly, sitting down next to me. "There's nothing to worry about. I won't be alone. I'm going with another boy and two girls."

"What!" I cried, rising. I looked at him squarely. "Does mother know about this part of it?"

"Yes," he said, shrugging his shoulders. "But it makes no difference. She still doesn't approve."

"I should think not!" I exclaimed. "Who are these girls, Bernatz? What kind of families do they come from—letting them go off on a trip with two fellows?"

Bernatz blushed. "Honestly, Helena. You sound just like Mother. As I explained to Mother, our relationship with these girls is completely platonic!"

I gave him a very dubious look and we both burst out laughing.

"I swear it!" he insisted.

"All right, Bernatz, all right," I said. "Although the trip sounds more unsavory than even before, you are obviously determined to go. I'll do my best to quiet Mother."

So Bernatz left for his hitch-hiking tour of Europe, but I was not so successful in calming Mother. I told her that she was worrying far too much over this trip. Undoubtedly it was natural that he, like other young people, should wish to explore the world. The thought of danger never occurred to them and this, too, was part of being young. She should be proud, I pointed out, that Bernatz was so clever and resourceful as to make his own way on such a journey. Certainly he would come back safely. Thus I attempted to soften her concern.

But she still worried about him. And due to his strange itinerary, his letters were infrequent, which did not help matters at all. Mother was always fretting about him.

20

Long before Bernatz had left, my mother had complained of feeling tired and sleepy all day long. This condition had not improved, but had become even more pronounced. I persuaded her to go with me to the family physician for a checkup, and she agreed. Following the examination, the doctor told me that her heart, which had been rather weak for years, had become even more so. It was vital that she take care of herself now, he warned. He advised her to rest and to avoid any kind of excitement.

It was easy to make sure that Mother avoided physical exertion. She had a very competent maid and had not had to do housework for some years now. But we could not control her inner life, which she often concealed from us. And true to her pattern, she continued to take things too seriously and to worry.

She suffered her first heart attack just about a month after our visit to the doctor. Fortunately it was a mild attack and she recovered from it in a short time. But all of us were frightened and each one in the family did not spare himself in giving Mother attention. Even Mela and Stela, so recently recalcitrant, now did everything in their power to make things pleasant at home, and helped to nurse her.

It seemed understood that the family must stick together at this time. There was a natural impulse toward cohesion from

185

all sides. That same summer, the entire family rented a big house at Bad Voeslau. Sisters and sisters-in-law came with all their children. Hanna came with Esther, George, and Robert, I with Ingrid and Gerda, Ellen with Henry, and Olga with her Eddie. With the help of two maids, we managed to keep the big household running very well.

For the first time, Mother agreed to spend the summer with us. I could not help but reflect bitterly on the decline in her which caused this agreement. Nevertheless, it was a pleasure to set her up in a sunny room with its own balcony. All of us were so happy to have her close, so relieved to have access to her and to see that she was properly cared for. So perceptible was this sense of relief that Hanna, Olga, and I discussed it from time to time. In the past our mother had eluded every attention we had tried to press upon her. Her selflessness remained incomprehensible to the three of us, even with the years.

So we contented ourselves with this summer when she gave herself over to us. It was a joy to see Mother with her grand-children. All of us seemed to thrive there.

The husbands drove in from Vienna on the weekends. Thus Saturday and Sunday were the two liveliest days of those summer weeks. Jim, Josef, Friedrich, and Leon seemed to sense the excitement which they added to the house, and always seemed jovial. When Monday came, a lull ensued, but it too was pleasant, a tranquality flooded with sunshine and unhurried swimming, with children napping and long remin-iscent talks with Mother often presiding.

For the children, that summer was a paradise, for they had not only the house, the pools, and the garden, but each other. Hanna's George was a little older than Olga's Eddie, and those two boys got along famously. Ingrid and Robert were exactly the same age and mostly stuck together, as did Gerda and Henry, who were also peers. Esther, the oldest of the lot, bossed everyone around. But I believe she loved my Ingrid the most. Ingrid attracted everyone with her sunny disposition.

She seemed almost immune to worry and was an optimist always. She glided through these young years with a marvelous gaiety which communicated itself easily to others, winning them. And while Ingrid's positive attitude was a delight in those untroubled days, it was to prove an even greater asset in helping her to face difficulties in the years to come. Her looks had always fit her personality accurately. She was rosy and plump and golden-haired, with perfect little features and gray-blue eyes.

Our Gerda was entirely different, both in nature and appearance. While Gerda, too, was a happy child, she expressed it much less effusively. Her face, too, differed sharply from Ingrid's. Gerda's was oval and narrow, with penetrating, large, dark blue eyes set off by straight hair that was darker blonde. She had an unusually beautiful mouth. But where Ingrid was lighthearted, Gerda was very sensitive. She had a tenderness of feeling, which could be touched off easily. And Gerda had a penchant, early, for dainty sentiment. Mother had predicted that this second daughter of ours would be "brainy." And time was quickly proving that pronouncement a valid one. Gerda was early demonstrating an artistic flair, even that summer in Bad Voeslau. In addition, she had a well-developed sense of humor and liked to talk a great deal. Here at the resort she was well supplied with an audience, because Henry was a good and loyal listener. But Eddie, who was older and very intelligent, often disagreed with certain of Gerda's statements and even went so far as to disparage some of them. Debates of a kind would follow. We mothers were amused at the spectacle of those two children arguing a a subject. They regarded themselves with the seriousness of diplomats. We never really found out what they were discussing with such ardor.

Our stay in Bad Voeslau was progressing serenely when it was interrupted with a shock. My father, who suffered from sciatica, had gone to a mountain resort — Bad Gastein — for a cure, as he did every summer. One day, as Hanna and I were talking together in the kitchen, we heard someone at the front door. Hanna walked out of the kitchen to see who had come in. A scream and a thud followed.

I dashed into the front room to find Hanna standing over father, who had collapsed upon entering the house. His face and hands were crimson.

My hand flew to my mouth as Hanna knelt beside him.

"Why, he's burned, Helena. I believe he's burned!" she whispered incredulously.

"I'll call the doctor," I said, going to the phone at once.

Our father was indeed ill. He had a temperature of 105 and only his basically sound constitution pulled him through that fever. Hanna had been correct in her diagnosis. But we had to wait a couple of days before Father was strong enough to tell us what had happened.

In Bad Gastein, he had been walking one day, and when he became weary, he decided to lay down briefly and to sunbathe. Inadvertently, he had fallen asleep on a mountain top, the target of violent sun rays. When he awoke, he felt that he was on fire all over his body. But for some reason, he did not seek aid in Bad Gastein. Injured, he instinctively sought his family. Somehow, he had persevered as far as the railroad station, where he had caught a train to Bad Voeslau.

We gasped at his story. It had such a childlike, homing instinct about it. Tears were running down my face as he finished it.

Fortunately, he began to improve almost at once. We were able to keep his presence unknown to Mother only for one day. All of us were afraid of exciting her. But on the second day, as Hanna and I leaned over him conspiratorially, with the doctor on the other side of the bed, she tiptoed into the room, in her slippers.

"Mother!" I exclaimed. "Now don't be alarmed. Father is just sunburned but he's going to be all right.

She walked directly to him as Hanna and I shrank back, her eyes missing nothing. Father stared back, and then slowly began to smile at her.

She sighed deeply, her hand at her breast. "Yes, I see, Helena, Hanna, your father will get well. You should have told me, daughters. . . ." And then turning to Father, she murmured, "You could have been burned to death!"

After that the recuperation progressed rapidly and completely. But soon we had a new worry. Bernatz, from whom we had at least heard intermittently at the beginning of his journey, had now been silent for weeks. Mother began to look anxiously for letters, mumbling furiously at the start of the anxiety and growing silent with fear as the length of time increased. The rest of us were uneasy, too, but cajoled mother into believing we were not, not in the least.

Then, one August afternoon when we were all sitting on the porch and the children were playing in the garden, Esther came rushing over with excitement: "Uncle Bernatz is here!"

My mother rose and pulled all her strength together, and, of us all, ran fastest down those steps to greet her youngest son. She embraced him, crying, "Bernatz, Bernatz!" and she wept for joy.

When this wild welcome had quieted, Bernatz sat down with us and recounted some of his experiences.

He and his group had walked a great deal and were often picked up by cars on their way from one village to another. To sustain themselves, they worked on a farm where they had slept in a barn. In the cities, they had worked in various places to earn money for food and shelter. Once they had even been given shelter by friendly people who had refused to charge them for it.

It was not long, however, before they discovered that it was easier for two to be picked up on the road than four, and accordingly, decided to separate. Eventually, by the same reasoning, Bernatz separated from his partner and made the balance of the trip alone.

He had visited many cities in France, Italy, Switzerland, Belgium, and Scandinavia. But Bernatz was clearly satisfied and rather relieved to be back with his family. As he told his story, he sat next to mother and kept pressing her hand. I thought he looked somehow more mature than when he had left.

Bernatz stayed with us for the balance of the summer. Now our family circle at Bad Voeslau was truly complete. His little nephews and nieces were particularly fascinated with Bernatz and they kept him busy with their demands. He had to keep telling the story of his journeys over and over (embroidering the facts, I suspect) to these round-eyed little innocents. And before long, Uncle Bernatz appeared to them like a hero from a fairy tale.

21

In 1930, the depression hit Vienna. People lost money in the banks, which collapsed, and also in the stock market, where Jim was not spared. Unemployment grew steadily among the working class.

Who, in these circumstances, could think of going to the movies? At the same time, a change was evolving in the movie industry itself. "Talkies" had come into existence, and now the projectors had to be changed from silent films to sound. Such a change involved the expenditure of a lot of money. This was the worst situation movie owners had ever had to face. Jim was no longer able to maintain the high rent for the two movies, the Stadt-Kino and the Turm-Kino, and was forced to give them up. The Marian, which he owned with Josef, he kept.

Olga, who was a partner in the Stadt-Kino, now took over the management of this movie. Olga had always been an intelligent woman; now she proved herself also to be capable. In the beginning, she had to struggle with circumstances, as the others did. But the new role was a great challenge for Olga. It made her feel very important and it helped to compensate for Friedrich's financial failure, which was being felt more than ever in these days of the depression. Olga tended to overdo her role a bit and became rather dominating.

As for Jim and me, we had to give up our expensive apartment at this time and sell much of our beautiful furniture. We kept only our bedroom suite, the children's things, and three Persian carpets—one large one and two little ones. The magnificent Steinway, purchased on Ingrid's first birthday, was now traded in for a much more modest piano.

We now moved to a four-room apartment on the Mariahilferstrasse. From our top-floor window, we could see the Hofburg and City Hall. It was near the Ringstrasse and close to two lovely parks. We had been fortunate, at this time of depression, to find a buyer to take over the old apartment and to buy the furniture from us. This buyer had come to us in the form of a certain Dr. Westheimer, a physician. He needed a large apartment for both an office suite and living quarters, and was glad to take advantage of Jim's cheap offer.

Dr. Westheimer was a man in his late thirties. He was a bachelor. As we came to know him better, we soon understood why he was unmarried. He struck up an acquaintance with Jim during our business transactions and, upon discovering that if he dropped in at Jim's movie for a chat he gained a free admission, he began to show signs of serious friendship. This was our first clue to certain traits of his: he was an unmitigated miser, so stingy that the thought of sharing his bounty with a wife was unbearable, precluding any real consideration of marriage. In addition, he was a pedant. Nevertheless, if one overlooked these qualities, one found a few others in Westheimer which were likeable. And dwelling upon these latter, Jim in time became a rather close friend of his.

This period of transition was a hard one. The one movie which Jim and Josef continued to hold needed maintenance and yielded next to nothing during the depression. Accordingly, Jim had to seek extra income to keep the family going. He did not have to wait long before a chance presented itself. Since he was well known in the film industry for his capability, Jim was offered a position as sales manager with

Universal Pictures by a Mr. Raab, who managed the Vienna branch of this American company.

Meanwhile, movie owners had to hurry the process of changing their projectors from silent to sound. First talkies began to arrive in Vienna from America. Jim was busy selling them, and he did very well. Raab, who was a clever man, predicted that the movie business would again flourish, once talkies were well-established and the economy improved. He and Jim had become quite friendly, and had grown to respect each other for good business sense. Raab got the idea that he and Jim should go into business together, and he suggested that they jointly rent a movie theater. Accordingly, they rented the Park-Kino, with which they did quite well. The first movie they showed there was *Singing Fool,* starring Al Jolsen, which was a smash success. Jim managed his involvement with the Park-Kino without giving up or neglecting his job with Universal Pictures. He enjoyed working for this company very much.

The Viennese were delighted with the new wonder from America. Who had ever imagined in the past that people on the screen would actually be able to talk? As the depression gradually loosened its grip on the economy, the movie industry, like all the others, came back to life again.

Olga had managed to weather the crisis and now the Stadt-Kino began to make a good profit again, which she attributed to her capable management. She continued to run gangster and western type films, which Jim had initiated there. Now, she and her family moved to a large apartment, situated close to the movie. Olga enjoyed furnishing it in the latest style.

During this new era of prosperity, Olga gave birth to a baby girl, Herta. Since the Landeses could now afford to keep a nurse for the children, Olga quickly resumed her management of the Stadt-Kino. She busied herself with selecting films, while Leon managed the theater in the afternoons during the performances. Now Bernatz entered into the scheme of things there. He had no interest in seeking a job elsewhere and insisted on the role of bookkeeper at the movie. Mother subequently intervened with Olga on behalf of Bernatz, and Olga finally agreed. But these two, Olga and Bernatz, did not get along well together. Bernatz resented Olga's dominating attitude toward him, while Olga resented the fact that Bernatz invited his girl friends to attend the movie gratis any time the impulse struck him.

Each came to my mother, complaining bitterly of the other. Their protests seemed rather petty on the face of it, yet both were deeply resentful of the other. In the end, my mother had to assume her role of referee to smooth out the differences.

22

VIENNA RECOVERED FROM THE DEPRESSION FAR MORE RAPIDLY than cities in other parts of the Western world. Prosperity followed the decline. And life in Vienna before Hitler's era was an easy one.

In those days, the coffeehouse was almost an institution in Vienna and was extremely popular as a place of relaxation. The extent to which this was so was revealed by the presence of specially bound newspapers and magazines which were provided for the customers to peruse, hours on end, while sipping their coffee. Jim was among those who enjoyed spending a spare hour reading the paper in a coffeehouse.

Every middle-class housewife could afford at least one maid. The servants took full charge of the home and children, leaving the wife a lady of leisure. The men, too, moved at a slower pace now. At noontime, husbands—like Jim—often came home for an unhurried lunch and had enough time to take a short nap before returning to work. In our apartment, we would spend the noon hour enjoying the children together, delighting in their little tales and antics.

I fell into the category of women who had plenty of free time. In the mornings, Ingrid and Gerda went to school. In the afternoons, a French governess came to take care of them. I could do with the hours whatever I wished. Many women spent them in the coffeehouses, where they socialized endlessly. Card playing was popular, too. Then there were also the five o'clock teas, where one could dance and even flirt.

As for myself, I was not interested in so much frivolity. Work appealed to me more. Since the upswing of economic affairs, Jim and Josef had rented another movie house— Schelder Kino—and I, together with Hanna, managed this theater.

Hanna and I shared an outside interest, too. It was called WIZO, which was the Women's International Zionist Organization in Vienna. Hanna was president of this group for the Sixth and Seventh Districts, and I was a member. Being Zionists—and we had never ceased to be—we were eager to contribute our time to any cause which this European branch of Hadassah sponsored. We also belonged to the regular Zionist Organization.

Hanna was very active, especially in fund-raising and in arranging parties for every occasion. I was more a cog in the wheel, only contributing money or attending the parties she arranged. But by giving her time off from her duties at "our" movie, I helped her to accomplish her work for the cause to which she was so devoted. And in this manner, I was kept busy all day long. For I still had my home to manage, even with help there. And I made sure that it was well-supervised, that things ran smoothly for the girls in my absence. The French governess who came in the afternoons was very pleased with their behaviour and cooperation. But the piano teacher complained that neither Ingrid nor Gerda practiced enough and that they were making slow progress. Their Jewish education also had to be attended to. Accordingly, I took them to services at the synagogue every *Shabbas,* and Hanna's Robert always came with us.

Although Ingrid and Gerda were of different natures, they loved each other very much, and got along most of the time. They were able to play together nicely, but sometimes they did quarrel. When they complained to me, each seeking my support, I told them to settle the dispute between themselves, which they did. When they misbehaved, I chose to punish them by refusing to speak to them for a while, which hurt them most. When this happened, they often wrote me a letter of explanation, which they slipped under the door of my bedroom. These letters were written in such sweet and funny tones that, invariably, I had to laugh. They ended by telling me that they would prefer to be beaten — anything! — only please, speak to them.

How much we enjoyed our daughters! They alone were a consistent source of hope through inconsistent years. The vicissitudes of married life became more clear with the passage of time, and now, again, our situation began to improve. The prosperity which had been so astonishingly ours before the depression began to build again as a new epoch began. Mr. Raab had predicted it would. The era of lavish movie premieres ensued, beginning a new type of social event.

These previews were held for the press and specially-invited guests who might promote the new picture. Elaborate banquets frequently followed the showings, with many leading stars in attendance.

The premiere for *Three Smart Girls,* with Deanna Durbin, was an especially big affair. The picture was a great financial success for Universal Pictures. Later, Joe Pasternak, a young Hungarian producer, made the movie *Paprika* in Vienna, with a Hungarian actress called Franciska Gaal. This, too, was a success for the company.

I had occasion to meet Pasternak and his wife at an artists' ball. Jim and I were introduced to them by Raab and his wife, who were on very friendly terms with the Pasternaks. I was very impressed with his youth, the boyish and slender picture of him, for he was already such a successful producer. Jim and I were invited to join the Raabs and the Pasternaks after the ball and, for some reason, I quickly declined.

For some time, since Jim had become a partner with Raab, I had been discovering things about myself. Most of these discoveries had been provoked by my acquaintance with Mrs. Raab, a woman as unlike me as any I can imagine. Mrs. Raab was a highly sophisticated woman whose social interests were deeply invested in the movie world from which her husband's income originated. She talked glibly and had a storehouse of witticisms at her fingertips. She was not overwhelmed by big names — at least not in the sense that she could not rise to the occasion of their company. Always eager to broaden her horizons, she was particularly fond of extending them to celebrities. In this way, she resembled her husband, who had always struck me as a little opportunistic.

On the night of the invitation to join them with the Pasternaks, I began to examine my role as Jim's social partner in a way that I had never done as sharply before. Perhaps it was Mrs. Raab's aggressiveness that called forth my instinct to withdraw that evening. As soon as the invitation was issued, I seemed to know in advance that I would be out of my element if I joined the group, that I would certainly be ill at ease. What clarified this most sharply was Mrs. Raab's contrasting enthusiasm over the prospect of sitting down intimately with people like the Pasternaks. Mrs. Raab, furthermore, had long regarded me with a certain condescension of which I was well aware. I was too retiring to be bothered with, as far as she was concerned, did not have the "knowhow" which she possessed, and thus, by implication, was of little or no value socially. I almost enjoyed her snubbing me because I couldn't stand the woman. Her transparent ambition was repellent to me. Still, I envied her self-possession. I don't deny it. And I was aware that I, Helena Hilsen, could not emulate her in this respect. I examined all this, thought it through, and as Jim's social scope began to expand with the booming movie world I decided, with a certain complacency, simply to be myself, to accept only those invitations which I found comfortable, and to accept the fact that my husband would occasionally enjoy an evening without my company. If there was a little of the Lwow girl which had failed to be erased by these many years in Vienna, I did not care.

And why should I? My home, my children, were a whole world to me. They could have stood without any embellishment, let alone the hectic round of pleasures which were vital to Mrs. Raab! And as for Jim, his image of me, of our life together, was clear and established. I don't believe I ever thought it threatened by outside interests. He was so manifestly fond of us, so proud of the girls, so sensitive to my feelings in every respect.

I wondered privately if Mrs. Raab's inner life was as secure as mine, why she felt it necessary to put on such airs in front of me.

Once, at a banquet, she came upon me, laughing and talking with a group of people. Aside she remarked to me, "I didn't know you could have such a good time in company!"

I really loathed her. No doubt she tried to imply that I was not adequate to the role imposed by being Jim's wife. She would have liked to see me fretting and troubled, and, had I been the type, I suppose I could have started wondering about him.

For at this point in his maturity and his career, Jim shed at least the superficial layer of puritanism which had clung to him since I first had known him. He branched out socially, more than ever before, and things which might have seemed daring or out of order to him before now became commonplace. Not only did he go out with other people to nightclubs, as he had with the Raabs, but he often went to five o'clock teas, which were so popular in Vienna. On weekdays, he often had to entertain customers from out of town, or movie owners from other cities in Austria, and he found it convenient to take them to these teas. On Saturdays, and even on a Sunday afternoon sometimes, Dr. Westheimer would call him and they would arrange to meet for a bit of leisure. On those days, I was tied up at the Schelder-Kino and I did not object to Jim's enjoying hours independent of my company. I couldn't tie up my husband all the time. It would have been poor psychology even if it had been possible. I knew he liked to dance, that he did dance at the teas, and it concerned me not at all.

On the evenings after he had been with Westheimer, he always picked me up at the theater and we went out together, to a show, a night club, or a coffeehouse.

Once, as we were seated in a restaurant, he grinned slyly at me and said, "Who do you think I saw at the Kursalon last week? Dancing, of course," he added.

"It's not hard to guess," I replied. "Ellen?"

"Correct."

"With Leon?"

"Naturally not," Jim replied.

I leaned over very confidentially. "What would you say," I asked, "if you walked into one of those five o'clock teas and found me dancing there — innocently, of course, like many one meets there?"

"I would turn you out of the place at once," he said, frowning seriously at the idea. He seemed to squirm a little.

"So! And why, may I ask? Other married women go to these things, quite alone and without their husbands!"

"But you are my wife, and you are different," he stated matter-of-factly.

"In that case," I replied, "how is it that you go alone, without me?"

"There is no comparison, Helena!" he asserted. "You know my character, backwards and forwards. I am not easily tempted. But women — and yes, even you, perhaps — are more vulnerable, being of a weaker nature. I watch all those women while they flirt at those teas. Often that is not the end of it. Clandestine meetings follow, sometimes affairs. . . ."

"Tut, tut!" I mocked. "So I am to remain exactly the same as when you met me in Lwow?" I teased.

"Exactly!" he repeated, not smiling now. "You have understood me well."

I had to laugh at that point, for Jim's face, at the mere contemplation of frivolity on my part, had taken on a forlorn expression.

"Don't worry. I haven't the slightest interest in the teas or in flirting. I have no need to seek extra pleasure. My family and home more than suffice."

And this was the truth of the matter. Those wives who could be found lingering there in the late afternoon were mostly dissatisfied wives. They sought relief from boredom. Typical of these malcontents was my sister-in-law, Ellen, who, with her friends, frequented these teas and was seen dancing at them. She was always delighted at a chance encounter with Jim, whom she admired, and would greet him with enthusiasm. Leon knew how Ellen spent her free time and was profoundly jealous. There had been a number of arguments between them on this subjct, but Ellen refused to give up her pleasure, claiming that it was really beyond reproach. Since Leon could not prevent her going by force, he had to console himself as best he could.

Every Sunday morning had a holiday spirit about it for us. In spring, we would take the girls in the car to Cobensl, a lovely hill on the outskirts of the city, near the Vienna Woods. Atop this hill was a restaurant with a garden, where we were served and relaxed together as a family. En route to this spot, we would pass Grinzing, a spot which had been popular even in the Old Vienna, and which is beloved by the Viennese to this day. It is wonderfully scenic, filled with restaurants and folk-singing, suggesting in its graciousness an older, more care-free existence.

In wintertime, on Sunday mornings, Jim took us all to the Ringstrasse, where there was a promenade used for walking and socializing. There, Jim delighted in every opportunity to present Ingrid and Gerda to an acquaintance. The little girls felt their father's pride in them and were deeply pleased by it. It was obvious that they adored their handsome daddy.

These times were at the core of our lives and these enjoyments were the fruits of our existence.

But this life was disturbed by the terror of the growing Nazi Party, whose propaganda advocated hatred toward the Jews. Thus, the Hackenkreuzler, as they called themselves (Swastika Men) being a legal organization, began to terrorize the Jews. They threw a bomb into a jewelry store owned by a Jew. The man, whose name was Futterweit, was killed instantly. Technically, he was the first Jewish victim of the Nazis in Austria. At the same time, vandalism was committed in Jewish cemeteries and stink bombs were thrown into movies owned by Jews.

Our family was not spared in these incidents, but at least we fought back. Once, Josef caught two Nazis throwing stink bombs in the Marien-Kino. He was so outraged that he gave them a beating, and handed them over to the police. These two men, who received prison sentences, swore that they would seek to revenge themselves against Josef.

Another incident occurred during the High Holidays, while some Jews were returning from the synagogue on Taborstrasse. My father, Saul, and Bernatz were among these, walking peacefully along, when a truckload of brown-shirted Nazis drove up to attack them. My brothers and other young Jewish boys threw themselves into the fight with the Nazis and struck back. There were many bloody heads on both sides.

This incident caused my brother Saul to consult with

General Sommer, who was commander of the Jewish War Veterans. General Sommer asked Saul to organize a group of Jewish boys for the purpose of defending Jewish life and property against the Nazi assaults. Saul managed to get together a group of 250 boys in Leopoldstadt. And since they did not have any funds to buy proper uniforms, my father financed this group.

Other districts in Vienna also had such groups. They called themselves Youth Bund of the Jewish War Veterans, and they stationed guards in cemeteries and in the streets. Since the groups were not aggressive, but defensive in nature, they were permitted to do these things by the government. However, they were forbidden to carry weapons. When necessary, they had to fight with their fists. And although these groups were small in number, they fought back vigorously when attacked.

23

By 1933, Hitler had succeeded in taking over Germany.
The actual persecution of Jews had not yet begun, although
many restrictions were placed on them. We Jews in Vienna
heard of their plight and sensed that it was the forerunner of
more ominous things for them. But it was terribly difficult
to imagine the same fate for ourselves, or to believe that our
government would ever submit to a Nazi take-over.

Thus, when Jim received an offer to buy a larger movie
house, he responded to the proposition as if things were normal,
as ever. A certain Mr. Klaus, who owned the huge Steffel-Kino,
offered to sell it to Jim, with very attractive terms. If we made
a fairly substantial down-payment, he would let us pay off the
rest in monthly sums derived from our profit.

"But," I protested, "where on earth would we get the money
for such a large down-payment?"

"By selling the Marian-Kino, Helena," Jim explained. "I've
already talked it over with Josef. Why not? This is such a rare
opportunity . . . to own such a tremendous theater! It's like a
dream. And this Klaus seems a prince of a fellow—intelligent,
sympathetic. He won't lose money after all, either. But the
terms of payment—where can we possibly get another chance
like this?"

So Jim went ahead and sold our smaller Marian-Kino, using
the money for the down-payment on Klaus theater, the biggest

venture we had ever contemplated. On the day of the actual purchase of the new movie, I waited at home and felt extremely nervous. Whispered rumblings of the Nazi threat seemed to reverberate in my head. Were we logical to disregard them? What implications had they, after all?

When Jim returned from signing the purchase contract with Klaus, he was elated. I hated to mar his mood with a pessimistic thought, but I could not resist mentioning my feelings.

"How does Josef feel about the new movie?" I began

"He's delighted. You should have seen his face when he signed today! Josef was beaming."

"And the future?" I asked. "Do you and Josef feel so sure that nothing will interfere with your personal business affairs?"

"Oh, you mean the Nazis? Well, we have looked ahead even to that eventuality. This Klaus is a man you can level with, Helena. Josef and I told him outright that we wanted some assurance as to the safety of this purchase. And we have a special clause written into the contract which assures it — no matter what political change occurs in Austria."

"A special clause!" I repeated. "But how clever of you . . . What does it say?"

"The clause states that in event of Nazi control of Austria, Klaus, who is gentile, will take over the Steffel-Kino — in name only, of course. In actuality, he will be only technically the owner, and we will continue to draw an income from our property, even if Jews no longer are allowed to own anything. So you see, Helena! You and the children won't starve."

"Nor Josef and Hanna either!" I marveled softly. "You really have a great deal of foresight, Jim."

How naïve we were! Looking back, I cannot imagine how we did not recognize the danger signs for what they were; I marvel at our blindness at their approach. We simply could not get it through our heads that an abrupt halt could come to a way of life which was good and which seemed continuous.

This purchase was to prove the greatest mistake of Jim's life. With the money he spent on Klaus' theater, we might have emigrated to America. For actually, Nazism was even now growing stronger in Vienna, with Hitler established as Fuehrer in Germany. His propaganda was spreading everywhere. But since this process was gradual and did not strike in every quarter at the same time, most of the Jews in Vienna continued to live as before.

One among us did, however, see the handwriting on the wall, and this one was my mother. Perhaps age, which gave her the position of retrospect rather than involvement such as the young enjoy, enabled her to evaluate the symptoms of moral decay in Vienna. When Hanna and I visited with her, she warned us of the deepening of these symptoms. For the moment, she was endowed with a keener sense of historical past and progression than Hanna or I or any of our generation, I suspect. Her life, since the heart attack following my brother's death, had slowed sufficiently to allow her time for reflection and analysis. She had been no stranger to change, having had to adapt herself countless times to the interruptions of events beyond her control.

The day that Jim and Josef bought the new movie house, I went to see Mother, to tell her the news. In the past, she had always been exuberant over any forward move which I, or any of her children, had made. Thus I approached her with the usual eagerness that such an occasion would imply. But as she listened, her expression tightened, a gravity filling her eyes. She stared at me incredulously.

"What can you be thinking of!" she whispered, aghast.

"What do you mean, Mother?" I asked, confused at the depression which had overtaken her.

"Is this a time to be buying movie houses, with all Europe in a turmoil from this madman, this Hitler?"

"Oh!" I exclaimed. "This is what's bothering you? He

won't affect us Mother. That whole business will blow over soon. And Berlin is not Vienna," I concluded.

"Berlin is not Vienna!" she repeated. "They are already here, Helena. They don't have to come from Berlin anymore. The Nazi heart is pounding now in Austrian breasts. How is it that my children don't see what is so clearly evident?"

Her breathing had become labored during this discussion and inwardly I grew alarmed. I had never imagined in my naïve excitement that I was to bring such profound anxiety to my mother. I cautioned her to relax and lie down for a while.

Still brooding, she complied, while I went to the kitchen to make tea. But there was to be no interlude of forgetfulness; Hanna burst in, bearing the same excitement which I had brought only fifteen minutes before. I grasped her wrist with a warning squeeze.

But Hanna's protests were like my own. There was a paralysis of foresight among the young. The wisdom of age could not alter that paralysis.

After soothing Mother and attempting to reassure her with optimistic thoughts, Hanna and I left so that she might sleep awhile. We were far more anxious over the state of her health than over the imminent threat to Viennese Jewry.

She had been cautioned by her doctors to take life very slowly now, to rest most of the time. But Hanna and I, who, I believe, understood her better than our siblings, knew with regret that our mother was incapable of taking life easy while she was still able to function at all.

Two weeks after this incident, Mother was stricken with a second heart attack. Hanna and I were beside ourselves, and now spent every possible moment with her, leaving the business to our husbands.

Now the whole family was alerted to her illness. Father, Mela, and Stela were in attendance day and night. Olga,

Hanna, and I visited constantly. And Father, usually so light-hearted, was suddenly grave with concern.

But mother was to rally again. She recovered from this second heart attack in four weeks, and she was able to spend most of her time out of bed. When summer came, Jim rented a cottage in Baden, near Vienna, and we arranged that Mother should come with us.

The cottage in Baden was situated on a hill and was surrounded with one large and three smaller cottages with gardens. The large cottage was inhabited by the owner of the place, an older lady called Mrs. Wolf. This particular summer, Mrs. Wolf received visitors who were of extreme interest and of some worry to us. Her son, with his wife and children, arrived at her house suddenly one summer day. They had fled from Berlin, where they lived. The outbreak of anti-Semitic incidents there, while still sporadic and still restrained in their nature, had nevertheless been alarming enough for this young family to uproot itself. The gradual encroachment of Nazi control over Jewish businesses, the occasional beatings and increasing disappearances of certain Jewish individuals, had been terrifying, although not yet universal in extent.

Jim and I listened to the tales of this couple with a kind of mounting terror. Berlin was really a nightmare to contemplate. And things were growing worse for the Jews there all the time, we were assured. What were the implications? Were these Nazis then to be victorious, to continue unstifled by the forces of reason, which we had always been so certain would vanquish them? And if the Nazis were to remain in control of Berlin, what then of Austria? We questioned the young Wolfs endlessly as to the incidents in Berlin. We were especially worried since we had cousins there, too.

"Not everyone runs away as we have done," the young man said, as we sat in the garden in the lovely Baden moonlight. "Some can adjust to anything. It's an apathy amounting to disease. They don't see that a literal inferno is building in Germany, a fire that will eat away their lives."

We listened to Wolf with a certain detachment. Our disturbance over the encounter with the young Wolfs was fleeting. We, ourselves, may even have sensed that it was too fleeting, that we should have forced ourselves to consider the whole idea of Nazism at greater length.

But here in Baden it was so peaceful. It was a lovely resort, larger than Bad Voeslau but similar to it, and it boasted a spa and even a gambling casino, though none of us frequented it. Mother enjoyed the atmosphere of Baden very much and was glad she had come with us. She would recline in her beach chair, set in the shadows, and breathe in the good air. Meanwhile, Ingrid and Gerda had discovered the Wolf's two little girls, and the four of them played together. Ingrid was now six and Gerda four. The summer was developing nicely, everything seeming to arrange itself, when Jim surprised me one weekend with the announcement that we were going to Lwow to visit his parents. They had not, he reminded me, ever seen either Ingrid or Gerda.

I was not too happy with this news, for it meant leaving Mother here in Baden. She did have a very dependable maid who would care for her in our absence, and I had to console myself with this fact. For I couldn't refuse Jim. He had a duty to his family, too. They, in every letter, begged Jim to come with his family. In Vienna, I talked with Hanna, who assured me that she would visit Mother often and keep in telephone contact with her constantly, and urged me to go to Lwow with a free mind. Mother, always wise in her gentleness, also urged me to go without a worry. She was feeling much better than before.

After making all the necessary preparations, we left for Lwow. Jim's parents and family were overjoyed when we arrived. Eight years had passed since our last visit to them.

The length of time showed in their faces; they had aged perceptibly.

Lonek had married in this interval and already had a son and a daughter. Wilhelm had reached his goal in the city theater. He became an actor and now played major roles in operettas under the name of Wilhelm Willinsky. He, too, had married, and was the father of one son. Fred, the youngest boy, had finished the Hebrew gymnasium and was attending the commercial academy.

Lwow itself looked to Jim and me as it had eight years before. But for Ingrid and Gerda the visit was very exciting; they saw a city which was not their own. We showed them around, eager to incorporate them into our past. We pointed out the house where I had lived, and where "Mummy" and "Daddy" had met and fallen in love.

On our second day in Lwow we paid a visit to Sala Brand. Her second husband's name, by coincidence, was also Brand. Now Ingrid and Gerda met their cousin, Addie, for the first time. He was eleven years old. Jim and I took to him at once, for he was an appealing child. Addie was a fine, rather delicate boy with good manners. Sala had done a good job with him, but she was concerned with his future. One of the reasons for her concern was lack of money. She and her second husband did not do well at all, and now they had a three-year-old boy, too. There was little future to be found for a boy in Lwow anymore, she told me.

"Why not send him to Vienna, Sala?" I suggested. "He could have everything there. And it would mean so much to my parents if he could live with them."

"To Vienna!" she cried. "But how could I let him go, Helena? How could I give up my boy?"

I understood how she felt, of course. But Sala gradually came to consider the idea of letting Addie go to live with his grandparents. She knew that they were in a position to do things for him, and that here in Lwow, on her husband's income, he would have little to anticipate.

She began to decide on it while Jim and I were still in Lwow.

"Yes, I am considering it seriously, now. Only, I must wait at least another year. But tell your mother I may send Addie to Vienna."

24

AFTER HAVING HEARD THE OMINOUS REPORTS ABOUT THE plight of German Jews from Mr. Wolf in Baden, we were easily influenced by the optimism we encountered in Lwow. Human nature is inclined to believe in good, rather than bad predictions. And in our old home town in Poland, we had found everything normal. We could detect no sign of excitement or apprehension over Hitler's domination of Germany. In Lwow, this was regarded as strictly a German affair; no one suspected that it might spread as far as Poland. It was not that the Jews in Lwow were indifferent to their fellow Jews in Germany. It was simply that they could not imagine that much real suffering for the Jews could take place in Germany. They themselves were the traditional victims — they, the Polish Jews, were the ones who had endured anti-Semitic persecutions in their own country. As for the Germans, was it not well known that they were a highly cultured people? One could hardly imagine that their anti-Semitic acts could equal, let alone exceed, those of the Poles! No, the Polish Jews could not conceive of any such possibility, nor be concerned with it. And as for the Polish gentiles, they were not too alarmed about Hitler, either. There had existed an enmity between Poland and Germany for years. Should Germany attack, or seek to take over Poland, it was generally assumed that the Western countries (England and America) would rush to Poland's defense.

All of this was derived by Jim and me from various inhabitants of Lwow during our visit there in summer 1933. Mentally, we welcomed this absence of fear, easily falling in with it, however vague its rational foundations.

Returning to Vienna in the fall, we found no visible changes, which confirmed our optimism. Movies were still well-frequented, and things ran smoothly for us.

About this time we had to give up the management of the Schelder-Kino, which we, together with Josef, had only rented. The owner of this theater now wished her married daughter to run it. Thus Josef, by himself, decided to start a new venture, by renting a large movie house called Amelon-Kino. He was quite enterprising at that time. He was already involved in a business service called *"Pendlerei."* Josef employed men, who, on motorcycles, delivered rolls with single film reels from one theater to another. Often the same picture was being shown in two theaters at the same time, using only one film, and so the timing of the *"Pendlerei"* operation had to be exact to insure a successfully continuing program.

Hanna now helped Josef in the new, large movie. Josef even employed young Bernatz, who was only too glad to leave both Olga and the Stadt-Kino. It seemed a satisfactory solution to his problem. Since Josef and Hanna were now absorbed with the new theater and with *"Pendlerei,"* I had to help out at the Steffel-Kino, afternoons.

Greta, who had come through her hysterectomy with complete success, now visited me frequently. She would stop by at the Steffel-Kino, late in the afternoon, and we would go to a nearby coffeehouse where we could talk and sip the good Viennese coffee with *Schlagobers* (whipped cream). It was wonderful to see her in good health again, and sometimes I was reminded of the earlier years of our friendship, when an unceasing strain of gaiety seemed to emanate from Greta. But the years had wrought their change, and soon I perceived a new trouble was afoot with my friend. When her anxiety became increasingly more apparent, I encouraged Greta to unburden herself to me.

Greta laughed sadly. "I always seem to involve you in my unhappiness, Helena. Still, what choice is there? You are my only real friend and it is such a relief to know I can speak—" She stopped abruptly, as if considering the manner in which to continue.

I pressed her hand across the table.

"Good heavens, Greta! You can certainly tell me anything you wish. For whatever it is worth, I understand you . . . better, I suspect, than most."

"You're wonderful, Helena. And I'm so happy that Jim appreciates you. He mounts you on a pedestal, always has, but it is no more than you deserve, after all."

"I am no more deserving than you, surely."

"That may or may not be. Whatever the case may be, there is certainly a difference between our husbands. I have had to face this fact ruthlessly. Erich is basically a good person, Helena. And this basic goodness has always made him attractive to people in general. It comes through in his friendliness, his smile. He's the kind everybody loves. But to live with him as a man! To know the frivolity, the utter lack of responsibility of which Erich is capable! Helena, it would have driven a woman like you mad. Because you see, the contradiction is always there, the goodness—yes, he has always been good to me, ironically good, even at the height of one of his adulteries. And as for taking marriage seriously, he is simply not capable of this!" she concluded, her voice rising.

"But you have known this all along, Greta!" I mumured frowning.

"Yes."

"And you told me you had even learned to accept it. You had taken on a certain sophisticated point of view. . . ."

"Accept it! What woman really can accept the fact that she's not enough for her own husband? Yes, Helena, I did try to feel that way, it's true. But when I had the operation, he was so wonderful then . . . I kept hoping that he would give up that way of life, be content with me and Kurt. But you see, far from having given it up, he has become even worse now!"

I leaned forward, alarmed at her expession.

"Have you any proof, Greta?"

"Yes!" she exclaimed with bitterness, and glanced around briefly, to see if anyone could overhear us.

"I am really ashamed to tell even you. He has gone too far this time. It was not enough that he did not take me seriously. He became terribly indiscreet, in addition!"

"How?" I asked.

Greta looked down at the table, biting her lip.

"When I came home from summer vacation, I found evidence of his other relationships right in my apartment! The carelessness of the man—the indifference! You will admit, Helena, that a certain callousness is necessary for a man to overlook a slip, perhaps a hairbrush of the other woman?"

"Good God!" I muttered. "It is really hard to believe."

Greta sighed. "So you see, the situation has become intolerable, even for Greta the sophisticate. I have decided to divorce Erich," she pronounced.

There was little I could say after that. In her present frame of mind, there was no point in trying to dissuade Greta from this course of action. And after this new, really offensive information about Erich's insensitivity, I scarcely knew whether I wanted to dissuade her. Also, there was a certainty, a finality, in Greta's tone. Evidently, she had made the decision after much deliberation.

A number of weeks passed after that conversation and I heard nothing more from Greta. I tried to phone her a number of times, but there was never an answer, so I assumed she must have taken the boy on a trip.

One day, after an absence of two months, she appeared at the Steffel-Kino. She embraced me quickly and said, "Helena, let's go back to that coffee shop — are you free? — I have to tell you so much!"

Seated at the same table, I was frankly not surprised to hear her say.

"It is done. The divorce decree is final. Yes, Helena, I'm free now. And looking for a place to live. A place just for Kurt and me."

She began to talk of her plans, of the type of apartment she was seeking, and I saw clearly that she was ready to make a strong effort to have a successful single life. I told her that I would help her hunt for a suitable place to live.

But, ironically, Erich lost his job with Twentieth Century Fox only a few weeks after the divorce became final. A brief and frenzied round of job-hunting ensued which resulted in nothing. He had been prosperous enough before, but he had lived too high, with their Vienna apartment and the Kritzendorf bungalow, and had put next to nothing aside. In no time, the man was fairly desperate, and no relief was in sight. It became obvious that he could never maintain two households now. And, characteristically, Greta was extremely sympathetic. A kind of decline affected Erich, and Greta felt a heartbreaking loyalty to him, however unjustified it may have been. She wanted to help him, somehow.

Accordingly, a very bizarre situation began to develop with the Schelmans. While Greta remained adamant in her decision to remain divorced from Erich, she decided to remain under the same roof with him, for the sake of financial expediency.

They lived together as friends, only. The physical side of

their relationship was a dead issue, Greta assured me. And I believed her. For when she relinquished completely both her rights and duties as Erich's wife, she was able to manifest a steady and congenial attitude toward him and it was strangely without rancor for the past.

And Kurt, their son, actually benefited from the situation. For he was not separated, as he had feared, from the father he adored, and his mother seemed more at peace with her situation than she had been in years.

But Erich's financial dilemma had to be met somehow, or else he would not even be able to maintain the one apartment which continued to house them all.

It was Jim who finally found a solution for him. He managed to get Erich a job with Universal Pictures as a salesman. In this capacity, Erich traveled to other cities in Austria, selling films for a company. But he maintained this position only for a few months. His nerves were going bad and he worked poorly. When he was fired from Universal, Erich suffered a nervous breakdown.

The decline in his morale had been mounting for a long time. It could not be attributed to the divorce, or to any one thing. Like all breakdowns of this type, it stemmed from a lack of inner resource.

I was horrified to learn one night that Erich had tried to commit suicide by taking an overdose of sleeping pills. Greta had discovered the situation in time and saved him. She nursed him back to health with an almost maternal ardor.

When Erich was better, I visited him at their apartment. Greta hovered about protectively. The picture of those two was touching in the extreme. Erich sat up in bed when I entered and smiled broadly.

"Helena! How good of you to come," he said warmly.

When we talked things over, he told how grateful he was

that Greta had remained with him. She was, and always would be, he knew, his best friend.

Before I left, Greta took me aside and begged me never to tell anyone — even Jim — of Erich's suicide attempt. I marveled at her loyalty to him, to his sense of dignity. I kissed Greta and assured her of my silence in the matter.

Erich's nervous state improved and he began to function again. But in the next few months, search as he might, luck seemed to elude him when it came to a job. He found nothing, and Greta saw gradually that desperate measures were needed, merely to keep food on the table. She had already sold her jewelry, piece by piece. Now she was forced to sell some of their furniture, which was all they had left to show of their former life. She got what she could for the better and least fundamental pieces. But in no time at all, the money from this sacrifice melted away, too.

Now the problem of Kurt, their thirteen-year-old son loomed up ahead of the Schelmans. He was a bright boy and certainly should be allowed to continue his education. But the gymnasium required some tuition, and such money would have to be raised.

The only resource remaining to Greta was her piano. This instrument, a concert grand of some magnificence, was the only object to which Greta had clung tenaciously up to now. Music had always been part of her life, a heritage from her pianist mother, and this great black piano had been given to her by Erich shortly after their marriage. It stood in their living room, polished wood, like the rest of the furniture. But when Greta put her hand to those keys, the piano seemed to take on an almost organic quality. And the music which her deft fingers evoked had the power to lift Greta out of her troubles, elevating her into its own higher sphere. Her expression while playing was extremely mobile, in direct relation to the sounds. Now she would beam with a kind of ecstasy; then she knit her brows in tune with grave melodies.

Once I had commented, while watching her play, "It is God's gift, Greta, to understand music. It gives one an extra piece of life."

Now this extra piece of life had to be relinquished. For Greta had finally decided to sell her piano. There seemed no choice if they were to do right by Kurt. When the men came to carry away the piano, they carried away Greta's joy. It seemed tragic indeed. Yet it was not the worst fate which either Greta or Erich Shelman were destined to suffer.

25

THE YEAR 1934 WAS CHARGED WITH EXCITING EVENTS FOR the Austrian people. On February 12th, I was at home with the children when I heard detonations outside. I could not imagine what was going on. Instinctively, I went to the telephone and called Jim at the office.

He listened to me and then said, "I know what it is all about, Helena. Just stay calm. I'll be home in a few minutes."

He rushed home in a taxi and he stayed with us all afternoon and evening. And he explained the cause of the shooting we had heard with such amazement and alarm.

We knew that there was a conflict between the *Schutzbund*, the army of the Social Democrats, and the *Heimwehr*, the army of the Christian Socials. Dollfuss, who was Chancellor of Austria and thus the most important political figure in the country, wanted to smash the Social Democrats, now the weaker party, who were in strong opposition to establishing an authoritarian state in Austria. The result had been an armed eruption.

The next day we read a chilling account of it in the papers. The *Schutzbund* had barricaded themselves in municipal buildings. These were large modern housing projects which the Social Democrats had built for the workers. The largest and best known was Karl Marx Hof. Here the Christian Social *Heimwehr* attacked the *Schutzbund* with machine guns and field artillery. Women and children were trapped and could not be evacuated. The horrifying result was several hundred dead and wounded.

The tragedy continued when the defeated *Schutzbundlers* had to face a court martial. Their leaders were branded as rebels and executed by hanging. The rest of the captured were sent to a detention camp in Wöllensdorf. This defeat marked the end of Social Democrat power in Austria.

Dollfuss and the Christian Social Party did not want the *"Anschluss,"* the annexation of the country to Germany. Rather, they preferred an independent fascist Austria. They went so far as to declare the Nazi Party illegal in Austria, and Nazis were persecuted when caught acting against the regime.

Perhaps the spread of the Nazi party in Austria could have been avoided if the two major political parties had worked together for an understanding. There is a folk saying to the effect that where two are fighting, the third is the winner.

Thus, despite the fact that it was technically illegal, the Nazi party thrived in Austria. There was an established background of anti-Semitism there which the Nazis could exploit, a sentiment which had been under cover when times were *gemuetlich*. Now the most barbaric notions ever fostered by those who hated Jews could come to the fore. The Nazis promised that they would re-distribute Jewish property.

Still, all this remained underground for the present. It was a great political dichotomy. One form of fascism reigned, objecting on grounds of national sovereignty to the other. The time was not yet ripe for Nazis to emerge in full form in Austria.

After the armed incident, things quieted down again, tension decreased, and, superficially, life ran smoothly again.

Personally, we proceeded with our everyday way of life as we always had. By the summer, I even dared to go on vacation as usual, with Ingrid and Gerda. We went, in fact, even farther

than before, choosing a Yugoslavian seashore resort called
Novi. On July 25, as I was resting on the beach, I read in the
newspaper that the Nazis had tried to overthrow the Austrian
regime. Dollfuss had been shot. I read the headlines twice and
then jumped up, flinging the paper aside, trembling. A kind
of desperation overcame me. I was afraid they would take
over the whole of Austria. I had a fleeting vision of myself,
with the girls, cut off from Jim, who had remained there. I
managed to get a phone call through to Vienna, to Jim. Thank
God, the Dollfuss regime was still in control of the country
and many Austrian Nazis had been put into jail.

I rushed back to Vienna with Ingrid and Gerda, grateful
to be close to Jim and near to my mother.

There were two surprises waiting for me when we arrived
in Vienna. The first was a letter from Sala Brand, advising
me that she had decided to send Addie to Vienna after all.
He was thirteen now, had been Bar Mitzvah, and had passed,
according to Jewish custom, into the beginning of the years of
his manhood. Actually, Addie himself had made the decision,
she wrote. Having passed the event of his Bar Mitzvah, Addie
had decided that he no longer wished to be a burden to his
stepfather, whose circumstances continued to be poor indeed;
also, Addie was old enough to see now that Lwow could offer
him little in the way of a future, whereas Vienna excited his
young mind. Here, there were more opportunities to learn a
trade and to become independent. As I read Sala's letter, I
was surprised to find no mention of the political unrest here
in Austria, no fear of sending Addie into the midst of it. After
all, Sala was an intelligent person and surely must be reading
of Austrian incidents in the Lwow newspapers. I really was
confused by the absence of comment on her part.

Evidently in Poland, now as two years ago, they still did
not believe that Hitler was a real threat. Why should they,
when we Austrian Jews, so close to the danger, refused to

believe it? I had not been back in Vienna more than a few
weeks when I perceived a marked change in the city's atmosphere. People like me could no longer delude themselves that
life was flowing on its normal course. There was a new tension
in Vienna, an undercurrent of strained feeling toward the Jews.
This feeling had not yet erupted in any of our Christian
friends and, on the surface, they were as friendly to us as ever
and went out with us as before. But the wave of anti-Semitism
which emanated from Germany seemed destined to inundate
the simplest heart with fear and suspicion. I knew, for already
I struggled with both.

The second surprise which awaited me in these dubious days
was the arrival of a female cousin, Fanny, from America.
She had come to Vienna just for a pleasure trip — a piece of
information which astounded me. Wasn't her father afraid to
let her travel into such a highly charged political climate?
Apparently not. Fanny herself explained it to me. Americans
did not particularly anticipate any general change in the
state of Europe just because Hitler was in control of Germany.
This was an internal affair belonging to Germany alone. No
other country had the right to interefere. No, her father had
not been at all alarmed about her trip to Vienna.

Fanny stayed with us for two months. These two months
were significant ones for my brother, Saul, for a romance of a
sort developed between him and the American cousin. Almost
as soon as she arrived, Saul began to squire Fanny around
town, making sure that the girl enjoyed Vienna. He was
extremely gallant in this undertaking, and at first we merely
regarded the situation as one between host and tourist. But
after the first couple of weeks, it became clear that Fanny was
looking at Saul in a very serious light. He was young and
eligible and, back in New York, there was a dowry waiting for
Fanny. During their Viennese outings, she filled Saul's head
with stories of America's beauty, its endless opportunities for

personal achievement. And Saul was impressed. The whole idea of America had always excited him.

I watched the romance between Saul and Fanny with a certain skepticism. There was something about its swiftness, its brevity, and its open practicality which was not entirely to my liking. But then, I was an incurable romantic. When they finally announced that they would marry, they were both very pleased and excited, but neither could have been said to be in love. They had simply discovered each other at a time when they could satisfy certain needs each had of the other. For Fanny, marriage would mean the release of her dowry money; for Saul, marriage to Fanny would mean an immediate passport to America as the husband of a U.S. citizen. I, in the end, had to shrug my shoulders philosophically and to give them my blessings. These were strange and turbulent times. Who was to judge the ethics of any situation these days?

My mother, for her part, was delighted with the news of their engagement. She, who more than any of us felt the rising threat of Nazism, was grateful for the prospect that at least one of her children would leave Austria.

The wedding of Saul and Fanny was held in the synagogue where all the rest of us had been married. Mother was too weak to attend, but she was present at the small reception which was held at home. She was happy to have lived to see her sixth child married. Soon after the wedding, Saul and Fanny left for the United States. He was the first of my siblings to go there.

26

Several months after Saul's departure for America, young Addie arrived at my parents' home. It had been a long and emotional trip for the boy, journeying from Lwow to Vienna. Each mile had widened the division between himself and the mother he relinquished. We all knew how Sala Brand had nurtured and adored her half-orphaned son since his birth. Addie's closeness to his mother had been readily perceived each time Jim and I had visited them in Lwow. When he arrived in Vienna, at the age of thirteen and a half, his situation was clearly a sensitive one.

All of us reached out to meet that state and we were successful, I believe. The mere sight of that slender, brownhaired boy, almost as tall as his father had been, and reminding us so much of him, was enough to make us love him at once. A tenderness went out to him from each of us. And when he looked up at us with Sala's sad gray-blue eyes, he seemed to see that a haven was existing for him here. among his father's people. We all loved Addie from the beginning and he in turn showed us an affection which might only have been expected had he grown up with us.

For my mother, it was both pain and joy to behold the child of her eldest son, whom she had lost so untimely and unforgettably. She could not enjoy him too actively, however.

For by the time of Addie's arrival she was already very weak and was confined to bed much of the time.

Mela, who had taken over the running of the household after Mother's first heart attack, was in complete charge by now, and Addie became her charge. Though not the most affectionate of his aunts, she was the authority figure in that household now, and the boy instinctively depended upon her to direct his activities. Stela, as always, merely seemed to echo Mela's sentiments on just about every subject.

It was decided that Addie should attend school for the time being and learn German, since he would now be living in Austria.

In his leisure hours, Addie formed a strong friendship with Hanna's son, George, who was exactly his age. The two of them became constant companions and seemed more like brothers than cousins. Eddie Landes, Olga's boy, spent a great deal of time with them, too. And Addie drew close to all of his aunts, uncles, and cousins. At our home, he was a frequent visitor and seemed to adore Ingrid and Gerda, who made his visits so gay.

But as the months of Addie's apprenticeship advanced, my mother grew weaker than ever before. Mela, Stela, and Father administered to her constantly, and all were aware that the end was not far away.

One day, when I was visiting Mother, who had been feeling particularly low, Mela entered rather abruptly, accompanied by a man who carried a briefcase. Mela asked me to leave Mother's room for a while and, mystified, I complied. As I left the room, my father followed the other two inside.

Waiting in the dining room, I was very apprehensive. I could not imagine why Mela and this stranger had entered the room with such solemnity and had asked me to leave. What was happening to my mother? Was she even more seriously ill at the moment than I already knew?

After a short time, the three of them came out of the room. Mela went off to the kitchen. But my father spotted me, waiting, and, seeing my worried expression, patted my hand and spoke to me.

"Mother's all right, Helena," he assured me.

"But who was that man?" I asked, frowning.

"That was Schorr's attorney."

"Schorr's attorney! And what was he doing here?"

"He brought a prepared will for Mother to sign. . . . and for me to sign."

"A prepared will!" I gasped, rather horrified. I gazed burningly in the direction of the kitchen. How could Mela have been quite this crass? "And you signed it?" I asked my father.

"Yes," he said, shrugging his shoulders, as if to question my wild expression.

"You read it first, of course?"

"No, as a matter of fact. What should I read it for? I trust my own daughter!"

I sighed and closed my eyes briefly, seeing how things had fallen into place.

"And Mother—did she sign?"

"Yes, willingly. She didn't even ask what it was all about. She was so tired, she just wanted to be left alone."

These last words of his brought angry tears to my eyes. I cared nothing about the will itself, but I was furious at Mela for arranging this signing when my mother lay so weak and vulnerable. I was even a little angry with my gentle father, for cooperating with Mela's plan.

Soon after this incident, my mother suffered her third heart attack. This time, the doctor insisted that she be sent to a sanitorium. As usual, she resisted the idea. But my father, usually so passive, was now devastated with worry over her. And for his sake, Mother finally agreed to go to the sanitorium. The sanitorium was in the country near Vienna.

When I visited her there, I found her deep in thought. She admired everything around her, the splendor of nature, which she had never had time to reflect upon, the shadings of the sky, the colorings of birds and flowers. How beautiful God's earth seemed! She knew well that this was her last summer. In the fall, she was happy to come home and lie in her own bed again.

Her heart grew weaker and weaker. She now took on a fight with this heart to prolong life as much as possible. She struggled to postpone the inevitable. She was not afraid of dying, for she believed sincerely that those who had lived according to the will of God were rewarded in heaven. But she was sensitive to all of us — her children and grandchildren — and did not want to hurt us by the fact of her dying.

Winter came and she had to spend all her time in bed. I came to see her daily. I winced when I beheld my mother — she had shrunk to the size of a ten-year-old. I sat down beside her, took her in my arms, and whispered to myself: "I still have her. I still have her!"

She knew when her time to die approached. She called me nearer one day, because she could only whisper: "My dear Helena, promise me that you will not upset yourself and cry. You know, I, too, had a mother. You have a husband and family who need you." I promised.

The next morning, the phone rang and I was summoned to her bedside.

When I arrived, her bed stood in the center of the room, surrounded by my brothers and sisters. The doctor sat beside her. Her blue eyes wandered around, as if she were seeking someone. I sat down near her on the bed. The doctor handed me a wet handkerchief with sugar, which I put into her mouth to prevent it from drying. We could hear my father sobbing in the next room.

I kept my eyes glued to her face, so as not to lose a single glance. First she had seemed to recognize us and mumbled inaudible words. But little by little, her eyes started to fade and her life flickered and died away. In contrast to her life of struggle, her death was very peaceful.

The day of her burial was in January. The funeral service was held in the cemetery chapel. I was dimly conscious of many people present, seemingly all in black like the family. My total impression within the chapel was one of shadow and blackness moving like a dark cloud. The rabbi began the eulogy. But instead of his words, I heard the last phrases which my mother had spoken, admonishing me against grief and weeping.

"No, dear Mother. I will try to keep my promise not to weep, although it is a hard thing. But how do I control the anguish of my heart?"

And then I saw Jim slip from my side to the black-draped casket which contained her. Leon, Josef, Friedrich, and Bernatz joined him. Then they lifted the casket, for they, her close ones, were the pallbearers, which was as it should be with a respected person. My sisters and I, heavily veiled, followed them slowly through the cemetery to the grave. The tombstones were covered with frozen snow, which seemed to again accentuate that blackness of our mourning garb, and that of the crowd which followed the family in a silent procession. When the casket was lowered, I threw some earth on it and whispered : "Sleep well, beloved Mother. You worked so hard in life. You deserve a good rest."

The next day many people came to pay their respects. All of us were mourning at my father's house, seated on low stools. Her death was attended like that of a great person. The people who came in throngs to the house spoke of my mother and her kindness. We discovered good deeds of hers which we had never known about. One woman told of my mother bringing her broth and chicken when she was ill. Another told how my mother had given her an unlimited supply of bread when she was too poor to buy any.

I recalled her words to me : "When you help others, do it in such a way that no one should ever know."

27

After Mother's death, Mela took over all the family affairs in addition to running the household, which she had been doing for some time now. Her dominant position, which now emerged full-blown, actually had been building for years. First, she had been influential with Stela, who was only slightly younger than herself, but who, unfailingly, became one mind with any scheme of Mela's. Then Schorr had entered the picture and under his guidance Mela's authoritative streak was sparked, tested, and finally realized. Mother's physical weakness during her last years, coupled with Father's passivity, merely had provided the setting, acting as expedients to Mela's slowly, but inevitably evolving role. She was the oldest female left in the house when Mother became ill. And the rest had simply followed

One of her first gestures of authority after Mother's death was to reveal to the rest of the family the contents of the will which had been so surreptitiously planned, prepared, and signed. And it was easy to see why the whole procedure had been veiled in such secrecy.

The matzoh factory—a big enterprise by now—was willed to Mela alone. The 50 per cent of the Stadt-Kino which did not belong to Leon and Olga was to be divided as follows: 25 per cent for Stela and 25 per cent to be broken up between Saul, Bernatz, and young Addie. My father's portion (it was typical of his passive role that he should be dealt a "portion" by his own children) was a monthly income which would nicely cover all his basic needs and which was designed to continue as long as he should live. When Saul had left for America, Father had given up the bread bakery, which they had run together. So now, at seventy-one, Father was fully a retired man.

The reaction to "Mela's Will," as we came to regard it, was various and interesting. Hanna, Olga, Leon, and I had pretty well realized that we would be left nothing. We really did not object, for we had received what we considered a fair share in earlier years. But the manner in which the will had been arranged and executed, the memory of our frail and shrunken mother confronted with that attorney of Schorr's, left a very bad taste in our mouths. Mela and Stela—but especially Mela—had irrevocably damaged the relationships they had with us older ones. How could it be otherwise? A certain malice aforethought had precipitated many wounded feelings, all unnecessarily. Personally, I felt very strained toward Mela and was little inclined to try to bridge the gap that separated us from sisterly feelings. Hanna had been alienated by her, too.

All of us shared a sorrow when Mother died, however, whose depth and reality could not be questioned. Personally, I did take one legacy after her passing; it was the book she had so cherished all through her lifetime—her bible, the Jewish *C'enuh Urenuh*. This book had lent her wisdom all through her active years and, when she became ill, had been a source of consolation to her. It was the most precious thing she could have left me.

Our mourning was heavy and deep. We went through all of the usual rites, wore black, and felt separated from the rest of the world by our grief.

It was father who weaned us away from mourning too long. He told us that according to Jewish tradition one abandoned strict mourning after thirty days. It was correct and wholesome to resume a normal life. For his part, he adjusted admirably. He had much leisure time on his hands now and, after a decent interval, became a devotee of the coffeehouses. He began to enjoy his old age, relaxing in those places, meeting old cronies there for card-playing and talk.

But I think his favorite diversion was visiting his grandchildren. Like Mother, he measured his well-being in them, in their sweetness, laughter and good health. He was perfectly satisfied that Mela had arranged everything financially. I suspect he was even relieved not to have been bothered with the responsibility. And as for his share, he deemed just anything which his daughter endorsed.

Young Addie had now become completely Mela's ward. To whom else should he turn, in that house, for guidance? And yet she was far from being his substitute mother. She was not particularly demonstrative of affection to the boy, although, in all fairness, she did feel quite a bit for him. But, as before, all of us gave Addie affection, even though we did not share the same roof. Mela's role seemed that of director.

Accordingly, the boy sought her opinion on every significant point and paid heed to it when rendered. This was clear whenever I visited him. On these occasions, Mela and I scarcely exchanged a word. She would, in fact, absent herself from the room while Addie, Father, and I chatted. I was sorry that we were hardly on speaking terms, but in time grew used to it, and hardened.

But a subject arose, concerning Addie's future, which finally broke the silence on my part. Mela for some time had turned her thinking to Addie's education and the subsequent work for which it would prepare him. Hanna's George, who was Addie's dearest friend, was now enrolled in the gymnasium. But according to Mela, Addie had not shown any scholarly inclination up to now. He was a rather poor student, as she saw it—even if he had not been, of what use was a pure academic background? To what practical end could it be put?

She, Mela, had thought of a trade for Addie. Auto mechanics was what she had in mind. I winced when I first heard of it. Yet Addie himself appeared to like the idea. He was young, eager to be self-sufficient, and no doubt had that impatience of youth which is blind to what a lifetime of a certain activity will be like. And Mela did not lie about his academic ability. He was clearly not an eager student. So between Mela's energetic practicality and Addie's enthusiasm, the plan came to fruition and the boy was sent to an auto mechanic to apprentice in this field.

When he finished his learning period, he found work readily, as Mela had predicted he would. I was shopping one day near the garage where Addie was employed and stopped by, briefly, to see him there.

He did not see me approaching, for he was lying on the ground staring up at the bottom of a car, his hand buried inside of it. Somehow, this picture of him hurt me. I felt a start of guilt, first for my long-deceased brother and, second, for Sala Brand, who had relinquished the boy to us for heaven knew what glorious future in Vienna. We should have done more, I was thinking. I, personally, should have intercepted Mela's slick planning, taken more upon myself and Jim.

But just then, the boy stood up and greeted me, obviously in good spirits. He took me by the arm, showed me around, described his duties with enthusiasm.

"You are happy here, Addie?" I asked dubiously.

"Very much, Aunt Helena. I take to this work naturally. I do it well."

"Yes, one enjoys what one does easily," I enjoined, thinking, "But he is only sixteen!"

I perhaps should have let things go at that. But the memory of Addie working in the garage continued to plague me. I discussed it with Jim several times in the next few days. Something about the picture of him there was just not right.

By the end of the week, I decided to go and see Mela about it. It would be difficult from several points of view. First of all, we were hardly on speaking terms. Secondly, I, like the rest, had let Mela assume most of the responsibility for Addie's guidance. Nevertheless, I was determined to clear the air on this subject.

"So, you are worried about Addie, Helena. Why?"

"An auto mechanic, Mela! Really, is it good enough? He's only sixteen. He has no idea of status, of how long a life can be . . . of the limitations he will suffer in comparison, say, to George."

"George?" she repeated, raising her eyebrows.

My temper flared a bit.

"Oh, I know. George is not an orphan! But didn't we take Addie to us just for that very reason? Just to see that he should have all the benefits that Sala couldn't give him?"

Now Mela jumped to her feet, furious. "Is that what you think—you and Hanna and the rest? That I treat him like an orphan, that I lower the boy? How blind can you be? He simply wasn't a student! Not everyone can be, you know. And as for status, he makes a clean and honorable living. Isn't it enough? I would have done him a worse injustice by setting up impossible goals for him!"

Her voice rang with a sincerity of protest. She was clearly on the defensive, not only about Addie, but about all the unspoken things which kept us from communicating most of the time.

Now, from anger and excitement, she was almost in tears. I suddenly believed all that she said, believed she had done what she felt was right for the boy. And who was I to say otherwise? I had no right to spell out standards for him. That was the duty of his own nature.

"Maybe I'm mistaken, Mela. . . . Somehow, the picture of him in those dirty overalls, with greasy tools. . . . I don't know. But yes, you are right. He seems happy enough. But I had to see your point of view, you understand?"

"Of course, Helena. I'm glad you spoke. I don't want it said that I, personally, would deny Addie any opportunity he really wanted. Was it not I who saw that he was included in Mother's will?"

And so the matter ended, and time seemed to hold up Mela's views.

After that incident, I, like the rest, conceded to Mela's total authority in what had been my parents' home. She managed it well and, in addition, proved an excellent business woman with her new possession, the matzoh factory.

28

THE DEATH OF MY MOTHER TOOK A GREAT TOLL OF MY NERVES. For some time following her funeral, I was subject to periods of weeping. Just when I thought I had begun to adjust to her absence, I would regress back to intense grief, as if the long months of her illness had never existed, never prepared me for a world in which she was not alive. Now Ingrid and Gerda observed my moods. It is true that the children had loved their grandmother. But Ingrid, eight, and Gerda, only six, were confounded rather than heartbroken by the spectacle of her death. My tears, on the other hand, were communicable, and seemed to devastate them. Neighbors would find them crying, and when they asked the reason would be told that "Mommy is so unhappy."

Jim was disturbed by my depressed state, and felt that I should seek distraction. Ultimately, in the summer of 1935, he persuaded me to go away with the girls to Riccione on the Italian Riviera.

Thus, quite unexpectedly, we were to spend an unforgettable summer even in these chaotic times. Italy, with its sun and antiquity was offered to me like a shimmering jewel to explore with my daughters.

En route to Riccione, we stopped at Venice, and, like a confirmation of a tourist's dream, a group of folk musicians by the hotel entrance were singing, "*Wien, Wien Nur Du*

Allein," praising our Vienna. We felt as if we had been personally welcomed.

Venice was so different from Vienna. Here there was no tension perceptible, no undercurrent of anti-Semitism to make one feel stealthy or possibly despised. The magnificence, the color of the city itself, with its canals, outdoor cafés, and golden cathedrals, seemed to form a background only for the wondrous warmth of the people who lived in it. Indeed, it was impossible not to feel uplifted in this atmosphere of spontaneous music, laughter, and languid time. The little girls followed me around as though on a tour through heaven.

What Ingrid and Gerda did not see, happily, was a political and personal difference which we ourselves were experiencing in Italy. Whereas in Vienna, particularly since the inception of the Nazi movement, a Jew felt on the Viennese streets a frequent self-consciousness as a Jew, here there did not exist even the potential for such a feeling. Not only were the Italians unconcerned about one's origins but, in addition, we Jews shared with them a certain physical similarity, both being Mediterraneans, and it would have been hard to single us out, even if someone were seeking to. Thus I enjoyed this lovely anonymity, smiling at the innocent faces of Ingrid and Gerda, who felt only the warmth and beauty of Venice, too young to be grateful for this extra dimension.

A few days later, having arrived at Riccione, our seaside destination, I found that the same atmosphere prevailed. Although Mussolini was in power here and was known to be a fascist, it was my impression that his brand of fascism was in no way synonymous with Hitler's—I doubted that the Italian mentality would tolerate it. My opinion was soon to be borne out by the fact that Il Duce himself was vacationing in his own villa only a quarter of a mile from the hotel where we were staying. We could observe his family enjoying themselves, swimming in the blue Adriatic, from our beach. His sons could often be seen on the streets of Riccione.

It was during that very summer, however, that Mussolini's forces invaded Ethiopia. One day, I was sitting in the hotel restaurant with the girls. An Italian officer and his wife were sitting at the table next to us. Ingrid and Gerda were absorbed in studying the plates of these two, which were filled with raw oysters. They were wondering what those little animals were. Gerda was daring enough to approach them and ask if these things could really be eaten. The gentleman offered some to us to try, but we declined. Then he started a conversation with me in broken German

"Where are you from?" he inquired of me courteously.

"Vienna," I replied.

"Ah, Vienna, A wonderful city! But how are things there, now?"

"They are . . . ." I stopped abruptly and considered the paradox of this sociable exchange. Like two citizens of the world were we really to exchange opinions? I almost had to laugh. The nature of this man seemed so good, so amiable, that I had been about to complain of the tension at home, forgetting that he, as an officer, must be considered part of the Axis.

"The city has suffered much change, much turmoil," I offered, rather evasively.

"So it is everywhere, really!" the officer said. "Even now, I have to uproot myself. My regiment is leaving tomorrow for Ethiopia, to fight Haile Selassie. For what, I ask myself!" He cast an already nostalgic look around him. "One would prefer to stay right here in Riccione. After all, it's summer."

"Why do you go then?" Gerda burst forth suddenly.

We all laughed at her, while the officer shrugged and gestured to me that the child seemed to know better than the powers that were.

Later, I thought again of this congenial encounter. Experiences like this one made it impossible to be anything but perfectly comfortable in Italy that summer.

And with Gerda as a liason between us and the world, there were plenty of encounters. This younger daughter of mine was always striking up conversations with strangers who happened to appeal to her. She would promptly introduce them to me and Ingrid, often involving us for whole afternoons. Ingrid used to giggle at Gerda's forwardness — she herself was too bashful for this kind of thing.

Early in July, I had noticed a rather handsome young couple, probably honeymooners, who were staying at our hotel. I heard them being paged once as Mr. and Mrs. Katz; thus I guessed them to be Jewish, probably German Jews.

I was very curious about Mr. and Mrs. Katz. First of all, I had not realized that German Jews were in a sufficiently normal state to be taking trips to the Italian Riviera. Rumors had led me to believe that in 1935 the German Jewish plight was gravely worsening. Still, the presence of the Katz couple would seem to contradict what I had heard. Perhaps, I thought, things are really not so bad in Germany. But this young couple provoked interest in still another way — they were terribly aloof for some reason, apparently desiring no contact or discussion with any of the other hotel guests. As the weeks passed, their isolation was so marked as to seem a gesture of hiding. I regretted this, for I would have liked to engage them in conversation. But whenever I thought of doing so, their faces bore a prohibitive expression which cut off my impulse.

One day on the beach, I glanced over my shoulder and saw that the young couple had their chairs close to us. Unlike the other times I had observed them, they seemed in a freer mood. They were laughing together, like young people in love, having lost sight, for the moment, of their environment and whatever it was they were shunning.

I saw my opportunity and took it. Ingrid and Gerda were playing together in the sand. I walked over to the couple.

"Excuse me," I began. They looked up quickly, their smiles freezing.

"May I sit down?" I continued, already regretting that I had begun. "I couldn't help noticing such two attractive young people. We are staying in the same hotel. You are on your honeymoon?"

The girl, smiling tentatively, but maintaining the tightness of expression, nodded.

"I am from Vienna," I offered, "and I am a Jewess. Your name, Katz. . . ." I mumbled a little awkwardly, for their faces, so tense, were alarming. "Well, I assumed that you, too, were Jewish, and I have so wished for a chance to speak to some Jews from Germany. We in Austria have heard such terrible things—we are so concerned. Of course one never knows how much is true. I hope you will not mind my intruding this way, but if one could be told the real situation. . . ."

"The situation is perhaps not as bad as you have heard," the young man said tersely, casting down his eyes.

Clearly, he would have preferred to say nothing, but felt obliged now to give me some answer.

"I see, of course, that you are free to travel," I mentioned.

"Yes," Mrs. Katz replied, changing her position nervously. "We are still free to travel."

"But the businesses!" I insisted. "We heard that all Jewish-owned business had been confiscated by the Nazis."

"Not entirely," replied the man, defensively. "There are commissioners who have taken over these businesses, it is true. But the owner is compensated."

I stared at this boy incredulously. What was making him adopt this tone, this attitude which was an apology for his enemies?

I was about to resume my interrogation, despite their

strangeness, when Mrs. Katz glanced at her watch. "We have to go in now. We haven't had lunch yet."

They excused themselves and I returned to the children, shaken from the fear that I had read in the faces of these two young German Jews. For them, the world had become so fraught with potential danger, so conspiratorial, that they were terrified of me, a sympathetic friend! So things were not bad in Germany?

About a week later, our month in Riccione came to an end. I took the girls to Velden at Woertersee, a magnificent Alpine resort in the Austrian province of Kaernten. We spent two weeks there with my sister-in-law, Ellen, and her son, Henry. But, coming from Italy, we felt the change of atmosphere immediately. Ellen began to warn me, even at the platform where she came to meet us. But she needn't have bothered. Within an hour, I felt it : anti-Semitism, like a poison spray, had infested this lovely mountain retreat. Slogans and swastikas defiled the sides of buildings. *"Juden Heraus!"* (Out, Jews!) was a frequent sidewalk decoration. Shaken from these preliminaries, I left Ingrid and Gerda with their aunt, while I went to rent a room for us. The first guest house I approached had no vacancy. The second one did have a room to rent, which I requested to see. The landlady hesitated and shifted her feet, observing me.

"Have you been here, to this house before?" she asked, studying me crudely.

"No," I replied, "but a friend of mine, Mrs. Raab, spent several summers here and recommended it highly."

The landlady narrowed her eyes. "Mrs. Raab!" she echoed crudely. "Oh, no. I don't take Jews in my house anymore."

I was so outraged and humiliated by this experience that it was only Ellen, who in her persistence managed to find us a room in the same place where she was staying, who prevailed upon me to stay in Velden. I was glad to leave the place a week later when we moved on to Semmering, where Jim was to join me and the girls.

It was a relief to be a whole family again, and to see Jim vacationing for a change. But Semmering itself was a relief after Velden, which had become so odiously provincial. Semmering drew its tourists from all over the world, because of its mountainous beauty, its crystal air, and its lovely hotels. Because of the heterogeneous nature of its clientele, Semmering seemed devoid of the anti-Jewish sentiments to which I had just been subjected.

A number of our Christian friends were, in fact, vacationing there at the same time. Mr. and Mrs. Borwitz, owners of the Kranz-Kino were, like us, staying at the Suedbahn Hotel. How strange it was, I thought, that Jews can be here, as we are, with Christian friends like the Borwitz couple, acting as though nothing had changed. Are they aware, as we are, that in some quarters of Europe we are despised?

Whatever their awareness, Mr. and Mrs. Borwitz gave no indication of it. That evening, we dined with them at an outdoor cafe. While studying the menu, however, my eyes beheld a symbol drawn in white chalk on a stone wall opposite our table. It was a swastika. My heart sank within me, and my expression must have fallen, too, for Mr. Borwitz noticed the swastika, as did his wife. They averted their eyes instantly, as I did. It would have been almost impolite to discuss it with Jim and me.

So it was really here, too, this poison! I looked at Mrs. Borwitz, thinking of the way she shifted in her chair, her shoulders erect. She was, as far as I knew, a friend. Yet did her shoulders square themselves with a certain satisfaction? Was she not glad—indeed must she not be—that she was Christian and not one of these Jews who were being singled out for contempt? I tried to change my thoughts and managed to appear relatively gay. But the evening had been ruined for me. How can one really banish the sight of a swastika from one's mind?

I put this question to the mayor of Semmering, a Mr. Feigerl, whom we had known for years in Vienna, where he was a frequent visitor and patron of our movie house. He had seen Jim and me sitting with the girls in a restaurant one day and had invited us to his table. He was a kindly man and no Nazi sympathizer. Freely, therefore, I described to him my experience in Velden, the terrified and secretive Berlin couple I'd met in Riccione, the swastika even in friendly Semmering.

"Where can it all lead?" I asked Mr. Feigerl.

"It will lead where it seems to lead," Mr. Feigerl responded.

"Whatever I, or people like me may feel, the tide is set. Only a fool can tell himself now that the Nazis are not a growing force in Austria. They are a slow malignancy, preying upon the need to despise, having a blinding vision of power. Morality is being devoured here. God help us all! They are only too well received here!"

Jim grew tense while the mayor spoke. So here it was! A Christian friend, a non-Jew, was spelling it out for us. I thought momentarily of our self-delusions; yet even while I did so, thoughts of returning to Vienna, for which I was now slightly homesick, engendered the urge for still more delusions.

"If I could," he confided, in a low voice, "I'd leave Austria, myself. If I were Jewish," he continued, looking into Jim's eyes, "I'd fly out of the country!"

"Then you are convinced," asked Jim, "that nothing but the worst can be in store for the Austrian Jew?"

"I see no other direction to events as they unfold," he said unhappily.

"Then," I ventured, my voice strained, "Austria will be another Germany?"

"Wait," cautioned Mr. Feigerl, gesturing patience. "We see an early Germany now," he added ominously.

I glanced in sudden fear at Ingrid and Gerda, who sat with

us at the table like two adorable dolls. Their little faces were lifted politely, following our conversation, comprehending nothing. I reached out to hug them suddenly, then caught myself, afraid of communicating my distress.

If all he says is true, I thought, then indeed those with any sense among us should pick up and run, find shores that are not hostile. America had been a haven for many!

But while I began to think, for once, of taking really concrete steps to leave, the truth of our plight hit me with double force. I was kidding myself! We had no cash with which to leave the country. All of our capital had been invested in the Steffel-Kino, that venture which had so tormented my prescient mother. I fought against weeping, as the children grew restless beside me. As for selling the movie, the idea was a crude joke. Times were such that no Jew would dream of buying it and as for a gentile buyer, that was out of the question, too. It was known in Vienna, by now, that it was not a time for buying. Since the Nazi movement was continually gaining momentum in Austria, many non-Jews who were Nazi sympathizers felt that eventually all Jewish property might be confiscated and that they, without paying for it at all, might become its new owners. Thus the movie house became a leaden thing, hardly yielding an income and bearing an unknown destiny.

Could we have gone to America at that point, with what little we had? Probably so, had we been willing to arrive almost penniless in a strange country. Yes, we could have managed the fare for a voyage. But in my naïve and confused state, such an idea was untenable. We were not yet sufficiently desperate to settle for flight alone. While there was still, ostensibly, a life to be lived in Vienna, we could indulge ourselves with the concept that it was necessary to have capital with which to re-establish oneself in a new place.

So, as we left Semmering a few days later, even the candid

mayor had failed to penetrate our stubborn determination to
to maintain what still remained untouched in Vienna.
Such blindness was a kind of marvel to be wondered at later.

29

THIS BLINDNESS WAS UNIVERSAL AMONG VIENNESE JEWS. IT must have been, for I did not hear of any of them leaving during the year of 1936. The coffeehouses—always indicative of the times—were still crowded. We had put our hopes into the Austrian chancellor, Schuschnig, who followed the assassinated Dollfuss. Although Dollfuss' regime had been a fascist one, it had also been anti-Nazi and against the *Anschluss* of Austria by the Reich.

Schuschnig was a man of more liberal thinking. He deplored race hatred and considered the Jews fellow Austrians. Schuschnig tried desperately, during the three and a half years of his regime, to keep Austria from Hitler's grasp. He made trips to all the big Austrian cities and delivered speeches attempting to explain the true character of Nazism. Unfortunately, the minds of thousands had already been poisoned by the underground of Nazi propaganda and he could not reach them.

The arrival of Schuschnig was always heralded by a lavish reception. In one of these cities, Schuschnig asked the mayor : "How many Social Democrats are in your city?" "Twenty per cent," the mayor replied. "And how many Christian Socialists?" "Fifty per cent." "And how many Nazis?" "Oh !" responded the mayor, "we are all Nazis !"

The story was whispered and circulated around as a joke. For us Jews it was a bitter humor. In any case, it indicated all too well the temper of the times in Austria.

With it all, however, the surface did not yet break. Christian friends still socialized with us, fellow theater owners and their wives. And we continued to drift as we had before, absorbed in our own worries and excitements. For at this time there was a great deal of commotion in the offices of Universal Pictures and changes were taking place there.

A certain Mr. Regler, who was the American comptroller of Universal, had made a special trip to Vienna to check the books of this branch. The profits of this branch appeared to be less than they should be. Being loyal to the company, Regler of course had to find out the cause. After much careful investigation and deliberation, he reluctantly revealed that Mr. Raab the worldly one, was at fault. A steadily growing involvement with things outside of Universal Pictures had fostered a neglect by Raab of his duties there which resulted, it was revealed, in a rather flagrant mismanagement of his duties.

After this, Mr. Schiller, who was supervisor for Universal over Czechoslovakia, Hungary, and Austria, arrived to study the situation. He discovered that Raab and his wife had been living too high a life—the kind that always lead to dissipation of a sort. Jim soon learned that a decision was being made jointly by Regler and Schiller. Raab was to be fired. Jim, honest and conscientious through the years, seemed to those two a perfect replacement. On the day he was told, Jim came home in a strange mood.

"Helena, congratulate me. Today I became manager of the Vienna branch of Universal Pictures."

I could not help but be happy that he was advanced. I kissed him and held him close.

"I'm very happy for you, Jim."

But he appeared anything but happy as the evening progressed. After the children retired, he fell into a silence which was clearly morose.

"What's the matter, Jim?" You should be feeling good tonight."

"Oh for heaven's sake, Helena. How can I? Raab is my friend—with everything, my friend and business associate! It's awful to think of building on his defeat."

I sighed and pressed his hand.

"It's true, Jim. Yet if you had refused, they would only have hired someone else for the position. It's not as if they'd ever take Raab back again."

And so it was settled, and in time, Jim enjoyed his enlarged responsibilities. As always, he was concerned, perhaps too seriously, with the welfare of the children, and encouraged me to plan a healthful summer vacation for them.

After thinking over the several prospects before me, I again chose Italy, because I loved that country. This time, I took my daughters to Laurana, a rocky beach resort on the wonderful, blue Adriatic sea. And with us that summer came Esther, my very special niece.

We spent a beautiful summer in Laurana. The three girls and I became lovingly familiar with the place. Along the beach there was one large and many smaller hotels. This strip was separated from the town. But we investigated the town, as well, admiring its little houses on narrow streets. The girls were enthralled with its idyllic quality, with the linen hanging from one side of a window to the other.

Ingrid laughingly refered to one of the narrow streets we traversed as "Broadway." She was familiar with this street in New York from one of the movies she had seen. I smiled at my eldest daughter, seeing the first efforts toward worldly associations set in.

And Laurana was a good place to be worldly in mind, for its clientele was very international.

Esther was now seventeen, nearly a woman. Accordingly, I took her to a dance one evening there. While we were seated at our table, a gentleman approached us and asked Esther to dance.

I watched them conversing, pleased that Esther could hold her own, as it were, in this adult scene. When she returned, she started to laugh and could hardly stop.

"He took me for an Oriental, Aunt Helena!" she giggled. "And he spoke to me in French. . . ." She paused, and then laughed anew. "Why French, I really don't know! In any case, I assumed, naturally, that he was a Frenchman, and blurted out a few poor words in that language—" Here she stopped to choke on mirth again. "This hair of mine, so black and curly, apparently misled him. . . . Oh, it's too funny! The end was that he turned out to be from Vienna. And when I mentioned that I was too, the poor man was really downcast. He had hoped for something more exotic, I guess!"

Yes, the international flavor was everywhere and escaped no one. I had my own little encounter, only a few days after Esther's. One evening a gentleman asked me to dance. I saw no harm it it, and agreed. As we danced, he began to speak English to me and told me he was an American. To my delight, I found that I could still speak a little English, which I had studied so many years before. I informed the man that I was from Vienna. He perked up his head as we danced on.

"And how are things in Vienna?" he queried.

"You mean, of course, with the Nazis?" I managed to say in English.

At the word *Nazis,* he looked me straight in the eye.

"Are you Jewish, then?" he asked.

"Yes," I replied, smiling at his immediate association of the words *Nazi* and *Jewish.*

"But I'm an American Jew!" he announced in a delightful, bubbling Yiddish.

I burst out laughing at his sudden Yiddish. It was too much. And I had strained myself so with the English!

But later, we talked seriously, this American Jew and I.

"I'm in Europe strictly for pleasure," he informed me.

"And what is American sentiment these days?" I inquired. "How do they feel about Germany and Hitler? Is there any alarm there?"

Our conversation was now held entirely in Yiddish.

"Not the slightest," he informed me. "Hitlerism won't spread. Really, we don't see how it can. As for America, well, she is separated from Europe by the Atlantic Ocean. Germany hardly seems to constitute a threat," he concluded with some complacency.

"But what if Hitler should take over all of Europe?" I demanded.

My American companion shrugged. "He won't," he assured me. "He only seeks to reunite the German people."

"And the Jews?" I pressed on.

"Oh, all of that is only propaganda. Don't believe what you heard about the Jews in Germany."

"Indeed!" I responded.

So this was the opinion of American Jews? It was incredible. I did my best to enlighten this deluded American, but my efforts were not well taken, I suppose. No one wishes to trade optimism for dread.

The next day, I met some acquaintances of ours from Vienna in a little outdoor coffeehouse, where I was enjoying the hour with Ingrid, Gerda, and Esther. This couple was called Gruber and they were very pleased to see me and joined our table. I told them about the American Jew I had met and described to them his point of view. They listened, frowning.

"And what do you make of all of this?" I asked.

Mr. Gruber sighed. "For the time being, we are safe, I feel, in Vienna."

"But you have a brother in Australia," I pointed out. "Why not go there, where it is certainly safer?"

"Yes, it is true I have a brother there. He has asked us to come. But Australia is so far away. One simply can't imagine picking up and running off to it, simply because the times ring of an uncertain conclusion. Only if the worst came to the worst would we actually leave for Australia," he said honestly.

It had been a full and interesting summer as well as a healthful one. Coming home, I did not realize that this was to be the last prosperous year for us in Vienna.

It was, largely, a pleasant year, like so many which had preceded it. I attended what was to be my last social affair in December, when Jim staged a big reception for a Mr. Cowdin, Chairman of the Board of Directors of Universal, in the Bristol Hotel.

I enjoyed the affair very much, using my English again with the Cowdins, and pleased not to be so rusty after all. It did not occur to me at any time during that evening that I might soon find it essential to improve my ability with the English language.

30

In 1937, THE SITUATION IN VIENNA BECAME PERCEPTIBLY worse. No Jew could delude himself about Nazism any more. This terrifying force gained momentum by the day, enveloping us slowly. Technically, it was still illegal to be a Nazi in Austria; in actuality, the strength and numbers of Austrian Nazis grew steadily, until now they came to the surface with their malice. Huge swastikas were smeared on walls and buildings; anti-Jewish signs and slogans were found pasted on Jewish-owned shops.

Jim's job with Universal Pictures was not troubled, which was indeed fortunate. For our personal holdings diminished, meanwhile, by the day. Little by little we were growing poor. As the times worsened, our Steffel-Kino was almost empty most of the time. Many gentiles, affected by Nazi propaganda, deliberately avoided our movie. Our Jewish patrons had diminished in number also, since they, like us, were growing poor through mounting discrimination in all fields of endeavor. Jim grew tense and strained as the predicament deepened. His job with Universal Pictures, while a blessing of stability in the midst of Viennese turmoil, was not, however, so highly paying a position. We had always subsidized our living expenses with the income from our own movie house. Now there was nothing left but his salary, and, in addition, our movie house was operating now at a terrible deficit.

Thus it became a daily matter of anguished calculating. How were we to keep the movie house to which fewer and fewer customers came? The building had to be maintained, the employees still had to be paid, the films that were shown cost money. I was tormented, seeing Jim's anxiety. I feared he would become ill. Why did we not simply close this movie house, which, far from profiting us, was now our heaviest liability? I can only attribute our tenacity, our willingness to keep it at any cost, to this overall delusion which had caused us to remain in Vienna in the first place. We were instinctively sure that the theater, like the situation in Austria, was coming into better days, and that, surely, this change was right around the corner. And since the last of our money had been so optimistically invested in the Steffel-Kino, closing it was somehow unthinkable and would have constituted the most final defeat for us.

In the midst of this decline, we were suddenly shocked by a catastrophe which no one of us could ever have anticipated. Josef was suddenly bankrupt. And we were involved. The news came like a thunderbolt. There had never been a hint of insolvency. On the contrary, Josef's optimistic mood led everyone to believe his financial state was a prosperous one. In this spirit, he had approached Jim a year before, asking him to sign a certificate of guarantee for a tremendous loan which Josef wished to make for business purposes. Jim, who trusted Josef, and who was as convinced as anyone of Josef's solvency, signed readily. It seemed a small favor at the time—a mere signature for one's own brother-in-law. Josef had a way of making one feel very good about doing favors for him, of banishing any doubts from the minds of those from whom he sought help. Jim was sure that Josef was handling his business affairs properly.

When the news of Josef's bankruptcy came, it brought with it our own financial ruin. Jim had co-signed with Josef for a tremendous loan. Josef, it was now revealed, was not only penniless, but was beseiged by creditors on all sides. Not only had Jim been dragged into this mess but others in the family as well—Olga, Leon, Saul. Each, in his turn, had been approached by Josef in his optimism, in his blindness, to add signatures to loan statements. Each, like Jim, had complied. No one had questioned Josef's reliability. His façade had been too perfect, too convincing!

It took Josef's bankruptcy and our implication in it for us to discover the real man behind the sporting personality. Only now did we read his character for the first time.

And even now, one could not say that Josef was evil, that he had meant harm to a single one of us—even to Jim, whom he had ruined. Rather it was an irresponsibility akin to a kind of hopeful madness that had prompted Josef from one folly to ever greater ones. Hanna had always been disturbed by Josef's lack of education. But none of us ever suspected that he was less capable in business than he had led us all to believe he was.

Where had this nightmare begun to weave itself? How far back did it go? I believe it started when Josef rented the Amelon-Kino. He certainly expected to make a lot of money on this big movie and had immediately taken on the manner and attitude of a man who is *going places*! Not satisfied with his *"Pendlerei"* and the partnership in the Steffel-Kino with Jim, Josef had decided to make his fortune on the Amelon-Kino. When this theater was offered for rent, Josef was determined to have it. To get it, however, he needed a large sum of money to invest. And so that miracle of delusion—his excellent reputation—came into play and served him. He was able to borrow almost any amount from professional usurers, at high interest. When payment became due on the first loan, Josef borrowed money from a second usurer to pay it back. And so it went, this incredible irresponsibility, all based on a fantastic assumption that it would all be well in the end, that a sudden prosperity would save the day, cover all debts, and make real for Josef the posture he had already established and maintained. Meanwhile, he ran his businesses without any concrete knowledge of their assets or their liabilities. His optimism was prodigious, his humor good and always a prop to the prevailing concept of him.

Perhaps Josef could have juggled his affairs so as to survive, had not the times been against him. But in 1934, his Amelon-Kino, which was owned by the Social Democrats, was closed by the Christian Socials, who had just taken over the government. Determined to regain possession of this theater, on which he had so counted, Josef's borrowing was a frantic but futile attempt to bribe the authorities in power.

Hanna had been as ignorant as we of the real truth of her husband's financial state. Josef appeared prosperous and she, as his wife, had lived accordingly. He was a good husband and father and had never refused her anything. And Hanna was ambitious, particularly where the children were concerned. Their education was a matter of some significance to her. Thus, she had sent George to a gymnasium and Esther to a private lyceum and later to the Commercial Academy. All of these pursuits had cost money. Beyond them were lesser tangibles— piano lessons, suitable clothes. Hanna had accepted Josef's money for all of these things in the belief that he could afford everything. Josef had even presented her with jewels from time to time. I had secretly observed that Josef had a habit of buying something expensive for Hanna when he heard that I had just received something from Jim. He had always emulated Jim and it had been rather touching to see him reproduce these gestures.

Josef had lived like a sport. He was a man who had a sense of well-being if at any given moment his pockets were full, even if the money should have been in the hands of his creditors. The immediate possession of it was sufficient to make him

The family in Przemysl (1902). With mother and father are the five children: (from top to bottom) Leon, Hanna, Abram, Olga, and (seated) myself.

Jim at eighteen.

The family photographed in 1911 in Lwow. From left to right, Mother, Olga, Abram, Hanna, Leon, myself; second row, Mela, Saul, Stela, and Bernatz on Father's lap.

Eighteen years old—the photo I gave to Jim.

Abram as a soldier.

Jim and I on our wedding day.

At last, a baby—1926.

Abram and Sala on their wedding day.

*In Franzensbad—Greta and I (with the umbrella on the right)
with friends.*

At the Film Ball.

The photo, taken at a masked ball, which Greta later used to identify me at Franzensbad.

Gerda and Ingrid—carefree days, 1931.

Youthbund guarding the cemetery against Nazi vandalism (1933).

The Youthbund guard the cemetery. My brother Saul is at the extreme left.

The family, when life was still good to us (1934).

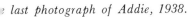

e last photograph of Addie, 1938.

Addie and girlfriend at Hachshara, 1938.

Ingrid and Gerda before departing for England, 1939.

Just before Father's escape to Colombia (1939); left to right, myself, Olga, Father, and Hanna.

The arrival in New York of Gerda and Ingrid (back row),
December 10, 1943.

Grave and monument to the martyred Jews of Yugoslavia.

feel rich, to make him generous. He loved, in fact, to hand out money, and contributed handsomely to various charities.

When he began to sink, Josef came first to Jim, later to the others. And who could have refused him, with that good, innocent face, when he asked for a favor? His uniqueness lay in his ability to make everyone like him so well, to act so unhesitatingly on his behalf. The last things anyone had doubted were his honesty and reliability.

The truth shocked all of us, literally numbed us at first. We had difficulty grasping the depths of it. It was compounded for Jim and me with the temper of the times, so quickly it seemed to turn on us and reverse our fortunes, our most essential security. It wrapped itself up with the decline of our business, with the rise and spread of Nazism. It was, like these other forces, a fact apart from us, yet hopelssly involving us against our will and, God knew, our design. In a way, it was the final blow.

Yet Hanna was hurt most of all. She was left poverty-stricken with three children. Her disillusionment with Josef could not be mapped. It choked her, recalled to her the nameless dissatisfaction of her earlier years, when, despite wanting to, she had failed to fall in love with Josef.

Her final humiliation came when Josef was sentenced to three years in jail. This occurred despite the help of everyone in the family who had co-signed for Josef; each of us was making good the amount his name was attached to. It was not we who let Josef down, but a certain friend of his. This man, a solid business friend, who had respected and loved Josef, had lent him a large amount, like all the others, with implicit faith in his ability to make good on it. And although this man had been compensated now, his outrage at Josef's duplicity was too vast for so simple a solution. He had been bitterly disillusioned. It was as though Josef had been a symbol of his own gullibility and, cheated, he sought vengeance.

Thus it was at the hands of a former friend who had adored him that Josef was brought to trial for fraud. That he was actually sentenced was due to the fact that the presiding judge was an illegal Nazi. None of us could do more than we had done. Legally, he was beyond our reach. At the conclusion of the trial, my brother-in-law was sentenced to jail.

Now Hanna knew her worst days. And the children had to be told. George was sixteen, Esther eighteen, and Robert just eleven. What was a mother to say? How to explain this sudden phenomenon, explain the relation between a father's largesse and his ultimate disgrace? Hanna suffered on every front. She was now ashamed to meet people. She was well known in Jewish circles as an honorable woman, an ardent Zionist, a devoted Hadassah worker; now she had been degraded by her own husband.

As for Jim, he was harmed financially more than anyone because he had co-signed for the biggest loan of all and now had to repay it. Having no immediate funds to dissolve the debt, he managed to arrange with Josef's creditor to pay off the amount in installments. This burden shook Jim's sense of security to the roots. Everything was at stake for us. I felt, as the days passed and I watched him suffer, that his health was my only concern, the restoration of his tranquility the only wealth I wished back again.

I tried to soothe him.

"There is no reason to despair," I murmured absently, stroking his hair. "It will work out, somehow."

"But Helena, the first installment is due in a week and I've nothing to pay it with!"

"You shall have the money when the time comes, Jim. Look, we really don't need the car, do we? We can sell it!"

By that statement, I meant that I, personally, would sell our Fiat. I knew that Jim could not bear the act of doing so, would take it much more symbolically than I would.

Accordingly, I sold the car several days later for a fairly reasonable price. In the end, we were both relieved. The money was there, in the house, in time for the first installment.

But it seemed that little time passed before Jim manifested a terrible nervousness again and I realized that the second installment was imminent.

I went into my bedroom late one evening while Jim was reading in the parlor. Ingrid and Gerda were sound asleep. Furtively, I opened the top drawer of my dresser and drew out my jewel box, a handsome leather square. Within this box, my fingers touched the adornments of a love which had persisted through the commonplace things of married life. The jewelry had been purchased by Jim for me during the prosperous years we had shared. Frankly, it had overwhelmed me at first. I was a woman of humble origins who had never expected or solicited these things. But Jim was the kind of man who had wanted his wife to have jewels if he was in a position to buy them. Certainly, I had been gratified, like any woman, to own beautiful things. Now, however, when I was on the verge of relinquishing them, I felt no regret at all. I was glad to have them to pawn, if only I could ease Jim's anxiety. Little did we dream when these baubles were purchased that they would ever be traded in to help us survive.

The next day, I took a bus to the Doroteum, the large state-owned pawn exchange. Unlike American cities, which have many small pawnshops where one can deal in privacy, there was only one such place in Vienna. It was a huge open place, where things were pawned and purchased, the large crowds present assuring an audience, and a number of unsavory characters as witnesses, to any transaction. It was the most humiliating experience I had known up to that time. Giving up the jewelry meant nothing; but being there was degrading.

When my turn came to speak at the counter, I presented a diamond watch, several diamond rings of varying sizes and shapes, gold bracelets, and a pair of diamond earrings. I smiled to myself as I presented the earrings, for only with them had I felt a certain female weakness. I had detached the tops, which were two diamond stones, and had hidden away the pearls which had hung from them, along with chains of diamond chips connecting them. My reasons for retaining these two things were not entirely clear to me. Did I want a keepsake to remind me of that carefree and abundant life, or was this merely that bit of acquisitiveness which all women are supposed to feel?

I received the money, the pawn tickets, and quickly left the vast hall, where so many eyes followed my movements.

In the bus, going home, I felt perspiration on my forehead and my heart was pounding furiously. I struggled to overcome my feeling of shame, of involvement in that crass and terrible hall which I had left.

By evening, I was composed. After Ingrid and Gerda had retired for the night, I presented Jim with the money I had received for the jewelry. I advised him of its source, since there was no other explanation.

A look of pain crossed his face, as I put the money into his hand. But I clutched his shoulder and demanded that he be realistic, not sentimental. I told him I was glad to have owned these things so that they could be put to practical use for us now.

"You have a generous soul, Helena," he said, and his tone indicated that he was forced to accept the situation and knew it.

"Oh!" I laughed, embarrassed. "We'll redeem these pawn tickets one day. You'll see, Jim."

Yet with all this, the jewelry, by itself, had not yielded enough to cover all of our debts. Within two weeks, I was to return to that hateful scene of barter three times more, armed with three Persian rugs and, finally, my fur coat and silverware.

The money from the pawned items, coupled with a part of Jim's salary from Universal, saved us from total catastrophe. But we lived very close, and after making the payments on Josef's debt and paying the bills on our profitless property we were just about able to pay the rent and buy our food. But Jim had rallied his spirits, perhaps because I had helped. He had nearly fallen prey to a breakdown when Josef's story had been revealed. Now he was sustained because he accepted the situation and because we managed, somehow, to make every payment of the great debt when it came due.

Hanna's adjustment was poor. She was full of rancor toward Josef, who was now in jail. At first, I wondered if she were not being too merciless in her consideration of him. But after visiting her, I understood better what she was feeling.

"I visited him yesterday, Helena," she told me.

We were sipping tea in her parlor. The children were out of the house.

"How does he seem, Hanna?"

"Relieved. Yes, he seems relieved. His dual role is over. I never knew he was carrying it . . . that smiling face! Did any of us guess? But now I see a relaxation about Josef that wasn't there. It makes me sick!"

"Poor man!" I cried, inadvertently. "How he must have suffered, Hanna, living in terror of exposure. The burden of that guilt!"

"The burden of his fantasy?" she retorted. "And who asked him to carry such a burden, to delude himself like a madman and involve all of us? Why didn't he come to me, tell me how things stood? I would have cut down the household expenses, taken the children out of private school — anything! Helena, I could have helped him, if only he had confided in me. And this is the one thing I can't forgive him for."

"I understand your bitterness, Hanna. You're suffering so much now. But you mustn't condemn Josef. Not that he did the right thing! But his intention, Hanna! Was it ever bad?"

Hanna gave me an astonished look.

"Honestly, Helena! How can you feel a shred of sympathy for Josef? He's all but ruined Jim. . . . But then it's foolish to ask how you can feel it. That's Josef's maddening secret, isn't it? To remain loved in the face of any misery he causes? Yes, that is his secret. And so maddening, so infuriating is that quality to me now, that I can't bear to think of it!"

I bit my lip, deliberating a reply.

"Look, you'll have to think only of what makes you feel positive toward Josef now. Because one thing is certain: if Josef never needed your support before, he certainly needs it now. You will have to see him, Hanna."

"But what of the children? How can I explain it to them? They love their father! Esther is eighteen now — a young lady! George is already sixteen and even Robert, who is eleven, must be convinced there's something wrong with his father. What can I tell them when even I don't fully understand this horror that suddenly took over our lives?

I took her hand firmly in mine.

"I know what you must tell them, Hanna — and tell it to yourself, at the same time," I said fiercely. "Their father is not in jail because he is a criminal, but because he was a dreamer. He wanted his family to have a comfortable life and his desire for this became so urgent that he chose the wrong way to achieve it. Many people go bankrupt. Josef was unfortunate to be sentenced to jail, that's all."

"You make it all sound so simple, Helena," Hanna remarked, with a fleeting smile.

"It has to be simple, for you, for the children. It has to be seen only in this light, or you will devastate yourself. Do what I say, Hanna. Take the children and go to see Josef. He is there now, isolated, accepting his punishment. Perhaps this punishment will help him to emerge with a clear sense of reality. So much is to be hoped. But for now, he needs to know that you and the children still love him, still belong to him."

Hanna's eyes filled briefly.

"All right, Helena. You are right, of course. I will see Josef and take the children, too. Only one thing — will you come with us? It would help so much. . . ."

"I'll go with you tomorrow to see Josef."

The next day, Hanna and I, together with her children, went to visit the imprisoned Josef. The jail was a special building which housed only those who had committed mild misdeameanors. This fact was a relief to Hanna.

We were all permitted to see him, and it was a second point of relief to find Josef dressed in his own clothes rather than some ghastly uniform which we might have imagined. He was very happy to see us and smiled as we filed into place in the large reception room where the prisoners' visitors were received. There was a large barrier between Josef and us, but it was possible to talk.

I had been very tense as we entered, fearing that Josef would weep when he saw the children, but he showed little emotion and was in a relatively relaxed state.

He talked to us for quite a while and told us how sorry he was that he had made us all suffer. Evidently he had thought much about it during these past weeks. But when he spoke of the future, of the time when he would be released from this place and begin his life anew, Josef's face lit up.

"You'll see," he assured us. "I'll make it up to you then!"

Incredibly, he was as optimistic as ever. And, as before, it was somehow impossible to feel any rancor towards the man while in his presence. Even now, a certain radiant warmth which emanated from Josef thawed the reserves of hostility and resentment which had been built up in Hanna.

Thus, when we left, my sister turned to me and said, "I feel much better, now that I've seen him. I'm so grateful to you,

Helena, for urging me to go. I only hope that Olga feels as benevolently toward us as you do."

Olga was very sympathetic toward Hanna and her plight. But Olga was to face further miseries after Josef's catastrophic exposure. She was called home one day from the movie. Friedrich had collapsed to the ground and could not be raised. The doctor pronounced a stroke. Friedrich was paralyzed and his speech was gone.

I rushed to the scene to comfort my sister. More than ever, her self-sufficient spirit was needed now. And, as always, Olga persevered. She pulled herself together, hired a nurse to stay with Friedrich and tend him. Olga resumed her work at the Stadt-Kino with greater intensity than before. She was the sole breadwinner of her family now.

When I went to see Friedrich, the scene in his room was heartbreaking. The two children—twelve-year-old Eddie and seven-year-old Herta—sat by his bed, talking to him with a strained eagerness to be understood. They loved their father dearly, and desperately tried to understand his babbling. Neither comprehended the gravity of Friedrich's illness, but Olga, of course, understood it well.

I did not know whom to pity more, Olga with her stricken husband or Hanna in her poverty with Josef in jail.

31

Politically, we were still free to walk the streets of Vienna. With Schuschnigg in power, the official attitude was that Nazism was not to be tolerated. It was within the Austrian population itself, as I have indicated before, that the fever of the new cult was becoming epidemic in scope. Thus, despite the official doctrine, small riots occurred here and there, and sub-surface anti-Semitism was rife.

But since it was on the surface that we existed, we continued to work and worry about our individual affairs, about Hanna and Olga and Friedrich, about Ingrid's toothache and Gerda's latest cold, about each other, as we always had.

Our financial situation remained very poor, but Jim's adjustment improved with the months, at least slightly. And then there was the national situation to talk of, to worry about, to contemplate the future of. This vastly more encompassing situation probably threw our personal travail into perspective for us, even while it contributed to it. In retrospect it is hard to explain how it could be so, but at that point we continued to live our usual daily lives. Jim and I sought out our friends as before and even such diversions as we could still afford.

Spring came and its eternal beauty touched us as it always had, warmed our tense faces even while we thought of installments which were due, of poor immobile Friedrich and destitute Hanna. There was no denying the season. It came on relentlessly, indifferent to the vicissitudes, the folly of human affairs. Summer began to approach and, walking in the sun, I mused lazily on scenes of former years. Now I would not have dared to dream of leaving the country, as I had in the past. Nor would I have had the means to do so.

In May, Greta came to visit us. I thought she looked poorly, and I kept thinking of the bartered Steinway, which neither of us mentioned. She had grown pale during the winter of 1937, and her clothes, so different from the old days when she was marvelously chic, looked shabby and unfashionable.

Jim and I knew that Erich had never recovered after their divorce and the loss of his job at Universal. The Schelmans were in very bad straits, even worse than ours. By now, they had sold almost everything they owned, just to keep going from month to month. All that remained to them, in fact, was a small bungalow in a summer colony in Kritzendorf, on the shores of the Danube, near Vienna. They retained this bungalow only because they had found it impossible to sell.

Greta's visit had to do with this bungalow. She talked around the subject for a while, shifting restlessly in her chair, and finally came to the point. Knowing that I would now be financially unable to take Ingrid and Gerda to a summer spot, she had come to invite me to stay with her at Kritzendorf, which, she pointed out, was so close to home, yet so lovely.

As Jim and I listened to Greta's invitation, we both realized that in addition to our company, Greta was implicitly seeking our help in maintaining this bungalow, perhaps even in providing her family with food.

The idea of going to a resort took some getting used to. Resorts were a luxury for the prosperous. All of us were poor now, stretching budgets, pawning non-essentials. Yet Greta had the bungalow, needed us there, and the place would be so good for the girls.

In the end, it seemed sensible and right that I should join

Greta and Kurt with my two girls. Jim and Erich would come on weekends to be with all of us at Kritzendorf.

As the time to leave drew near, I was grateful for one more summer vacation. It was the only pleasant thing we had had to anticipate for a long time. It came as a contradiction to the pattern of decline and sorrow which our year had followed so relentlessly. And although this contradiction was but an extended moment and not to be taken as any indication of change in our plight or Greta's, I was very enthusiastic over the plan.

Kritzendorf on the Danube was uniquely beautiful, a river beach nestled in tall, slender trees. The bungalows amidst these trees were close together and looked like birdhouses among them, for they were elevated on wooden pillars against the danger of flood.

This was a friendly summer colony, even in 1937. Ingrid and Gerda found many playmates there and flourished on the beach as they would have in any other year. Ingrid's blonde hair turned platinum in the sun. Gerda became sunburned. They enjoyed the set-up we had arranged; they loved "Auntie Greta," as they called her. Ingrid at this time was eleven, Gerda nine. Greta's boy, Kurt, was fifteen and a scholarly lad. He and the girls got along together beautifully, and he even tutored Ingrid in mathematics, with which she had difficulty.

So again I, with my dear ones, encountered this deceiving serenity for yet another summer. Here in Kritzendorf, coffee-houses and cafes near the beach were crowded and full of laughter. People danced to the "Blue Danube Waltz." Music and dancing were everyday things. Tension and peril seemed unreal in this atmosphere.

But Greta and I soon became aware that symptoms of danger existed right on the shores of the Danube. Every afternoon, it was our habit to go for extensive walks, taking Ingrid and Gerda along. Amidst the scenery of trees and gardens, we discovered that a large courtyard had become the training ground for a Nazi camp. These were Austrian men with Nazi sentiments, who had organized themselves and were now conducting militant drills, goose-stepping with fearful precision. What an anomaly this seemed! And why did these men prepare? Obviously for the day when the Nazis would take over Austria completely.

The first time Greta and I passed this camp, we stood frozen to the spot, full of despair. Looking inside the gates, we observed them. They wore *brown khaki* uniforms with swastikas on their sleeves. They saluted their commander with "*Heil Hitler!*" as they marched past us.

"Who are these soldiers, Mother?" asked Ingrid, turning to me. "Are they preparing for a war?"

I glanced at Greta questioningly. She shrugged and then nodded to me, indicating that we were of one mind, that the truth could no longer be withheld from the children.

"They are soldiers who have their own ideas," I told her. "But this is not the Austrian Army!" I added, as if to convince myself. "Well, if you must know Ingrid, they are Nazis, about whom one hears so much in Vienna."

"The Nazis who hate the Jews?" Gerda piped in suddenly.

I looked at her in astonishment. Jim and I had tried so hard to keep the girls apart from these things while they were still officially illegal.

"Who told you that?" I asked her.

"My friends at school," she answered directly.

So Greta and I were fooling ourselves. Even eight-year-olds were kept informed these days. Fortunately, Ingrid and Gerda were not able to interpret things with any depth or accuracy yet. Now they ran ahead of us playfully.

Greta turned to me slowly. "So you see, Helena, how strong they are getting. Before long, they will overrun us."

I nodded. "I also see," I said to Greta, "that they are well-trained and well-supported by Nazi Germany. Still, I can't help feeling, Greta, that Austrians are not as bad as Germans. Haven't the Austrians always been known as *gemuetlich*? Why it's a national characteristic, this warm-heartedness! Jim and I have so many Austrian friends who have never shown a trace of anti-Semitism toward us," I protested.

"Wait!" Greta cautioned me softly. "When the Nazis take over Austria you will see some turn-about when true loyalties begin to come out. Remember, Helena, while Nazism is technically illegal, the climate is not ripe for the discreet sympathizer. But your friends, I'm afraid, will show their true faces."

"No!" I insisted. "I can't believe that people change overnight, that their warmth masks this contempt. How can it be possible? If it were so, then nothing would be real anymore!"

So it was in idyllic Kritzendorf that the truth was to confront us. In Vienna, such drills could not have gone on in the open. Here by the Danube, the so-called underground blatantly prepared for the mastery of all Austria. How strange to see all those brown uniforms bordering the blue river!

By the time we returned to Vienna in the fall, then, the sword of Damocles hung over our heads. The inevitability of Nazi control seemed assured. Our imaginations, however, could not begin to formulate a picture of precisely what this would imply for us.

PART III
The Hitler Era

32

THE YEAR 1938 WAS A PRELUDE NOT ONLY TO THE DESTRUC-tion of European Jews, but also to World War II. Hitler's aim, of course, was to dominate the whole world and to this end he planned and prepared systematically. He believed that Providence had singled him out for this role and he was deter-mined to shape the world according to his will. And everything went according to plan. He now felt powerful enough to begin his expansion. With his propaganda and preparations, it seemed that he could undermine every country. The first to surrender was Austria.

Hitler ordered Chancellor Schuschnigg to Berchtesgaden for a "talk." Schuschnigg complied, believing a discussion would actually follow. But the interview was not to consist of negotia-tions. Schuschnigg received an ultimatum: Hitler demanded that all imprisoned Nazis — including Dolfuss' murderers — were to be given amnesty at once. Also, the Nazi, Seyss-Inquart, was to be made Minister of Interior. Schuschnigg could do nothing but sign these dictated demands and to capitulate under the threat of armed attack. A waning last hope for Mussolini's help now expired completely for Schuschnigg. His expectation of French and English intervention had already been abandoned. Thus he was forced to resign.

We knew from the newspapers and the radio much that was occurring. We also knew that disaster was approaching with

273

quick steps. On the evening of March 11th, Schuschnigg made his last radio speech, and Jim and I listened. He told the Austrian people that he had to yield to force, since Austria was not prepared to shed blood. He took leave of the Austrian people with the words: "God protect Austria." His voice trembled with tears over the air and the sorrow was transmitted to us. Jim and I shed tears, too.

Jim turned gravely to me and said, "So you can see, Helena, that the last illusion is now dispelled. For us, normal life is over. We must now be prepared for the worst."

Even as I brooded over Jim's remarks, the public reaction to Schuschnigg's speech began to resound. Austrian Nazis began to crowd the streets and shout: *"Sieg Heil!"; "Heil Hitler!"; "Judah Perish!"* At first the police appeared to oppose them, but, slowly, even they joined hands with them.

On that same evening of March 11th, I stood before our Staffel-Kino in the Mariahilfer Strasse, dazedly watching a group of Austrian Nazis marching and shouting: *"Sieg Heil! Heil Hitler!"* Behind them, I saw mounted policemen and many pedestrians cheering and giving the Hitler salute. People standing all around me were responding fervently.

Suddenly I looked at the man standing next to me. It was Seidl, one of our most loyal ushers. A swastika glared from his chest and his arm was raised in a salute with the others. I gazed at him with a transfixed horror.

I went into the movie house. The Jewish employees were huddling together in despair, asking each other, "What is going to happen to us now? What is to be done?" We had a feeling that we were all tumbling into an abyss.

Looking around, it suddenly occurred to me that none of our gentile employees were present. No wonder that these who remained looked to me now for some word, some assurance! So Seidl was not unique—all of them had run out on us.

This realization made my knees weak. It was as if the walls and furniture had been conspiring against us all along.

I went home and found that Jim had returned from his office, too. We looked at each other and at Ingrid and Gerda, who seemed nervous from the excitement which they did not yet comprehend.

Ingrid and Gerda were very confused as to exactly what was taking place. For this, Jim and I were grateful. It would be sufficiently clear to them later on. For Jim and me, this day was odious because it spelled defeat and made a mockery of everything we had tried to do for our two daughters.

These considerations left us unnerved, dizzy with insomnia. It ended with the two of us having to take sleeping pills to calm down. As I was finally dropping off to sleep, I said to Jim: "When we wake up in the morning, I hope we discover that we have had a bad dream and find that everything is as it used to be."

But the next day, things became worse. German troops marched into Vienna and passed through the Mariahilfer Strasse, cheering and laughing. We heard and saw everything from our window because we lived on this main street. They sang the Horst Wessel song — "When the Jewish blood flows, everything will be good." "Today Germany belongs to us, tomorrow the whole world!" they chanted in unison.

We trembled as we heard them, their song as ominous as a funeral dirge. Below us, in the street, the Austrian people cheered the Nazis.

And then the Fuehrer was expected in Vienna. The Nazis had made preparations to receive him. Flags were hoisted over the city, particularly in the main streets. Every landlord had to have a flag on his house. The Mariahilfer Strasse, which the Fuehrer and his staff were to pass through, was beautifully decorated. Every three or four yards a white pillar had been erected. These the *Hitlerjugend* (Hitler Youth) had adorned with wreaths of green leaves and topped with a gold swastika. The whole Mariahilfer Strasse was filled with such pillars. Vast banners were stretched across the Mariahilfer Strasse, from streetlamp to streetlamp, bearing three consecutive signs:

"WIR DANKEN UNSEREN FUEHRER" (We thank our Fuehrer)

"EIN VOLK EIN REICH EIN FUEHRER" (One nation one empire one Fuehrer)

"SIEG HEIL"

The unforgettable day came. Austrian gentiles poured into the street. The air was electric with anticipation. Mitzi, our loyal maid, grabbed Ingrid and Gerda, saying, "Let's go downstairs and see our Fuehrer!" And before I could stop them, they were down the stairs to join the throng. Mitzi, completely ignorant of Nazi ideology, was simply caught up in the excitement.

Jim joined me at the window and we watched the spectacle below. People now lined up on both sides of the street. But the Gestapo also did their duty. They were stationed every ten feet, one with his face turned to the street; the next one with his face toward the people, in order to watch closely that nothing might happen to the Fuehrer.

Jim and I stood there and watched it all from behind our closed apartment window. (It was forbidden to open the windows.) As the scene evolved, we saw the symbolic enactment of every shunned fear we had known in recent years. Cars arrived. After a few preceding him, Hitler came, standing, his arm raised for his famous salute. He was like a triumphant hero in this pose, and yet different from any hero in history one could call to mind.

I gazed at him and thought, "It is true what they say of him —he imagines himself superhuman. Anyone can see it! Of course, his luck can't last forever. But God knows which of us will survive to see it end!"

After the parade, Ingrid, Gerda, and Mitzi clambered back

upstairs, thoroughly impressed. My poor girls had not the slightest inkling of what all this meant.

Now I went down into the street. There were still many people about. Everyone seemed so pleased and happy. I walked among them, incredulous still, for they were my countrymen.

"My God!" I thought. "How is it possible that one part of humanity can be so exultant while the other is so deeply unhappy?"

We Jews now knew what to expect. During the first days, the Nazis were busy celebrating their victory. But very soon they began to persecute the Jews. The first step was to round up young and old Jews and Jewesses in the streets or in their homes and force them to scrub the streets and barracks.

Now our family desperately kept contact with each other by telephone. Each of us lived in fear of hearing that some humiliation had been forced upon the other. Stela, my youngest sister, was finally singled out and was made to scrub a barrack.

My father was luckier. He had been sitting in a coffeehouse with his friends, as usual, when a few SA men entered the place and rounded all of them up. One of the SA men turned out to be a former schoolmate of Bernatz's. He recognized my father and sent him home. His friends, however, were taken away.

Hanna's predicament worried me most of all. She seemed so vulnerable, alone in her home with the children. Once, when I arrived at her apartment, I found her trembling. The SS men had just been there, looking for Josef.

"My God!" I breathed, sinking into a chair. "What did you tell them, Hanna?"

Hanna paced the room excitedly. "I lied, Helena. If I had told them he was in jail, they would have gone there directly. So I said that some SA men had picked him up."

"And they let it go at that?"

"Amazingly enough, they did. But why not? There is such chaos in Vienna now. Every uniformed Nazi is like a commander in his own right, choosing prey where he will." She shook her head in wonderment, her hands trembling still.

"If only this will be the end of it. Do you think they'll forget to come back, Hanna?"

"It is possible, Helena. Other Nazis have taken him, they think. Maybe it will be a closed issue. My God, what an irony it would be if Josef's jail sentence should be the thing that saves him!" she said, with burning eyes.

The following week Greta came to see me. She told me how she had been sitting in a coffeehouse in the Neubaugasse when the Nazis invaded the place. Here, too, the Jews were rounded up. One Nazi turned to Greta and asked, "Are you Jewish?" Greta replied that she was. Accordingly, they had treated her as they had the others. All of them were taken to Gestapo headquarters. The male Jews were detained there, but the women were sent home.

"Greta!" I exclaimed. "Why didn't you tell them you are not Jewish — only half Jewish? They would still regard you as a non-Jew if you have Aryan blood."

There was a long pause.

"What is the use of that, Helena? If ever before I have felt part one thing and part another, I now feel I belong entirely to the Jewish people. What do I have in common with these gentiles who commit such inhuman offenses?"

Greta considered what had already transpired in Austria as inhuman. She, like the rest of us, could not have conceived of the atrocities which were to evolve from these first, comparatively benevolent days of Nazi life in Austria.

But the persecution continued constantly, surrounding us always, depicting our despised status in the new order. Jewish stores were smeared with "Judah Perish!" and similar slogans. Nazis seized storekeepers and put signs around their necks which read : "I am a dirty Jew. Don't buy at this store." They forced many Jews to carry these signs and drove them through the streets. Many non-Jews enjoyed this spectacle.

And yet this was only the beginning of the persecution. The Nazis next imposed a fine of several million schillings upon certain Jews who were reported to have given money to Schuschnigg's regime; this fine was to be their punishment. But a terrible blow to all Jews came next : the *Kultusgemeinde* was closed, its high officials sent away to concentration camps. The Jews were now deprived of their last support. Without the *Kultusgemeinde*, they had no representatives who could take care of their affairs. Now, any Nazi might approach a Jew in the street and box his ears or spit in his face. These were not uncommon occurrences. Fiendish Jew-baiting continued. Jews with obviously Semitic faces were the most frequent victims. Then the Nazis came up with a new idea for Jewish persecution. Many Nazi maids accused their masters of "Race Shame." The accused ones were promptly taken to concentrations camps, with no opportunity to defend their innocence.

33

I HAVE INDICATED THAT WE JEWS HAD BEGUN TO ACKNOWL-
edge the real truth of our situation in Austria. Before this, we
had told ourselves that the world would oppose Hitler's
schemes. And our hopes, our wildest illusions were tenaciously
held until the last day before the Nazis took over the country.
Only then did illusion yield to despair. And in this state a
number of Jews committed suicide, choosing death as an escape
from Nazi inhumanity. Perhaps their helplessness was the most
demoralizing factor. How could the Jews, individuals singled
out here and there, stand up heroically against the Nazis and
defend themselves when even the Austrian regime with its
army had yielded to Hitler?

Now the Jewish cemetery was crowded as never before.
Since my mother's death, it had been my habit to visit her
grave and that of my brother Abram regularly, once a month.
I had always left the scene with a sense of tranquility. Now in
these times of duress, I found myself seeking out the cemetery
with frequency. It was customary among certain Jews to pray
at the grave of a beloved one, or else at the grave of a rabbi,
seeking God's help in times of danger. I believed that the pure
soul of my mother rested now among the souls of our great
Patriarchs, as was indicated in the *Yiskor* (memorial) prayers.

Standing by my mother's grave, dimly aware of many others
kneeling or standing by other graves, I prayed for our salvation

from the Nazi nightmare, prayed for the survival of my children, of my people. I did not really see how this salvation could come about, but I prayed and hoped.

Often, as I walked through the cemetery, I witnessed tragic scenes. I saw funerals of the suicides and heard the lamentations of their survivors. But the most heartbreaking scene there took place when four coffins were carried to two open graves. In one of the coffins, a six-year-old child had been placed with its mother. This whole family had committed suicide after suffering Nazi maltreatment.

At this point, our financial situation grew worse from day to day. Since Klaus had taken over full control of the Steffel-Kino, we no longer received a penny from that place. The only thing sustaining us now was Jim's salary from Universal—a godsend, we felt, because it was derived from an American company. But this fact proved unimportant to the Nazis.

One day an SA man who was known as an inferior supernumerary appeared at the office of Universal, turned Jim out, and took over his job on the spot. Nazis were doing this everywhere; this much we knew. It was a matter of indifference to them if any Jew starved to death for lack of income. But with Universal being American, we had hoped they would not dare. We had hoped in vain.

Now we were left without income or money. There remained only one valuable which I had not pawned—Jim's old-fashioned gold watch.

We were reduced to selling our pawn tickets. One of my neighbors, who had always been on friendly terms with us, bought up all the pawntickets for a fraction of their worth. Word must have gotten around in the neighborhood: the Hilsens are getting desperate for money, they have a few beautiful things. Other neighbors soon came to the apartment, bargain-hunting. The women picked up things that they liked —pieces of silver, crystal, and china. They bought them for a pittance. But even at that we were lucky to have customers. It was strange that these women, so familiar to us, had never before appeared to us as Nazis. Now, without exception, they wore swastika badges.

It was also part of the Nazi program to take over all Jewish businesses and property. They appointed a commissioner for every Jewish shop. He took charge of all the property belonging to that particular Jew, but he did not give him any money to live on. If a Nazi commissioner wanted to take over a Jewish business, he sent the owner to the concentration camp Dachau.

Jim turned over the Steffel-Kino to Mr. Klaus immediately, according to our agreement. Klaus, it was now revealed, had been a Nazi all along and he now refused to give us any money from the movie. And contrary to our original arrangement with him, he now became not technically but literally the owner of our property. As for that little clause which we had so naïvely believed would sustain us if these circumstances should ever come into being, it might as well have never been made part of the contract. Klaus, even if he had wanted to, was powerless to give us a penny now, for the new Nazi law forbade it. Under the circumstances, we were fortunate that Klaus was well-disposed toward us in general. For he had it in his power to send us off to a concentration camp at any time he might wish to.

The Nazis were relentless in investigating Jewish property which had been given over to the control of a Nazi commissioner. They made every detail of the transaction their business.

One day, two SS men came to our apartment looking for Jim. Mitzi and the girls were at home. Jim, Dr. Westheimer, and I were at a nearby park. The SS men looked under the beds and in closets, thinking that Jim had hidden himself. Loyal Mitzi was indignant.

"Herr Hilsen has not committed a crime that he must hide!" she remarked.

She sent Ingrid out to the park to fetch us home. I was afraid to let Jim go and insisted on going home alone instead. At the apartment, I asked the SS men what they wanted. They ordered Jim to appear at the Steffel-Kino within an hour to show them the papers which would confirm the fact that we had relinquished all rights to the property. Complying with the order, Jim was able to show them sufficient evidence of what they wanted; they let him go home, saying, as he left, that they would confirm all this with Klaus. Klaus must have corroborated all that Jim explained, since we were not disturbed again about this particular matter.

Olga was less fortunate. Right after the Nazis had occupied Austria, Mr. Borwitz, our gentile friend from Semmering went to the Stadt-Kino, presented himself to Olga, and announced that he was now the commissioner of the theater. Borwitz ordered Olga to hand over certain past profits to him. This she promptly refused to do. She explained that the little bit of money which she had taken, long before the Nazi occupation, from this dwindling enterprise, was barely enough to provide food for her children and her paralyzed husband. When she persisted in her refusal to yield the money, Borwitz threatened to have Olga sent to a concentration camp.

In desperation, she sought out Jim. He knew Borwitz. Had they not had, at one time, a certain rapport, a certain friendship? Olga was beside herself. If she were sent to a concentration camp, not only her children but Friedrich, so cruelly invalided, would be left starving. Thus Jim approached Borwitz and somehow the man, who had always liked us, was touched by his appeal. He would abstain from sending Mrs. Landes to a concentration camp, and would permit her to keep the sum in dispute. We wilted with relief.

But this brush with disaster was enough to galvanize Olga

into determined action. She was the first of us to act quickly to save her children before it was too late. Olga composed a desperate letter to Friedrich's uncle, the Chief Rabbi of Johannesburg, begging him to send a permit for Eddie which would enable him to leave Vienna. At the same time she wrote to Friedrich's relatives in England, describing the grave situation and asking them to take Helga.

These letters to relatives in other, safer places were the first steps that any of us could take. The relatives were the most obvious source of sympathy and possible salvation.

Bernatz, too, had penned such a letter shortly after the Nazi occupation. He wrote to our brother Saul, in America, asking him to send affidavits, to save as many of his family as he could. Unfortunately, Saul had not prospered in the New World, which his fiancée had made to seem so glittering for him. He worked in Brooklyn as a baker and earned only enough to support himself. His marriage had dissolved after one year when he and his bride, who had married for expediency, discovered that they were most incompatible. Thus, Saul, though urgently desiring to help Bernatz and the rest of us, was not able to do it alone. Other letters had to be written. But who was left? Although we had other relatives in America, there was only one, besides Saul, with whom we had maintained a correspondence over the years. This was my father's brother, Henoch, who, when I was a child in Przemysl, had emigrated to America. Like Saul, Uncle Henoch was far from being rich. He managed to make a modest living for his wife and children by working as a machine operator in a slacks factory. His eldest son, Harry, however, knew and cultivated more prosperous relatives. Eventually, they helped Saul to get some affidavits.

They succeeded in sending three, for Bernatz, George, and young Addie. What rejoicing these affidavits caused! Every affidavit meant the life of a member of the family saved.

Shortly after Bernatz had received his affidavit, he paid me a visit. At that particular hour, Jim was out in the park with the children. I was delighted to see my brother.

"I wish I could offer you a *Sachertorte,* Bernatz," I said wistfully, "as in the good days. . . ."

Bernatz sighed, and took a seat. "Yes, Helena. Those days when all we had to think about in a morning was a good piece of cake and pleasant conversation are gone. But we mustn't lose our heads by giving into despair. All clarity can vanish if this happens. Now we have to do something to save ourselves!" he concluded ardently.

In his speech Bernatz was as vibrant, as compelling as ever. The charm which had won over so many women was still in force, even in these dark days. I smiled to myself wearily.

"Clarity, Bernatz? Save ourselves? Come now, who is being unrealistic? To whom can we turn for affidavits now? Saul has exhausted the only possibilities. You know there is no chance for any one of the rest of us to get one!"

"Even so," he said, rising, "tell me this. Have you gone to the United States consulate to register for a visa?"

"Why—why, no . . . but what earthly good would a visa do one without an affidavit, Bernatz?"

Now Bernatz took my hands firmly in his.

"Listen to me, Helena," he said. "Go immediately to the consulate and register. It can't harm you to do so, and to fail to do so may prove fatal. How can you be certain? Maybe you will get an affidavit somehow, but without registration, you would be lacking the visa! So many Jews have registered there. You must do the same. I insist!"

"Bernatz . . ." I began to protest again.

"Helena, you will go right away. Now, so that I can see you leaving. There will be a long waiting list for the quota as it is, and every minute counts."

So under pressure from Bernatz, I dressed hastily and rushed to the American consulate. There was a long line waiting for registration. I waited my turn and received my registration card. The date was April 28, 1938. And as fate was to design it, Bernatz's visit and talk had come like a miracle, impelling my action on that day. For one day later would have been too late.

This was because Jim and I, although Austrian citizens, belonged to the Polish quota, having been born in that country. This was the case of many Jews in Vienna who had escaped from Galicia during World War I and had, like us, remained here. Thus the number of people registering for the Polish quota was tremendous, and, to complicate matters, the Polish quota was a small one compared to those for other countries. Those who registered first had the best chance of getting out of Austria. And there had already been a multitude preceding me in the one month since Hitler had occupied the country. My registration date was April 28th. And the people who had registered from March through this date were to be spread over a period of two years, to receive their visas. At the close of the day on April 28th, the quota for that year was exhausted, and the people registering on April 29th would have to wait one year more than we (by which time the war was to be in progress, with all communications and travel cut off).

My next visit from Bernatz was his farewell visit, but it was not for the departure we had all been anticipating. He had discovered that there was a tremendous waiting list and that it would take at least a year or two before he would be able to get his visa for America.

"Let us face the truth," he said. "A year or two are ideas that have no meaning for us Jews anymore, in terms of waiting. Every new hour can prove fatal for any one of us. Helena, I have decided not to wait!"

Bernatz had decided to go with friends to Cologne and to try to pass across the border into Belgium. He left in May.

34

THERE CAME A SUDDEN GLEAM OF HOPE FOR THE JEWS IN these sinister days. The President of the United States had proposed a conference of the representatives of all European and American countries. They were to discuss the possibilities of helping the Jews by receiving them in different countries. This conference, which was to take place in Evian, was scheduled for July. But it was spring when we learned of it, and there would be a long wait before we would learn the result of their talks. We were afraid it might turn out unfavorably.

Meanwhile, each day brought new measures against the Jews in Austria. A Jew was no longer permitted to keep a gentile maid. This applied, of course, to our Mitzi, who had been with us for five years. Ingrid and Gerda adored her, and Mitzi was so much a part of our household now that she seemed more like a relative than a servant. With tears in her eyes, she made her farewell at the door, where two modest valises stood. I watched as the girls sprang to embrace her, thinking, "We would have had to let go anyway, now. There's not enough to pay her wages."

Jewish children were now forbidden to attend their regular classes, lest they contaminate the "Aryan" children by sitting next to them. They were transferred to Jewish schools.

When I brought Gerda to her new school, she cried bitterly

in her new surroundings. She had loved her former teacher and her friends in the old school. Everything here was foreign to her. I struggled with tears myself on that day—not because the school was exclusively Jewish, but because this segregating action was designed to humiliate children like Gerda to show them they were a breed inferior to the "Aryan" one. Fortunately, the children adjusted quickly and made new friends. Indeed, the adaptability of my girls proved a blessing in these times, as did their extreme youth, which made the truth of our situation incomprehensible to both of them. Ingrid, for example, now eleven, still maintained the carefree disposition of her former years. She had a best friend, Marianne Selinger, who consumed much of her time. Together they shared a boyfriend, Herbert Hahn, who was fourteen. This trio stuck together constantly and, while the Nazis tightened the net over Viennese Jewry, they were concerned only with the subtleties of their mutual romance.

They met sometimes in our apartment, sometimes at the Selingers', and occasionally in the park. Gerda yearned to join them, but they rejected her as being still a child. She resented this quite a bit. Once in a while, therefore, they made a concession and took her along to the park with them.

On one such occasion, the four of them returned, flushed and excited, and burst into our apartment. They told us that a man in a uniform which people call SA had approached them.

"Are you Jewish?" he had demanded to know.

The children had, of course, said yes. And promptly they had been turned out of the park.

"Why did he make us leave, Mother?" asked Gerda. "We were playing nicely."

"It was when we told him we were Jewish that he made us go," Ingrid reflected. "Daddy, why did he ask us if we were Jewish?"

Poor children! They still did not realize the gravity of our situation. Even when we told them things outright, they were not able to comprehend them. Perhaps it was because the souls of children are too simple to grasp such diabolical deviousness as the Nazis could perform. And how could I, their mother, begin to explain Hitler's theory that the Jews were an inferior race and expect them to understand it? I do not really remember what I told them on that particular day. I only recall it as their final visit to the park which was so much a part of their lives.

Not only parks were closed to Jews now, but the mere privilege of sitting on a bench in the Ringstrasse was prohibited. Movies and other entertainments were also forbidden. But we were little concerned with pleasure at this time. Survival was foremost in our thoughts.

Jim was now a man without occupation. Since he could not stay at home all day, he often went out. I was uneasy every time he set foot outside the door.

One day, he failed to return at the expected time. As the minutes passed, I grew anxious. The possibilities of being *taken,* simply taken off the streets and condemned to some camp were now great in Vienna. My fears took a dozen forms.

At last he limped into the doorway. His leg was hideously swollen. My hand flew to my mouth, and he cast his eyes down.

"It's not the end, Helena. I am home, at least," he said.

Without looking directly at me, he told me that the Nazis had chased Jews in the street where he was walking. He had started to run in order to escape, had fallen and injured his leg. Fortunately, he had succeeded in escaping. After five minutes at home, however, he discovered that he was unable to walk and we had to call a doctor. Jim still had a right to hospitalization, but the Jewish doctors had all been dismissed. We looked through the list of non-Jewish physicians and found

one who had an oddly Jewish name—Schoenberg. I phoned
him and asked if he would come to treat Jim.

When Dr. Schoenberg arrived, the first thing we noticed
about him was the large swastika band on his sleeve. He went
about his business pleasantly, however, and after a thorough
examination of Jim's leg pronounced it broken. Jim had to
wear a cast for several weeks. This accident and the accidental
choice of Dr. Schoenberg were acts of Providence, I am now
convinced, for they were to save us from future disaster.

Only much later did Jim reveal to me the true cause of his
broken leg. As he had stepped out of our building that morning,
he had been seized by two SS men who demanded to know
if he had been manager at Universal Pictures. Jim told them
he had been. They took him into a house and threw him down
a flight of stairs to the cellar. He remained there, in agony
with his broken leg, lying in total darkness. Later the SS men
picked him up and took him to the Gestapo office where he
was questioned by others as well. Jim was accused of having
shown the movie *All Quiet on the Western Front,* Erich Maria
Remarque's story, which was banned by the Nazis. Jim
explained that at the time this picture was run, another man
had been manager at Universal. By a wild coincidence, one
of the SS men present had known Raab, knew Jim's statement
to be true, and confirmed it. As a result, he was released and
sent home. This was still another remarkable escape from the
axe's edge.

35

DURING THESE FIRST MONTHS OF HEIGHTENING DESPERATION, when a typical Jewish family lost first its life's savings, next its weekly income, and finally was reduced to the search daily for bread, the *Kultusgemeinde,* with the help of the American Joint Distribution Committee and Hias, reopened. They established and opened community kitchens where needy Jews could receive cooked food to take home. Unfortunately, nearly all the Jews were needy by now, the formerly rich as pauperized as the humble. We had been systematically robbed into a state of starvation. The Nazis were completely indifferent to the fact that we had been stripped of all means of survival. They did not care! How often did I ponder that phenomenon? Would I ever grow old enough to comprehend their behavior?

For me, as for the others, the time came when there was no longer enough food to set the table, and I went to the kitchen, which was annexed to our synagogue, to attend in line. This was a terrible feeling, like a bad joke, at first, giving me the sensations of both unreality and protest simultaneously. I was violently embarrassed at first whenever I met an acquaintance of mine as I stood in line. Often, she, too, having been well off in former times, was ashamed to see me. None of us was used to this role yet, was willing to grasp its full implications. But in time, I, with the rest, adapted myself to standing in line for free food. I was beginning to discover a power of adaptation in all of us which I could never have believed possible.

Jim had discouraged me from thinking about the food line too much.

"It is not the worst thing that has happened to us, Helena. We must pray to God that nothing worse occurs."

But serving the food I had brought from the kitchen was still another matter. Ingrid and Gerda watched me dish it out into their plates and uttered not a word at first. But both withdrew from it with distinct aversion. It had about it the smell of institutional cooking. Both refused to touch it—and no wonder! They were not used to that kind of food. After much coaxing from Jim and me, they swallowed it with tears in their eyes.

Those meals were a misery. The poor children had now begun to realize how serious our situation had become. First, they had been abruptly ejected from their schools; then they had been turned out of their beloved park; their parents had become tense and thin and altogether different, and now even food was no longer to be taken for granted. Yes, for Ingrid and Gerda the times were clearly spelled out now. They had been singled out, were despised, deprived, and belonged to two haunted-looking people. So it was with Jewish families.

When Jews met their friends these days, they tried to console each other with rumors that Hitler had cancer in his throat, that he was expected to die any day, which would of course result in a coup that would restore the Jewish status quo. I suppose that most of us knew this was wishful thinking.

Less fantastic, however, was the hope we had pinned to the conference scheduled at Evian, France, which was to take place in July. This conference, whose purpose was to resolve the Jewish refugee problem by finding specific countries to receive them, had been in the back of our minds for months, like something in reserve to keep us going.

As the actual date of the conference approached, I grew quite optimistic and was constantly speaking of it to Jim.

"Just think," I said, "of what a great reversal could come from this conference. If the free countries—and God knows there are so many!—really open their doors to us, everything would be different. It would be like a statement from them refusing to condone Hitler's immorality."

"A statement, yes. But will they make such a statement Helena?" Jim asked quietly, with a remote despair in his expression.

"They must!" I replied.

"Why?"

"Because it's implicit that a democracy behave in this manner!" I answered ardently, but his doubt of the conference's outcome had only mirrored some secret misgivings of my own. I turned my face slightly and Jim rose.

"Look, Helena. What you say is true. Humane behavior may reasonably be expected from democracies meeting to discuss a group needing rescue. Only, don't have such certainty, dear! We just don't know how far they'll go or what, if anything, they'll do. If it should somehow fail. . . ."

"Oh God," I protested, "it simply can't fail!"

And yet, the Evian Conference turned out to be a fiasco. With a kind of numb horror, we read accounts of it in the Nazi newspapers on July 8th, which delightedly scoffed at the conference and were pleased to be able to inform their readers that *no* country wanted to receive the Jews. At once, there was a wholesale lowering of spirits among Viennese Jews. A sense of betrayal tore at us. How could they be so indifferent? Was it to appease Hitler, or to avoid offending him by showing sympathy toward the Jews? It seemed incredible; yet what else could one make of it? Only one thing remained clear. We realized we were aboard a sinking ship and that everyone who could should save himself.

Almost everybody tried to go abroad. Many succeeded in passing across the Czechoslovakian border.

The separation of Jewish husbands and wives was now a common thing. The separation of Jewish children from their parents occurred everywhere. When any individual had a chance to leave Vienna, he usually left, for it meant he might survive. Or if there was an order for someone to leave, cutting him off from his whole family, he of course had no choice but to obey it.

Such was the case with our friend, Erich Schelman. He came to our apartment and showed us his order to leave Austria within two days. This order was typical of the diabolical Nazi commands we Jews received daily. While Erich was ordered to leave Vienna, he was at the same time not permitted to leave it, having no papers to get out with, and having no country which would receive him.

Thus Erich, like others trapped in this mad contradiction, made hasty plans to take the only course left to him for survival: he would attempt to leave Austria by slipping over the border illegally to France. Greta would now be left behind with seventeen-year-old Kurt. Kurt had been one of the lucky ones. Through his girlfriend, he had acquired an affidavit to America and, having been born in Vienna, stood a good chance of leaving within a short time.

Erich's departure was swift. With mumbled and unreal words, he took leave of Greta, his divorced wife who never left him, of Kurt, the pride of his own defeated life. Stoically, Greta helped him prepare to go. If he remained, he would be killed.

As soon as he left, Greta gave up their apartment and moved in with us, bringing Kurt with her. They occupied the living room. Soon afterward, Kurt left for America. Greta rejoiced and we wept tears of joy with her. One among us went to certain safety.

With her son gone, Greta grew restless. But she was deeply involved with us now, since she was living in our home. Jim's leg was still in a cast, and his health seemed generally to decline with the injury. Greta saw the way things were with the four of us : we were trapped in Vienna. But I, in turn, was sensitive to Greta and saw the desire to leave form within her. She said nothing at first, but rather threw herself in deeper with us, helping me serve Jim, trying to amuse the girls. Finally, I approached her.

"Greta, if you can think of a way to save yourself, then do so. There is nothing to keep you here now, with Kurt gone."

"Nothing to keep me here! But how can I leave you with a sick husband and two children? If only you had someone who was arranging something for all of you. As it is . . ."

I grasped her shoulders. "Greta, I haven't given up hope yet. Not every stone is yet turned for us. But meanwhile, you are one person. And one alone travels easiest. Take your opportunity while you can. You will see—both your family and mine will be out of Austria soon, and whoever is in the best position to help the other then will do so!"

We wept bitterly during that conversation, feeling at every point that a seeming truth was in fact a lie. Nevertheless, Greta left for France, illegally, two weeks later.

Then came an order from the Gestapo that all Jews who were Polish citizens and who had visas must leave at once; those without visas who were unable to get one were put into a concentration camp. This order did not apply to us, for we were Austrian citizens.

My friend Helka, however, was a Polish citizen and did get a visa for herself and her daughter. We were immensely pleased for her. This meant she could finally be reunited with her husband in Warsaw. And with what enthusiasm did she anticipate her departure! She seemed to forget entirely the forlorn parade of lovers who had substituted for the remote husband all these years. Suddenly, linked with the idea of safety, he became the most desirable man on the face of the earth for Helka. Her only regret was that she must leave her parents behind in terrorized Vienna.

One by one our friends were leaving us behind. And always for a new reason. Now many men received an order from the Gestapo to leave Austria within a few days or be sent to a concentration camp. But this order contained its special quali-fication. In order to leave, it was necessary to have a valid passport and a permit to enter a foreign country. To receive a passport, you had to possess a certificate saying that you had paid all your taxes. This the Gestapo blithely demanded, knowing full well that the Jews had been robbed of their means. Most of this group, therefore, was unable to pay the taxes which would have yielded them a passport. Some of them passed the borders illegally at terrible risk.

Any Jew who had relatives in the United States frantically cabled asking for affidavits. It was the happiest of all solutions to receive such an affidavit and to be able to emigrate to America.

The Jews in Poland, as yet untouched by the Nazis, and having not the slightest premonition of what lay ahead for Poland, were now in a position to pity us Austrian Jews. Letters from worried Polish relatives poured into Vienna, expressing anxiety for their dear ones. Among these letters were those from Jim's family in Lwow and from Sala Brand. Jim's family wanted to know if we were all right, if they could help us in any way. The news had obviously terrified them. But after considering our answer carefully, Jim and I decided simply to tell them that we were all right. As for help, they were power-less to help us and we realized it. Our letters consequently glided over the worst facts in order to make them feel better.

Sala Brand was terrified now about the well-being of her son Addie. It struck her as a terrible irony that she had sent her boy to Vienna so that he would have security and happiness, only to find him trapped where his life was in danger every day. Her letters were full of despair. To me she wrote saying that she wanted Addie to come home to Lwow, where he would be safe. I answered her at once, telling her that Addie had an affidavit which would enable him to go to America (certainly a safer spot than any country in Europe!). Unfortunately, I advised her, he would have to wait for his quota, since he had been born in Lwow. In her next letter, Sala confided to me that she had written a letter to Mrs. Eleanor Roosevelt, who, she knew from reading, was a great humanitarian. Her letter had been penned from the point of view of one mother to another. Sala had described her suffering at the time of Addie's birth, the sorrow of raising the boy without a father, and she asked Mrs. Roosevelt to help save this dearest son of hers. Sala specifically requested that Mrs. Roosevelt obtain a visa for Addie, so that he would not have to wait for his quota. Later, I heard from Sala again. She had received a very sympathetic answer from Mrs. Roosevelt. Unfortunately, she had advised her that it was not within her power to change the law about quotas, as much as she wished it were. She would have liked to save not only Addie, but thousands like him. Probably, Mrs. Roosevelt had been bombarded with such requests constantly.

36

THE OUTCOME OF THE EVIAN CONFERENCE STRENGTHENED THE
Nazi position in their treatment of Jews. Obviously, the Jews
were, as they claimed, an inferior race which should be dis-
posed of; otherwise, why had no country made arrangements
to receive them? The indifference of other countries to the
Jewish plight made the Nazis feel justified not only about past
actions, but new ones as well.

They indicated this by imposing on us even greater pressure
than before and new persecutions. But now it was literally
broadcast. The air reverberated and trembled with pronouncements of hate. They put loudspeakers on all the main streets in
Vienna and ordered the Austrians to listen to them. In the
OpernRing near the Vienna Opera, one such loudspeaker had
been erected.

Jim and I stood there one evening and heard speeches by
Hitler and Goebbels. A large crowd had gathered to hear the
malignant accusations against Jews, and the bloodcurdling
promises.

"I always keep my promise," Hitler advised them. "And I
have promised to wipe out the Jews."

Like trapped rats, we stood there, watching the intent faces
of our countrymen as the speech went on. Jim, leaning on his
crutches, shook violently. I grasped his arm to steady him, only
to find I needed support myself.

Now the words had been said. Evasion was a thing of the past with the Nazis. Annihilation was their goal and they announced it for all of us to hear.

It is no wonder that a new wave of suicides broke out among the Jews. All hope for survival seemed gone.

Since the night of the speeches, I had noticed a new and marked decline in Jim's spirit. He who had always been so active and orderly had become progressively more demoralized as the weeks passed, and his leg remained in the cast. Since the Jewish crisis had been mounting simultaneously, it was almost as if the cast on his leg became symbolical for him; it was a token of our paralyzed condition, of our helplessness to fight back or even to run away. His health seemed poor now. Often he had chills, as though running a fever, but without other symptoms.

The day after Hitler's speech rang out on the OpernRing, Jim caught my hand as I walked past him in the living room and held me to the spot.

"Helena," he muttered distractedly. "There isn't a chance for us to leave this hell. Why wait till they kill us? Should we not, as others have, take our lives?"

I sprang at him and screamed.

"Have you gone mad? Kill our children? Did you suppose we could kill ourselves and leave them behind for the Nazis? Oh, no, Jim. It's not that simple!"

Probably, I did not take him seriously at that time or I could not have maintained my own strength. But his words, his physical attitude, finally made me realize that Jim had lost his nerve. Sometime between the day he had been thrown down a flight of stairs to a filthy cellar and the night of Hitler's promise to exterminate us all, his core of courage had broken. Futility began to claim him and because I loved him so, because our daughters needed him to have nerve now, I determined that he should find it again and with my help.

For one thing, the violence of my reaction to his words had alarmed Jim. My scream had frightened him, bringing him close to familiar things again, to concern for me, for what I was thinking.

I wept hysterically, grateful perhaps that he had given me legitimate cause. I felt that I had stored up these tears for years on end.

Later, I sat beside him, thinking out loud, examining our problem. "Above all, we must not give ourselves over to desperation as we did today," I stated emphatically. "Somehow, I'm convinced that there is a source of help as yet untapped. You know that I've registered with the U.S. consulate. Now this was a very important step, Jim. If you could only think of somebody we could write to and ask for an affidavit!"

"But Helena, dear Helena, you know quite well that I have no relatives there. Saul, your brother, has always been the only one. . . ."

"Saul! Didn't I tell you that, in addition to George, Bernatz, and Addie, Saul got Leon and his family an affidavit through some relatives of Harry's?"

Jim groaned. Another door closed.

"But Jim," I continued eagerly. "You miss the point of this. The fact is that none of these gave up. They didn't give in and they kept trying!"

"That's all fine . . . but with whom can one try at this point?" he demanded.

I leaned forward eagerly. "Think of somebody from Universal you could write to, Jim!" I offered.

There was a long silence. Jim closed his eyes and rubbed his forehead.

"Look," he breathed softly, at last. "Maybe there is someone. I have one idea. You remember Joe Pasternak, of course?"

I nodded.

"Well he's in Hollywood, now. I knew him only briefly when he was here in Vienna, but he seemed an awfully decent man. The Raabs spent a few good evenings with Pasternak, remember?"

"Yes, Jim."

"I'm quite sure Pasternak would remember me if I wrote," he speculated.

"Then do write, for God's sake, Jim!" I begged, rising. "He surely will understand our situation and help us."

"He may," Jim considered, "have already been besieged with such requests. . . ."

"Never mind. You must try at least."

So Jim wrote to Pasternak and we waited breathlessly for his answer. He wrote immediately, sending very sincere regrets that he would be unable to supply us with affidavits, since he had already done so for a number of his relatives and close friends in Austria and was not able to provide any more.

"We should have known he'd of course take care of his nearest and dearest," Jim said. I saw his posture droop and I almost shouted.

"Never mind! How were we to know for certain he had relatives here? It was worth a try—anything is. That's all we've got now! Pasternak probably felt terrible. He was an awfully nice man. You can see from his letter how much he would have liked to say yes."

"I'll agree to that," Jim said. "He was a good kind of man."

But now, with no letter to anticipate, our situation remained ominously unchanged, and each day heightened our danger.

On one of my sleepless nights, an idea struck me. Why not ask the vice-president of Universal Pictures, Mr. Seidelman, to send us affidavits? But no. Jim did not know Seidelman, for he had started to work for the company shortly before Hitler had invaded Austria. I also knew that Jim would never permit me to trouble him with our problem. Jim had such stubborn pride when it came to bothering strangers! But, without telling him, I contacted Mr. Schiller in Prague, who did know Seidelman, and I described our desperate situation. I asked him if he would please write to Mr. Seidelman requesting that he help us and send the necessary papers.

Before long, I received an answer from Prague. Mr. Schiller had forwarded my letter to the United States. He was sure that Mr. Seidelman would find a way to help us. And he was right. Shortly thereafter, we received a letter from Mr. Seidelman, stating that he was willing to do everything to help us. Two weeks later we were notified by the American consulate that our affidavits had arrived.

This was the first happy day for us since Hitler had occupied Austria. This was our first hope of actually being saved from Hitler's hell. It would be impossible to describe the gratitude we felt toward Mr. Seidelman. Ingrid and Gerda, elated at seeing their weary parents happy again, spoke ecstatically of going to America, of fleeing from these bad men, the Nazis.

But things did not work out as fast as we expected them to. We had hoped that we would be able to leave for the United States as soon as the necessary papers had arrived. But many people had registered at the American consulate and the quotas were very quickly exhausted — especially the Polish quota, to which we belonged. People besieged the American consulate in order to learn when their turn would come. This was the reason they finally closed the consulate. A sign was posted on the door on which all quotas, the registration days, and date of issue of the visas were written.

I nearly fainted when I read that it would be two whole long years. But Jim and I consoled one another, saying that some relief might come for our quota. And as disappointed as we were, Jim and I were among the happier people, because we had some hope—however remote—of leaving the country.

37

DURING THESE DAYS, WHEN ANY NAZI IN UNIFORM COULD SEIZE a Jew from any place and do whatever he liked with him, we walked in constant fear. We were the hunted, although we lived in the open still, like others. And there were contradictions in the situation. Although we could not have imagined it worse than it was at the moment, worse indeed was yet to come. Mass annihilation was not yet set into motion; rather, these early days betokened tragedy on an individual level. Hitler was not yet at his boldest and so attempts were made at this time by some to save those whose destinies could still be salvaged.

Thus the *Kultusgemeinde,* with the help of the Hias, set up a number of different courses of study to be undertaken by Jews who had the possibility of going to the United States. These courses taught various trades so that one might be self-sufficient upon arrival in America and not be a burden to those who had sponsored his affidavit.

After talking it over with Jim, I decided to enroll in a course with my sister Mela. It was a study of corsetry. I attended classes faithfully and followed the teacher's instructions to the letter. How annoying I might have found this at another, earlier phase of life in Vienna! Now, the thought that this trade was linked with the idea of escape endeared it to me. I would become a corsetier. For what other occupation would I be suited in America? And what of Jim? To what purpose

could his former talents be put in that new land? Would anyone care about his abilities? Indeed, when I thought of his
increasing spinal pain, of his chronic depressions, a faintness
came into my chest which I fought only by blocking out these
thoughts and working hard at anything.

The Palestine Office rented an old castle in Upper Austria,
called Schloss Thalheim, from its owner, and there founded
Hachshara, a vast farm where Jewish youth was taught agri-
culture, in preparation for a future in Palestine. Many young
girls and boys joined this group joyously. The project provided
a temporary escape from the ambience of Nazism and re-estab-
lished, while they were there, the illusion of normalcy. It is
difficult to realize that the Nazis permitted *Hachshara* to be
opened and maintained. Its leaders were, in fact, in constant
fear that the Gestapo would intervene at any time and dissolve
their efforts. But the children adhered to the atmosphere,
which was one of constructive optimism. They worked terribly
hard there, but none seemed to mind it. All spoke of going to
the Promised Land as their dearest wish. And so isolated was
this preparatory farm that, visiting them, one almost felt that
they were already there, away from Nazi pressure. In the evenings, they sang and danced the *horah* in high Jewish spirits
and enjoyed one another. Inevitably, some romances grew
out of this situation at Schloss Thalheim. And one of those
romances involved young Addie, who was working there. Now
seventeen, he fell in love with a girl who was part of his group.
Their dream was to go to Palestine, to marry, and to live in
simplicity and freedom there.

The question of departure from Austria for these young
people was at all times paramount. The *Hachshara* was under
the guidance of experienced people from the Palestine office.
Those people took care of organizing groups of boys and girls
and sending them to Palestine. However, England, which was
then the mandatory of Palestine, allowed only a certain quota

of these youngsters into Palestine. Here, too, unfortunately, the merciless quota system barred their way, preventing many Jewish youths from being saved. For those left behind, the claws of the Hitler Moloch awaited — a Moloch who seemed insatiable, everlastingly craving more victims.

Nevertheless, the boys and girls were optimistic. Each believed in his own salvation. When the preparation period on the farm was completed, the quota was first filled up, and those who remained outside of it were divided up. A few of these were sent illegally. The rest were sent to Holland, from where they hoped eventually to embark for Palestine to join those who had preceded them.

Addie did not make the quota. He learned this with an especially sinking heart, since his girl had been included and they were to be separated. He was sent to Holland.

But all of us were glad that Addie was going to Holland. I, who had felt so badly when his mother's letters beseeched me for news, now felt relieved. He would at least be out of Austria. Only that seemed to matter now.

Hanna had joined *Hachshara* for the duration, and cooked meals for seventy persons. My sister had always worked hard for causes she believed in, and now she exhausted herself serving these young people. To prepare such enormous quantities of food, to mix such immense containers of soup, was only part of her day. At night, she helped to organize the dancing group and helped lead the singing.

When Hanna came home one weekend, she described the set-up to me.

"My God! How can you do it, Hanna? Where do you find the strength, day after day?" I asked.

"I am happy in these surroundings, Helena — happier than I have been for sometime. The work keeps me occupied and it is good wholesome work. It gives me little time to think about myself. I had reached the point where looking backward was impossible and looking ahead a mystery, perhaps a nightmare. Here I think from moment to moment. From meal to activity. It is good for me and it is good that I help the young people."

Her daughter Esther, now twenty-one, took care of the two younger brothers while Hanna was thus employed. Esther, like many her age, went to the *Kultusgemeinde* and learned that England was admitting women up to the age of forty-five into the country as housekeepers. Esther procured the address of Bloomsburyhouse, the committee in London which took care of Jewish people who wanted to come to England as domestics. Having decided to take this course of action for herself, she wrote to this place and waited for an answer. George, who had an affidavit to America, was waiting for his quota. Fortunately, his wait was not a long one.

Right after Esther had written to England, Olga received an answer from the Chief Rabbi in Johannesburg and simultaneously heard from the relatives in England. At first, because she could not really visualize her children's departure, she was overjoyed. There was good news from both sources. The Cottons, Friedrich's relatives in Birmingham, had agreed to take Helga and had enclosed the permit for her in their letter. From Johannesburg came word that arrangements were being made with haste for Eddie and that Olga should await confirmation.

So Olga's little Helga was the first of the young children to leave us. Once Olga had found relief in the news that her daughter would be saved, she now had to find the heart to relinquish her. I tried to identify myself with Olga in my thoughts, thinking with emotion of having to send off one or both of my girls. I did not know how I could stand it. But I said none of this to Olga. The rational must prevail now, and the rational insisted on survival.

I accompanied Olga to see Helga off. Olga was trembling visibly but tried to control herself so as not to upset her daughter when the moment came to say goodbye. Helga, only an eight-year-old child, did not comprehend the gravity of the situation, or its strangeness. At the station, she took me aside and whispered, "Try to console my mother and father, please, Auntie!" She was excited about the trip and was not afraid to leave.

"I will tell everybody in England what bad people the Nazis are and how they are treating us," she said to Olga. "Please don't worry, Mother. The English people are good. They will help us all!"

Olga, choking on tears when the train was at last out of sight, clutched my arm as we walked away.

"The pain of seeing her go—but with it all, I'm lucky, Helena, lucky to send her where she'll be safe! Now I won't rest until Eddie leaves Vienna, too."

Olga did not have long to wait for this second departure. Two weeks later, she received another communication from the Chief Rabbi of Johannesburg. He had decided to "adopt" Eddie in order to be able to bring him to Johannesburg at once.

Eddie, now a boy of thirteen, was quite jovial over his prospects. The journey before him seemed most exciting; the idea of actually going to another continent was highly alluring. His head was full of geography and exotic scenes. Like Helga, he failed to recognize fully the circumstances of his exit, and now one heard him boast proudly: "I will be the first in the family to pass the equator."

38

So the weeks progressed. We lived in constant fear, never knowing what the next day would bring. We were afraid that the bell might ring at any time, that an SS man would stand at the door to take Jim to a concentration camp. What, really, was to prevent it from happening?

Jim was now actually ill and had to stay in bed all of the time. The pains in his back, which he had suffered since the Nazis threw him down a flight of stairs, became acute. I again phoned the Nazi doctor with the "Jewish" name who had treated him right after the accident. He was very courteous when I phoned and came to the apartment at once. This time he treated Jim as a private patient, for Jews had automatically lost their hospitalization rights. He examined Jim thoroughly, and left his bedside frowning.

"I've given him an injection," he told me. "But he will need continued treatment, Mrs. Hilsen."

After that, Dr. Schoenberg visited Jim every other day, giving him further injections for his spinal condition. Already overwhelmed with his kindness of his manner, with his readiness to be bothered with Jim, who was after all only a Jew, we were really amazed when Dr. Schoenberg began to stay a bit longer, after the treatments were made, and chat with us. Among other things, he told us that he was a medical police officer. Then he talked to us about ourselves. He seemed to want to cultivate us!

The injections, unfortunately, brought little relief to Jim. He suffered intensely during those days, but was very patient. I almost wished at times he would protest loudly. But he was afraid of articulating the severity of his plight, afraid of compounding it for me with the incessant burden of terror under which we daily struggled.

Instead of screaming, he lay in bed and read the papers, listened to the radio, and, in better moments, studied English. The two of us were always eager to listen to Radio Austria from Paris or Strassbourg, where people spoke against Hitler. Ingrid and Gerda, sensing our enthusiasm, would huddle around Jim's bed to listen also. From this source alone, we hoped to hear better news. With the newspapers, one had to read between the lines.

Ingrid and Gerda still were attending the Jewish school. And I still went daily to the public kitchen to get food for the four of us. While I stood in line there, people discussed affidavits, quotas, and expressed their worries. There was no one untroubled in that line.

Frequently, I ran into Mrs. Selinger, Marianne's mother, as I stood waiting my turn. Invariably, we discussed our children, who were our deepest concern. The theme was usually affidavits and the latest tale of woe concerning them. But one day Mrs. Selinger blithely informed me that she had an affidavit for her entire family which had been supplied by distant relatives in New York.

"How wonderful!" I exclaimed. "You must be so relieved, Mrs. Selinger. When will you leave, then?"

"Leave?" she echoed vaguely. "Who said we are leaving? My husband, frankly, is in no hurry to leave Austria."

"But Vienna has become a death sentence for all of us!" I muttered. "What do you mean, not in a hurry?"

The woman sighed, partly in resignation. "My husband is an optimist," she said. "Every day he pronounces the deliverance of Austria from Hitler — he believes it is close at hand, and that we Jews will soon be restored to our former status here. If that is so, then of course, there is no need to rush away. . . ." It was clear she half believed this herself.

I restrained myself from shaking Mrs. Selinger harshly. I closed my eyes and struggled for the right response.

"We all suffered those illusions," I told her. "We all maintained this blindness until the day the Nazis took over Vienna. But as a mother I can tell you, if you value Marianne you will regard your affidavit as a blessing from God and act upon it swiftly!"

I turned about quickly then, leaving Mrs. Selinger trembling and confused. The incident depressed me for hours.

A few days later, Jim received a summons to appear at the local draft board. This was utterly confusing. We did not understand why a Jew should be called to report to the army. Since our doctor was a medical officer, I asked him to give me a certificate with a legal stamp, stating that Jim was sick and unable to appear at the local board. To our immense relief, the doctor complied with our request, as kindly as he had heeded our previous calls for help. He made out a statement, declaring that Jim's leg was broken and that he was suffering from a serious disease in his back; therefore, it was not possible for him to get out of bed.

On the specified day, I appeared at the draft board and presented this certificate on Jim's behalf. As the SS man behind the desk read it, I almost fainted with fear that he would either laugh or be furious at the thought of excusing a Jew, however ill he might be.

But the man was quite busy and read my paper hastily.

"All right, all right," he said, dismissing me quickly.

I rushed out of the building, thanking God as I did so that

I'd had sufficient presence of mind to hang on to the medical certificate, which might come in handy again.

Later that week, Jim and I had news from my sister Mela. Like everyone else, Mela was trying to get out of Vienna. She was making attempts not only for herself, but for Stela and my father as well.

"With money," she advised me, "one can procure visas for Colombia."

I laughed sarcastically. "With money indeed! And who has money anymore?"

"We do—a bit, anyway, Thanks to Schorr."

"Schorr!" I gasped. "But he's gone—escaped to Switzerland, hasn't he?"

"Exactly," replied Mela with satisfaction. "And because of that—his having got away—Stela, Father, and I have something left. You all despised Schorr in the past, Helena. You resented his interfering. I can see how things might have looked to you before, but now you can see that Stela and I were right in depending on him. When he left for Switzerland, right after Schuschnigg's abdication, he managed to take some of our funds with him. Stela and I have maintained contact with him steadily. He is arranging for all of us to go to South America now."

This interview was taking place in my father's home, and Mela spoke to me in the deepest confidence we had shared since the time before Mother died.

In the greater strife of a whole people, our family dissensions had pretty well dissolved.

"Colombia—South America—It's so far away, Mela."

"Schorr says that's what's good about it. He doesn't think any place in Europe is safe anymore."

"He's probably right," I said.

Mela rose and began calculating. "It will take time, of course. There will be many formalities to go through—legal or illegal as the case may be—visas don't come overnight."

"But your going is certain?"

"Yes, Helena."

"Thank God—and yes, Schorr, too. Three more of us are saved."

We embraced quickly, and I left.

One by one they were leaving, relatives and friends. After rejoicing with them, I would imagine their departure, their plunge into unknown lands, the resurrection of their lives on alien streets. Then another image sometimes haunted me : I saw all of them gone, an evacuated Vienna, save for four spectres who never managed to leave. That particular vision was one which I fought and scorned and never believed in. First of all, Vienna would never be fully evacuated of Jews, since many of those who had attempted illegal exit and failed had been forced to return.

Bernatz, we discovered that week, had succeeded. One of his friends came to us and described my brother's experiences since he had left Vienna. Bernatz had tried three times to cross the Belgian border near Aachen. The third time he had succeeded. Some in his group had been caught by the Nazis and taken back to Austria. Others had been shot. A few lucky ones, like Bernatz, were safe in Belgium now. Jim and I broke the news to Ingrid and Gerda when they came home from school that day. They were very happy, being, as they were, so fond of Uncle Bernatz. But I observed their small, bright faces as Jim recounted my brother's courageous attempts at the Belgian border, and it struck me that the children were equating this latest adventure of Bernatz's with the earlier one, his hitch-hiking tour of Europe, which had so enchanted them. Of course, they were children, no different in what they could grasp from other children. I don't know why it depressed me so. I should have been glad for that fact.

I phoned Mela to inform all of them at home of Bernatz's

safety. In turn, I was to receive some surprising news.

"Stela was married yesterday," Mela told me on the telephone.

"Married! But to whom?"

"Eli Taub, her old boyfriend . . . you remember him?"

"Of .course. But I thought she hadn't seen him for years," I replied.

"She hadn't. But he started coming around again, a few weeks ago, out of nowhere, really. Then yesterday, with little ado, they simply went down to the *Kultusgemeinde* and were married by the rabbi there."

"In this chaos, too!" I considered. "Well, more power to them. I hope Stela will be happy with him. But tell me, Mela, how is your visa situation progressing? What will happen now?"

"We can only get two visas at this time, Helena, and now that Stela is a bride, I want her and Eli to get out first. Father wants it that way, too. It's the least we can do for them. Anyway, once they get to Colombia, they are sending permits for Father and me. We will simply follow them later."

Two weeks later, Stela, with her bridegroom, left for Bogotá, Colombia.

Another autumn came, and with it Rosh Hashana and Yom Kippur. Incredibly, the Leopoldstadt synagogue, to which my father had always belonged, still held services. On Rosh Hashana, I decided to attend, even though Jim was unable to go with me.

During the services on the New Year, many people burst into tears; others lamented steadily. No one present was without anguish. We prayed together in desperation, absorbed in our grief.

Suddenly, the Nazis entered. People rose and screamed and the Nazis started to attack individuals and throw them outside.

A few left quietly, with a resignation that said they had known all along this was too much to hope for.

Most of the Jews of Vienna had lived here in this section of Leopoldstadt. Since the occupation, however, it looked like a cemetery. Streets were empty, stores were closed. The deadly silence was broken, from time to time, by the shrill cries of women and children as the Gestapo wrecked their homes and took the husbands and fathers away to concentration camps.

Abruptly, it worsened. An order was issued stating that all Jews had to appear at police stations to receive identification cards bearing their fingerprints. All women and girls had to adopt the name "Sarah" and the men and boys the name "Israel." On this occasion the Nazis flagrantly molested the people in the Jewish district. The incident became known for its infamy. The girls were forced to undress and had to remain naked in front of the Nazis while they took blood tests in order to study their race theory. We were spared from this particular horror by our address.

Since it was Hitler's aim to dominate the world, Austria alone was a mere crumb. The Nazis had never stopped singing: "Today Germany belongs to us — tomorrow the whole world." Their next step in this scheme was to demand the Sudetenland. At this point, we fervently hoped that France and England — with America's support — would stop Hitler with a strong, decisive protest. We felt that such a protest might work, since Hitler had not yet reached the highest degree of his strength and it was generally known that he feared America. Tense with this hope, we listened avidly to our radio, only to hear that Chamberlain had come to Munich and signed a peace pact with Hitler. The news was incredible! A feeling of outrage stole over Jim and me as we sat there, and right after the broadcast a neighbor burst in shouting, "Have you heard? Chamberlain *appeased* Hitler!"

A chaotic scene ensued. The three of us, echoing each other's anger and disappointment, began to thrust furious questions into the air: "Why did Chamberlain sign this pact? What's happened to this British diplomat — aren't they supposed to be the most astute in the world! Has Chamberlain been struck by blindness or senility? Why? Why?"

We were confounded; we could not understand. Was it possible that Chamberlain was so shortsighted as to believe Hitler's assertion that he wanted only to reunite the Germans? The last war alone should have taught the world a lesson. The Germans' cry had always been *Lebensraum*. Had they not, during World War I, barbarously overrun Belgium in order to attack France from there? Now, Hitler was not demanding *Lebensraum*, but was flagrantly attempting world domination. It was obvious that Chamberlain had actually removed an obstacle from Hitler's maniacal path of conquest by coming to terms with him.

The Jews were the first victims of his *drang* (drive) to power. With them he had clearly shown the world how he could deal with helpless human beings. Yet no one had seemed to care. They were only Jews. How Hitler must have rejoiced in the indifference of other countries to his treatment of Jews! How free and unhindered he must now feel to pursue any insidious plan. Why wasn't the world protesting?

On September 29, 1938, we read in the newspaper that the "Sudetenland was occupied by our troops." The Austrian Nazis celebrated this victory, attained without any loss of life. And again, they could be heard singing, "Today Germany belongs to us — tomorrow, the whole world," as well as the *Horst Wessel* song about Jewish blood running in the streets.

Thus, the prospects for the Jews grew more hopeless. In all sanity, one had to be prepared for the worst. Yet, as one drowning grasps at a straw, I tried to console myself with the possession of an affidavit to America. I thought less about the quota system, which rendered it worthless for almost two years.

39

November 10, 1938.

The Jewish disaster deepened. A Jewish boy, Grynszpan, killed Herr vom Rath, the secretary of the German Embassy in Paris on November 7th. The Nazi hordes were always delighted with such an incident; it tended to justify not only an outbreak but an extension of their bestiality. When the news of Herr Rath's death was released, all hell broke loose.

The 10th of November, in 1938, will always be a black date in Jewish history. An everlasting memory of horror and torture, it will be sustained in the minds of those Jews who, like me, survived this day under Hitler.

In the morning, Jewish homes were invaded by the Nazis, ostensibly to search for guns. It was pretty well known that the Jews had no guns. All men found at home were rounded up, while many green cars waited outside, filling up with these victims.

We waited our turn and it came. Three storm troopers burst into the front door. I stood up as they entered, and spoke to them. Jim was still bed-ridden and helpless. I had insisted the girls stay in his room.

Immediately, the storm troopers asked for my husband. When I told them he was ill and in bed, they accused me of pretending. I remembered the medical certificate which Dr. Schoenberg had given us. Jerkily, I walked to the desk and withdrew it from a drawer. They studied it; I waited, the pounding in my ears was so violent that it deafened me to the muffled voices of the children in the bedroom, whom Jim was trying to keep silent.

The legal seal bearing the swastika impressed them. But they made a total search of the place before they would leave. They kicked open the door to the room where Jim was lying in bed. Ingrid and Gerda were frozen at the appearance of the men. Every drawer in the apartment was opened and ransacked. But even as I watched them, I was grateful. From the window, I saw my neighbor's husband being herded with several others into a green car. "The certificate, the certificate!" I rejoiced wildly. "It has saved Jim twice now!"

When they finally left us, I went into the bedroom, embraced Jim and the girls. The place looked so wild and strange with everything torn up.

I sat at the foot of Jim's bed and looked closely at him.

"Your injury," I said, "which made me sick to contemplate at first, has saved you in the end from torture, maybe death."

"I was thinking so when I heard you showing them the certificate," Jim said.

"And Dr. Schoenberg, what if we hadn't called him that day?"

"I would have long since been taken, Helena. I don't doubt it. Look at that car . . how many are they taking?" he said, looking through the window.

"Hanna is lucky Josef is not home this morning," I mused ironically. Then I jumped to my feet. "Hanna! Why, she's all alone and unprotected. I'm going to her, Jim. She may be in need of someone. . . ."

As I left the apartment, Olga phoned to find out how we had fared. I ran all the way to Hanna's, with terrible visions of her being molested.

Hanna was sitting quietly when I rushed in.

"Thank God!" I panted. "I was afraid they had done something to you," I confessed, collapsing into a chair.

"No, I am not hurt. But they took the last money I had, Helena. The last bit. They found it and they took it."

While she was describing this robbery, George came in from the street.

"Mother! They have set our synagogue on fire!"

Hanna jumped to her feet and began to weep suddenly. It was as if news of this less personal, but symbolic tragedy had released the outrage she had been feeling all morning.

"Please, Mother, don't be so upset—what's the use?" George said.

I ran out into the street. I don't know why. I ran toward the synagogue, which was adjacent to the kitchen where I stood in line each day for food. Both of them belonged to the *Kultusgemeinde*.

I stood in the crowd watching the orange flame consume our synagogue. Many non-Jews were watching the spectacle. Among their voices, I heard an old woman protest: "But this is a house of worship!"

I wheeled around and stared at her with burning eyes. Her words, so unexpected here, made my head spin. I bent over, coughing from smoke. I wanted to cry out, to answer her protest. Wildly, as I watched the flames, I thought of her words as handwriting on the wall for Hitler, who, in my feverish thoughts, was like the doomed Belshazzar. When the smoke became too much for me, I ran away from the scene muttering, *"Mene Mene Tekel Upharsin!"*

It was on the next day, and during the days that followed, that we were to learn all that had transpired on that November 10th. All synagogues, not only ours, had been burned, as well as the chapel at the cemetery.

We heard from George's friend, who with his sick father had been taken to a room crowded with Jewish victims. There were so many people there that no one could move. Wedged together, they were kept there all day and all night without food. A few of these people had become so desperate in this hideous trap that they jumped out of the window. At this point the Gestapo put several men against the wall and threatened to shoot them. This silenced the hysterical.

In another spot, on the same day, Tauber, a former colleague of Jim's, was forced to run up and down three flights of stairs continuously until he fainted. The SS men poured cold water over him until he revived, then made him begin all over again. As a finish, they tramped on his stomach with their heavy boots. Then he was released, a physical wreck, grateful, withal, not to have been sent to a concentration camp.

The Gestapo had established an emigrations office in the great castle belonging to Baron Eugene Rothschild, in the Prinz Eugen Strasse. Those Jews who had the possibility of leaving Austria had to apply for their passports there. Always, there was a long line of people in front, waiting their turn.

On November 10th, my brother Leon had been standing in line in front of the castle. Leon, a lucky one who did not have to wait for a quota (he had registered in 1921, when he had first intended to go to the U.S.A.), had hope of leaving Austria soon, since he had an affidavit from Saul. But as he stood in line on that day, the Gestapo halted them and rounded up all the Jews there. The group was taken to a cellar where they were beaten mercilessly; with bleeding heads, they were dumped into trucks and driven off to concentration camps. Leon, with the others, had been taken to this cellar. By a miracle of chance, however, he was recognized by one of the SS men as the owner of the Stadt-Kino, where the officer had for years been a steady patron. There had been several moments of conflict for the officer, as he stood there, first eyeing Leon, then ignoring him, then reviewing him. Abruptly he had turned and in swift silence directed Leon to a side door through which my brother escaped. The incident was a source of wonder and conversation in the family for months thereafter.

Also on November 10th, the Nazis attacked all the public kitchens where destitute Jews procured their meals. All the food was flung into the streets. Of necessity, the kitchens were closed for one week following the incident. Many faced near-starvation, since this was their last source of food.

When they reopened. I went again to get our food, but the whole scene was transformed. The place where the synagogue had stood was nothing now but a heap of black bricks. It looked like a crematorium, and as I stood waiting for poor-smelling food (the quality of which worsened as Nazi violence increased), the sight of ashes and the odor was galling. Conversation became infrequent among us women there. What, really, could we say to each other now? There was nothing to do but watch and wait.

40

THE 10TH OF NOVEMBER HAD RELEASED A PANIC WHICH thousands and suppressed in order to keep going from day to day. Now there was a wholesale urge for exodus from Vienna. Every office connected with departure of any kind was choked with swarms of terrified Jews. Many people like us, who had affidavits but had to wait for quotas, simply could wait no longer and plunged into maniacal routes of escape. When news of their capture came to us, it was like hearing of suicide.

Dr. Westheimer, that strange parsimonious character who had become, unexplainably, so close to Jim, visited us constantly. He was badly off these days, a man bedeviled with terror. One morning, he had interesting information.

"Jim, Helena, I'm going to Shanghai!"

"To Shanghai! But you only have three more months before your visa for America comes through. Why go to the Orient?" Jim said.

"America? The Orient? Does it matter where I go? In three months I may be a corpse. I can't stand this waiting any more. I feel that I'm going insane here!"

"Doctor," I beseeched.

"No," he said. "It's true. I almost took my life last week. Only this news — that one can go easily to Shanghai — kept me from doing it. I thought it was all up."

Nervously, motioning with his hands, he told us that

321

entrance into Shanghai was a relatively simple business. They put up few barriers or conditions. He had, he confessed, hidden just enough money from the Nazis to make the trip.

"This Shanghai retreat is becoming quite popular, actually," Jim conceded. "I've heard of several others going there, just in the past week."

"You see?" cried Westheimer, suddenly jubilant. "I really struck on something . . . believe me, I've been making plans every minute since I decided. It's a good place to go for many reasons." He paused, then added, "They're letting me take my furniture with me."

"Your furniture?" I repeated incredulously. I was more amazed that he could think of it than that he would be permitted to take it.

He laughed. "Well, perhaps I should say *your* furniture, Helena. It did begin with you . . . but you know how attached I am to familiar things. It's going to make a world of difference, having my things there in a strange setting."

I turned away, too astonished to continue the discussion. This was the most bizarre idea, shipping suites of Louis XVI furniture to Shanghai while escaping from Nazi butchers. Only Westheimer could have thought of it, would have the money saved to do it, or would want to be bothered with the burden of it. "These pieces of gilded wood," I thought, "which Jim and I relinquished so easily in poor times, have become Westheimer's wife and children!"

So our poor friend made his preparations. He was to leave within ten days. On subsequent visits, he became most enthusiastic about living in China. He thought it would be quite an opportunity to see the exotic. His point of view, his manic babbling, reminded me of my little niece and nephew, when they had gone away.

Westheimer really belonged to no one. He had one married brother, it was true, but had not been able to maintain close relationship with him. Objects, apparently, proved safer, more reliable than people for him. Yet strangely, with all his amused tolerance, Jim had developed a genuine fondness for the doctor over the years. I must have felt something for him, too, for when he left I kept feeling sadness and relief.

It would be preposterous to pretend that Jim and I were unaffected by the profound wave of terror that had swept over Vienna. We felt our vulnerability afresh and we were desperately afraid for our children. But it was the children, I believe, who forced upon us whatever stoicism or sanity we maintained. For Ingrid and Gerda, we kept up a front. And because of them, we still believed in miracles.

But the days were long and the thoughts were anxious. Westheimer had fled to China, rather than wait a mere three months for a visa to America. We had more than a year to wait. Did it make sense that we could stay here that long and survive?

Two months passed. And one day brought a letter from Westheimer, now in Shanghai. Jim tore open the envelope eagerly. I waited patiently, watching him as he read the letter.

"Dear God!" Jim muttered, looking up at me. "His furniture's been lost, Helena. . . . How does he put it? Let's see . . . somewhere en route . . ."

"It was inevitable," I said.

"But read the letter. The man's just crestfallen!" Jim said, handing it to me.

I took the letter and read it. Westheimer told a sad story all around. He was not adjusting well to life in Shanghai. The climate did not agree with him; he doubted if he would ever get used to the food. As for the furniture, he had almost written an elegy.

"There is one positive note," I remarked. "He's found work in a medical laboratory there. In time, this may help him to like the place."

But a few weeks later, a stranger visited us. He turned out to be Westheimer's brother.

"I know how close he was to Mr. Hilsen," the man said. "I thought you'd want to know. He has committed suicide. We got word yesterday, from Shanghai. They are sending me an urn with his ashes."

He told us that Westheimer had injected poison into his veins while at work in his Chinese laboratory.

Jim and I were dejected for days afterward. My husband had somehow grown to love that foolish, penny-pinching man. Their hours at the five o'clock teas had been lingering, perfectly pleasant. As for me, I was thunderstruck with the futility of his whole venture. I kept thinking of his jubilation as the time to sail came close. An exotic adventure, he had meant it to be.

Our spirits were lifted about a week later via a letter from Greta. She had succeeded in crossing the border to France. Once in Paris, she had managed to find Erich. She did not say, but I guessed it must have been an extraordinary reunion. Unfortunately, it did not last very long, for Erich, who was without means, had been sent by the Refugee Committee to Marseilles.

Left alone again, Greta had procured a position with a French–Jewish family near Paris. She was now employed in the capacity of governess and piano teacher to the children. They treated her, she wrote, as a member of the family. Greta was apparently quite pleased with this solution. The rest of her letter was about us. She was terribly worried about us, had heard all the recent reports of mass arrests and beatings. What were our prospects for leaving, she wanted to know.

I reread her letter several times. It was good to know she was safe in France.

And then there was further good news in our own family, here in Vienna. The passports for Leon, Ellen, and the child had come through. They were leaving (legally, too!) for the United States.

Jim and I could not see enough of them before they left. When would I see Leon again? Good, patient Leon who had been my big brother since Abram died so many years ago. The Leon who had relinquished his Palestinian life in order to comfort his bereft mother. And I would miss Ellen, too!

When they came to say good-bye, there were many emotions in the air. On the one hand, it was impossible to conceal their mounting excitement over the departure to America. On the other, our having to remain in Vienna rankled their thoughts. Ellen, always so fond of Jim, was disturbed at his injury and helplessness, and lingered at his bedside for a while, talking to him. During this final visit of theirs, I noticed an improvement in the relations between Leon and his wife. Like other dissenting relationships, theirs had tended to heal, at least temporarily, under the threat of danger. Ellen was sweeter, less condescending toward Leon now.

When they left us, Leon was anxious and troubled. But there was no course open to them but to pursue their own salvation at this time.

Hanna's eldest boy, George, sailed shortly after Leon and his family. I thought Hanna took his departure beautifully. She began talking, very quickly, I thought, about Esther going next, as if she could hardly wait until her next child was despatched into safety. I looked at her curiously, thinking, "This is merely an adaptation to reality. In another way, her heart is all but breaking."

Esther had now received her permit to go to England. She promised Hanna that as soon as she arrived in England, she would get her a permit, too. Esther was to work as a domestic. This was a fairly popular way out with women in Vienna in these days.

But Hanna was far more concerned with placing Robert,

her other son, than with her own escape. She frantically wrote letters to WIZO in England, asking if they could help place the boy there.

Olga was now at peace on this subject. Both her children were safe and wrote to her faithfully. Their letters said that they were happy with their relatives. The Cottons in Birmingham, who had taken Helga, even wrote to Olga, offering to send her a permit.

Without thinking, when I heard this, I blurted out, "Take the permit then, Olga! Stela has left, Mela and Father are going. Leon and Saul are in America. Bernatz is safe in Belgium. Why should you stay here to be . . ."

"Helena!" she exclaimed. "What about Friedrich? Could I save myself and leave an invalid to the mercy of the Gestapo? No. As long as I can keep my apartment, I will stay with Friedrich and take care of him as always."

"Of course, Olga. That is the only thing you can do."

This subject of Jews retaining their apartments was a kind of haphazard business. Many Jews had already been forced to give up their apartments to move in with Jewish friends. Others, by no design at all, still held theirs.

Before long, however, Olga was singled out and told to evacuate her premises. The long-dreaded news was devastating. Olga, always so composed in the face of adversity, now was frantic. Where was she to go with a paralyzed and helpless husband? She could not nurse him in some tiny corner of a shared apartment. At my suggestion, she sought help from the *Kultusgemeinde,* which tried to aid those who had lost their homes. After many formalities, they helped Olga to place Friedrich in the Home for the Aged and Infirm, which they owned. Relieved as she was to place Friedrich safely where he could receive care, the nature of the Home struck her as desolate. Its name did not help. I tried to console her.

"Forget that they call it the Home for the Aged," I advised

her. "Be realistic, Olga. There is no other place as suitable for Friedrich, at least in these times."

I did not add, in conversation, what we both knew well: that Friedrich was incurable anyway.

4 1

THE YEAR 1938 WAS OVER. FOR THE JEWS IT HAD BEEN A year of degradation, suspense, and suffering. For the Nazis it had been a year of jubilation, celebration, and persecution of the most helpless of peoples. We hardly expected that 1939, the new year, would be a better one for us. It was clear that more terror and suffering were inevitably to follow.

At the time when Olga had been forced to surrender her apartment, many other Jewish families had received similar orders from the Gestapo and were homeless until they moved in with Jewish families who still retained rooms. Having placed Friedrich in the Home, Olga moved in with Mela and Father. Because of the situation, Jim and I rented our living room to one such ousted family named Kish. It was awkward, of course, but we hardly considered that point. Our whole life had become a constant readjustment since the Nazi occupation; to relinquish privacy seemed a small thing. Furthermore, the Kish family was very pleasant and we rather enjoyed their company.

Mrs. Kish had already received a permit to go to England as a domestic. Mr. Kish and their twelve-year-old son were to stay on and wait until Mrs. Kish managed to get permits in England for the two of them. These plans filled our conversations for the most part.

One day, however, a new proposition came to light. Mr.

Kish came home from the *Kultusgemeinde* burning with information. He sought me out as I was washing dishes.

"Mrs. Hilsen! What I have not discovered today! A special children's committee at the *Kultusgemeinde* is registering kids for transports to England—also France and Holland. Listen, I'm not going to wait for details! I'm registering my boy immediately. Now what about your daughters, Mrs. Hilsen?"

"My daughters?" I repeated, trembling.

"Of course," he said impatiently. "That's what the committee's working for!"

I rushed into the bedroom, fearful and excited. Jim shifted in bed and eyed me apprehensively.

"What's the matter, Helena? You seem frightened."

I sat on the edge of the bed and surveyed my husband. Thoughts were jamming through my head incoherently, one fighting the other. This was the first time I had ever considered being separated from Ingrid and Gerda. I had found brave words to utter to my sisters when they relinquished their young in order to save them; now, I suddenly discovered that the thought of letting my own go from me was all but unbearable. Still, here was Jim, bedridden, locked in Vienna. Our visas to America were nearly two years away. How many of us Jews would be allowed to live for two more years?

I took Jim's hand.

"Mr. Kish just told me some news, Jim. It seems that children can now be registered for transports to England, France, or Holland. He is going to register his boy. If we wish, we can register Ingrid and Gerda. . . ."

"They might really go?" he asked, incredulously.

"Yes."

We both fell silent for a few moments.

"So there is to be a choice, after all, for them?" he murmured.

"Apparently. But it is we who must make the decision. What shall I do, Jim? Should I register Ingrid and Gerda?"

"Yes, Helena. Of course you must. And as soon as you can."

"But how can we possibly part from them, knowing nothing of their destination, of how they will manage away from us. My God, who will take care of them? They are nine and eleven years old now . . . and I've never been separated from them for a single day!"

Jim's voice was sad but firm. "Helena, I have heard you tell others to be realistic. Now it is your turn. It is useless to consider the details of their destiny when the choice may be no destiny at all. Their lives are at stake, Helena! We never know, here in Vienna, what new move, what deprivation or attack the Nazis will think up. No matter what happens to us, the children must be saved. Go, Helena, and right away. Register the girls."

I lost no time after that and hurried over to the *Kultusgemeinde*. All the way, I kept envisioning my hand, holding a pen, writing the magic names on that list of salvation.

But when I found the right desk at the *Kultusgemeinde*, I found that it was not so simple. The Children's Committee Office informed me that at present no one could register. For the future, they were hoping . . . I left the place sadly. It was so indefinite, so improbable!

By now, Olga's two children were in safe places. Eddie wrote a letter from Johannesburg, describing his uncle's warm welcome and the exciting journey to Africa. He had passed the equator and now made intelligent comparisons between Johannesburg and Vienna. He sounded quite happy, but did not fail to add, at the end, that he hoped to be back with Mommy and Daddy again. Nevertheless, it was painful to read the letter, knowing how dubious the reunion between Eddie and his parents actually was. Who knew if it would ever take place? Still, Eddie was safe. What of my two children?

When I had been unable to register the girls immediately, I had felt great disappointment, but also a secret relief. I would be able to keep them with me a little longer, I felt. I entered their room each night and watched them sleeping there, grateful to be able to look at them.

But as the times worsened, the idea of the children's transport became easier for me to accept, and I prayed that the plan would materialize. The girls were really not happy any more. They had never adjusted to the inferior food we had to eat every day. Their home was troubled and overcrowded. The friends who came there were full of anguish and fear. And as the days progressed, I wished only to register them as soon as possible.

It was Olga who finally made this possible. While at the *Kultusgemeinde,* she discovered that the Director of the Children's Committee was an old friend of hers. They were now registering a limited number of children. She implored her to include Ingrid and Gerda on the first transport out. The Director had agreed.

The transport was to leave for Britain in the near future. So now we waited. We were impatient for a call which would summon us to the *Kultusgemeinde.* But no call came.

Then strangely, I heard one day that several children's transports had already left for Britain without our ever having been advised. I called Olga at once and asked her to look into the situation.

Olga went directly to her friend, the Director, who, in turn, was amazed to discover that Ingrid and Gerda were still in Vienna. They examined the list and found out that two other sisters with the same last name had been sent instead of my children. The children who had already left were to be handled by the Refugee Children's Committee in England, and the children were to be sent to camps where they would be cared for in groups.

"Olga, I can't wait now. I am so eager for them to get out!"

"The next transport, Helena. The Director has promised me. There will be no mistake this time. The delay has been good for you. You are more ready now — are you not?"

I comforted myself with Olga's words.

"Now that we have investigated the children's situation, Helena, I must tell you of a decision I am forced to make," she confessed, handing me a letter.

The letter was from Helga, in England. She had written that she was well cared for and hoped to see her mother soon. There was also a letter from the Cottons, her guardians, and in this was enclosed a permit for Olga to enter England.

My face lit up when I saw the permit.

"Olga, what a blessing! You can leave Vienna and be with Helga too!"

But Olga burst into tears.

"That's just it. I can't leave Vienna! Friedrich is here. Whom does he have in this world? I was hoping they would send two permits, so that I might take Friedrich with me." She wept.

Had Olga really thought of taking Friedrich? It was doubtful that the man could survive the trip. I took a long look at Olga's face. How she had aged in this one year! How drawn and middle-aged was her expression. But did Hanna or I look any better?

"Each time you visit Friedrich," I said out loud, "you tell me how relieved you are that he is in the Home. He receives medical care and decent food. The atmosphere enables him to rest. He couldn't endure travel even if you had the permit, Olga!"

"I know," she conceded.

"You can't really help Friedrich by staying on here. Except for your visits, he's out of your hands now. But your children do need you. If you save yourself, you can reclaim Helga and work toward a reunion with Eddie. But if you remain in Vienna and lose your life, the suffering of those two will be immeasurable!"

Olga rose and wiped her eyes. "Of course, I will have to use the permit. Thank you, Helena, for helping me to clarify my purposes. I will act for the children and for myself. . . . Ah, but it is hell to be torn in two directions!"

Olga remained emotionally disturbed on the subject of leaving Friedrich behind in Vienna, however. At her request, I accompanied her, two days later, to the Home for the Aged and Infirm.

Friedrich Landes had aged so vastly since his stroke that he really looked old and gray. I smiled at him, hoping that the change in him did not register in my face. The truth was, in spite of Olga's protests, that Friedrich's presence in the Home was hopelessly appropriate.

Hanna's emotional status was somewhat better than Olga's at this time. A permit for Robert had arrived. He would now be able to go to England through the efforts of WIZO. Once he got to Britain, WIZO would send him to a private boarding home. Hanna was especially pleased because Robert's permit had arrived before Esther left; now the two of them could leave together, on the same train. Hanna had substantial hope of going to England fairly soon herself, so she was not at all miserable at their departure. She seemed quite happy, in fact. Her only remaining source of concern was Josef. His plight, of course, was not as bad as Friedrich's. At least Josef continued to enjoy good health, even in prison. And as far as safety was concerned, it had long since been evident that Josef was safer from the Nazis in jail than he would have been on the outside.

Hanna had told the children not to visit him before they left for England. It would have upset both them and Josef too much. But after Esther and Robert were gone, Hanna herself went to the prison to see Josef.

He was greatly relieved to hear that all the children were now safely out of Vienna. Hanna told him about Esther's plan to procure a permit for herself. But she also told Josef that she was loathe to leave Vienna when his own destiny was unknown. Josef was touched at her reluctance to leave him behind, but he would not hear of her staying. Always an optimist, Josef was not too worried about his own future. Hanna could not help noticing that he was in excellent health and that he was probably eating better in jail than any of us were on the outside.

42

Time went on, bringing with it a slight improvement of Jim's leg and the departure of Mrs. Kish, our boarder, for England. It failed, however, to bring any notice from the Children's Committee regarding departure for Ingrid and Gerda.

"I, too, am waiting anxiously all these weeks," Mr. Kish said to me. "Nothing more has come for my son. I had hoped he could leave right after his mother went away."

"I'm not going to sit around and wait any longer," I announced, stripping off my apron. "I'm going to the *Kultusgemeinde* this afternoon to see what I can find out."

When I arrived there, I was genuinely surprised to encounter Mrs. Selinger, whom I had not seen since the day I had snapped at her in the food line.

"What brings you here today, Mrs. Selinger?" I asked, noticing how harried and excited she looked.

"I'm here to register Marianne for the Children's Transport," she replied.

"You want to send Marianne away? I thought your husband felt it was unnecessary, that we would all be free of the Nazis before long."

"He no longer believes that, you may be sure, Mrs. Hilsen. Not after November 10th! We want to send Marianne away as soon as possible. We've also written to the States to our sponsor, asking for additional papers for ourselves. We have quite lost hope that Hitler's end is close at hand," she concluded.

After this discussion, we both went to make inquiries at the Children's Committee Office. And both of us were crestfallen to learn that all transports to England had been stopped. Now, only children who had been individually claimed by English families which would adopt them temporarily had a chance to leave Austria. We were told, however, that we could register our children for transports going to France or Holland.

I walked home in a state of utter depression. I had been dreaming of the girls in England. The idea of that country, of its people, seemed particularly benevolent, somehow.

I found Jim up and about. He was able to walk now with the help of a cane, although he still suffered chronic seizures of pain in the spine. I told him the latest information.

"France or Holland!" he said. "Maybe we'll choose Holland," he speculated. "After all, Addie's there, living peacefully enough in Utrecht, isn't he? Only last week he wrote of the kindness he received from that Jewish family he's staying with. Didn't he describe the Dutch as extremely sympathetic? They've been wonderful to the refugees."

"I know, Jim. But every time Addie writes to us, I read something between the lines. It's as if he finds Holland a very temporary kind of haven. Invariably, he ends his letters by saying he will take the first chance he gets to leave for Palestine," I noted.

"That's true."

"And besides, there was something about their going to England that seemed to be just right. We had grown to feel so good about it!" I said.

"Not to mention the little scheme I've been nurturing! We still have hope, after all, of leaving Vienna ourselves. We could have picked up the girls in England, on our way to America."

"Oh, Jim, what can we do now?"

"I don't know. But it's got to be England, Helena. We've simply got to make it England!"

After that, I phoned Olga and told her what I had learned at the *Kultusgemeinde*. She advised me to write a letter to the committee in Birmingham, asking them to look for two families willing to take in my two girls until our chance to leave for America came. I wrote immediately.

Jim and I were overjoyed when, after a short time, the committee answered, saying that two kind-hearted families — the Coupes and the Cresswells — had agreed to take Ingrid and Gerda into their English homes. A bit later, we received splendid letters from Mr. Coupe and Mr. Cresswell, both from Birmingham, expressing eagerness to receive the children. Our relief could not be measured then. The children would be going to good people; they would be well cared for and at least relatively happy.

The *Kultusgemeinde* took care of all the formalities pertaining to the departures of Ingrid and Gerda. Soon I was notified to submit the children for physical examinations, and I took them to the *Kultusgemeinde* for that purpose. Many mothers were waiting there for the doctor when we arrived. We witnessed a most upsetting scene: many women, with babies in their arms were crowding to a door. Ingrid and Gerda, watching them, grew tense beside me.

"What is it all about?" I asked a lady sitting near us.

This lady, who was pale and wasted-looking, turned wearily to me.

"Two rich women from the United States have come here, to Vienna, to adopt two babies. The two will be chosen from that mob," she explained.

I glanced up quickly at the young mothers again, pressing forward eagerly. "My God, how can they give up those babies?" I thought, watching their faces. "They may never see them again—even if they do they'll have no identity for the children. They won't be remembered. . . . But if it means life, survival, it's worth it, of course! Oh, why am I differentiating? I am nearly in the same boat with my two. But, thank God, they are older, not quite so vulnerable, not infants, at least!" Every mother there was desperate to have her child chosen.

Soon we were distracted from this scene; our turn came for the medical examinations. After these were finished, we were informed that Gerda had been registered for the next transport, which was to leave Vienna on March 25th. The news was upsetting. I had hoped both girls could leave on the same transport; but it was not to be.

A week before Gerda left, I had to take her luggage to the *Kultusgemeinde* in the Seitenstattengasse, where a customs officer was to examine it.

It was terrifying now to enter the large hall. Once it had been the oldest, most beautiful synagogue in Vienna. But on November 10th, it, with all other synagogues, had been razed. Only bare, fire-blackened walls and broken balconies remained. On this day, mothers and fathers with white, drawn faces rushed about, bearing suitcases, and lined up tensely before customs officers. These were all Nazis now, Hitler's servants managing the *Kultusgemeinde*. They processed us harshly, with peremptory gestures, alarming the confused ones still further. The formalities which I and the rest had to go through on that day were painful. But relief followed the ordeal of processing; Gerda was leaving for safety.

The day before Gerda's departure I took her "shopping." I managed to buy her only a few basic things. These at least symbolized the provisions I would have liked to make for her.

On the way, she remarked to me, "Mummy, I'm walking on these streets for the last time." Gerda was now ten years old.

When I tucked her in bed that night, she asked me to lie

down next to her for a while. We hugged each other, and she murmured only, "Mummy dear!" Neither of us spoke another word, fearing an outpouring of tears which we strove to avoid for each other's sake.

I could not sleep all night. I kept thinking of the next day, of Gerda's empty bed. She would be far away from us, out of our hands. My second daughter, so serious and sensitive since infancy—how would she take this break, how would she adjust to an entirely different world?

Jim accompanied us to the station. I was grateful that he could walk on that day, even though he limped. He was tense from the effort of controlling himself. Only I knew, from our whisperings of the night before, the intensity of his suffering. Sweat broke out on his forehead as I gave last-minute advice to Gerda. His blond hair was soaked.

We went to the station by trolley car. I sat opposite Gerda to keep her face in mind as long as possible. Her dark blue eyes seemed so large and strange.

I kept thinking: "Will I see you again, my child, when will I see you again?"

At the station we found many other parents assembled there with departing children. There were also a few babies being cared for by a nurse. All the children wore tags around their necks for purposes of identification. The *Kultusgemeinde* had arranged everything well.

Now parents and relatives pressed forward to be as close as possible to their children, not wanting to miss a second of this final, precious time with them. We did the same.

Then a man who was in charge of their departure ordered the children to board the trains. I felt my face drain. Gerda lifted her face for one last kiss and was gone. Relatives were now told to remain in the waiting room.

We watched Gerda hurry away. Ingrid stood next to me and said, "Mummy, don't cry." I did not cry. At this point, we were permitted to go out to the train. I felt Jim take my hand as we walked to the tracks. His own hand was wet.

By now, all the children were seated in compartments. Gerda was spotted, standing at a window. She looked very excited. When the train began to move, we walked, then ran with it, until it rushed away from us and disappeared out of sight. Again, Ingrid examined my face.

"Are you crying now, Mummy?" she asked.

"Don't you see, my darling? I am not crying! I'm happy that Gerda left. So is your father. We would be happy to see you leaving Vienna too, very soon."

43

MARCH OF 1939, THE MONTH IN WHICH GERDA HAD LEFT FOR England, witnessed an increase of international woes. The Nazi pest spread again, demanding more victims. Again a small country which was unable to defend itself was simply overrun by the Nazis. And again there was no intervention to deter them. No country stepped in to halt Hitler's occupation of Czechoslovakia. We now had more fellow sufferers, and it seemed that a war would break out at any minute. But it soon appeared that this time, too, Hitler had attained his goal without a war.

My personal uneasiness at this time about the possibility of war was concerned with the fact that it might break out before Ingrid had a chance to leave for England. Jim and I waited impatiently for notification from the Children's Committee. All we wanted now was the assurance that she could leave soon. A few weeks passed; Mela received permits for herself and Father from Stela, who was safely arrived, and now the two prepared to leave for Bogotá.

Soon it was April, shortly before the Passover. I went to the public kitchen to get my ration of *matzoh*. These had been sent to the *Israelitische Kultusgemeinde* from the Joint Distribution Committee in America.

As I received my ration with a few words, I noticed tears spring suddenly to the eyes of the man who handed the *matzoh* to me. This man knew me well, for in the past it had been my father's habit to donate each year a few hundred pounds of *matzoh* for the *Kultusgemeinde* to distribute to the poor. Now I, his daughter, stood here and received charity.

When I reached home, Jim and Ingrid were very excited. A card from Gerda had come in the mail — our first communication from her since she left on the train. As I read the card, I teased Jim sarcastically about his elation. It was a very sad little piece, in fact. Gerda recounted her inability to sleep all night. How devastating that trip must have been for her! She had been longing for home, and was worried about all of us. There was not a description yet of her new surroundings, for the card had been written upon arrival.

"But that's the only part that matters, now!" Jim said. "She's arrived and she's safe. Of course it's hard at the beginning. Gerda would find it especially hard, I suppose."

Like Jim, I was pleased with having the card, no matter its melancholy tone. I hugged Ingrid as I reread it aloud. Jim, smiling, opened the package of *matzoh* I had brought home.

"Gerda's card comes in good season. Just in time for Passover. Something good to show the whole family."

We were actually holding a *Seder*. It was the last *Seder* we ever celebrated in our apartment. My father, now seventy-six years old, came, with his remaining children flocking around him — Hanna, Olga, Mela, myself, and Jim. Of all his grandchildren, only our Ingrid, twelve years old, remained in Vienna now. He spoke with awe and wonder of the flight the others had taken, of the fantastic trip which he and Mela were soon to make. Never had he dreamed that at his age he would be forced to leave for a distant country, that his children and grandchildren would be scattered all over the world.

As it progressed, the *Seder* became a sad affair. My father, always a traditionalist, wanted to observe the holiday as always. Accordingly, he turned to golden-haired Ingrid.

"You are the youngest here tonight," he commented. "It is fitting that you ask the four questions, Ingrid."

"I don't mind asking the questions, Grandpa," Ingrid replied. "But would you mind if I asked a few different ones tonight? There are so many on my mind."

"Ask, then, child."

Ingrid caught her breath a little self-consciously before speaking and colored slightly, the object of all the elders' attention. How lovely she had grown through all of this mess! Nothing had deterred her incipient blossoming, no condition, no apprehension had marred that promise.

"Grandpa," she began, "why are the Jews being treated in such a terrible way? Are they not the same human beings as non-Jews?"

"We are all God's children," he answered. "But among his offspring are good and bad. Certainly God will punish the evil."

"Will God save our people from the Nazis as he did from Pharoah's slavery?" Ingrid asked.

"Yes!" My father assured her. "When the time comes, He will perform miracles as in the old days. He will gather the scattered and bring them to the Promised Land, which again will become a land of milk and honey."

The rest of us sat by silently, drinking in Father's words, recognizing them as familiar euphemisms, but deriving comfort from them nevertheless. Perhaps, in the haphazard ways of history, there was a past pattern which might be repeated on our behalf. Each of us at that *Seder* was more than willing to believe in a good God who would help the oppressed. We knew we should not lose hope. Perhaps there would be a redemption for us!

On the second *Seder* eve, we all went to see Father and Mela off for Bogotá. The scene was wild with excitement and many tears were shed. The more remote the place of escape, the more improbable did reunions appear. Each thought this, but none said.

Still, as I watched their train moving slowly away I was happy that more of my family were saved.

44

Two weeks after Passover, it was Olga's turn to go. Her feelings about going to England had remained ambivalent right up to the last minute. Whenever the picture of Friedrich — gray, shrunken, paralyzed, babbling in an effort to speak — swept across her mind's eye, she had grown weak with a sense of bertaying him. When the appointed day came, only the idea of reclaiming her children had gotten her as far as the station.

As I stood with her, waiting for the train, she was rather silent for the first few minutes, lost in her own thoughts. Then she turned to me with an almost fierce expression.

"Look at me, Helena! Here I am blithely leaving Vienna for safety, abandoning Friedrich to public mercy, leaving all of you behind. Who knows if the rest of you will get out for certain. Oh, I tell you, it's not right, this going away!"

"Olga, Olga!" I murmured, taking her arm. "And here I was thinking I had convinced you it was right! Look all around you. Is there one present who is really happy? Those who leave are miserable and those who are left behind at least equally so. But no one who has the chance to go stays behind. You must not hurt yourself so with needless guilt! You did everything you could for Friedrich, Olga, and the children will be so happy to have at least one of their parents restored to them."

"You know what, Helena? I have a feeling that Friedrich wanted me to leave. When I went to see him yesterday, to say goodbye, he had such a pleased expression on his face — one of gratification almost. He mumbled something too, as if he were trying to tell me, 'Go to our children, Olga. They will need you.' Of course," she added, "I'm interpreting."

"I am sure you interpret correctly. I, for one, don't doubt that Friedrich understood the situation and wanted you to leave."

Olga turned to me abruptly, full face.

"Helena, promise me that you'll visit Friedrich."

"Yes, I will, Olga, as often as I can. I'll check up on him regularly and keep you advised of everything."

The buzzing of voices around us now swelled to a sudden noise as the train approached. Olga and I exchanged a last kiss, and she ran to the train with tears streaming down her face.

The next week, I went to visit Friedrich at the Home. In the lobby, a woman came toward me and asked what I was doing here. She seemed to know me. Finally, I recognized her as an old neighbor of my parents'. She was now married to the director of the Home.

She accompanied me to the ward where Friedrich's bed was situated. My brother-in-law seemed to recognize me. I noticed a faint smile form on his lips as I leaned toward him with a greeting.

When we left Friedrich, the woman showed me all around the establishment. All the beds were occupied with the aged and crippled. It was good to see, however, that they were still well cared for by the doctors and nurses here while such chaos reigned in other parts of Vienna. She led me to the garden and to the adjoining, centuries-old cemetery. I bent down trying to read some of the inscriptions on the gravestones, but most of the Hebrew engraving had been worn illegible by time. One stone in particular caught my attention there. There was a fish distinctly carved upon it with some Hebrew letters beneath it.

"What on earth does it mean?" I asked, astonished.

"No one knows for certain. But the story goes that a fish lies buried here — a fish who spoke with a human voice," she explained.

The mysterious stone with its strange legend, so close to the wards of ailing and dying men, alarmed me suddenly. As twilight pressed on, I felt a chill all over me.

But after I left the place, I spent little time contemplating it. Walking home I was absorbed in my own problems again. Jim was on my mind. His leg had improved, it was true. He could now walk again. But the spine injury never seemed really to diminish. It came and went, but its severity during attacks was frightening. "Perhaps his psychological state has impeded a full cure," I thought. "Ingrid is destined to leave soon. Once she, like Gerda, is safe, maybe Jim's health will improve."

Jim was waiting impatiently for me when I arrived at the apartment. He asked for Friedrich and I told him that Friedrich seemed slightly better and certainly content to be where he was.

Then Jim showed me the letter from Gerda which had arrived right after I left. I snatched up the paper and read avidly:

"Daddy, Mummy, how lucky we are! Just imagine, my English daddy is working for the same Universal picture company as you, Daddy, and Mr. Cresswell, who is taking Ingrid, is manager for the Metro-Goldwyn-Mayer Company in Birmingham! Can you believe it?"

Frankly, these facts seemed miraculous as well as wonderful to us. That a professional link should exist between the foster parents' present and Jim's past seemed to stabilize our hopes, to confirm our strange feeling that we and our daughters would somehow elude the worst. We now reflected endlessly over the fact that Gerda and Ingrid would have been sent to camps in London had their names not been confused with those two sisters who had taken their place on an earlier transport. Due to this delay only, they had remained in Vienna until the condition of being claimed by an individual family was required. And, consequently, these two lovely families had reached out to them.

Both the Coupes and the Cresswells were non-Jewish. Many non-Jews in England were, like these two families, showing the Jews that they still had friends on the face of the earth.

A couple of days after Gerda's letter arrived, Mrs. Selinger telephoned me to tell me her good news. She had received a notice from the Children's Committee informing her that Marianne had been claimed by a wealthy family in South-ampton, England. Marianne was scheduled, therefore, to leave with the next transport.

Ultimately, we, too, were notified that Ingrid's turn had come. She, too, was to prepare herself for departure on the next transport.

Again, I had to go the same way, repeat the same steps that I had taken when Gerda left. Ingrid made the separation and its preparations easier for me. She maintained the light touch which had been hers since childhood and she managed to convey to Jim and me that she was genuinely happy to be able to leave. She consoled us by talking of a reunion, which we would undoubtedly experience soon. She begged us not to worry. And, girlishly, she was pleased that Marianne Selinger, her friend, would travel with her on the same transport.

The day came swiftly. Jim and I stood on the platform and looked unceasingly at the window of the compartment where Ingrid was standing now. She nodded to us, her radiant face assuring us that she was happy. And, as with Gerda, we ran doggedly behind the moving train until it disappeared.

Slowly, we made our way home. Within it, everything

seemed empty and desolate. Even the Kish family was gone now. The son had left on an earlier transport and the father had left to join Mrs. Kish.

Jim and I felt strange in this new silence. Already, we ached to hear the voices of the children. But we felt reassured even in our loss, because they were safe. Let anything happen to us now! They were entrusted to good and noble people, with whom they would be happy.

Shortly after Ingrid had left for England, I met Herbert Hahn, the boyfriend she had "shared" with Marianne. The boy was in a sad state and readily told me it was due to the combined absence of the two girls.

"Tell me, Herbert," I said. "What are your chances of leaving Vienna?"

"None," he said quickly. "I live with my mother and grand-mother, you know . . . they have no connections anywhere. They did not even try to get out."

"But you?"

"I will stay with them."

I hurried down the street, away from Herbert Hahn, and when I spotted an empty doorway I hid my face against it and wept. I pitied him so; I pitied any Jewish child who was left behind.

Our days and nights continued to pass in anxiety. Jim felt better sometimes, but always seemed to relapse after a hopeful period. He still underwent medical treatments at the hands of Dr. Schoenberg, who had maintained his interest in Jim's condition.

Jim and I enjoyed a momentary lift when Ingrid's first letter arrived. It reflected fully the optimism of Ingrid's nature, her ability to be gay under the most trying of conditions. First, she described her journey to England. In her train compartment she had been delighted to find not only Marianne but also some other girls from their class at school. When she arrived at Birmingham, she at once spotted Gerda who was waiting for her. Gerda had run to her. They had embraced and kissed and cried. Then Gerda, pointing to the company which surrounded her, introduced Mr. and Mrs. Cresswell, "your new mummy and daddy." And this was followed by introductions to "my mummy and daddy," the Coupes. All of them went to a coffeehouse after that and had lunch together.

At lunch, Gerda, who could understand a few English words, tried, with the help of the little English–German dictionary I'd given her, to act as interpreter.

Ingrid wrote that she found this very funny, to see our Gerda in this important role. Jim and I laughed too as we read the letter. We could imagine Gerda, usually so fluent in her speech, coming to many abrupt halts while she stopped to consult the dictionary in order to continue.

Our sole joy now came from these letters from Gerda and Ingrid. Their news was always good, always cheering. We had no more reason to worry about either of them. We knew about the people who were caring for them. It seemed that they treated them as their own children.

45

THE CHILDREN HAD GONE AND OUR HOME WAS DIFFERENT. IT
had taken on countless changes in the past year, most of them
notable, but this change was the most profound we had to
accept. If I heard Jim sigh, If he saw me wince, it was scarcely
necessary to ask the cause. We ached to see or hear our absent
daughters; at the same time, we were so relieved that they were
out of Vienna, away from a situation which grew harsher from
day to day.

Hanna was the next to lose her apartment. This in itself was
not upsetting, since she hoped to leave for England soon. She
was able to move in with Jim and me, occupying the room
formerly shared by Ingrid and Gerda. But Hanna was facing
other problems. For one thing, the expected permit from Esther
in England had not yet arrived; it had been expected before
now. Further, it was necessary to be financially clear with the
government before leaving Austria. Each Jewish person who
was to obtain a passport had to submit an *Unbedenklichkeit*,
a receipt stating that all taxes had been paid by that individual.
Since Hanna had almost no money at all, she offered her
furniture, which fortunately covered the amount she owed.

On the same day that this fearsome worry had been lifted,
a letter came from Esther bringing new ones. Esther explained
that permits had now become quite difficult to get. A new
regulation in England admitted only those who came as

351

domestics, and these had to be *single*. The reason for this was that married women, once in England tended to claim their husbands and bring them over. At the moment, it seemed that England was not eager to admit more men.

"I give up!" Hanna vowed, throwing Esther's letter on the nearest table. "Look, I have a husband and I can't leave him here anyway. The whole idea's been a daydream."

She was ready, almost, to let fate fall where it would. Arranging the departures for her children, giving up her home, contemplating the ironic safety of Josef in prison — all these had taken their toll of Hanna, who undoubtedly had been pulling through on the promise of her own ultimate release. I refused to see her give way.

"You can't help Josef here!" I said urgently. "When he's released from prison, he'll find a way out for himself. Why, Josef with his cleverness could think of fifty ways that would never occur to us, Hanna!"

"That's true," she admitted with a tenuous smile.

"Furthermore, we all know he's safer in jail than any Jew on the outside. And Robert's just a child, Hanna. How much Robert needs you now, and Esther wants you out of danger! Oh, I had this trouble with Olga, too. So, for that matter did you! You saw that Olga had to leave Friedrich behind for her children. Now do the same for yours."

"But what about that little detail they require — my being a single woman?"

I was walking around the room excitedly. "Yes, there is that. Why not go to the *Kultusgemeinde*? They surely know about this new regulation, Hanna — they somehow know everything there. Someone there will be able to advise you."

Hanna took my advice and went to the *Kultusgemeinde* immediately. Jim came in. I told him the latest news and together we waited breathlessly for Hanna's return.

About two hours later she returned, flushed with excitement and conflict.

"Helena, Jim! It is so fantastic. I'm divorced from Josef. Can you believe it?"

"How?" I breathed, astonished.

Hanna sank into a chair, shaking her head.

"Well, you were right about the *Kultusgemeinde*. Helena. They were well aware of the new English regulation. Their answer to the problem is to issue a divorce through the rabbinical office to any woman whose obstacle is not being single."

"Good heavens!" Jim said, saddened by such a solution.

"Oh," Hanna burst out, beginning to weep. "It is so sad and so painful—a divorce, just for expediency!"

I went to Hanna and kissed her.

"Don't condemn this expediency. It is only sane. During the Spanish Inquisition, Jews converted to Christianity to save their lives. Later, those who had escaped to other countries returned to Judaism. By the same pattern, when you and Josef are reunited in a free country, you can remarry."

"I'm with you all the way, Hanna. And Helena is right in what she says. You know what an incurable romantic Helena is. If she approves of the idea, it can't be wrong," he concluded with a wink.

I smiled at Jim's remark, and at Hanna. But I was thinking how superfluous romance had really become, even for people like us, who were its former advocates. How gallant of Jim to have even brought it up. I knew his thinking well these days: he advised any to get out who could get out. As for means, his old rigidity did not enter into such considerations. No wonder he accepted Hanna's divorce. And well he might think anyone's escape a good thing. The near future held out no promise for himself or for me.

Our conversation with Hanna helped her I believe. Her

mind seemed easier after that about her departure, which she began to arrange.

Meanwhile, I continued to visit Friedrich Landes at the Home for the Aged and Infirm. I went often, as I had promised Olga I would. Friedrich had only one other visitor beside myself, his only sister, a Mrs. Walder. Her children were already safe in America. Her husband was dead. As far as I could gather, Friedrich's sister made no attempts to get out of Austria herself. But I was glad to see her there from time to time. Her presence made Friedrich seem less alone. I wrote to Olga, telling her of Friedrich's sister, saying that Friedrich's condition was unchanged, that he looked pleased when I came, and that he received good care as before. I really looked in on him often, and Hanna came with me sometimes.

From England, Olga replied that she was relieved that Friedrich was not deserted. Then she described her life there. She was working as a housekeeper in a private home. The hours were very long and the work very strenuous. She did not mind, however; she was grateful to be near Helga. Poor Olga, working as a maid at this stage of life! The bookish sister who had never been asked to do housework as a girl, who had had a maid of her own when married, now worked harder than any maid who had worked for the Landeses! I smiled bitterly, thinking of it. Still, she was lucky and she knew it. There was no reign of Nazi terror in England.

Jews in Vienna were being chased and uprooted from their apartments every day now. A chance acquaintance brought us together with a family called Riber at this time. They had just been ousted from a large apartment and were seeking shelter. They learned that we had a living room which was not being used at the moment. The family consisted of husband, wife, and a twenty-year-old daughter.

We were perfectly willing for them to move in but there was one little problem. After the Kish family had moved out, we had been lucky enough to sell all the living-room furniture. Only the piano, for which no customer was found, remained there.

The Ribers made light of this problem, however; they had things of their own which would do very well. So the three of them moved in, bringing with them two beds, one couch, a table and chairs. They had all the essentials. The piano, which looked bizarre amid this hodgepodge, I covered with a sheet.

Riber, an extrovert, soon felt at home in this terrible crowded room. He struck up a friendship at once with Jim and began to spend hours in his room. Together, the men listened to foreign radio stations and discussed the latest news. Riber, who had a hearty voice and ready laughter, puzzled me a bit.

Once I asked, "You've made some arrangements, I assume, to get out of Vienna?"

"Oh, yes. I wrote to my nephew in America some time ago, asking him for affidavits for the whole family."

"And did he send them?" asked Jim.

"No."

"But that's awful. Families are usually the first to send affidavits to their own relatives," I protested.

"Well," he said. "It wasn't an absolute refusal. But my nephew made conditions." He lowered his voice confidentially. "I own property, as it happens in Czernowitz, and my nephew knows of it. He wrote me a letter saying that he would send the three of us affidavits if I would transcribe the property in his name."

"Of course you agreed?" Jim said.

"Certainly not."

"But why?" I asked.

"This is the only property I have in the world. Czernowitz belongs to Rumania. It's the city I lived in and loved before the World War. I have every hope of returning there with my family after the world situation stabilizes a bit," he stated.

"Good God, Riber!" Jim said. "Who knows what any part of Europe will look like later on? The safest place is America, certainly!"

Riber straightened up. "I believe," he asserted, "that everything will be normal again in Europe. Hitler won't last long."

"Another optimist!" I thought bitterly. "No wonder he's always in such good spirits."

Still, I was glad that Riber and his family were there. Riber provided a certain heartening companionship for Jim. And it was good for my husband to have another man to talk with in these days. That the man was fearless and hopeful in these desperate times was also helpful, even if Jim knew his hope to be blind. Riber lent something positive to the atmosphere of our home.

For example, a day came when our doorbell rang with a fearful urgency. With so many of the family gone, we expected no one. I stiffened visibly with fear. But Riber, who was invariably calm and hopeful, said:

"Don't be frightened, Mrs. Hilsen! I'll bet it's a messenger, bringing some good news to you."

That guess seemed highly improbable to me, but I had no choice about answering the door.

As I did so, a gentleman stepped into the foyer. Noticing the terrified expression which I was unable to conceal, he smiled and said quickly, "Don't mind my swastika badge, please! I am forced to wear it, or else I shouldn't. My name is Genegel. I'm the manager of the Berlin office of Universal Pictures."

"I am relieved," I said. I shook violently, however, as I let him into Jim's room. Jim was in bed that day with spinal pains.

"This is Mr. Genegel, Jim."

"Genegel!" he repeated.

"You know my name?"

"Certainly. From the Berlin office, aren't you? You were referred to frequently here."

Mr. Genegel, meanwhile, had surveyed Jim, the general condition of the apartment, my terror at his arrival. He sat down next to Jim's bed.

"Look, I'm terribly sorry for you, Mr. Hilsen. We both have worked for the same company — occupied the same position — and here you are in this pitiable condition because you happen to be a Jew. Believe me, I deplore the Nazi sentiment, the Nazi treatment of Jews. They are inhuman . . . and the Austrians, I notice seem even worse than the Germans."

Jim was speechless for the moment. He just kept staring at the man.

Genegel cleared his throat and continued. "But why don't I get to the point? I've got good news for you, Mr. Hilsen. I received an order from Mr. Seidelman in New York. He's instructed me to close the Vienna branch of Universal. He has also granted a monthly allowance to you. It's to be sent regularly from the Berlin office."

"And you got permission to pay a Jew!" Jim asked, incredulous.

Genegel scratched his head and smiled.

"It wasn't easy, I'll confess. I had a lot of trouble getting that permission from the Nazi authorities — but finally did get it."

Jim sighed deeply. As for me, I had never stopped the trembling which began when the doorbell rang.

"Mr. Genegel," Jim said. "I don't know how to thank you. I'm sure my wife doesn't either. That you've endangered your own security by helping a Jew is evident."

"I only wish I could do more for you, Mr. Hilsen. Please write to me when you need my help. I'll do whatever I can for you."

Thus, the stranger departed. So we had more reason than

ever to be thankful to Mr. Seidelman. Not only had he sent affidavits for us but, having discovered our wait for the quota, he now helped us with money to live on. To have an income again, money that would come in regularly, seemed a miracle. I would not have to stand in the food lines any more!

But buying food was not so simple a matter as I had imagined. It was made very difficult for Jews. There was a regulation stating that they (who could buy at all) could buy food only between the hours of twelve and one o'clock P.M. At that hour, most of the food had been sold to gentiles.

But in this difficulty we found another non-Jewish friend who was moved by the myriad indignities we suffered. The superintendent of our building, like Mr. Genegel, was a gentile with a generous heart. He despised Nazi ideology and was daring enough to disdain wearing a swastika band. He had sent his son and daughter away to the country, rather than have them join the *Hitlerjugend*. He knew our situation well, and was distressed with the idea that although Jim was ill and needed nourishing food, we could rarely procure it.

Thus he began to stand in line for us at the markets, bringing us fish and other items of food. Whenever he brought his parcels to us, we had to smile, to be heartened. Every good non-Jew had to count for scores of unknown ones. We were infinitely grateful.

Adequately fed, for the moment, we continued to concentrate on the quota situation. I made another trip to the *Kultusgemeinde* to see if some fantastic chance had hastened the hour of our expected time. But no change had occurred and America was a long time off.

46

HITLER'S DEMANDS EXPANDED. HE WAS VERY STRONG NOW; everything was apparently within his reach. This time he chose Danzig. He staked everything on one card at a time and was always successful. He had taken the Rhineland, Austria, Czechoslovakia, the Sudetenland — why should he not get Danzig, too? And if Danzig succumbed without difficulty, he would continue in his demands.

The Austrian Nazis had not wanted war. They did not mind robbing and persecuting helpless Jews. That was an easy job. But in going to war they might lose their own lives. Nazi propaganda had appealed to their intense chauvinism at the beginning. They had expected to be personally enlarged by the German occupation.

But it was not to be so. Slowly now, they began to hate the Germans. And small wonder! For Austria had become a German province. All the Austrian government officials had been sent to small towns in Germany and all their jobs in Austria had been taken over by Germans. The Nazis had great difficulty in running the businesses which they had confiscated from Jews. They sold out the merchandise but were often unable to get other goods. In addition, Hitler demanded taxes from all the merchants. If they were unable to pay those taxes, their stores were closed by the government and the owners obliged to accept jobs in a war plant.

As these facts unfolded, dissatisfaction grew among the Austrian gentiles, but they could not alter the situation. However, they no longer said, "We thank our Fuehrer"; they had stopped being grateful to him.

Nevertheless, the Nazi poison had penetrated their minds. Goebbels' propaganda against the Jews had mounted, and had had the desired effect. He was prolific with new lies. One of them took the form of a flagrant exhibition, bearing the motto: COMMUNISM WITHOUT THE MASK.

Large posters, showing a communist stripping off his mask and revealing a caricatured Jewish face underneath, holding the Ten Commandments in one hand and the hammer and sickle in the other, were abundant. Pictures of Jews in the vilest and most despicable positions were everywhere. This was the new Nazi culture.

At the time of this exhibition, we had an unexpected visit from an old friend. Seidl, our former usher, had chosen to call on us.

When I opened the door, he was peeling off his swastika badge, which he had worn so proudly when the Nazis first took over.

Amazed at his appearance, I told him to come in. Jim was up and about that day. The three of us talked at length.

Seidl was terribly disillusioned with the Nazis, he confided. And further, he was ashamed of his original liking for them. He had come from the exhibition in a state of disgust. He had not realized what distortions they were capable of. He longed to leave Austria, but was powerless to do so. He wanted to make it clear that he would never have espoused the Nazi cause if he had recognized it for what it was.

It was August 23rd, 1939, when I was in a grocery store, trying to buy some food, that a woman rushed in excitedly and said: "Did you hear? Ribbentrop has left for Moscow. Now we'll be reunited with the Russians and all the Jews will be exterminated!"

She was unconcerned with the Communists, whom the Nazis hated; for her, it was more vital that the Jews be wiped out. This woman did not recognize me as Jewish. But the storekeeper, who had known me as a customer for years, knew. She looked at me without saying a word. What she was thinking, I could not tell.

But the message of her bloodthirsty newscarrier had come through. I felt blood running to my head. Somehow, I rushed home to tell Jim what I had heard.

"My God," Jim said. "If Ribbentrop has gone to Moscow, that means that Hitler wants to start a war. Ribbentrop has made the trip to preclude interference from Stalin."

And then Hanna rushed into the apartment, terrified also. She had just come from an office to get her papers for departure, the permit from Esther having arrived since her divorce. But today the man in the office had said to her, "Hurry up, Jewess! When the war breaks out, all the Jews here will be killed!"

"He was right, Hanna," I said. "Get out, for God's sake, while you can. It seems that war is imminent. When it breaks out it may be too late for you."

"Too late for me!" Hanna screamed. "Well what about you and Jim? What about Josef? Am I to leave you here trapped for the kill?" She began to sob hysterically.

I put my arms around her.

"Hanna, Hanna, if we are trapped for the kill, as you put it, then how can you help us by staying? You would only make us miserable by trapping yourself needlessly."

Thus it went, until she was quiet. Before she left, she elicited a promise from me to go with her for the last visit to Josef.

We found Josef looking much the same as ever. Since news of the times seeped into the jail regularly, he was greatly relieved that Hanna's departure for England was now a settled thing. As for the divorce, he understood completely. He genuinely hoped to rejoin her and their children. He seemed confident that it would happen eventually.

His optimistic mood during this final meeting was a great help to Hanna, who was frankly guilt-stricken. I watched Josef as he talked to his wife and thought, "How lucky Josef really is, having such a nature! Any dream seems possible to a mind like that. He has lived intimately with a score of delusions."

After that day, Hanna was busy running around town, settling everything for the departure. Meanwhile, I went to see Friedrich again.

When I entered his ward, I saw at once that his bed was empty. I rushed to the office to make an inquiry. They told me that they had been just about to inform me : Mr. Landes had passed away an hour ago.

"Dead?" I whispered.

"I'm afraid so, Mrs. Hilsen. His casket is about to be taken to the wagon — that goes to the cemetery chapel."

I rushed outside, thinking of Olga. How could I write this to her, and so soon, so soon! There, indeed, was Friedrich's casket being carried to the black wagon. It began to move and instinctively I followed it. The horses which drew the wagon moved slowly and I, the only one accompanying it, followed Friedrich's body for two blocks with a shocked and mute respect.

The next day, Friedrich's sister, Jim, Hanna, and I and a few random acquaintances attended Friedrich's funeral. There were a number of other funerals the same morning, and Friedrich's resting place was surrounded by many new graves.

Two days later, on August 30th, I took Hanna to the railway station. Her day had come. Hanna was the last of my family to leave and, as luck would have it, Jim was suffering a relapse of spinal pain that day and could not accompany us. Friedrich's funeral had depressed him and the indisposition had followed.

Hanna was controlled as we kissed goodbye. She had had so much guilt and emotion in the mere contemplation of her journey. Here was the last train which civilians could take to leave Vienna.

I walked from the Westbahnhof, the station, through the Mariahilferstrasse, on toward home. *"Auf Wiedersehen!"* sounded in my brain—an echo of Hanna's calling, "Will it be *auf wiedersehen?*"

For the first time, I thought, "No, there is no hope. Before, there might have been. Now the time is closing in on us. The others have left. Jim and I are left here, trapped, as Hanna feared!" I had never admitted this kind of hopelessness before. It was a new experience; it hollowed one out. A panorama of pictures swam through my mind. I began to visualize the worst. "How will Jim and I end?" I asked myself. There was a choice of visions, after all—torture in concentration camp, shooting, starvation; one could go on for quite a while.

Still, whatever was to come, Jim and I would be together until the last moment. That much, at least, seemed certain. My children and the rest of my family were in safety. I thanked God for that.

I walked without seeing where I walked. The people who passed me seemed like dream creatures. Somehow, I managed to get home.

There, Jim was waiting for me anxiously. He had been worried.

"It took you so long, Helena. Where were you?"

"Oh, I decided to walk home, Jim."

"You should have taken the trolley such a long distance!" he said. "Imagine walking all the way from the railroad station. You look exhausted."

"I am tired," I admitted, "but don't worry about it. I'll be all right. And Jim, don't give in. Friedrich is dead, Hanna is gone, and we are here. But we have to be strong, whatever happens to us."

47

On September 1, 1939, the dreaded, inevitable war broke out. Propaganda posters against Communists were still to be seen plastered on billboard pillars in the streets. Yet the Nazi press prized the treaty with their best friends, the Russians, which was to the mutual advantage of both Germany and Russia. Surely it had to be to the advantage of both Hitler and Stalin, since they had divided Poland between themselves, with the demarcation line at the Rivers Bug and San.

To enlighten their people, the Nazis ordered their population to listen to some radio speeches delivered by Hitler, Goering, and Goebbels. Austrians thronged to the large loudspeakers in the streets to hear the latest pronouncements. The mere expectation of the speeches had caused mass excitement and tension.

Jim and I, together with Mr. Riber, were sitting in front of our radio, listening. Hitler's dramatic voice, shouting, was transmitted.

First he accused Chamberlain and the Jews; they were responsible for the war which had broken out. He had asked for Danzig and the Corridor, he stated, with peaceful intentions, but they, the warmongers, prevented German territory from being annexed to the Reich. He continued sarcastically. As I remember, it went something like this:

"Chamberlain has warned me that the war will last four to

five years. I, too, have to say how long the war will last. So now I tell you it will be a *Blitzkreig* and we will be victorious. I am going now to the battlefield, to my soldiers. If something should happen to me there, I appoint Goering and Hess my successors."

As for Goering, his statement went : "Now, since Chamberlain has declared war our *Luftwaffe* will bomb London. But no bomb will ever fall on German cities. And since we are in a state of war with France, too, we will finish her off quickly."

Jim and I were reduced to a state of shock. So England, that haven of safety to which we had dispatched our children with such relief, was now to be bombed. The English population, containing within it the trusting bodies of Ingrid and Gerda, was in grave danger.

At once, communication with England was broken off. We received no more letters from our daughters. So a new terror became ours : their physical fate in England.

Meanwhile the Nazi press boasted of their victory over Poland. They were proceeding rapidly, without opposition. Next we read : "WARSAW BOMBED BY OUR GLORIOUS LUFT-WAFFE." On September 7th, they announced : "OUR LUFT-WAFFE BOMBED LONDON WITH GREAT SUCCESS !"

So it had happened. Goering's threat was quickly realized. Our misery was great indeed. Perhaps neither of us had quite believed it could happen.

The Austrian gentiles were not enthusiastic about the war. Food rationing, which had existed for some months, was now tightened. Blackout precautions were now taken. Light was blotted out with either black cloth or paper.

A neighbor of ours whose husband and son had been taken into the army complained bitterly, and asked naïvely, "Why didn't they just give him Danzig and the Corridor?" She had ceased to be an admirer of Hitler's. "We don't want a war," she said to me.

For the gentiles, there was much inconvenience, many impositions upon their personal lives which they had not foreseen in their original embracing of Nazi ideology. They knew the pain of war. No one could deny it. Still, their soldiers were armed, had a chance to defend themselves.

The Jews, on the other hand, were defenseless. Never organized, they were a dispersed prey for the Nazis. With the outbreak of the war, their plight worsened perceptibly. There was a new wave of regulations and persecutions.

The second Day of Atonement under Hitler's rule came. Without synagogues, the Jews prayed and fasted in their homes this year. A desperate mother saw the Gestapo pick up her son on Yom Kippur. Having fasted for twenty-four hours already, they forced him to continue the fast. Another mother wept relentlessly, day and night, because her two sons had been taken off to a concentration camp. The relatives of those taken to concentration camps now heard of the absent ones only when they received urns containing their ashes. I met an acquaintance of ours on the street whose husband was among those in concentration camp. I asked, automatically, if she had heard from her husband. She answered: "Thank God, I have not heard anything."

A new regulation was issued, stating that all Jews had to relinquish their radios and any silver, gold, or jewelry which still remained in their possession. A forlorn line of Jews formed in front of the police station with the remnants of their possessions in hand.

At this point, I still owned a pair of silver candlesticks. Earlier, I had hung on to them stubbornly, for they were a keepsake from my mother. I had wanted to regard them — something — as still precious. Now, I had to let them go.

But I refused to hand them over to the Nazis. Instead, I gave them as a gift to our superintendent, who stood in line for us at the markets. It was the least we could do, I felt, to show our recognition of his humanity.

When the war broke out, Jim and I were convinced that there would be no more possibility of leaving Vienna. That we would be killed by the Nazis seemed a relatively certain matter. It was only a question of time before they would get around to us.

What, after all, could we delude ourselves with now? There were no means of communication any more. Trains and ships did not exist, except for soldiers. The American consulate had ceased to issue visas any more.

As for our apartment, we knew that it, too, must be taken from us soon. Jim and I were the only Jews left in the building. The manager of the house soon came to us and told us that he had received an order from the Gestapo to throw out any Jews remaining in the building. But the man pitied us. He kept pulling at his chin and gesturing as he told us the situation.

"I tell you what," he said finally. "Rather than ask you to leave at once, I'll issue a regular eviction notice. This, with its legal procedures, will take time . . . you know the red tape! And that will postpone your leaving for awhile. . . ."

48

In October, the gates of immigration reopened unexpectedly. The American consulate started to operate and to issue visas again. And the *Kultusgemeinde* took great pains to help as many Jews as possible to leave Austria. Dutch, Italian, and American ships were at their disposal. As soon as the news reached us, I went hastily to the *Kultusgemeinde* to inquire when the next quota was due. Those people, I was told, who had registered at the beginning of April, 1938, and had all the necessary papers, could receive their visas now. Since we had registered on the 28th of April, we had the prospect of being considered in the not-too-distant future. The consulate also advised me that we would need some additional papers. I regretted having to trouble Mr. Seidelman again. We already owed so much to that benevolent stranger.

The notification from the consulate, however, quickened our hopes. The request for more papers took the prospect of leaving from the realm of the vague to that of the real. Postponements in the past had invariably depressed us, since no one knew what horrors an extra month could bring. Even now, we had no definite date promised to us. But that something was being processed for us — that they needed more papers — meant we might really leave Vienna alive.

A good number of our remaining friends got out at this time. As contrasted to theirs, our plight, even with its hope, seemed a bad one. When they came to say goodbye, several cried to see our condition, our lack of absolute certainty. A few treated us as if we were lost.

Hitler had pledged to exterminate the Jews. As his victories swelled, as a number of interferences he might have feared failed to materialize, it began to seem very likely that he could keep his word. Before the actual outbreak of war, Jewish persecutions had gone on willy-nilly, perpetrated by individuals and in small groups; this accounted for the inconsistencies of fates up to now. But with the fact of real war, there was nothing to deter the worst. According to his plan, Hitler had systematically prepared for the extermination of the Jews.

The Polish actions were the first steps in this mass murder. All Jews were to be rounded up and sent to Poland to be killed. The first Polish action started in Vienna in November, 1939. Perhaps the most fiendish aspect of this plan was to order the *Kultusgemeinde* to execute the task. The Nazis wanted the Jews themselves to send their own brothers to certain death. In their exasperation, many Jews cursed the *Kultusgemeinde* clerks, not realizing that they were defenseless tools of the Gestapo, which had an office right in the *Kultusgemeinde*. From there SS men controlled and dictated to the Jewish clerks in charge of deportation and other matters. And the Gestapo had ordered them to put two thousand Jews at their disposal for the first transport to Poland. So the *Kultusgemeinde,* which had a list of all Jewish inhabitants, sent their messengers to Jewish homes with summonses to appear at their offices.

At midnight our doorbell rang, nearly paralyzing us with fear. Mr. Riber, who was still with us, answered the door and brought us a summons for Jim to appear at once. I shook violently as I read the summons, thinking of friends who had just left Vienna. Why now, I thought wildly, just when we had hope again? Jim took the news more quietly than I, and he tried to calm me. He had no choice but to go at once. He rose from the bed, wincing with spinal aches, and dressed quickly. I would not let him go alone, and he finally agreed to let me accompany him. He took his cane and together we walked through the blacked-out streets to the *Kultusgemeinde*. It was a long walk from the Mariahilferstrasse. We passed the Babenberberstrasse, crossed the Burgring through Hofburg Helden Platz, Kohlmark Graben, and Rottenturmstrasse; from there, we turned to Seitenstettengasse, on which #4 was the *Israelitische Kultusgemeinde*. Despite the blacked-out streets, we had had no difficulty in finding our way here. I knew the streets well by now, after months and months of hounding the *Kultusgemeinde* offices for information of one kind or another. Nor were these desolate streets the least bit frightening to us on that night. Darkness had been our companion in the last month. The darkness of human minds, which awaited us within the building, was far more dangerous to Jim and me.

Inside, we found many other Jews who had been summoned to appear. A suppressed terror was almost palpable in the air. A physician was examining those who had been summoned; he was to decide which of these people were to leave.

Ultimately, Jim's turn to see the doctor came. I stayed behind in the waiting room, scarcely daring to think. But, immersed as I was in our own immediate plight, it was impossible to ignore the scenes going on in this room. I saw a young sick woman crying and lamenting, because her husband had to leave with this transport. Next to her stood her old mother who was attempting to console her, although (as their broken conversation revealed) this mother had received an urn containing her husband's ashes only a few days previously. He had been killed in a concentration camp.

Then the young husband came back into the room. He was to leave, he told them, the next morning. The young woman fainted upon receiving the news. As they strove to revive her,

Jim entered the room abruptly. I jumped to my feet and ran
to him.

"It's all right, Helena," he muttered to me, smiling. "I have
been exempted — from this transport, anyway."

Tears ran freely down my cheeks.

"Your back condition?" I whispered, as we swiftly began to
walk out of the place.

"My condition, of course."

By now the dark night air surrounded us again.

"It's too fantastic!" I said. "You might so easily have been
taken. Such sorrow as there was in that waiting room. . . . Why
have we been singled out? Why has fate decreed that you
should leave that place a free man tonight?" I wondered.

"Part, of course, is freakish luck," Jim said, as we quickened
our steps. "The rest, Helena, only God can explain."

The next morning we heard that the action had been completed. Each of the group which had been selected for the
Polish transport was allowed to take a mere pittance of money
and a small valise containing a few essentials. And thus
equipped, the first victims left for Poland that day.

Later, because we happened to know a policeman who used
to come to our movie frequently, we discovered the fate of that
transport, which he had accompanied: when the train had
passed the Polish frontier, it had stopped in a wood. The
Gestapo had chased all the Jews out of the train, robbed them
of their money and small trunks, and had fired on them. Many
were killed. Others had managed to escape. A few had swum
the River San and had reached the Russian part of Poland.

Two weeks later a second order was issued by the Gestapo
for another transport. And again the Jews were summoned to
register. Jim was not spared a summons this time either. But
now no medical examinations were to be given. If anyone was
too sick to join the transport, he was to bring a certificate from
a medical police officer stating so. Most medical police officers

were Nazis, of course, and not the least inclined to give out such certificates to Jews.

Frantically, we called Dr. Schoenberg, fearful that his office might not answer, that he might have vanished into some new movement since our last encounter. But mercifully, he answered the phone. Strangely, he was as eager to help us as before. He told us to come to his office at once. I saw that Jim was feeling ill as I put down the receiver.

"You're not well, are you?"

"It's all right, Helena. I can make it to his office."

But he winced as he turned away.

"It's pointless for you to go. He's not going to treat you today. I can get the certificate for you, Jim."

So I went to Schoenberg's office alone. I had grown used to doing things by myself since Jim was first incapacitated. The doctor greeted me warmly.

"How is your husband, Mrs. Hilsen?"

"Oh, much better, but there are always recurrences. Sometimes, I wonder if he will ever be really well again."

"These healings are always slow. Spine injuries are often subtle and devious. But I've seen other cases like this. Time will do it. After all, he's a relatively young man. But about this Polish transport, Mrs. Hilsen. . . ."

I described the situation to Dr. Schoenberg. Without another word, he prepared the necessary documents for me — supplying me with a duplicate if I should need it. I could not find enough words to thank him. But, in the end, he seemed to shrink at my excessive gratitude, and hastened me away with a slow smile.

Jim and I presented this certificate at the *Kultusgemeinde*. The clerk in charge looked at the certificate, then looked at Jim. He was apparently convinced. So the second Polish transport left without my husband on it.

But after a short time, a third summons was issued. This time a printed postal card came, bearing a threat from the Gestapo. If Jim did not show up for this third transport, there would be serious trouble. Without phoning, I rushed again to Schoenberg's office. I froze as I saw a large sign over the door— "CLOSED." Compelled, I rang the doorbell anyway. His wife, who would barely answer me, opened it and heard me out. Then she merely shook her head and closed the door, leaving me outside.

I entered the apartment trembling.

"Jim!" I blurted. "Schoenberg's office is closed! Something's happened—he must be in trouble. His wife came to the door. God, what a bitter face she had!"

A day or two later we discovered that Doctor Schoenberg had been taken away by the Gestapo. They had discovered that he was of Jewish descent and had been concealing it. So Jim and I had been correct in our intuitive choice of Schoenberg's name from the list of doctors so long ago.

Jim and I were miserable at the news of his capture and even fancied some misplaced guilt. Had Schoenberg's involvement with us had anything to do with his being found out? But no, that couldn't be, or else the Gestapo would have come for Jim by now, and even me. Still, the recollection of Schoenberg's compassion for us! How we were haunted by it. Probably he would have a terrible fate now. No doubt it had taken but one Gestapo officer to look twice at his name, detect its possible Jewishness, and Schoenberg had been undone.

But Jim still had to be saved, if possible, from going on the third Polish transport. Fortunately, we were still in possession of the duplicate certificate Schoenberg had given me that last time. It stated clearly that Mr. Hilsen would be unable to join any transport for months to come. This time, I decided to go without Jim. It might be more convincing if I said he was too ill to make it down to the *Kultusgemeinde*. This time, our hearts were literally in our mouths. Would the certificate work?

No one really knew how quickly Nazi information could spread. Suppose these Jewish clerks at the *Kultusgemeinde* had been supplied with a list of doctors whose certificates (like Schoenberg's) should be disqualified? Endless possibilities for failure occurred to us. Time itself was alarming. This was, after all, the third evasion of Poland which we were attempting. How long could our fantastic luck continue?

But when I, summoning all the poise left in me, presented the certificate at the *Kultusgemeinde*, the clerk in charge did not hesitate over it for a minute. He was glad that I had this means of preventing my husband from going on the transport and dismissed me with a smile. So another hurdle was gotten over. Jim was to be left alone for a while. I could scarcely believe it. Then, all of the transports were postponed until February, 1940.

49

THE STRAIN OF THESE PROCEEDINGS HAD FINALLY BEEN TOO much for my overtaxed nerves. Abruptly, I fell ill. I fainted. When I opened my eyes, everything seemed to be whirling at such a rate that it appeared I would be overwhelmed when all the objects tumbled down. I was forced to remain in bed. I remember that Jim managed to find a doctor who came to the apartment and left a prescription for me. Two weeks later, when I finally got out of bed, I was still dizzy and had to hold on to things everywhere to prevent myself from falling. Was this dizziness a retreat that some part of me was attempting? I must have suspected so, for gradually another part of me— my will—struggled for clarity and, slowly, I recovered my balance. Was it not essential to have balance if one was to realize the hope of leaving Austria, the dream of recovering one's children?

Shortly after I was well again, we received a legal notification to appear in court. This was the eviction procedure which the building manager had begun some time before in order to avoid ousting us at once. I went to the office of this manager. As before, he was extremely nice to me. He told me he was ashamed to be a German, that he could not stand the way the Nazis were treating the Jews. I told him that Jim and I had a prospect of leaving Vienna in about three months. It would mean everything to us if we could remain sheltered in our apartment until the day of our departure. The manager listened to my story carefully, quietly. At last he said, "I am with you, Mrs. Hilsen. And to show you my sincerity, I will go to court with you and ask the judge to postpone the eviction for three months."

This man kept his promise and his intervention worked. The judge granted his request. Then I had to sign a document stating that we would vacate our apartment on February 28th.

Now Jim and I turned our whole attention to the subject of leaving, praying that no new obstacle would arise to prevent it. Our original scheme of picking up the girls in England en route to America was now clearly out of the question, since England had gone to war with Germany. We could not even exchange letters with Ingrid and Gerda any more. So we revised our dream; once safe in the U.S.A., we would bring the girls over there.

One day the postman delivered a package to us which brought us quite a surprise. We were certainly expecting no packages in those days. A quick glance at the sender revealed that it had been sent by Schorr from Switzerland! The package contained some fine canned food and other tasty items which it would have been impossible for us to obtain in Vienna. Shortly thereafter, two more such packages came from Schorr. We were very thankful to receive these gifts from him. It was so strange to be the recipients of Schorr's thoughtfulness at this time. The man had always confounded us so. What made the gesture even more generous than it might appear was the realization that Schorr probably had little hope for our ultimate survival, having heard what he must have of Austria and its Jews. So it was especially nice of him to send food at this time to what he might have considered two potential ghosts.

With this added bit of sustenance, we concentrated fully upon the course of our quota problem. I haunted the *Kultus-gemeinde* to inquire which quota number was due. I was advised that the register days of April 15–20 were due now. Finally, I was told that the 28th of April was due. I was almost crazy with relief. We discovered that those who had registered on April 29th were so numerous that few had a chance to be included in the quota. We recalled how Bernatz had a year and a half before persuaded me to register on April 28th, and we shook our heads. . . . Another miracle.

The next day a letter arrived from Mr. Seidelman in New York. He told us that he had sent all necessary papers for us to the U.S. consulate. Jim and I kept rereading Mr. Seidelman's letter. It was real, tangible. Everything seemed to be finally working out. Next we were informed that the papers had arrived at the consulate in time; we would be able to go to the United States! A week later, we were notified by the American consulate to appear there for a medical examination on January 31st.

The Selingers were far less fortunate than we. They had written to their American sponsors for additional papers and had received no answer. As our departure became imminent, the Selingers visited us with increasing frequency, bemoaning their fate. Selinger now cursed himself for his former optimism, which had lost them their chance to go to America. He and his wife, having been born in Vienna, could have been among the first groups to leave. Now, as they began so late in the game to try to emigrate, they needed new affidavits. Indeed, the Selingers were now among the "lost ones," as we had been considered by those who sadly had left us behind.

Now that we were apparently due to leave, they begged us to look up their silent sponsor when we arrived in New York, to ask him to send the papers that would save them. Of course, I promised that I would see the man as soon as we arrived. And certainly, I would do so. I did not say out loud that it seemed to me far too late to begin such proceedings, that even our departure, so systematically arranged so long ago. seemed little short of a miracle.

50

It was now January, 1940. A year of terror, suffering, and hopelessness had miraculously culminated in our salvation. Before we left Austria, another person who had been saved by erratic fate re-entered our lives: Josef, my brother-in-law, was released from the prison which had shielded him from Nazi focus.

Josef, as might have been expected, emerged from prison unhurt and unchánged. In his familiar suit and coat, Josef looked to us exactly as he had before he was sentenced. Indeed, his mental and physical condition was far better than Jim's at this time. By contrast, Jim was exceedingly thin and his spirits could not be described as good, despite our happy turn of fate. Jim had just been through too much to be quite happy at this critical time. He had endured in "freedom" endless tortures of uncertainty, as had I. Josef, imprisoned and kept in ignorance, had been spared much that we experienced.

Now that he was back, Josef enjoyed describing his life in jail to Jim and me. He told us that the director of his division was a good man with a thoroughly human heart. He had taken a liking to Josef and had treated him very well, even seeing to it that Josef's diet was superior to that of the other prisoners.

Jim and I heard the story with amused wonder. Dear, unquenchable Josef! Who could fail to love him? Who could harbor ill will because he had nearly ruined us? With things as they were, we would have been ruined anyway. We begged him to stay with us for the little time we were to remain in our apartment.

But Josef was forced to decline the invitation. He was afraid of being seen, in our vicinity, by a certain Nazi who knew him from the past and who would surely kill him on sight.

So instead, Josef went to the Leopoldstadt section, where he stayed with a friend of his, who had been released somehow from Dachau and was waiting for his turn to go to America. Josef himself immediately began to seek some illegal way to get out of Vienna. There was not too much Jim and I could do to help him. I gave him a few oil paintings which remained in the apartment. Perhaps, with luck, he could sell them and get a little money for his basic needs. Josef took these, though reluctantly, and begged us not to worry about him. He was overjoyed that we would be able to leave Vienna soon.

We still owned the furniture from the children's bedroom, as well as the piano. Now, needing money badly, we tried to sell these things. A member of the Nazi party came to the apartment to look them over. He asked Jim what his business had been.

"The movie business," Jim replied.

"Indeed!" said the man. "Oh, I wanted to get a movie theater, myself. Why not? My illegal Nazi activity before the occupation was considerable. But at the office where all the Jewish property had been taken over, I was told that I did not deserve a movie theater because I'd only been in jail a few months, whereas other illegal Nazis had done much more for the Nazi effort. Imagine!"

It was difficult to imagine, indeed. I thought I understood him. Then Jim said, "What do you mean, exactly? How did it work?"

"Well," said the man, without a trace of self-consciousness, "you see, some Nazis who had killed our opponents during the

Schuschnigg regime were imprisoned for life. Of course, they were let out when the Nazis took over. But such people are considered more justifiably rewarded with valuable Jewish properties than I."

We were speechless. The man was so matter-of-fact that we felt no more emotion than he did. It was an old story to us, really. But it had been so bizarre to hear him tell it.

In the end, he agreed to buy our things, although he paid a very small sum for them.

Since we still did not have enough money to cover our passage, we wrote Mr. Genegel in Berlin, asking for the sum we needed. Genegel, having anticipated our need, had already obtained permission from Mr. Seidelman to get us additional funds and sent the sum immediately.

Now the time had come to complete all the formalities necessary for obtaining a valid passport to America. First, I had to get the *Unbedenklichkeit* — the receipt which stated that all one's taxes had been paid. To cover this, we had held something in reserve, banked on it, and drawn our dreams on the basis of it : some time ago, in the days of our well-being, we had taken out two insurance policies, each for $10,000, for Ingrid and Gerda. These policies had been meant to provide each daughter with a dowry. They were due in 1951 and, most important, they had been entirely paid up by Jim. Fortunately, this insurance company was making refunds on insurance policies to Jews like us who needed the money for taxes. The Nazi government did not interfere with these refunds, even though they were to Jews, since the money ended up being additional revenue for them.

I went to the insurance company and although they paid me a comparatively small amount on the two policies, I was happy to have the cash. Immediately, I took the money to the Internal Revenue office, where I was peremptorily told it was not enough. At this, I brought out a trump card — Jim's old-fashioned gold watch, which we had held on to tenaciously, even when half-starved. This, with the money, satisfied them, and I received our *Unbedenlichkeit*. It was like receiving a remedy to a serious illness.

Our next step was to go to the immigration office in the Rothschild castle. The Gestapo was taking care of everything. At the entrance, a young SS man, who snarled at Jews as if they were curs, was posted. As we went in, we saw an older woman entering the gates, with another young SS man directly behind her. The latted shouted suddenly :

"A Jewess dares to enter the door in front of me! Step back at once."

I could not help smiling ironically and thinking to myself, "Master Race!" But when I realized that my readiness for humor was relative to the closeness of my departure, the smile disappeared quickly from my lips. I hoped that no one had seen that smile. It could have been dangerous for me.

In the hall inside, people stood in line waiting their turn, forbidden either to talk or to look around. It was little wonder that looking around was forbidden, for the palace had been ravaged. Where, in former times, the most glorious works of art and Gobelins had hung, only raw marks where they had been ripped remained.

At last our turn came. We succeeded in obtaining passports and were delighted to leave the bare and mutilated palace.

The most important hurdle was still before us : the physical examination and the subsequent granting of visas. We had heard stories, sad ones, of people who had all their papers in order, but whose visas had been refused because they were medically unfit. An acquaintance of ours had, to everyone's astonishment, been refused a visa on such grounds. Her excitement during the medical examination had caused her to talk incessantly and her behavior was construed as highly neurotic. She was denied a visa. Her husband got his visa, but refused to leave his wife behind. The two remained in Vienna. They were sent to Poland, where they perished. Another case concerned a physician who did not get his visa. When he went home to tell his wife, to whom one had been granted, both committed suicide.

Everybody was afraid of being refused. But Jim had special fears in this matter. Could not the traces of his broken leg and spinal condition, which so ironically had saved him from several slaughters, now be the instrument of his denial? As if determined to be, as well as to appear, healthy and relatively strong, Jim stood more erectly and complained less of pain as the time for our examinations drew near. The American consulate would know nothing of his injury except what they discovered on his body.

On January 31st, the dreaded day, Jim looked marvelously well. He did not limp at all. I marveled and prayed when he went into the doctor. The examination seemed to take forever. Finally he emerged, beaming. He had passed. He was healthy enough to go to America. We had no difficulty in obtaining our visas. Our joy was indescribable.

Now that the way was certain, I took time to go to the cemetery. I sat for a long time near my mother's grave, contemplating the violent changes that had taken place since her death. I was convinced as I stood by Abram's grave, and Friedrich's too, that I would never return to Vienna to visit their graves again.

Our most vital business was settled now. Only the luggage remained to be taken care of. We had very little, really — only a few dresses, suits, linen, and bedding. After we had paid our expenses, we were rather demoralized to find that only $7.00 in cash was left to each of us. But that was all the Nazis permitted us to take along.

We were able to remain in our apartment till the end, since we had until February 28th to stay and were scheduled to leave on the 22nd. I had no regrets about leaving this once-beautiful city in which Jim and I had realized the hopes of our youth, had lived out our young love, and had been so happy. But the thought of every friend we left behind tore at us. Many, we knew, must perish.

It was especially difficult to say goodbye to the Ribers, who had been such warm and encouraging roomers, to the Selingers, who because of their optimism had trapped themselves in Vienna. It was horribly apparent that it was too late for them to get out, that they were almost certainly doomed.

On Wednesday, February 22, 1940, Jim and I left our apartment. It was early in the morning and still dark. Our good superintendent carried down our suitcases and put them in a taxi.

He and his wife stood in front of the house. Both of them cried and wished us good luck. In the taxi, we sat as in a dream. Then we arrived at the station. There were many Jews there, all jubilant, as were we, to be leaving.

Josef had come down to the station to see us off. We were not the last of the whole family to leave Vienna, after all. The sight of him brought such love, such warmth to us! Was this not the same Josef with whom we had shared so much of our life, who was so close to us? This Josef could not purposely harm anyone! Ever an over-confident child, he was even now delightedly disclosing his new plans to leave illegally for Yugoslavia. He was so glad that we were leaving for America.

So it was Josef, whom we had discounted, in part, from the whole scheme of Viennese life, whom we had hardly expected to see again, who came to see us off. We embraced and wept a little. Our eyes transmitted many warm and wonderful thoughts which were somehow unspeakable now.

"Good luck, Helena—Jim," Josef called as we boarded the train.

We took our seats in the compartment. The train began to

move and, at the same time, far away on the horizon, the sun sent out the first rays, showing that a new day had begun. Gradually, the darkness of night gave way to the light of the sun, which rose higher and higher, illuminating everything. It seemed to me that we had left chaos—night and darkness with their allies, fire, torture, and murder—behind us. And in that chaos, millions of innocent humans had been left to the mercy of Hitler. I looked at Jim and knew that he was torn with the same thought. He pressed my hand and we were both silent.

Before us was the sun, announcing hope and liberty for us. There was hope to be reunited with Ingrid and Gerda. There was hope of preserving our identities, of starting a new life, however difficult, in America, a place of genuine liberty.

51

EVEN ON THAT TRAIN LEAVING VIENNA WE WERE STILL NOT safe. As long as the train rode in Austrian territory, we could still be arrested in flight, removed from the train. SS men came to the compartments and looked everyone over. They asked questions, their eyes growing narrow. As one entered our compartment, we shrank with fear. Would we be singled out for some reason? At any station along the way, we were in danger of being removed and sent to our doom. So great was our apprehension on the first phase of this trip to liberty that we took no notice of the other people in our compartment. Jim and I sat terribly still, afraid to talk and hoping to be as obscure as possible.

After a few hours of this silence, a man boarded the train at one of the stations in Styria. He, too, was silent for a while. Then he began to talk to us in broken German. He was an Italian, he told us, who had been working in Germany. His family had been left behind in Italy.

"Mussolini," he said, "wants us to have many *bambinos*, but he does not supply us with work so that we can feed the little ones. So I went to Styria for a while—the Nazis offered Italians jobs there. But I was miserable there—no use pretending. I'm on my way back to Italy, now."

He knew that we were Jewish, that we were escaping. He was very sympathetic to our lot.

"Anti-Semitism has never taken hold with the Italians," he mentioned with some pride as he held out a box of food to us.

As we conversed with the Italian, we suddenly reached the Brenner Pass—the Italian-Austrian border. Abruptly, our status changed. We were in Italy! No one would touch us here. What an enormous relief not to see any SS men at the station. Italian border customs officers boarded the train and entered our compartment, chatting cheerfully as they went about their routine. So we could breathe freely at last, human beings again. How long had we been feeling somewhat less than that?

The train route through Italian soil was colorful and pleasant. We relaxed, viewed the scenery from the train window, chatted with relative ease.

"It won't be so impossible," I thought eagerly, "to rediscover ourselves!"

Ultimately, we reached our destination—the port of Genoa. With others, we climbed down from the train. And in the station, a porter came up to us.

"Hebrew?" he asked.

Jim nodded his head. Then the porter, pointing to himself, said, "Hebrew." He shook hands with Jim and, without a moment's hesitation, took our luggage and guided us out-of-doors. In front of the station, several men were waiting. Our porter took us to one of them, who was a representative of the Committee for Refugees. This man took us to a hotel, where we were to spend the night.

It was evening now in Genoa. Jim and I, who had begun the journey before daybreak, were exhausted, mostly from the various emotions which the day had brought. In our hotel room, we sank into exhausted sleep.

The next day, the man who had brought us to the hotel, himself a refugee from Austria who worked for the Committee now, appointed himself our guide for that day and showed us about the city.

Genoa was different from the places in Italy, like Riccione, which I had visited in former times. Although it was a port city, it was less southern than what I had seen before. But it had an intensely Italian charm, too. Its old buildings with arches everywhere seemed to dominate the scene. We enjoyed strolling through the narrow, winding streets and through the decorative colonnades, and sitting peacefully in the outdoor coffeehouses. Everywhere in Genoa, people were friendly. Nowhere did we perceive a trace of anti-Semitism, although Goebbels's propaganda must surely have reached the Italian people a long time before.

We recalled the boast of the Italian stranger on our train the day before. And I remembered the scenes in Riccione, during the days when Nazism was taking hold in Germany. There, too, the warmth, the basic humanity of the Italian seemed to preclude acceptance of such notions as race inferiority. It was incompatible with their nature, somehow. And now, even with the strong alliance between Germany and Italy, Nazi insanity had been unable to take hold here. How different from Austria!

That day and the one night in our hotel was all the time we spent in Genoa. By evening, it was time to board our ship, the S.S. *Manhattan*. The sensation of embarking on an American ship was almost an exalted one. We felt that we were already on American soil, the earth we had been dreaming of so long, so persistently. Actually, the ship, as our voyage began, moved and shook fitfully, unbalancing many, even slightly alarming those whose first voyage it was. But for Jim and me the ship was a nest of security. It was an American ship. What else could possibly matter?

Soon the violent undulations ceased. The ship began to

move smoothly through the Mediterranean waters. Jim and
I stood on deck, watching the beautiful view. I saw a sizeable
strip of light far away.

"That's the coast of France," Jim told me.

From that point on, the two of us became relaxed and
truly began to enjoy the voyage. Our fellow passengers consisted of a variety of types: there were a number of refugees,
like ourselves, elated in their escape from Hitler's hell; there
were a number of Americans on board, who, having made
trips to Europe as tourists, had been trapped by the outbreak
of the war; there were non-Jewish Europeans on board for a
number of different reasons. Everyone had his own story.

Enthusiasm, however, was the prevailing spirit. We felt and
transmitted it at the same time. Every Jew present, like us,
had had his miracles. Without them, not one would be aboard.

"I'm going to enjoy this trip!" Jim declared. "Let's try to
forget the past, at least temporarily, Helena. I want to feel
human again, don't you?" he asked anxiously.

And we did enjoy the trip. The food alone was a joy. We
had not eaten so handsomely in years. The excitement of going
to another continent was entirely new to us. The people, even
with their sad histories, were wonderful to talk to, because of
their current happiness aboard the *Manhattan*.

I peered ecstatically into the water from the sun-drenched
deck.

"Look, Jim! A fish is jumping out of the water!" I exclaimed.

"That's a sailfish," Jim said.

"How did you know that?"

"Oh," Jim said shrugging, "I studied all kinds of fish at
school."

"I never knew that."

It was a small thing but it impressed me. Under stress so

long in Vienna, everything, every concern which was not essential to daily existence, had slowly vanished from our conversations with each other. The need to survive had made them absurd. Now, so quickly, slow, easy and, if one desired, insignificant talk could fill an hour pleasantly, humanly.

"Remember, Jim, how we always thought we'd go to America, but under entirely different circumstances?"

"I do. The World's Fair, wasn't it? And weren't we hoping to visit your relatives?"

"Imagine it!" I said, frowning.

Jim put his arm around me. "You know the saying, Helena? 'Man plans and God commands'."

We had reached Gibraltar and the ship had stopped. We stared like two dreamers at the Rock of Gibraltar and across at the coast of Morocco, which seemed incredibly close. Suddenly, we noticed boats sailing toward our ship. Several men in uniform boarded her. Mad excitement became rife on board. Jim and I did not know what it was all about. Other passengers explained that some spies were on board the *Manhattan*. The British patrol had been ordered to arrest them.

After the British boats had dispersed, another group of little boats sailed over to our ship. These were small Moroccan boats filled with peddlers. They formed a most picturesque scene, these men and women in their colorful outfits, offering the passengers their goods. These were mostly shawls and Moroccan fabrics. Jim and I did not have any money to spend. But the scene was enchanting.

From Gibraltar, our ship sailed into the ocean. The next day was stormy and the passengers were ill and fearful from the violent rocking. Jim and I had chosen to lie still on deck until the violent sea wore itself out. As we lay there, an older woman on the deck chair next to me spoke to a younger one, who was her daughter.

"Let's go down. I'm afraid up here," she said in Polish.

"I am not afraid," I stated suddenly, in Polish, too. "Storms don't frighten me. I've looked into the eye of danger too many times. Storms threaten less than evil people do."

The two women were delighted with my Polish, forgot their fears of the storm, and began talking excitedly to me. They lived in Philadelphia, they told me. The two had taken a trip to Poland, which was their original home, and had been trapped by the Nazi occupation. They were delighted to be returning to Philadelphia. But my Polish, which had gone unused for so long, had pleased them. They asked me to speak some more to them in Polish. Somehow, from school days in Lwow, I called to memory a number of Polish patriotic poems which I had memorized as a girl. Stirred by their enthusiasm, the words poured from me easily. They were obviously very chauvinistic, these two.

"*Polska Bedzie!*" the elder said passionately after my recitation. "Poland will exist again!"

Her ardor, the strangeness of the encounter, made my eyes fill suddenly and I turned away from the two Polish women. Our dialogue, as the ship twisted in the night, had evoked recollections of Lwow for me, of the time when we had escaped from that town during World War I. That had taken place in 1914. Now, in 1940, we were fleeing from another war. But this time, as we escaped, the extermination of our people was proceeding on the shores we had left behind us.

PART IV
New York

52

On the evening of March 4, 1940, our ship approached
the harbor of New York. Jim and I stood on deck, hours in
advance, watching for glimpses of the city which grew slowly
visible to us. Holding hands, we spoke not at all, but gazed
with a kind of awe at the illuminated skyline. That brilliant
Manhattan panorama! What thoughts, what feelings, too,
considering the nature of our arrival. Two poverty-stricken
refugees, close now, sailing past the famous Lady of Liberty.
"And we are older, now, in the bargain!" I thought wearily.
But the lights were growing brighter; we could not fail to be
excited.

After a while, Jim broke the silence with sudden enthusiasm
in his voice.

"Helena, do you remember how, when we approached
Vienna back in 1914, we both stood by the window in our
compartment, admiring the view—the lights that came from
the buildings of Vienna?"

"Did you imagine I could forget it?" I asked, squeezing
his hand. "Didn't I say, 'What tremendous buildings!'? And
didn't I swear that Vienna must be the most beautiful place in
the world, Jim?"

"My God, how long ago that seems! We were so young,"
Jim remarked, his voice tinged with uncertainty.

"I know, I know. I was thinking of that just a while ago. There's no use pretending we are the same in any way now. Imagine, we are both forty-four years old, Jim! How quickly the time went. And who could count the changes in our lives since then?"

"Well, at least we weren't separated," Jim said. "Thank God for that. So many were and won't ever meet again on this earth. Look, we must be grateful! Here we are actually arriving in America! Our children are being well-cared for, and we'll bring them here as soon as it is humanly possible, Helena. Then we'll all have a new life. You'll see!"

By now, we had reached the famous Statue of Liberty, that benevolent stone lady with the torch. We murmured in excitement, with others who crowded on deck now. She had welcomed countless oppressed since her erection, but never before refugees like us, escaping from actual barbarism.

We approached the pier. The voices on deck grew more and more excited each moment.

"If only Leon and the others are there!" I said to Jim.

"If they received your letter, Helena, they will surely meet us."

"It's so crazy, Jim, arriving in a strange country with seven dollars in your pocket, no job, and—"

"Hush!" he said, putting his arm around me. "It will all work out, you'll see. Actually, this is the best position we've been in for some time," he noted with ironic humor curling his lips.

Then we had arrived at the pier. In the wild throng disembarking and waiting, I somewhere spotted Leon. I shouted at him joyously. There beside him, with lifted, expectant faces, were Ellen, his wife, my brother Saul, and a stranger whom I assumed to be my cousin Harry, the man who had helped Saul to get the affidavits.

When we disembarked it was so strange to see Harry for the first time; he bore a striking resemblance to Leon. The group of them now waved at us excitedly. And in that reunion with dear ones, in this country so far from our origins, we could only feel rich, favored by destiny. After the embracing, the happy tears, we extricated ourselves from the crowded pier. Saul hailed a taxi and we all climbed in.

We must see the city right away. Saul was insistent that we feel the very pulse of it at once. We did not fail to be impressed by the tour he offered. It was almost too much for us, as we drove through 42nd Street and Times Square to see so much light, such swarming traffic, such mobs of people. And then, to astonish us further, Saul took us to dine at Hector's Cafeteria. Those trays of gorgeous food! Who could have imagined such abundance? It was like a fantastic dream which must surely vanish at any moment.

Later, Saul drove us to Brooklyn, to the home of Uncle Henoch. This was to be our home temporarily. They had arranged it that way, once they knew we were really coming. I had not seen him since I was a small child. Nor would I have recognized Uncle Henoch now. As he and his wife came forward to welcome us so warmly, I had to struggle to reconcile his present face with the dim one in my recollection. Although fourteen years older than Henoch, Father was much better looking with his full head of grey hair, his tall stature, and his fine square beard. Uncle Henoch was a smaller man whose fate had been more modest. He had hit upon luck only once in his lifetime—the time he had won the sweepstake which paid his passage to America. Once in the land of opportunity, he had not been among those whose phenomenal fates and fortunes were so legendary in the old country.

No, Uncle Henoch had become a factory worker when he came to America and he had remained one. He sewed pants

in a clothing plant and he was poor. But he had married a
good-hearted woman who had been a warm and undemand-
ing helpmate. They had struggled together in New York and
had raised a few children, not unhappily. Henoch and his
family lived in an area of Brooklyn known as East New York.
They had moved into this large, quite pleasant apartment
after Leon came to America. They shared the rental, and
Leon, who had a job in engineering, did rather well. The
apartment consisted of six rooms and Jim and I stayed there
for the first few weeks. Saul who worked as a baker in uptown
Manhattan, had an apartment close to the bakery.

I can't imagine what Jim and I would have done without
Leon, Henoch, and the others who welcomed us so cordially
in the foreign city. With all our enthusiasm in coming to
America, we had still been frightened, penniless, scarcely able
to speak English. That apartment was indeed a haven. Once
secure in it, I discovered that I was exhausted from the trip,
from the wondering.

I relaxed but briefly. The voices of those left behind in
Vienna reverberated in my head; requests had been made of
us, of me. I had promised the Selingers and other Jewish
friends to look up their silent sponsors, to beg, if necessary,
for the needed papers which would save them. How could one
rest with those voices echoing, at odds with the peace which
was in Leon's apartment in the borough of Brooklyn? Jim and
I did not forget how we had waited so wildly for our own
papers to arrive. These others were still there, desperate to get
out. I would do what I could.

I explained the situation to my cousin Harry. Stirred with
sympathy at my stories, he put his car at my disposal and
offered himself as chauffeur. This was a great relief. New
York was so immense, had so many parts to it, that I felt I
should never have been able to follow subway instructions.

And the addresses given me by those in Vienna took me not only to Manhattan but to other boroughs as well. My list was not short. In addition to friends and acquaintances, I traveled on behalf of a few strangers, too. Right before we had left, a few of these, hearing of our good fortune, had approached me at the *Kultusgemeinde,* each with the same supplication : would I look up this sponsor, this relative? Life itself depended on it. A word in person from someone on their behalf would surely quicken a response.

I had not refused a single one and now that I was here I did not miss a single address, either for friend or stranger. I went to each one, explained the gravity, the urgency of the situation, asking them to act quickly. In each case, I elicited a promise that they would send the proper papers immediately.

At each interview, I presented the picture as if some hope were left. I believe I conveyed that feeling. But I was far from convinced of it myself. A sense of futility nagged at me before each encounter. My God, didn't I know it was far too late for papers now? Still, I couldn't be sure; it was moral and right to assume the opposite. If those who had sought help failed to be saved, it would not be because I had failed to act for them.

Finally, these urgent missions, with Harry's help, were finished. I spent more time at the apartment now with Jim, Leon, Ellen, Henoch and the others. It would be foolish to pretend that Jim and I were suddenly happy because we ourselves were safe. How could we be? Ingrid and Gerda were in England. England was at war with Germany and anything could happen. But we were comforted by their first letters, written in response to our cables advising them that we were alive and safe in New York. They rejoiced in our survival and assured us of their own well-being.

One of Jim's first acts had been to re-establish contact with his parents and Sala Brand in Lwow, from whom we had been cut off since the outbreak of the war. In 1940, Lwow was under Russian jurisdiction. Since America was not at war with Russia, letters could be exchanged between Poland and New York.

Jim's family replied with good news. The Russians were treating the Jews reasonably well—no worse, at least, than the native Poles had and certainly better than the Nazis would. For one thing, they could keep their usual jobs; Wilhelm, Jim's brother, was allowed to continue acting in plays at the city theater. The status quo (such as it was) remained, at least for the moment. Jim's relief was vast.

But from that same Lwow, Sala Brand wrote desperate letters. She was sick with worry over Addie. Could we not, in New York, write to him? Since Holland was still free, I was able to write directly to Addie at his Utrecht address. I described our arrival in New York and told him of his mother's letter, of her deep concern for him. My letter concluded by asking for an immediate reply describing his present situation.

We were overjoyed when we received a reply from Addie. He wrote he was well. But there, in Holland, where he had been fostered up to now, a change had come into his heart and mind. He no longer wished to take advantage of his affidavit for the United States. He had always wanted to go to Palestine. Now he was convinced that he belonged there. However, he was concerned with the fate of the Jewish family in Holland which had taken him in. The fate of the Netherlands now seemed profoundly in question. Would we, Jim and Helena, transfer his affidavit to their name? I wrote to Sala, my fragile sister-in-law, conveying this latest news of her son. I hoped my letter was reassuring. But I was to hear nothing more, either from Sala or from Addie.

Now it was also possible to write to Hanna, in London, for

the first time. Our communications had been broken at her departure, for the war had broken out at just the same time. I explained to Hanna that we had not seen George here, that he had enlisted in the army and was away at camp. I assured her that Josef was alive and well. Eager to post my letter and receive her reply, I promised a more detailed account in my next letter. At the same time I also wrote to Olga.

More letters arrived from Ingrid and Gerda. They were happy in Birmingham. They enjoyed seeing Aunt Olga and Helga on Sundays. Both of their letters were full of hope and life. Our spirits rose a little when we read them.

"Still," Jim said, as he put down Gerda's letter, "when you think. . . . they could be here with us now—here they would be safer. When I think of how we couldn't wait to dispatch them, Helena."

"Could we have possibly known we'd get out alive? Did we dare to gamble the girls on that improbability?" I said, my voice rising. "Oh, why torture ourselves on that point? We did what any sane parents would do. It is terrible not to have them—perhaps worse—yes worse—for a mother than a father. But they are alive and with good people who didn't *have* to take them in. Eventually, we'll get them over here."

We knew of course that there was no prospect for doing so now. The war was going on by sea and air. The trip could have been suicide. Our boat, embarking from Genoa, had come by a safer, southern route, which would not be open to them. Then, too, had they been able to come, how could we have received them? Two penniless guests! We were not even self-sufficient. We could only hope to become so in time.

Olga's reply followed the girls'. It, too, was full of reassurance, as well as crammed with information. Things were not as bad in England as the newspapers led one to fear. The English government certainly provided protection for its people. Olga sounded well-adjusted. She accepted her role as domestic servant. She had had to accept Friedrich's death. Her son was far away in Africa. Yet she was reassuring me!

"You can't imagine, Helena, how well certain things at least have worked out. I thought it luck enough that Helga and I were to be in Birmingham. That Ingrid and Gerda should have been placed in this city, too, made me feel a bit like their appointed guardian angel. Not that either of them really needs one, mind you! The Cresswells and the Coupes are doing their utmost. But on Sundays, Helena, your daughters belong to me and to Helga. We have a weekly reunion. We go to all kinds of English places together, and I like to feel that it links the two of them to you and to Jim, somehow. We speak of everything, but the talk always ends with the subject of you two. Always you are at the fore of their thinking. Never dream that their foster parents have weaned away their love for you, their identity with you. It simply could never be! Those relationships, while extraordinary, are entirely different. Helena, dear, I know how you must be feeling, but console your longing with these facts. . . ."

So they saw each other frequently and all was well! Olga looking after my absent girls! How we pictured their Sundays, Jim and I. Olga's letter kept us dreaming for days of Ingrid and Gerda. Indeed, my sister's "facts" had consoled us. As things stood, in relation to what might have occurred, I was a fortunate mother. But late at night, when I sometimes sat alone, the yearning for my children knew no reason, no comparison to other fates; how could I reconcile myself to being apart from them?

A few days later, Hanna's first letter from London was received by Jim and me with great excitement. She described her arrival there and the events which had followed it. Hanna had been in London only a short time when her daughter,

Esther, had married a boy whose parents had emigrated there from Poland after World War I. Esther and her bridegroom had helped Hanna to furnish an apartment, out of which she rented two rooms to a boarder for whom she also cooked. In this manner she kept herself, a landlandy now. She was very pleased about Esther, who seemed very happy and fulfilled in her new married state. I smiled sadly as I read the letter. I understood Hanna's anxiety about Esther; she had misgivings about her relationship with her eldest child, even to this day.

Robert, her youngest son, she explained, was still assigned to the home of his foster parents, despite the fact that his own mother was also living in London now. This was because Hanna hardly had enough to feed herself and could not have supported him in her pitiable state. But Robert spent every weekend with her, and for this she was grateful.

When I wrote back to her, I told her all about Josef. I described his release from prison, his visits to us, his seeing us off. I told Hanna of his plans to go illegally to Yugoslavia, of his high spirits when Jim and I had seen him last.

53

DURING OUR VOYAGE AND OUR BRIEF STAY IN THE HOME OF
Leon and Uncle Henoch, Jim and I had begun to recover our
shattered nerves. Our faces, gaunt with anguish and thin from
inadequate food in Vienna, now began to fill out slightly, to
relax in expression. Jim's general condition was much improved, but his back still gave him trouble. He was not yet
fit to work. That was evident to all and particularly troubling
to Jim, who was so eager to find a role for himself now. My
brother Leon had overheard a number of Jim's complaints
about spinal pain, and one day he spoke up.

"Look, there's no point in being a martyr, Jim. There are
excellent doctors in New York. Why not see one?"

Jim flushed at Leon's suggestion and I read his thoughts at
once: where on earth would he, who had neither shelter nor
bread of his own, find the money to pay a doctor?

Leon must have known what we were both concerned with,
for he quickly added, "By the way, there are some fine public
clinics here, too. And lots of people—newly arrived, like you
and Helena—go to them. They cost nothing and I've been
told they are staffed with very pleasant doctors and nurses."

That, of course, became the plan we followed. With Leon's
help, we found the address of a clinic in Brooklyn. I went there
with Jim. The clinic doctor, who heard the history of the

404

injury in detail, gave Jim a thorough examination. The doctor was a specialist, an orthopedist. He prescribed an orthopedic belt to support the back and to relieve the pain while it continued to mend.

This belt was a great success. It was the biggest step forward —it gave the first indication that the pain might really be conquered. Jim's confidence in himself soared when for days at a time he felt something like his old self again. I saw clearly in the contrast how close he had been to giving up hope that he ever would.

In a short time, he announced his readiness. "Helena, I want to see Mr. Seidelman."

"So soon! Shouldn't you wait another week? . . ."

"No, I'm feeling quite well, quite secure about this old body," he said, smiling. "And even if the man has no job to offer me, we owe him a debt of thanks. I've only been waiting to tell him so till I could walk in the door properly."

Since this was more than half the mission, I insisted upon going along. Had Mr. Seidelman not saved my life, too? I was quite nervous as we approached the offices of the Universal Picture Company. How peculiar to confront a stranger, here in the plush offices housed in Rockefeller Center, to thank him for saving one's life! He was a living legend to us, this Seidelman. I wondered if he could possibly know that, or whether we should even try to convey it to him.

He greeted us warmly. He was obviously very pleased to see us, to meet us finally, after all the urgent communications. To our delight, he knew German and spoke it well. That made it easy for us. We expressed our gratitude for the affidavits he had sent. We thanked him for saving our lives. The conversation flowed freely enough. It did not seem to me, however, that we could possibly thank him enough.

But the man did not want excessive gratitude from us. He

was gratified enough that we were here in New York City. He and Jim went on to discuss possibilities for employment.

"Look, Mr. Hilsen. I can promise you a job, all right. But it's going to have to be very modest at first. There's the problem of your English, first of all. Until you have good command of English there will be a language barrier. Secondly, the whole arrangement of things here in New York is entirely different than at the Vienna branch."

"I understand," Jim assured him quickly, "and I don't mind if it is a humble job. I have no illusions about what to expect. All I want is certainty, a sense of direction, you understand?"

Mr. Seidelman nodded. "It may be a few weeks before an opening comes up, but I'll see that you are notified immediately when it does."

Mr. Seidelman turned to me, then.

"What do you hear from your daughters, Mrs. Hilsen?"

"Why, they are quite well, thank you—but do you know where they are?" I asked curiously.

"Indeed I do!" Mr. Seidelman replied, smiling broadly. "In England, right?"

"But how on earth did you know?" I asked, astonished.

"It's quite a story," Mr. Seidelman told us. "You see, in 1939 I was attending a convention for the company in Liverpool. There, I had occasion to meet a certain Mr. Coupe, salesman for our branch in Birmingham. We began to talk of one thing and another, and then Coupe told me about young Gerda Hilsen, who was staying in his home. You should have heard him describe her! They are so fond of Gerda. He told me about Ingrid, too. Said they were two lovely girls."

Jim and I were enchanted with the story. It was an extra dividend in the long-anticipated meeting with Mr. Seidelman.

It was also the first time we learned of his deep interest in the fate of our daughters.

We left shortly after that and walked out to Fifth Avenue. How beautiful the city seemed to us! How full of promise! We were not foolish enough to identify ourselves—even our future selves—with the wealthy and the glamorous who strolled by us; no, we were too altered for that. But it hardly seemed to matter. Jim, whose life's career had been snatched away, who had been reduced to an invalid by Nazi brutality, was to have a job somewhere in the great office building we had just left. It was something real and positive after so long. It was good enough to make us feel buoyant on that day.

Now that the job situation had been settled, I could concentrate on other matters which had been pressing on my mind. One of these was Aunt Rosa.

My mother's sister, who had emigrated to America from Przemysl when I was a child, had been living in New York all these years. How well I remembered the first real wedding I had ever seen—Rosa's orthodox ceremony with the wildly joyous dancing that followed it. It was cities ago, worlds away in my past. But I had never forgotten that colorful young Aunt Rosa or her wedding, just before she left.

I announced my plans to visit her at home. Jim, who had never known her, offered to go with me, but I insisted on going alone. First, because I was shaky about the first encounter; and second, because I wanted the adventure of taking the subway by myself, all the way from Brooklyn to the Lower East Side of Manhattan. Cousin Harry gave me directions for going there and explained to me that the most important things to remember were "Uptown—Downtown."

On the subway, I studied the people sitting and standing, and tried to guess which nationalities they originated from. What a diversity there was, just in the one car! Looking around, I noticed a man seated, absorbed in reading a Jewish newspaper. I could scarcely believe my eyes! In Vienna, even before Hitler, no one would ever have read a Jewish newspaper in a public place. As my gaze continued, I spotted another man, this one reading a Spanish newspaper. No one seemed to take the slightest notice of either of these men. I couldn't get over it.

But I was to see even more when I got out of the subway at Essex and Delancey Streets. Here, before my incredulous eyes, were Jews walking about in their traditional orthodox outfits and hats, identical to those I'd seen years ago in Lwow. I had seen them, too, in one section of Leopoldstadt, before the Nazis had come. Here on Delancey Street, these black-garbed men were like a reincarnation of those earlier places and people.

"No," I thought, with swift passion, "Hitler can never wipe out the Jews! He has done so in the countries that he dominates, but here, in America, Jewish life, even orthodoxy, continues!"

In all of Jewish history it had been the same. When, in one country, Jewish life had been extinguished, it had found life and bloomed in another country. It accounted for Jewish survival over the generations.

Delancey Street was a panorama of life. Not only Jews walked here, but Italians, Irish, and immigrants of almost every nationality. These people were as yet unassimilated, but each, in his group, seemed at home here on the Lower East Side. As I walked toward Aunt Rosa's address, I even spotted a group of gypsies. In Europe, these were an ever-uprooted people, eternally homeless. But here they apparently settled down like everyone else.

So wandering and musing, I reached 31 Lewis Street, where Aunt Rosa lived. I was very disappointed to see the number

attached to an old, damaged two-story building. I remembered
that when I wrote the address on my mother's letter, I had
pictured Lewis Street as wide, lined with beautiful houses.
But perhaps Aunt Rose, like Uncle Henoch. . .

The inside of the building contained a narrow, dark hall-
way leading to an equally narrow staircase which I climbed
to the first floor. I rang the bell and soon an aged-looking
woman stood before me. I tried to control my face. Could this
be my Aunt Rosa? But good heavens, what had I expected
after thirty-seven years, a glowing bride? Hadn't Leon, who
had visited her, told me her age? I was annoyed with myself.

"I'm Helena, your niece," I said, and I embraced this
woman, feeling close to her. Her eyes, at least, were familiar.

"Helena." she repeated, returning my hug. "No use pretending I recognize you. You were a little child when I left
Przemysl."

I nodded, "I've never forgotten you, Aunt Rosa. The picture of your youth, your wedding, made such an impression
on me."

"Really?" She laughed. "It was so long ago, and you, I
know, have been through so much on your own. Leon told me."

"Yes, I've been through a lot. I've had a marriage of my
own, been separated from my two children, have emigrated
here, like you, finally. But of all those memories which the
mind retains out of the greater number it loses, your wedding
day, for some reason, has stayed with me. You know, I can
recall the song. . . ."

"The song?" she asked curiously. "What song?"

I started to sing thinly: "Brother, hitch the horses and run
after the young years . . ."

As I sang, my aunt began to join me. The years seemed to
peel away for a few moments.

"No," sighed Aunt Rosa. "The young years won't return

again. You know, of course, that my husband and I separated a long time ago?"

I nodded, then flushed. Perhaps I should not have spoken so of her wedding day.

But Aunt Rosa saw my expression. "No, no, Helena. I'm not sensitive about it. That happened years ago. Now, of course, my children are married so I live quite alone. I, too, went through dangers in my life, but what's the use of dwelling on it?"

We spoke, instead, of Mother, who had loved all of her family so much. Rosa spoke nostalgically of their girlhood, then of Mother's character as it had been maintained through the years.

"Even here in America, Helena, whomever I met who knew her from the other side praised her as a good woman, a pious woman."

I told Rosa about Mother's insight during the time her health was failing, described her apprehension about the Nazis which we younger ones ignored. I left out much, of course. No point in going into the business venture which Mother feared, no use to tell her all about Hanna and Josef, Olga and Friedrich.

Soon it was time to rush home. I had stayed longer than I planned to. I rose and pressed her hand.

"I'll come to see you again, Aunt Rosa."

Outside, it was beginning to get dark. But I found my way back with no difficulty. At Canal Street, where I had to change, a woman who had no foreign accent asked me directions. I was able to show her the right train, which amused me greatly. I had been in New York for three weeks.

When I reached home, Jim was terribly excited.

"I've been so worried. I thought you were surely lost on that maze of subways, Helena!"

"No, indeed. I had a wonderful trip. And that Lower East

Side! What an international place. It was extraordinary!"

And I began to describe what I had seen there. Harry overheard me.

"So you liked the East Side, Helena? I'll tell you what. Next
Sunday, I'm going to take you and Jim on a tour. You'll want
to see more of New York now."

Cousin Harry's tour the following Sunday began with
driving from Brooklyn to Manhattan. He drove us through
Prospect Park, over the Manhattan Bridge, and through the
Bowery. Then he showed us Chinatown. Jim and I viewed
this settlement—so completely Oriental, with its own shops and
people, some even in native dress—with astonishment.

"How is Chinatown regarded by the native Americans?"
Jim asked.

"Oh, everybody loves Chinatown. It's a novelty," Harry
answered casually.

For us, it was a wonder. Harry drove us through midtown
Manhattan, through Central Park, over into Harlem.

We looked out of the car windows curiously. "Is Harlem,
then, the Negro equivalent of Chinatown?" I asked.

"Not quite," Harry answered, frowning. "In Harlem I suppose there are many who would prefer to live outside of it,
but who cannot, for a variety of reasons. This is an area filled
with problems which even the wonderful Americans have not
yet learned to solve, Helena."

As we drove home, I said to Harry, "If Hitler ever conquered this country, he would wipe out millions. How many
would fail to be 'Aryans'?"

Harry laughed. "He will never get that powerful. So don't
worry about America. Although I must admit there is a Nazi
movement right here in New York, they aren't very strong."

"Yes," Jim said. "We heard about it in Vienna. The
Austrians of course would have one believe that the Nazi Party

in America is very strong. They even go so far as to claim that the Americans are their friends and support Hitler's aims."

"That's a lot of rot!" Harry said angrily.

"We thought it was unbelievable. But why then do the Americans tolerate such movements after seeing what Hitler has done in other countries?" I asked.

"America is a democracy, Helena. Our Constitution gives freedom of speech so that individuals can express their convictions."

"Even when those convictions teach hatred toward other fellow Americans of different faiths and colors?"

"But I told you, Helena. The Nazis are not strong here. No one intelligent pays any attention to them at all. It's not in the American temperament to be taken in with slogans— especially slogans based on hate. The American mind is a reasonable one, after all!" Harry asserted.

"Let's hope so," Jim said. "Once the Nazi Party in Austria was considered weak and insignificant, too, though. How do you know it is not quietly building itself up here, too?" Jim asked.

"Oh, really, Jim. That's preposterous! Most Americans loathe the Nazis, are terrified of them. There is simply no climate here for that kind of thing to take root. A handful of fanatics, lunatics, maybe. But the American people, as a whole? Never!"

Thus we argued back and forth, Jim and I needing much convincing, and Harry more than ready to keep his stand. We were so absorbed in the discussion that we hardly noticed when we had reached home.

54

IT WAS NOT SO EASY TO START A NEW LIFE IN NEW YORK. There were complications one had not anticipated. Here, life was much different from the one we knew even before Hitler's era. Under Hitler, there had been no life at all, only existence, a waiting period either for survival or death. Being treated as *Untermenschen* who had no right to live had left its mark; we had developed inferiority complexes which only now we clearly recognized as such. But they were there. Here, in peace and relative security, as Jim and I bgan to untangle our emotions and catalogue them, we found the complexes implanted; we could not shed them. That we were now impoverished refugees, living off the charity of relatives, did not help. I seemed to look up to every American, even the most ordinary I could see on the street, as someone on a vastly higher level than Jim or I. Each had a home of his own, a family that was all together, a job and a normal life. None of them had had the worthiness of his existence questioned, or had had to deport his children to save them from being exterminated. Now it seemed ages since we had known such a normal life. Our new role, our current adjustment, would be to work ourselves up, to become (was it even possible?) the equals of these others.

Our first step was to study the English language. We could already communicate a little in English, for we had taken every opportunity to study it in Vienna when conditions were so uncertain. Now Jim and I enrolled in a night course for foreigners in Brooklyn.

Work, which would make us independent, was the most vital point, of course. True to his work, Mr. Seidelman had seen to Jim. A few weeks after our talk, Jim received notification to report for work. As Mr. Seidelman had warned, the job was indeed modest, the salary alarmingly small. Jim would work in the accounting department of Universal Pictures. That part pleased him very much. He was so glad to work for his old company; it gave him a sense of continuity. As for his earnings, we would be able to support ourselves now, if I also managed to find a job which would supplement his. All in all, we were very grateful, once again, to Mr. Seidelman.

At home, Jim's job was a big topic for discussion. Leon and Ellen were so pleased that he had found a place for himself; Uncle Henoch, seeing Jim's relief, was delighted. Obviously, now that he would be a breadwinner once again, Jim would want to move out with me. But where? A whole apartment to ourselves was out of the question. The most we could aspire to at that time was a room. Leon and Henoch, together with their wives, held several discussions of the matter. Ultimately, they reached a decision. They would rent a larger apartment than this one, with a good extra room in it which Jim and I could rent from them. We would have kitchen privileges, and I would cook for Jim and myself. Jim and I liked the idea very much. It was comforting to remain with our close ones a while longer in this vast, strange city. Leon and Henoch found a larger apartment almost immediately and we all moved into it.

We were a surprisingly compatible group. Since the beginning, Henoch's wife had been wonderfully warm to us. As the eldest housewife present, she had made us feel literally at home, rather than like guests. Ellen, too, had taken us in readily. She and I got along well; we always had in the past, on summer vacations in Voslau, when our children were just babies, and later, too, when they were older. I had always liked Ellen so much, had hated to have my fondness damaged by her former treatment of my brother Leon.

Inevitably, I had been curious as to how their marriage was faring here in New York. They had been through so much together before they left Vienna that I had rather assumed that things would be vastly improved. And on the surface, at least, they were. Ellen seemed more polite to Leon, more deferential than she had been. It was hard to be certain of anything, of course. I had to realize that she would certainly be on good behavior while Jim and I were present in the apartment. Still, I was eager to think the best of Ellen. Perhaps, here in America, she was seeing Leon in a new light. Of all of us, only he had been able to find a job in his chosen profession right away. Engineering was a highly negotiable thing, a very specialized thing which transcended the national obstacles affecting men like Jim, for instance. I was certain that Ellen must have been impressed with that fact, certain that Leon's scientific ability, which she had somewhat disdained (for its lack of parlor-talk dazzle), must now impress her. But it was difficult to draw any conclusions. To me she was as charming as ever. Now in her early thirties, Ellen was still a beauty. Her hair was the same glossy black and her red cheeks only slightly less brilliant than when she was younger. Sometimes I thought I sensed a restlessness in her, a kind of stifled impatience which I had known in her before.

Added to that, she occasionally entertained, with Leon, a male visitor whose exact relationship to them remained a mystery to me.

Ellen and Leon had been in New York for over a year now. In that time, they had collected a few friends here — some old ones rediscovered from Vienna and a few Americans, too. But basically they were still refugees in status. It seemed to me that that status was designed to make a husband and wife cling together, designed to cast out petty differences in the need for common strength. These thoughts made me very confused about the man who came to visit Leon and Ellen, for in time it became clear that Ellen was the object of his attention.

He was a young Viennese man, very good-looking, who watched Ellen during his visits with a rather insinuating stare, as if something unspoken in the room existed between them. I tried to tell myself that I imagined this, that in any case it was none of my business.

But one night, after the man had left, my old aunt, Henoch's wife, approached me, worried and embarrassed. Indeed, she was agonized in getting the words out.

"That man—he's interested in Ellen. I think she likes him, too. And your brother . . . oh, that Leon! He just—just tolerates it!" she whispered, shaking her head.

Poor little gray woman! I had to suppress a smile at her woeful consternation, despite the sadness I felt at her information. I pressed her hand.

"Ellen has sometimes seemed flighty, Aunt. In the past it was so, too. But she and Leon have always remained together. Let us say nothing and hope for the best."

But my aunt was not so easily quieted. She was deeply disturbed over the flirtation she had seen between the two; she was annoyed at Leon for letting it continue.

A few days later, Leon and I were alone in the apartment. Leon was in an excellent mood and kept talking about Jim's good luck in finding a job with Universal. He had no doubt that Jim would rise quickly in New York, as he had in his youth in Vienna. Jim was, after all, a man of proven ability.

"Leon," I said abruptly. "Do you mind if I get very personal for a moment?"

"Not at all," my brother said, but he flushed nevertheless.

"I've been wondering about you and Ellen. It's a long time

and a world away from Vienna. The two of you were very young, of course . . . but have things changed between you? Are they better now, Leon?"

Leon stared thoughtfully at me for a moment, then broke into a smile.

"Look, Helena, why not say what you mean? It's that fellow who comes here every so often, isn't it? You think Ellen's attracted to him, is that it?"

"Well—I didn't know, really."

Leon laughed, for I was blushing now.

"You can relax about the whole thing, Helena. Really. He's a friend of mine, too, you know—not just Ellen's friend. And he's quite an interesting person. You can't blame Ellen for liking company now and then. She doesn't work—doesn't need to, with my salary and with Henry in school all day. She's delighted to have the monotony broken by a visitor or two. . . . What's wrong with that?"

"Nothing," I murmured.

"And as for our marriage," he said, looking up at me cheerfully, "it is going very well. Ellen and I understand each other, I think."

"Of course, Leon. I am reassured to hear you say so."

The truth of the matter was that I was far from reassured. But there was nothing I could do to change things for them and, indeed, I was pressured with problems of my own.

It was now my turn to go job hunting. My first thought was to utilize my knowledge of corset making, acquired back in Vienna at the *Kultusgemeinde*-sponsored course. But I soon discovered that my knowledge was of no value here in New York. They had a different method of making corsets and I could not offer the experience demanded by the manufacturers who advertised. I was advised to take a course which would teach me to work in a factory. Then I would be able to offer a real skill. This advice was gratefully taken and I enrolled in such a course at once.

My sister Mela, who had also taken the course in corsetry back in Vienna, was more successful in utilizing her skill in Bogotá. There she could apply the European methods. Not only was Mela a capable worker, but (as ever) she was an excellent business woman. In Bogotá, she found, Viennese girdles and brassieres were a novelty and in great demand. Within a short time Mela wrote to tell us that she had opened a shop of her own there and was training some of the native girls in the art of girdle sewing. Slowly Mela began to prosper in Bogotá. As for Stela, she was able to live adequately, too. Her husband was an automobile mechanic and there was a lot of work for people in that trade.

The sole complaint in Mela's letters dealt with the climate of Bogotá. Since the city had an elevation of 8600 feet, the air was extremely thin. She was troubled from time to time in adjusting to the climate. Father, who remained with her, found the adjustment impossible. Being, as she put it, an old man, he was too used to the European climate and did not seem to get acclimated in Bogotá, even with time. For the first time, she suggested that he should leave South America. No doubt he would fare much better in New York. . . . Would it be possible, Mela asked, for Jim and me to bring Father here? She would, of course, advance his passage.

Mela's request was alarming. Jim and I definitely had the impression that Father was not happy in Bogotá. But we ourselves were so new here, so unsettled, really. Nevertheless, I acted at once. I went to a cousin of Father's here in New York and sought his help. I asked him to sign an affidavit for Father, assuring him that the rest of us would be entirely responsible, of course, for Father's support. Our cousin agreed readily and all the necessary papers were supplied. Jim and I were a little nervous about his arrival; we wanted to do so much for him and there was so little we could do. One among us, however, was wild with anticipation. This was Uncle Henoch. He had not seen my father, his brother, for more than forty years.

In the autumn of 1940, my father arrived in New York. The group of us went down to the Grace Line pier to receive him. Jim and I thought he looked wonderfully well. He was smiling and hearty as we all embraced him.

"Leon, Helena, Jim, Ellen. . . . You don't know how wonderful it is to see you alive! After I left Vienna, I was crazy with worry about Jim and Helena, alone in that monstrous place. My prayers were answered!" he exclaimed.

And then he spotted Uncle Henoch, that small gray figure who had shyly lurked in the background while Father greeted his lost children.

"Henoch!" he called softly.

The two old men embraced. My father, tall and hearty though seventy-seven years of age, towered over the small and weary-looking Henoch, 14 years younger, who had been absent from him almost half a century. The two men wept on each other's shoulders.

A little later, Father described his adventure in crossing the ocean for a second time. He spoke of his brief life in Bogotá, of Port Barranquilla. The names sounded so exotic in his mouth. But to our surprise he had learned quite a bit of Spanish.

"Oh, the crossing this time—it was wonderful!" Father declared enthusiastically. "I must say people still seem to like me . . . I made a number of friends on the voyage."

"But making friends was always your specialty, Father," I teased, a remote panorama of his figure in a series of coffeehouses flashing across my mind.

It had been decided that for the time being Father would stay with the rest of us at the apartment. Uncle Henoch was happy, as was his wife, to welcome this particularly dear relative into their home.

"It is so wonderful to travel," Father said that night, nestled safely in one of Henoch's chairs. "But to live in New York—for years the city of my dreams—that is the real wonder!"

He began to tell us how for decades he had nurtured the dream of coming here.

"Way back in Przemysl," Father confided, "when I still had only two children, I was eager to emigrate to America."

"Why didn't you, Father?" I asked.

"Oh, your mother wouldn't let me, Helena. You know how women make roots."

I thought about his remarks for a moment, then stated, "It's lucky you didn't decide to leave Mother then. Otherwise where would I have been?"

Everybody laughed, perhaps Father most of all. It was good to have him here with us. He had retained his lightheartedness through all the years with their drastic changes. I did not quite know how we should all manage here, but there was not one among us who was not delighted that Father had joined us.

Mela was very happy when I wrote, informing her that Father was extremely welcome here and that he was happy. She also had some good news of her own: Schorr was on his way from Switzerland to Bogotá. After fifteen years of friendship, he and Mela were going to be married.

The news was stunning. It was completely unexpected and no one could begin to explain why Schorr and Mela (who, in fact, had never seemed explicitly lovers) had waited so long to consummate their relationship. All of us, however, were pleased. It was certainly good news. In her letter, Mela has asked that I go down to Schorr's ship, when it stopped in New York, to see him.

Father decided to accompany me. He was anxious to see his future son-in-law and Father had been Schorr's ally, even when the rest of us had disliked him. As we waited for the ship to come in, I could not avoid a moment's nervous reflection, considering my relationship to Schorr in the past. Would he remember that or hold grudges? Still, he had sent Jim and me food packages from Switzerland when we were stranded in Vienna. It was absurd to think he would resent me.

Presently, the ship arrived and Schorr's face approached us. There was not a trace of ill-will in his smile. His large frame having filled out in the intervening years, Schorr looked more manly and dashing than ever, with his confident expression and fine dark hair.

I held out the packages which this time I had brought to him (the very best we could afford) and, together with Father, greeted him as a close relative—my long-expected brother-in-law.

55

I HAD COMPLETED THE COURSE WHICH TAUGHT ME HOW TO operate a sewing machine. Again, I looked for ads in the newspapers, followed them up, was evaluated in a number of places, and rejected as too inexperienced. Finally, I was taken on in a brassiere factory in downtown Manhattan.

On the first day of the new job, I boarded the subway at rush hour. I had never done this before and was a little overwhelmed. People dashed as the rubber-edged doors closed, forced them apart, and squeezed into inches of space. Then the vehicle started and the mob within swayed violently, each groping for equilibrium. But none seemed troubled by it. I think I was more aware of this than anything. As I reached for a swinging loop, I thought, "Now I am a part of these people, really one of them."

When I left the subway I relaxed and walked to the address of my employer. I entered a very old seven-storey building which was depressing to look at. Within, there was a tiny elevator, so decrepit and overloaded that I caught my breath while it ascended. I reached my floor and walked out.

The factory itself was large and light. The sewing machines were operated by older women and by young girls. Here I found the same diversity of origin which could be seen on any subway; there were Negroes, Italians, Spaniards, and a few refugees like myself on the payroll. The experienced ones were fast on the piecework; the refugees had to be worked in.

At first I felt very strange at the factory, clumsy as compared to the others, sometimes blocking altogether on some simple task, always fearful of being too slow. Some of my co-workers seemed gruff and harsh; they made me most aware of my inexperience. But others sensed my dilemma and mumbled kindly things to me. Day by day, the walls, the machines, the faces became familiar to me, and as my work improved I grew accustomed to the factory. Before long, it seemed to me that I had been a factory worker for ages. I was used to the place; one might almost have said I was comfortable in the situation. It was merely another illustration of the rather frightening adaptability of which I and other humans were capable. In Lwow, I had lived the kind of life which was available to me and my family and had been reasonably happy there. In Vienna, my life had changed completely and I had risen to improved circumstances and accepted them quickly, as if I had never been without advantages. Under Hilter, I had become a nobody and had felt that way. Here in New York, I was a pieceworker in a factory and I was content to live the role of a simple American laborer, as if I had never known an easier life.

Indeed, my only immediate aim was to improve my skill, to be equal to the other workers, to be considered adequate. But the work was mechanical and when my anxiety over speed diminished, my mind was free to pursue its courses. I kept thinking of Ingrid and Gerda, of Hanna and Olga and Josef. I wondered often about Bernatz in Belgium, of young Addie in Holland and his poor mother, Sala. The more skill I gained at the factory, the freer I was to contemplate their fates.

In the case of Ingrid and Gerda, my thoughts were enmeshed not only with fears for their safety, but with a great sense of my own loss as well. I knew that I should be grateful that the girls were in good homes, lovingly cared for; I had

only to call to mind a desolate list of less fortunate Viennese
children to reinforce this reasoning. But reason had little to do
with an aching sensation that I carried about with me from
place to place, from day to day, rarely naming it to others.
My yearning for the sight and sound of my children was like
a physical vacuum which no substitute, no rationalizing would
fill. I came to know the sensation of it in waves, sometimes
diminished by busy labor at the factory or by momentary absorption in conversation with people. Sometimes the most unexpected word in one of those conversations would provoke my
longing, my constant heartache, and the emotion would come
over me. I wanted to shout, to protest that they belonged with
me, at my side where I could watch them grow and change—
for that was a mother's right. But I knew the futility of protest.
We had a long wait still ahead of us, Jim and I. It was something we had to live with, and in order not to appear ungrateful, we had to live with it silently, sensibly.

In addition to the ache, to the significant and forgivable
vacuum inside me, I harbored a number of other, rather petty
misgivings about the absence of Ingrid and Gerda. I would not
have admitted it then, but I was probably jealous not only of
their foster parents, but indeed of anyone who was forming
serious relationships with them in England. I was ashamed of
that feeling. Hadn't Olga assured me that we were always to
the fore of their thoughts? But how well grounded were our
images—Jim's and mine—in their minds? Did I not well know
how mental pictures faded bit by bit and were replaced by
others of the vital present? It was easy enough to assume that
I couldn't be replaced in my daughters' hearts by a foster
mother, but was that quite realistic? Surely, love given is felt
and eventually reciprocated. But good God, what did I want
— Ingrid and Gerda in a loveless environment? I juggled with
these contradictions constantly, always in private. But were

they any less than human? Were they not, in fact, the forces of reason and love at odds with each other?

The worst was that time, rather than serving as balm for the wound, tended to widen it. The longer they were away, the more of them had eluded me. The worse the war became, the thinner grew our chances for bringing them over from Birmingham to New York. To offset my preoccupation with the children, I threw myself vigorously into my daily life, reasoning that each step forward that we made somehow brought the day of reunion closer. We would have to be functioning smoothly here, if only to receive them back properly.

Jim, meanwhile, was quite happy in his new job. The change in him was remarkable. Despite the extreme modesty of his position in the accounting department, it presented something positive and concrete to him. His surroundings in Rockefeller Plaza were far more pleasant than mine in the brassiere factory, and Mr. Seidelman had told him that in time he could certainly advance. Slowly, the new circumstances worked a transformation in Jim. The awful pain, the defeat which had marked him that last year in Vienna, vanished by degrees. He stood upright again. Jim was still handsome. Daily, he rode the subway from Brooklyn to midtown Manhattan and entered the glamorous offices where he was employed. Now, in the evenings, he was more vibrant again, more his old self. Nothing could have pleased me more. With the change in attitude and prospect, his health improved constantly.

Both of us had made great progess with our English. I took a two-hour lesson every Sunday. Jim could already read *The New York Times* each day, and both of us listened to the radio in the evenings, comprehending most of what we heard. As in Vienna, our prime interest in the radio was the daily news of the war events. In May, 1940, we were alarmed with the news that the Netherlands and Belgium had been overrun by the Nazis.

"My God!" I said to Jim. "Addie, Bernatz, and the rest who 'escaped' from Vienna to those places—they're trapped now! They'll meet the same fate they would have had in Austria. Or maybe they got out. . . . Oh, Jim! Do you think so? Addie was trying to get to Palestine. And Bernatz, he's always been so clever. . . ."

In the midst of these dismal broodings, Saul telephoned us with extraordinary news. He had just received a cable from Bernatz. The day was May 8th. Bernatz had advised him that he had finally procured his visas for the United States and was embarking for New York on a ship called the *Bateau Grace* on May 15th, from St. Nazaire, France. Elated, we began to await his arrival. No one's joy at Bernatiz' cable exceeded that of my father, however. He was wild with anticipation.

But on May 20th, we read in the paper with profound shock the following item : "*Bateau Grace* sunk by the *Luftwaffe*." If Bernatz had embarked on this ship, he was surely among the drowned. And since he had cabled that he was going to take this ship, how could we reasonably doubt that he had been aboard? Still, we speculated that perhaps he had been unable to reach the ship at the appointed hour. But in that case he would be trapped by the Nazis in Brussels! In either case, everything seemed to say that Bernatz, my brother, was lost.

In desperation, I contacted the Red Cross. Wracking my brains for details, I gave them all the information we had about Bernatz. At the same time, I made an inquiry about Addie, giving his last known address in Holland. The Red Cross people promised to advise me of any information they could discover concerning these two. After that, we could do nothing but wait for an answer.

I continued to work, to sew at the factory with the other women, to speak to Henoch and the rest at home. Leon was tense with worry over Bernatz by now. The days were immeasurably long.

Finally, we received a card from the Red Cross. Addie, they had discovered, was seized by the Nazis in Utrecht. They had been unable to discover anything beyond that—either what had happened to him or where he had been taken. About Bernatz they had been unable to learn anything at all.

"My God!" I muttered. "Addie seized by the Nazis! That means only one thing—death by torture! Nineteen years old . . . he wanted so to go to Palestine. Wasn't he dreaming of a happy future there with that girl of his? Oh, they had dreams, those two. They were going to till the soil of our forefathers like free human beings." I noted Leon's ashen face, Jim's bowed head, while I spoke.

"It was the quota that prevented him from getting out in time!" I shouted suddenly. "Yes, the quota system—it's cost many Jewish lives. And Sala? She will die on the spot when she hears this about her Addie."

56

WE HAD NO WAY OF KNOWING IF SALA EVER RECEIVED NEWS
of Addie's seizure; there were no more letters from her. For
ourselves, the news of his fate, the anxiety about Bernatz and
the others, were factors that had to be lived with, assimilated
into our daily lives in New York. Here in America, the war in
Europe was the prime topic of conversation wherever one
went. People were fearful of war and the name of Hitler
inspired terror and aversion. If Hitler had admirers in the
United States, as the Austrian Nazis claimed, they certainly
were not in the majority.

Jim and I went daily to our jobs, both of which were in
Manhattan. The long ride from Henoch's Brooklyn apartment
was quite wearying and, in time, both of us wished we lived
closer to our work. Also, the apartment was quite crowded
now, with Father living there with us. He needed a room of
his own but there was none left to give him. After talking the
situation over, Jim and I decided to look for a room in Manhattan. This would simplify our commuting and would enable
Father to take over our room at Henoch's.

We looked up the advertisements in a refugee paper called
Aufbau (Reconstruction), and through them we found a room
on West 100th Street. Some refugees, like our new landlords,
made a living renting out single rooms of a large apartment to

fellow refugees. Jim and I paid a modest rental for a room with kitchen privileges.

After work each day, I did the shopping and then cooked dinner for Jim and myself. Every roomer had his specific time for using the kitchen and the bathroom. The situation was far from comfortable, adding up daily to a number of petty tensions. But this was the life of the refugee for his first years in the United States and we were grateful to have it. After all, it was pleasant to walk around the neighborhood. We could sit on benches in Riverside Park on a summer evening, breathe the summer air and watch the ships move on the Hudson River. And since there were a number of refugees, like ourselves, living in the area, there was always someone to talk to if one cared for conversation.

The Viennese refugees had a desire to reconstruct some semblance of their former life in the better days in Vienna. This fact was recognized by a Viennese man who rented a vacant restaurant on West 103rd Street and ran it as a Viennese coffeehouse. As soon as word of this place spread to our kind, it was quickly patronized and soon was always crowded in the evenings. Everybody who went there was eager to meet some former friend or acquaintance from the past. When such a meeting took place, the greeting heard was almost invariably, "Thank God! You, too, are safe here!"

Jim and I liked the new coffeehouse and took to dropping in there during our summer evening walks. It cost very little to relax over a cup of coffee there. Most of the patrons were, like ourselves, very poor and rather shabbily dressed.

One evening, however, a rather beautiful woman, dressed expensively and chicly, glided into the coffeehouse as we were sitting there, spotted us, and walked directly to our table.

"Mr. Hilsen!" she cried joyously. "Are you a fantasy or are you actually sitting there? Good heavens, it's wonderful to see you!"

Jim, who had flushed deeply, obviously recognized the lady at once. He rose and extended his hand. "Hello, Liesl. . . . I'm glad to see you got out of Vienna, too. . . . But you've never met my wife. . . ."

He proceeded to introduce me to the lady, so glamorous in this refugee corner although apparently a refugee herself.

"May I sit down?" she said to me.

"Of course. Please do."

The lady called Liesl sank into a chair at our table and surveyed Jim rather boldly. "You haven't changed much, Mr. Hilsen. You're as handsome as ever, I'm afraid," she stated, laughing a little.

"Actually I was very ill in Vienna, Liesl. You should have seen me before we left! But I've recovered rather well here."

"He was suffering for a long time," I put in.

"And your two sweet girls—where are they?" she asked.

"In England, with foster families. We hope to bring them here as soon as it is possible," Jim stated.

As their conversation progressed, I was burning with curiosity over the identity of this "Liesl" who seemed to know my husband so well, who was aware of Ingrid and Gerda, and who, for the life of me, I could not remember in the slightest.

"You know my daughters?" I asked.

"No. I don't really know them, but Mr. Hilsen used to show me pictures of them—very proudly, I might add—when I met him in a coffeehouse."

I stared at her.

"Why," she continued, "I remember when he told me you were expecting your first baby!"

Now I looked at her with astonishment. It was all so confusing, but I hesitated to ask more questions.

Liesl, who by this time had sensed my bewilderment, laughed softly and said, "You are wondering who I am? Well, I'm going to tell you my story, Mrs. Hilsen. Years ago, in sane times, I would have kept it all inside. But now, pride is not the same thing. All perspectives have changed. For some reason, it's not painful for me anymore, and I'm sure it won't hurt you to know it."

Liesl lit a cigarette and smiled at me.

"In 1926," she began, "I was extremely young, only twenty. But I had already tasted the bitterness of life. I had married even younger than that. I had chosen my husband with all the inexperience of youth, making an absurd choice, really. After a year, we had a little boy, whom I adored. But I was not to enjoy motherhood for very long. My little boy died when he was a few months old. After his death, the basic incompatibility between my husband and me started to show itself as it had never done. Our loss, instead of uniting us, drove us to loathe each other. Our scenes were ghastly; we simply could not communicate. After a while, we both agreed to a divorce.

"All this by the time you were twenty?" I said.

She nodded. "But wait, there is far more."

The waiter brought our coffee then. Liesl sipped from her cup thoughtfully while we waited for her to continue; I kept wondering what the story of her life had to do with Jim.

"After the divorce, I almost went to pieces. My nerves were shot and I was horribly disillusioned. But because I was so young, I found strength to continue in that fact alone. With so many good years still ahead of me, I was determined to find some happiness."

Liesl paused briefly to puff at her cigarette. Jim had been listening intently. He made no comment now, but waited for her to continue. It was to me that she was telling the story. Her implication at the start had been that Jim knew it from long ago. At this point something familiar began to tug at my memory, but it wasn't clear.

"And did you find that happiness?" I asked.

She shook her head. "No. I was destined to suffer even more

profoundly, in an entirely different way . . . but to keep up the story—I was determined to forget my troubles. My sister, to help, took me about to coffeehouses, movie theaters, and a variety of entertainments where I might meet people. I loved movies, as it happened, and gradually became a steady customer at the Turm-Kino, where the best pictures were shown. One time when I was there, I was struck by the appearance of a very distinguished-looking and handsome man. I found out that he was the owner of the theater and that his name was Mr. Hilsen. After that, I came to the theatre more frequently than ever. I used to take a seat in the lobby next to the manager's office and watch Mr. Hilsen going in and out of his office. I was like a moonstruck kid. Having never exchanged a word with the man, I began to fantasy a whole life with him. I felt myself to be madly in love with him. . . . Well, I didn't have the nerve to speak up. The more my fantasy about him grew, the more in awe of him I was. There was only one way to communicate : I wrote letters to Mr. Hilsen. And what letters they were! Full of passionate love. . . . What a fool I must have seemed!"

And suddenly I remembered the letters. Jim had showed them to me, years ago. How I had pitied the author! I was about to say out loud that Jim had shown them to me, but as I looked at Liesl's face, I decided against it.

"Finally," she continued, "I did talk to Mr. Hilsen. I told him everything about my past, my disillusionment. I told him I was in love with him and wanted him. . . ."She stopped briefly, this time smiling at Jim. Then she turned to me again. "Your husband was wonderful. He was very sympathetic, and managed to reject me so nicely that my dignity never suffered from it. He told me that he was already happily married, that he and his wife were expecting their first baby. Of course this new picture of his life broke my fantasy. I had simply not envisioned a family in my dreams of him. But he advised me well.

He asked me to stop coming to the theater—it would only be self-destructive. He encouraged me about my chances for making another marriage, a happy one. He put me in a positive state of mind."

"And of course," I said, "you did meet another man?"

"In time, yes. I did not forget Mr. Hilsen so quickly, even though I stopped going to his theater. But some time later, I met a very good-looking man, a gentile, who held an important position. He fell in love with me and eventually we got married."

"Thank heavens—a happy ending!" I commented, relieved.

Liesl smiled bitterly and shook her head.

"No, Mrs. Hilsen. That was not the happy ending. It is true, we were quite happy, this man and I, for the first few years. We seemed to understand each other and lived quite harmoniously. But then the Nazi party grew strong in Austria and as it bloomed there was something in its ideology that attracted my husband. Elements in him which I had never known—irrational ones—found their realization in the Nazi fever. Yes! He joined the party and became an ardent member. In no time, this affiliation became the motive for every thought and feeling he experienced. My husband transformed before my eyes. He changed from a reasonable human being into a monster full of vile slogans, all of which he believed. Of course, it was just a short time before he turned on me. Our whole past relationship, the love he had apparently felt for me, was abruptly repudiated. It was as if an entirely different man existed in the form which had been dear and familiar to me. It was a nightmare. First he called me a rotten Jewess and other names of loathing. Later, he began to strike me for being one."

"My God!" I said. "That surely was the height of your suffering."

"Of course I had to leave him," Liesl continued. "When I

could stand no more I left him and divorced him. That was in 1937. In 1938, Hitler took over Austria and the Austrian Nazis. I was lucky. I was able to leave Vienna that year and come to America. Had I stayed there after the occupation, my husband might have done real physical harm to me. He had become a vengeful monster."

"This part of your story, Liesl, I did not know," Jim said, looking sadly at the woman.

"No," she agreed. "This was after your time."

"But now," I urged her on, "you look so well. When you entered the coffee shop, I couldn't help noticing your walk, your lovely clothes. Everything about you today bespeaks well-being."

"Yes, it is true. I am well off now and reasonably happy. Here, in New York, I had made my first sound marriage, no longer young, it is true, but middle age must mean something also, no? I've been married for two years now. My husband is an American. He is wealthy and he adores me. He is a sincere and good-hearted man, and for the first time in my life, I am quite happy."

"So there is a happy end, after all," I mused.

"Yes, after all those years. But I never forgot Mr. Hilsen. You see, he was a kind of symbol for me of the desirable but unattainable man of integrity. When it became obvious that he would never be untrue to his wife, I was wildly jealous of you, Mrs. Hilsen. I considered you the luckiest woman in the world to have his fidelity. Now that I've met you, I can understand his faithfulness. I even think," she added with a twinkling smile, "that I prefer you to Mr. Hilsen."

I thanked her for the remark and we continued to examine her strange experiences, the timeliness of her departure from Vienna.

"But of course," Jim remarked, "there is no one sitting in

this coffee shop who did not have his private miracle. Without them, not a single one would be here."

When we parted from Liesl on that strange evening, we promised to meet again in this place. The incident excited my imagination for days, bringing on a reconsideration of topics I had considered romantic and superfluous for some time now.

57

It was now the summer of 1940. The days were hot, and by evening we sought the relief of the benches by the Hudson River. There we sat endlessly, our talk punctuated by long silences about which it was unnecessary to question each other. We lived in peace and security; this much was true. But we carried about with us an inner life which deplored the past and was fearful of the present. The fates of Addie, Josef and the Schelmans had penetrated into the movements of our lives, our thinking. Now Bernatz was forever in our minds. Although everything seemed to indicate that he had been drowned on the sunken *Bateau Grace,* I refused to believe it without official confirmation. Who could believe Bernatz gone, merely because a vessel he had boarded sank? A jolly, adventurous vision of him played continually in my mind; his bold and merry blue eyes, his lively movements, the handsome face which always seemed to command its own destiny; the full head of sandy hair, so boyish after all. No, I did not believe my brother Bernatz was dead, but I was partly afraid that he might be. And so life went on for us in New York. Since our arrival there had never been a day untouched by dread for our dear ones left behind.

In Europe, the Netherlands and Belgium had been overrun. Within those countries, Hitler's forces held the power of life and death over the Jews and any gentiles whom they chose to exterminate. France was to be next.

At this time, the people of England were in greater peril than ever before. Their stubborn and wonderful strength, their failure to fall at the very outset of the war had enraged Hitler. Furiously, he attempted to finish England in a Blitzkrieg, throwing tons of new bombs over her cities. All of this was related in the New York newspapers. Jim and I lived in an agony of anxiety over Ingrid and Gerda. They knew our terror well, and each letter from them was an attempt at consoling us. Indeed, we were consoled by the letters, but only briefly. New headlines would terrify us until the next letter. Invariably, the girls' letters were written in good spirits and were full of assurance that they were safe and well. In June, Ingrid wrote sad news: Mr. Cresswell, her foster father, had passed away. Jim and I mourned the death of this noble stranger. We had felt very close to him; he had loved our daughter and she loved him, too.

The only good news possible in those days was hearing from a dear one who had survived. Even such news of a remote friend was wildly heartening.

When my brother Saul received a letter postmarked Lisbon, it proved to be from Bernatz. The joy of the family could not be measured. It was as if Bernatz had emerged from the world beyond. Personally, I rejoiced that my intuition concerning him had been right. Bernatz simply had to be alive!

There was no explanation in his letter of his survival. These were hurried times, not made for story telling. Now, he asked Saul for a new affidavit; his old one had expired. He assured him that he was safe and well in Portugal; he would tell us more when he arrived in New York.

Saul related all the information to Jim and me, and I lost no time in seeing to Bernatz's request. Again, I sought out my father's cousin, who was wealthy enough to sign still another affidavit. And again, this cousin agreed readily and with kindness. In a couple of weeks, I gathered all the necessary papers together and sent them to Bernatz in Lisbon. Now, at least we could relax a little about him. On June 22nd, the New York papers carried shocking headlines—Hitler had launched an attack on Russia. Power-drunk now, he evidently believed that he could conquer Russia as quickly as he had the smaller European countries. The German army, we read, now marched through that part of Poland which was occupied by Russia, trampling down everything on the way to their goal.

The part occupied by Russia . . . this meant Lwow! Jim's whole family—Sala Brand—all our friends. What would become of them? Would a single one be left alive? More horror for the Jews of Eastern Europe!

With the German invasion of Russia, the emotional climate in America changed perceptibly. No foreigner could fail to feel it. Anxiety grew; attitudes were changing. In our jobs, in the park, or wherever we had a chance to speak with native Americans, the change of tone was evident. Previously, there had been a more isolationist attitude: "This is a European war. We don't want to interfere, to send our boys overseas."

Now the same people who had made these statements began to recognize the danger of Hitler's expansion as a reality which threatened them. Did not the Nazis believe in their song: "Today Germany is ours, tomorrow the whole world?" Who had believed he would get this far?

There was a fear of war; no one wanted it, of course. But there was a new determination to fight, if necessary, to protect the democracy. As the horrors of dictatorship became daily more evident, the preciousness of the home-scene became vivid in contrast. Everywhere Americans were tense now, waiting.

Europe, meanwhile, was under the fire and sword of the German army. Neighboring countries, as yet unoccupied, lived in dread of invasion.

Still there was a trickle, even at this late hour, of people lucky enough to have visas for America, lucky enough to leave Europe. America was a haven for those in peril. And our Bernatz was among those favored few who was to get out of Europe alive.

58

HITLER, ELATED WITH HIS VICTORIES, NOW BOASTED THAT HE would soon invade England by land. With a brazen strategy, the Germans hoped to weaken and cow the British in advance, to make the invasion an easy one. The aerial invasion of England tormented Jim and me with this irony: we had despatched our children to that place, thinking we ourselves were doomed. Now we were in America, the safest place of all, and the children were in danger of being killed by bombs. Yet their letters continued to be optimistic and reassuring.

In a letter from Ingrid, we read that she had been in contact with her old friend, Marianne Selinger, who was in Southampton. Marianne, with her foster parents, was very well, indeed; but the child was consumed with fear for her parents in Vienna. My hands grew cold as I read this. I had sought out their affidavits on this side; the papers had been promised. I remembered the Selinger's begging faces, before Jim and I left Vienna. And I recalled that I had known somehow that it was too late for them. Perhaps I was wrong? Perhaps the Selingers had gotten out of Austria even at that late date? At the moment, there was no way of finding out.

The *Luftwaffe* continued to bomb English cities, with greater force each time. We followed the progress of the war feverishly, in the press and on the radio, over which we listened most eagerly to the commentaries of Gabriel Heatter. He discussed the bombings that destroyed English buildings, killed English people. Yet he always concluded his program with the words: "And the sky over England is still in our hands," from which we derived some consolation and hope.

One evening, when I had left the factory, I bought the evening paper before going down the subway steps. When I glanced down at the paper, the black headline struck me like a thunder clap: BIRMINGHAM BOMBED! I clutched the railing and continued downstairs, trying not to faint. On the platform, my subway pulled in and I rushed into it, holding the newspaper.

The subway began to move, and I thought, "Ingrid and Gerda may have been killed by the bomb!" I did not feel tears running down my cheeks; I had little awareness of myself. But a man who was sitting next to me was moved by the sight of me.

"Why are you crying?" he asked softly. I looked at him and saw that he was embarrassed, that asking me had cost him something.

"May I help—in some way?" he offered.

I thanked him for his sympathy, then pointed to the headline.

"My children are there," I said simply.

When I reached home, I found Jim overwrought. He had seen the evening papers. Leon and Ellen hovered about, trembling and fearing to suggest anything. Uncle Henoch kept shaking his head and closing his eyes.

Jim and I cabled the girls at once, asking that they cable back immediately to tell us how things were with them. After that message was sent, we lived through an agonized week of suspense during which no word came from either of them. We were nearly out of our minds.

Then their answers came and we were assured they were perfectly all right. They had been unable to reach us sooner because the bombs had damaged the telegraphic equipment in Birmingham. Soon after their cables, we received letters from each of the girls assuring us again that they were alive and well.

Ingrid wrote describing her air raid experience. When the sirens had blasted, Mrs. Cresswell had grabbed her arm and the two had begun to run to the shelter. Just as they had reached the basement shelter of the house, there was an explosion. One wing of their home had been struck by a bomb. "So you see, Mommy and Daddy, we are really fine," Ingrid wrote cheerfully, "and quite safe with our good shelter." I laughed with tears in my eyes at Ingrid's naiveté.

Our worries extended to Hanna and Olga, too. We wrote to each of them, asking for immediate replies to assure us that they were still all right.

Hanna's reply informed us that Robert had been evacuated from London when it was bombed, as had many other children. Hanna herself had little fear of bombs, she wrote. She did not even bother to go to the air raid shelter when the siren blasted away. The English people were very brave and well-trained to meet the current emergencies. Morale was extremely high there. This same high morale was perceptible in Hanna's own letter.

In her letter, Olga seemed to confirm the more general information we had about England. Morale was high throughout the nation. They had little fear of German bombs. Hitler, she assured us, could never conquer such a brave people, especially with a man like Churchill at the head of the government.

So the high spirit of the British was still being maintained! This was a great consolation to us. We felt reassured. The British would never be demoralized into surrender, no matter how relentless Hitler's aim to defeat them by pouring bombs on their cities.

By the middle of June, Hitler moved forward again, with *Blitzkrieg* as the basis of his strategy, his goal to crush his enemies with lightning swiftness. We were stricken by the radio announcement that Paris was occupied. Greta, Erich, and many others who had escaped Vienna to find refuge there were destined to be doomed, after all.

Nevertheless, in the hope that Greta was still safe with the family she lived with in a small town near Paris, I wrote to her at once. But about two weeks later, my unopened letter was returned with something in French stamped on it. Obviously, Greta was no longer at this address. The unopened letter was ominous in my hand. Immediately, I contacted the Red Cross.

I inquired about Greta and Erich Schelman, giving their last known whereabouts and other pertinent information I had about them.

One day, when I came into the apartment, I found Jim sunk in gloom.

"My God, what is it?"

Seeing my terror, he quickly said, "No, the girls are all right. It's something else. A card came from the Red Cross, Helena. It gave the answers to your queries about the Schelmans. . . ."

I sank into a chair.

"They are dead," I said.

My husband nodded. "Greta, with that Jewish family she lived with, was seized by the Nazis. They were taken to an extermination camp in Poland."

"Oh my God!"

"Do you want to hear the rest?"

"What is the use of waiting for it?"

"Well, then, Erich—from Marseilles, he was sent to Gurse, a concentration camp in Southern France. From there, they assume, to Poland."

We sat in silence for a long time. I do not know what Jim was thinking, but for me the whole wild magic of our young married years, the good gay life in Vienna, were inextricably bound up with Greta and Erich. The sweet prosperity, the warmth and worldliness of those days with their velvet masked balls, their cunning flirtations—all of them were Greta's era and Erich's. How their marital conflicts had pained and confused us! And Greta's love for Erich after their divorce—what love could have been more eloquent, even robbed of its sexual role? Erich's professional decline, their mutual love of the little boy—we had lived it all with them. They were kin to us, it seemed to me there in that silent room.

Abruptly, I rose and threw myself sobbing in Jim's arms.

"What is the use of controlling oneself! If the Schelmans are dead, a little of us, Jim, has died along with them!"

Jim held me close. He tried to console me.

"But I kept thinking, Helena, after the card game, maybe Erich actually met Greta in one of those infamous places. . . ."

59

THE YEAR 1940 WAS DRAWING TO ITS END. IT COULD AC-
curately be said that Jim and I had adapted ourselves completely to the new life. Though still refugees, we were gradually
coming to feel ourselves as more and more a part of the American people. We began to reflect much of their thinking, many
of their enthusiasms. The coming election was indicative of
this. True, we were not yet citizens and neither of us possessed
the right to vote. But it was our first experience with an
American presidential election, with all its campaign fever,
build-up, speeches, and last-minute hopes. We were spectators
to the machinery of a democratic government in motion and
we found it no less than marvelous. In Europe, there had been
nothing to approximate it.

In Vienna, we had read that President Roosevelt was hated
by the Nazis. They spelled his name "Rosenfeld" to make it
sound Jewish, and they claimed that the man was mostly influenced by Jews and Negroes.

Here we saw how popular Roosevelt was. He was more than
the usual presidential figure in America. Having served two
dramatic terms already, he had taken on the proportions of a
living legend. The excitement over the election was encountered everywhere, and one person infected the next with anticipation. For Jim and me, it was a sensation to follow the election returns. We kept the radio on nearly all night, spellbound.

In the morning we were overjoyed to hear that Roosevelt had been elected for a third term.

The coming year was full of sensational events in the European war theater. Across the Atlantic, Hitler was spreading to the north, south, east, and west in his victorious drive. In those countries he had conquered, great cities were destroyed, large numbers of the population mercilessly killed, and other portions of them used for slave labor.

But for the Jews, Hitler had contrived something special. The promised extermination was now in full swing. In Austria, even with deportations to Poland, the exact fates of many who were led off to concentration camps had been only vaguely known. Rarely had any facts about them been certain once they had disappeared from our sight. But now there was wholesale news about the Polish extermination camps. They had names like Bergen-Belsen, Tremblinka, and Auschwitz. The latter was that little town we had passed, back in 1914, en route to Vienna from Lwow. Now it was the most infamous extermination camp of all, known in every corner of the world for furnaces that burned Jewish flesh, alive as well as dead. Stories of starvation, thirst, vermin-filled huts crowded with the prospective victims came through to us now, here in New York. Before now, the details had not been known. No doubt there were worse stories, as yet to be unfolded, connected with these camps. The worst stories always concerned the helpless, somehow : children so young they had not yet learned their parents' names; elderly men and women too feeble to protest their captivity.

But still one heard about Jews who tried to escape this fate. A particularly poignant report involved a group who managed to hire a flimsy boat and from Bremen attempted to cross the Atlantic. Actually, none of them had a specific destination; they had embarked only with the hope of finding a country which would take them in and save their lives. But they had

no luck, this crew. Not one country in this hemisphere would
admit them, since none of them had valid visas. Was a visa
more important than a human life? Or was this just a fiendish-
ly inopportune working of laws, perfectly just in saner eras?

When Jim and I heard that this group on the boat had been
forced to return to Bremen and give themselves up to the Nazis,
we simply could not make peace with any rationale about
quota systems. The crew had literally been tossed back to the
lions.

From Rumania, too, similar escape voyages were attempted.
Jews boarded illegal vessels and, by way of the Danube and the
Black Sea, through the Dardanelles and into the Mediterranean, tried, ultimately, to reach Palestine. One such vessel,
overloaded, sank, drowning whole families with little children
and aged grandparents. Another vessel actually reached Palestine.

When the Nazis occupied Yugoslavia in April, 1941, our
thoughts turned at once to Josef. Like a number of other Jews,
he had illegally crossed the border to that country, thinking to
save himself from the Nazis. But for the moment it was impossible to discover anything about him. Things were chaotic in
Yugoslavia now.

From time to time, Jim and I met new refugees in New
York, who had been able to come here from Italy. In 1938,
they explained, Italy had admitted those Jews who wished to
come there, as long as they could bring with them an amount
of money which would guarantee their self-support. Those who
had gone into Italy at that time had lived quite peacefully,
had been very well treated by the Italian people. Therefore,
when Yugoslavia was seized by the Nazis in 1941, Jews
streamed into Italy, illegally of course. There, the Italian
authorities, with the help of Jewish groups supported by the
American Joint Distribution Committee, opened camps for the
Jewish refugees. They were given food and were treated most

humanely by the Italian overseers. The Italians, clearly, were not enemies of the Jews.

The murder and deportation of Jews in Italy began only when the Germans became masters of Italy. And though forced by the Nazis to do their bidding, the Italians never accepted this barbarous way of treating fellow humans. On the contrary, they did much to counteract it. Many individual Italians saved Jews by hiding them in their homes, in woods, in mountains. And they brought them food. Whatever an Italian did for a Jew, then, he did at the risk of his own life. There were wonderful stories of priests and monks who hid Jews away in their remote monasteries, deep in the countryside. These sounded like fairy tales of medieval knights rescuing the innocent from a world of evil. For my part, I readily believed every story of Italian benevolence. I knew the Italian people well, I felt, and their humanity was real.

The days and weeks passed. We worked, we wrote letters, and still there was no word of either Bernatz or Josef. Then, one day, a letter came from Hanna. Hanna had heard about Josef. A man had written to her at Esther's English address— the one I had given Josef when we said goodbye to him.

This man had met Josef in Yugoslavia. The two had become friends. In Yugoslavia they had been supported by various interested organizations. They had lived poorly, but they had lived. Until the Nazis took over, they had been quite free to walk on the streets unmolested. They had been grateful for that.

When the Nazis had taken over Yugoslavia, they had not even bothered to round up the Jews there in order to send them to an extermination camp. In that country, it was simpler to shoot them down like wild animals, right in the vicinity.

At the outset of these shootings, several groups of Jews had taken it into their heads to go on foot to the Italian border. If they reached the border, they would try to pass it, illegally.

Josef, it seemed, and his friend who wrote the letter, had begun this arduous trek. But at a certain point, Josef had told the man to continue without him. He was on the verge of collapse. His spirits were very low and his shoes were torn beyond wearing. He simply could not go on. The letter to Hanna had concluded with the information that Josef, trapped in Yugoslavia, had perished.

The rest of Hanna's letter contained her reaction. It pained her terribly to think of Josef, that incorrigible optimist, at the mercy of two torn shoes, beaten in spirit at last. I read on and on and thanked God that Hanna had Esther close to her to sustain her now.

My tears, too, were goaded by the special ironic horror of Josef's death. And that night, the contemplation of years shared with Hanna's husband could not fail to coincide with our sorrow.

The only good news possible in those days was hearing from a dear one who had survived. News of even a remote friend was wildly heartening.

60

On the evening of April 17, 1941, our telephone rang. I rushed to answer it and heard a familiar voice:

"Hello, Helena! Can you guess who this is?"

"Bernatz!" I shouted into the phone. How fabulous it was to hear his voice. I was elated, but not really surprised. We had been expecting him momentarily.

"Where are you?"

"At Uncle Henoch's home," he answered.

"Already at Henoch's. Why didn't you let us know when you were coming? Jim and I would have met you at the boat."

"I did send Leon a cable," Bernatz explained, "but he never got it. A friend of mine happened to be at the pier, waiting for a relative of his own who had failed to arrive on the same ship —the *Nyassa*. He did recognize me, however, and he took me to Leon's home."

"Bernatz, you're incorrigible! An adventure at every corner, I swear you've an extra sense which keeps you always with the fantastic!"

My brother laughed richly over the wire. I felt a bit choked up thinking of my father's joy, of Leon's when Bernatz had walked into their home the night before.

"Well, I shall prove," Bernatz continued, "that I am very much alive. You can't imagine how anxious I am to see you and Jim. I want to come tomorrow . . . all right?"

450

"All right! We can hardly wait to feast our eyes on you. Please come early. Come to dinner. We've wondered and worried about you so, Bernatz. . . ."

Bernatz arrived promptly the next evening, and we did indeed feast our eyes on him. He had changed greatly since I last saw him, in May, 1938. My "baby" brother, now over thirty, was very manly, perhaps more handsome than ever. His face was deeply suntanned from the voyage and from some outdoor life which must have preceded it. His thick sandy hair was almost blonde from the sun, and his blue eyes were brilliant gazing out of that tan face.

"You don't look as if you've returned from the beyond," I remarked. "I'm afraid you look terribly well!"

But as we talked, I saw new expressions working in his face, which clearly betrayed his sufferings of the last few years. There were lines, too, engraved from anxiety.

At first there was so much to say. The three of us babbled all at once, interrupting one another, then laughing. But I had to remind him of one vitally serious fact.

"Of course you know, Bernatz, that if you hadn't insisted that I go to the American consulate and register, when you visited me, in April, '38, Jim and I wouldn't be sitting here with you now. We surely would not be counted among the living."

A serious silence came over the three of us. Bernatz flushed slightly.

"I am so glad to have been the instrument of your salvation."

"Listen to him!" I shrieked. "Well, you were one of them. I'm afraid we had a few others, too. . . . But your cleverness, Bernatz—surely it saved your own life, too?"

Bernatz settled back in his chair. "Yes. Acting according to my common sense and its dictates saved my life, I must admit, in a number of dangerous situations."

"Or is it luck—merely fate—that the three of us are sitting here alive tonight?" Jim interjected, his eyes remote.

Bernatz shrugged. "Whatever guided our destinies, Jim, it is good to be alive."

"Perhaps you can appreciate it even more than we, Bernatz. After all, you were on the other side so much longer and . . ."

"Yes. I faced death many times, Helena," my brother said softly.

"So we had feared. But now tell us your story. It is time and we deserve it. Could I ever count the hours we've been speculating about your whereabouts or your plight?"

"Where shall I begin?" asked Bernatz, smiling.

"From the very beginning. From Vienna, when you left in May, 1938."

"I warn you both," Bernatz said, leaning forward. "It will be a nerve-wracking story, an exhausting one."

"We are strong enough to hear it," Jim assured him. "We want to know what went on in Europe after we left."

Bernatz sighed. "Very well, then. When I left Vienna," he began, "I went to Cologne. From there, I went to Aachen in order to cross the border to Belgium illegally. We were a group of several friends. There was constant danger because of the German frontier patrol. Twice we attempted and did not succeed. Some fellows in our group returned to Vienna, thinking it hopeless. But two friends and I refused to give up and tried a third time. This time, we succeeded in crossing the German border by finding a different road. But this new road had led us to woods. After resting there for about an hour, we rose and began to walk. Covering several miles we spotted no sign of human life. Soon it was midday. We walked endlessly, seeing nothing but trees. We realized this was a no man's land and a dull panic began to gnaw at us. By this time we were hungry and thirsty. We could not seek help from trees. The sensations were similar to those one must feel being lost in a desert where one would inevitably perish. I turned to my friend abruptly and said, 'We've got to go away from here, no matter what is waiting for us elsewhere.' My friend felt the same way.

We lost no time. As long as we were still able to walk, we took the only road we saw, having no idea where it led. By evening, we had reached the end of the road. From afar, we saw a pale light.

"Is it a *fata morgana*—a mirage?" my friend demanded.

We walked faster, to get near this light, afraid of losing it altogether. At last we reached the place it came from—no mirage, but a little house—a Belgian border post. Exhausted, we entered it and gave ourselves up as Austrian Jewish refugees. We were prostrate with fatigue. The Belgian officer in charge was very decent. He gave us something to eat, let us revive ourselves there, and then, to our astonishment, released us onto Belgian soil. He did not have to do this, you know. We were there illegally. He risked his position in letting us go."

I nodded, but hurried him on. "So you were now on Belgian soil?"

"Yes," said Bernatz. "And from there we were free to take the next train to Brussels."

"Brussels!" Jim repeated. "And how was it there?"

"Oh, there were many refugees from Austria, from Germany, in Brussels. Jews, who had no money and were not permitted to work, were supported during this period by Hias and by certain Belgian Jews who were wealthy. There were many refugees there, like me, who only wished to stay there until their quota was due and their visas procured for the United States. I was rather unfortunate in this respect: having been born in Lwow, I had to wait two years for my quota. But the time went by, not badly. At last, on May 8th, I got my visa and immediately made arrangements to sail on the *Bateau Grace,* which I was supposed to board on May 15th."

"That's when you must have cabled Saul!" I murmured.

"But we read the ship was sunk by the Germans on May 20th.

Then we heard nothing from you! Can you imagine what we were going through?"

"I will explain," Bernatz continued. "On May 10th, Hitler invaded Belgium. At once, the Belgian police issued the order: 'All foreigners must report to the nearest police station.' Since I fell into this category, I followed the order. From the police station, we aliens were sent to a camp in Etterbeck, where thousands had already been rounded up by the police all over the country. This was not a concentration camp or an extermination camp, but a camp for prisoners of war.

"And what a variety was gathered there! There were people from Spain, from neutral countries, the Hapsburg family was present . . . but most of the people were Jewish refugees. Ironically, the Jews were considered Germans, for some ungodly reason, and, as such, enemies of Belgium. After a thorough investigation of the people in camp, they began to release some. First the Hapsburg family left, then the nationals from neutral countries. But of the Jewish bulk which remained, they released only those individuals who could show their visas to another country, not occupied by Hitler.

"As luck would have it, I had left all my documents at home. I explained to the officer in charge that I had my visa to America. He would not listen to me. But I refused to give up. The French which I had perfected some time before now stood me in good stead. In that language, I kept hammering away at the man, trying to convince him of the truth of my assertion, that I had really left my visa at home!

"I don't know whether he finally believed me or just wanted to get rid of me, but he gave me a *Laissez Passer*, to leave the camp."

"Whew!" Jim said, shaking his head.

"Those who remained in the camp," Bernatz continued, "and there were thousands of them, were put into cattle trains and sent to St. Cyprian and Gurs in Southern France."

"And your fluent French spared you from joining them?" I said incredulously.

"That," said Jim grinning, "and a fantastic amount of nerve. But go on, Bernatz."

"Once on the street," Bernatz described, "I breathed the clear air of a beautiful May day. But it was not so simple any more. I was conscious of a profound change of status now. I no longer felt myself to be a free man, and, indeed, in the usual sense, I was not. With the Belgians, I was considered a German; with the invading Nazis, I had the familiar status of the hunted Jew. Imagine the paradox! That the Belgians and French should think us inimical to them! Nevertheless, it was so, and in order to survive I had to gather all my wits about me. It was evident that I must leave Brussels at once. Fortunately, I still had, as I had claimed, my affidavit and visa to America, which miraculously lay untouched in my room. But as my grateful eyes fell on these documents, they took in some other details which had not mattered before : my passport was a German one and, further, it was marked with a J for Jew! Now I had to get busy. Wherever there was a mark pointing to either my Jewish or 'German' origins, I crossed them out with heavy ink. The passport had to be destroyed altogether. On my 'Good Conduct Letter,' which was issued by the Belgian police and attached to the affidavit, I crossed out the words '*Nationalité Allemande.*' These precautions were to save me on several occasions from either severe embarrassment or death by a firing squad."

I caught my breath audibly and Bernatz turned his charming smile on me.

"Wait!" he cautioned, and then went on. "After making my corrections, I gathered up the papers, a toothbrush, and only the barest essentials, leaving all of my possessions behind. Outside, I walked toward the railroad station.

"My first thought was to reach the train to St. Nazaire,

hoping to get to the ship—the *Bateau Grace*—in time for its scheduled departure. Actually, the hour of that departure had already come, but in a state of wild hope I imagined that they were holding the ship at the pier, waiting for the one absent passenger—me! As I walked, the streets in Brussels were desolate. No cars, street cars, or taxis could be seen on the Boulevard Adolphe Max. Then I spotted a great procession of weary people making their way like a defeated herd. Belgian police were watching them. Now I recognized them—they were my people, the group I had left. Like captive enemies, they were on their way to prison camps in St. Cyprian and Gurs.

"At the railroad station, I bought a ticket to Paris. The train I boarded was crowded with Belgian civilians who were trying to escape from Hitler's forces to the south of France. The train began to move. I tried to sit back and relax, but it was impossible. Twenty-five miles from Brussels, the train jolted to an abrupt halt and everyone had to get out. There was wild murmuring among the protests. Rumors of explanation were rife. Some said an imminent air raid was the cause of our stop. Others claimed that military transports had interrupted us. Many insisted that a search for fifth columnists was the reason. Everywhere people eyed each other suspiciously. The air was thick with distrust and uneasiness. I became alarmed, thinking of my own dubious status, so easily misinterpreted. I hardly dared to open my mouth and speak to anyone. Even with my perfected French there might be some hint of the alien in my speech. By now, everyone was out of the train, and no one knew where to go. So I joined other people on the road toward nowhere. Now that the train was emptied, I saw thousands of Belgian refugees. There were old ones, young ones, bawling infants. As we walked aimlessly on, refugees from other cities joined us, pouring into the road, thickening the tragic parade. Again, my status had changed. Wordlessly, I had become a Belgian refugee, plodding along with the other natives of this country which had sheltered me for a while. In addition to those of us who went on foot, there were cars, crammed with every thinkable item; there were bicycles packed so that they kept tipping their riders over. The scene was confusing. One became tired just watching it. But I walked on with the others.

"Then we were forced to change from this road to another one. The Belgian army soldiers pushed us onto the new one and later onto another one when the second became blocked. We kept being shunted back and forth. No one knew where we were going, but all of us wanted to go to the South of France away from the Nazis. There was a dimly held opinion that we were moving in that direction. With time, the thickening parade of refugees became a panorama of grief and anguish. As exhaustion mounted, people threw their baggage away, the cries of children were unceasing. Somewhere on this trek, I decided to trade my watch for a bicycle. My opportunity came sooner than I had hoped. Later that day, I was standing by an entrance to a farm, resting briefly. There I fell into conversation with the farmer's son. The youth was quick to realize the value of my gold watch and, since his family did not intend to evacuate, he willingly gave me his bicycle in exchange for it.

"I began to pedal with wild enthusiasm. My thought now was to somehow reach that ship with the aid of the bicycle. I couldn't move fast enough. No one could establish a pace of his own. In that chaos, not even knowing where we were driving, I had to give in, to let myself be carried along with the stream.

"After three days on the road with thousands of refugees, I learned from some others that we were now 10 miles south of Dunkirk. Actually I was lucky to have gotten this far. On the road, people were being checked by the Belgian security officers at the French-Belgian border. They were looking for spies. Had I not blotted out the German aspect of my affidavit, I would inevitably have faced a firing squad at any of those points.

"Then I was sitting with a group. We were resting briefly.

I had not eaten anything for two days. The parade of weary people passed us as we sat there, filling us with sadness. Suddenly, I heard women's voices shouting terribly. I turned my face to the direction of the noise and witnessed the most horrible scene. Two mothers were fighting over a dirty carrot they had found in the field. Each wanted it for her hungry child."

"Terrible. . ." I interrupted, and a chill went over my body.

"Yes," Bernatz nodded. "I'll never forget that scene. But those things come about easily when a people is suddenly uprooted. After a while, I got on my bike again and joined the others in the drive toward the south. Suddenly, we were blocked by a stream of other refugees, coming from the South! Excitedly, they were telling our group not to continue; they were just fleeing the Germans who were moving toward the north! Our group, in turn, advised them that the Germans were coming from the north. A wild confusion was set up. The people were desperate. Where to move, what to do! Then abruptly, from nowhere, we heard machine gun fire. It came from not far away. Instinctively, I threw myself down in a nearby pit. The shooting became more intense and was closer. Then there was silence for a while. I crawled up out of my hole. What a sight was before me! Dead bodies of young and old were scattered all over the field near the road. Some, alive, were running madly to seek cover. Then, to my horror, I saw German tanks and cars with swastikas coming in our direction. Then officers, mounted on them, spoke to the mob. Everyone was ordered to return at once to their homes. By now it had become evident that we were right in the midst of the battle of Dunkirk, which had fallen to the Nazis. As the officers' voices droned on, I turned away to think for a moment. Incredulously, I heard a curiously familiar voice call joyfully, 'Bernatzi!'

"When I raised my face, I thought my heart would turn to stone. One of the Nazi officers was running toward me with

happy recognition and I saw that he was a classmate of mine
from Vienna.

" 'Bernatzi!' he repeated, clutching my shoulder warmly. I
was so paralyzed with fear that I can't remember how I
answered him. He was gone in a second, having pressed a
package of cigarettes into my hand. I was afraid to lift my
head. That Bernatzi had sounded fearfully like *Nazi,* and
which of these poor Belgian refugees would stop to believe that
I was not a spy after that warm greeting from a German
officer? But, miraculously, no one had seen, no one had heard.
The old classmate, who did not bother to remember I was
Jewish, had vanished. My Belgian comrades turned home-
ward.

"I went back to Brussels then. With Paris taken and Dunkirk taken there was no more retreat. In Brussels itself, the
Germans were drunk with their victory and ignored the civilians for the most part. This fact enabled me to start getting my
Spanish and Portuguese visa. I had kept my American visa
safe through everything. So, on my birthday, September 23rd,
1940, I crossed the French-Spanish border, en route to Portugal. I readily admit that on that day I considered myself being
born for the second time," he concluded, grinning.

As Bernatz finished his story, Jim and I felt ourselves almost
to be waking from a terrifying dream. We had followed every
word with intensity.

"Bernatz," I commented weakly, "this story is quite different from the one you told us in Voslau—your hitchhiking
adventure as a student who wanted to see Europe!"

"It is a different Europe, too," Bernatz said sadly. "The
people, life, culture, and beauty—all destroyed by the villainy
of the power-mad. . . . Thank God we're in America now and
can enjoy all this which in Europe is lost."

61

On December 7, 1941, the announcement came over the radio that Japan had attacked Pearl Harbor. On the way to work the next day, a wave of intense excitement swept over the subway Jim and I were riding. Our pulses had quickened with the rest; all around us a variety of emotions were at play. First of all, there was a sense of outrage; few had believed America would actually suffer an attack of this sort. Then there was the inevitable retaliatory spirit. On this day, wherever one went, little was left of earlier isolationism, despite the fact that young boys might prefer to continue their lives at home than go to war, or that mothers' hearts would break in sending them.

Hitler and Mussolini, true to their agreement with their Axis partner Japan, declared war on the United States. So in the end, World War II could not be avoided by the free countries, no matter how great their desire for peace. The power-madness of the aggressors reached for them all. Now the American boys had to go and fight and defend their way of life. And with them, many refugee boys I heard of enlisted, eager to fight the Nazis who had ruthlessly murdered members of their families.

Among these new young Americans was my nephew George, Hanna's elder son. Having been in the army before Pearl Harbor, George was one of the first soldiers to be sent overseas. The boy had reason enough to want to fight the Nazis. His father's death was a new and unhealed wound.

460

When George arrived in New York before embarking with his company, he came to say goodbye to us. How much he had changed since we saw him last! (My heart sank as I thought: "Have my girls changed as much?") George had grown very tall; in his khaki uniform he resembled Josef as he had looked in his Austrian military uniform in World War I. Josef in khaki, courting Hanna when on leave! Suddenly I was looking at George with Hanna's eyes and I had to turn my face quickly, so as not to depress the boy. Instead, I mustered up a hearty voice.

"How well you look, George! It seems ages since we saw you last. Here you are, an American soldier—you can fight back."

"I mean to, Aunt Helena."

"Poor Addie . . . he couldn't defend himself!"

"I think of him often . . . oh, you can't imagine how glad I am to be able to fight the Nazis out in the open, after what we went through in Vienna. I only hope I can get a hold of one, face to face and say, 'Here's a Jew who lived to fight you. You took no risks butchering the defenseless ones. But here on the battlefield, it's different. And we're going to fight you to the end.' "

Thus Hanna's boy went off to war, a soldier inspired by tragedy of the past and new-found freedom. Pearl Harbor had changed things for everyone. Now that total war was on, the hope of bringing Ingrid and Gerda over from England diminished. The crossing could be suicide now. Accordingly, there was no choice but to wait and to console ourselves with the letters they sent us. We were grateful that they were well, that their education had not been interrupted. Gerda was making good progress at school. And Ingrid had moved. Mrs. Cresswell, after losing her husband, had moved from Birmingham to Glasgow, where there was less danger from bombings. In

Glasgow, Ingrid enrolled in a commercial school to prepare herself for office work.

Three years had now passed since I had seen my daughters. And those were just the years when children change into girlhood. Ingrid was fifteen now; Gerda was thirteen. Jim and I had missed watching their development.

We received pictures from them which clearly showed how they had changed. Both had grown taller. Gerda's narrow face still revealed that seriousness, that sensitivity we knew so well, while Ingrid's photograph revealed the familiar smile on her round face. These pictures were to substitute for the presence of our girls for the time being. I carried them with me always, showed them off to the other women at my factory, glanced at them hungrily during breaks.

Since I was now a reasonably experienced worker, I changed jobs, procuring one in mid-Manhattan so that my subway connections would be easier. At about this time, Jim and I decided to move again. This time we aspired to a room with its own bath and cooking facilities.

But one day, while perusing the ads, Jim said, "Why don't we look for an apartment, Helena?"

"An apartment!"

"Oh, a very modest one, of course. We might find something reasonable. The point is, shouldn't we be preparing some sort of home for the girls when they arrive?"

An invisible tremor went over me. I had thought of this before and had rejected it.

"No, Jim. I don't want to. Not yet."

"But why not, as long as we're moving?"

I sat down beside him, staring ahead of me.

"Who knows how long it will take before they're able to come here, Jim? There's so much uncertainty before us. Between the bombs falling on England and the possibility of their crossing, I don't know which frightens me most!"

"I know," Jim said, "but we can reasonably assume that it won't be too long before they can come here. Even now, such crossings are being arranged."

"All right, then, let me add something else," I said abruptly. "I am superstitious about preparing an apartment for them in advance. Yes, I'm afraid we might challenge fate by doing it!"

Jim was looking at me with a strange expression and I laughed merely to alleviate the tension.

"How can I explain it, Jim? I'm like a pregnant woman who is afraid to buy the crib before the baby comes."

In the end, we did take just a room. It was more comfortable than our previous one and it was located on West 111th Street. This room had a kitchenette as well as its own bath. For my part, I was perfectly satisfied. When the girls came, we would rent another room for them in the same house until we found an apartment. In the meantime, perhaps we could save just a bit by paying less rent.

Our income was still very small. Jim had to work overtime on Saturdays to earn a little extra money. On those days I visited Father and the others in Brooklyn. Father had adjusted beautifully to life in Henoch's apartment. The forty-years separation between brothers had melted away in a simple and beautiful camaraderie. Perhaps Henoch's wife had made it possible, too. It would be difficult to imagine a less selfish individual than she.

Frequently, on a Saturday afternoon, I met Bernatz there also. Already having a good command of English, he was working as an assistant manager at an MGM movie theater, and he liked his job. His occupation was the same that he had had in Vienna, and that was a good break.

But Bernatz had the talent of adaptability. It is a gift that few possess. But those who have it make themselves at home in any environment. Linguistic ability is only part of it. One found Bernatz, for example, not only speaking almost perfect

English, but in no time at all possessing a command of American colloquialisms which were still quite baffling to the rest of us. He seemed to have an intuitive grasp of the American scene, of the people here, which I found amazing.

One Saturday, at Henoch's, Bernatz and I were "practising" our English together, and I teased him about it.

"You adjust almost too quickly, Bernatz!" I protested laughingly.

"Why 'too quickly'?" asked my brother, grinning.

"Well, it's a little disconcerting. The way you've picked up English, certain American habits and points of view. . . . I could never have done it!"

"Oh, it's really just a matter of confidence, Helena, confidence in one's approach to these things."

"But a special kind of confidence, isn't it? I suppose you were born with it."

"Maybe. But why should it bother you, Helena — my adjustment to life in New York?"

I took a good look at Bernatz, ignoring his teasing smile.

"I'm not really sure. But I feel almost uneasy about it. . . . Perhaps I'm afraid you're preparing for a new adventure!"

Bernatz laughed. "Certainly not," he assured me.

"No?" I eyed him dubiously. "Then why not try the biggest adventure of all? Why don't you get married, Bernatz?" I asked seriously.

"Oh that!" he said, coloring slightly. He rose and lit a cigarette. "I haven't discounted the possibility."

"No, but you don't make up your mind to do it, either," I remarked. "What about this girl of yours—the one who lives in the Bronx"

"Erna?"

"Yes, the one you brought here for dinner. She is lovely, Bernatz. I would grab her if I were you. And she is obviously in love with you," I pointed out, not mentioning that this had been the case countless times before in Vienna.

"Erna is wonderful," Bernatz agreed. "I am quite serious about her, if you want to know, Helena, more serious than I've ever been before. But even now, every time I think I'm ready to ask her, a kind of restlessness seizes me, makes me feel uncertain, not quite ready."

"You are over thirty," I reminded him, "and I suspect your wild oats have been sowed for some time. There are satisfactions within married life that cannot be found elsewhere, you know."

"I know, I know," he said softly, nodding to me.

I laughed a little.

"Maybe you are spoiled. Maybe we are all guilty of spoiling you, the baby of the family, the best looking of us all. Good Lord, the fuss we made over you! And as if that were not enough, women spoiled you, too. Yes! Since you were an adolescent, girls have been making fools of themselves over you. It's no wonder you haven't married, brother. They've made it too easy for you, I think."

At this, Bernatz protested vigorously. He was not spoiled, nor was he a confirmed bachelor. His handsome ruddy face kept grinning apologetically while he insisted.

"Prove it then," I challenged him. "Let us see what you will do about your Erna. I will await the announcement of your engagement," I stated coolly.

We left the subject at that and I went home. I knew that Bernatz had continued to court Erna after that day and genuinely hoped to hear of an alliance.

But our next news of Bernatz was to be of an entirely different nature. One Saturday, he burst into the Brooklyn apartment, full of excitement.

"I've been drafted," he announced, not without pride.

I received the information with astonishment. I hadn't

thought too much about this possibility. Now I heard Bernatz mentioning "Camp Pickett" and "basic training" to the entranced family audience.

"It's in Blackstone,, Virginia," he said.

And as I watched his beaming ruddy face, I could not help thinking, "You rascal! Saved again from the altar!" But I felt it best not to say this out loud.

Bernatz was to leave shortly for basic training. He was delighted at the prospect. I sighed with a certain resignation, for he seemed destined to be ever the adventurer. As a civilian, he had already learned what war meant. He had been caught in fire between two fighting armies. He had seen action and battle deaths. In the process of escaping the Nazis he had looked death in the face a number of times, nearly trapped through no design of his own.

In the U.S. Army, he would at least know when he was about to fight the enemy. It would mean fighting to save more lives than his own; he would help, he felt, to preserve freedom and human dignity.

Needless to say, we were immensely proud of him.

62

In 1942, THE WAR WAS IN FULL FORCE. HARDLY A SPOT IN Europe was not in danger. In spite of this, ships still crossed the ocean, bearing not only soldiers to Europe, but refugees from England to America. Those who managed to get visas at this late hour took chances willingly. Such ships were accompanied by convoys of battleships to protect them from being sunk by German submarines. But despite this precaution, some of these ships were sunk and the hopeful refugee passengers never reached the shores of New York to greet their anxious relatives.

At this time the Refugee Children's Committee in London, which had maintained a list of the children it had placed, contacted those parents who were in America now, asking if they were willing to give their consent for their children to be enlisted for a transport to the United States. Like the others, Jim and I received such a letter in regard to Ingrid and Gerda. The request for our permission set up a terrible dilemma for us. On one side, there was great and constant danger in England of the girls being killed by the bombs of the *Luftwaffe*. Then again, the danger of their being torpedoed on the ocean was just as great.

The need to make this decision was shattering. Jim and I were wildly restless day and night, discussing the two alterna-

467

tives. How on earth were we to make such a decision? The fate of our girls apparently had been placed in our hands.

"If we give our consent for the transport and they are drowned, we will blame ourselves," Jim said.

"Blame ourselves!" I repeated. "I couldn't go on living if that happened, Jim."

He nodded. "Nor do I think I could, Helena," he admitted.

Such conclusions then led us to reconsider the situation in England. But if they were killed by bombs in that country, would we not also blame ourselves for having withheld permission for the transport? The conflict was hideous to bear. Either way was filled with possible calamity, and we, who lived for the sight of them, now had to choose.

Then, just during the days when we were debating the whole issue with ourselves, we read an electrifying news item. A ship bearing a children's transport to New York had been torpedoed and sunk! The parents of those children, who had given their consent, were never to see them again on this earth. Their grief must have been unfathomable.

This news drove me nearly out of my mind. The picture of the sinking ship pursued me day and night. Once that week I was lying in bed in the dark, so immersed in fear that I could not tell—did I dream or imagine it? I saw a sinking ship. A mass of children were screaming for help. Among them, I saw Ingrid and Gerda, calling, "Mummy, help!"

I jumped out of bed and felt sweat all over my body.

"Jim, wake up . . . Jim!"

He started violently as he woke, betraying his own state.

Brokenly, I described to him the scene I had either dreamed or imagined. He pressed my hands knowingly.

"Poor Helena! But I'm hardly better off. I've scarcely slept all these nights since the letter came from the Refugee Committee."

Nevertheless, that night was the turning point. Our fear of a ship being torpedoed had finally proved strongest; we both decided not to give our consent at this time.

At the offices of Universal the next day, Jim was called into Mr. Seidelman's office. Mr. Seidelman had, since our first New York meeting, been deeply interested in the plight of our children. In this matter, as in the matter of our own flight from Vienna, Seidelman assumed a very protective role.

When Jim entered his office, he asked, "Well, have you decided? Will you and your wife give your consent for the transport?"

Jim sighed deeply. "No, Mr. Seidelman. We simply can't bring ourselves to do it."

"Good—now that you've decided, I'll be frank. I would not sign at this time myself. The situation with ships is too bad. You are wise to wait till the crossing is safer. . . . But look here, I've something to tell you. You know Daff, our sales manager?"

Jim nodded.

"Well, Daff is leaving for England in a few days, going on business. And I've asked him to look up both your girls, if possible, and to do anything for them that seems necessary."

Jim was indeed heartened by this information, and he had a long talk with Daff before the latter left for England. Jim was glad to bring the news home to me. I guess I had been a rather pitiful soul of late and he was glad for anything that would console me. Both of us were immensely gratified to have such good benefactors.

About three weeks after that, Jim came home radiant from the office one evening.

"Good news?" I asked.

"Very good," he told me. "Daff is back from England, safely, thank God."

"So soon? But don't make me wait. I'm dying to hear everything."

"Well, sit down then, Helena. It's quite a story."

"Daff had to attend to some business in Glasgow," Jim began. "And of course he knew Ingrid was living there. But first he went to our branch office there to ask Mr. Ancill, our manager, to help him contact the Hilsen children. Mr. Ancill quietly listened to this and then, without saying a word, rang the buzzer on his desk. Soon a girl came into the office and Ancill turned to Daff, saying, 'Here is Ingrid Hilsen.' Then he proceded to introduce the two."

"Ingrid has a job at Universal?" I shrieked.

Jim laughed at my outburst, nodding. "Wait, you must hear this part! Daff could hardly believe his eyes, Helena. He was expecting Ingrid Hilsen to be a child and there stood a beautiful young lady of sixteen before him. You should have heard him rave about her—so tall, such blonde, wavy hair . . . the red cheeks and fair skin! He was really impressed."

I wiped my eyes. "That we should never have seen this young lady!" I murmured, but then controlled myself. "I'm sorry, Jim. Continue, please!"

"Well, Daff, as I said, was flabbergasted. 'Are you actually Ingrid Hilsen?' he asked her, still not believing it.

" 'Yes,' Ingrid told him.

" 'But your daddy didn't tell me you were working for our company!' Daff insisted.

"Well, Ingrid said I probably hadn't received her latest letter. She told him she'd gotten the job with Universal in Glasgow by the purest coincidence. He asked her if she liked the job and she was very enthusiastic. But most of all, Helena, she wanted to know if Daff thought Mr. Seidelman would give her a job in New York when she came here. Daff assured her that he would."

"Then she is like us, perhaps? Dreaming of a reunion?" I murmured.

Jim put his arm around me. "Can you doubt it?" he admonished softly.

"No, of course not. But go on. There is more."

"I was never so proud in my life, Helena, as I stood there and heard Daff describing his encounter with our Ingrid. To think that she went through all those uncertain years and has emerged with such charm and sweetness as he described! Do you know what he said to me at the end? 'Mr. Hilsen, that encounter with your daughter was one of the most memorable experiences I've ever had. I don't think I'll ever forget the impression it made on me.' "

By this time, tears were streaming down my face. I had followed every word that Jim had uttered, had felt myself an invisible witness to the scene between Ingrid and Mr. Daff.

In a few days, a letter arrived from Ingrid herself, describing with enthusiasm her meeting with Mr. Daff, and informing us that he had promised her a New York job with Universal.

"How wonderful," she wrote, "it will be to work in the same company with Daddy! Gerda and I are so happy that you two are safe in America. We never stop being grateful for this. Only recently we heard something which was a terrible reminder. Our friend, Marianne Selinger, who as you know is with foster parents here, has not been as lucky as Gerda and me. She has received terrible news from the Red Cross. Both her parents had been deported from Vienna in 1940 to an extermination camp in Poland. And imagine! All this time, Marianne has been talking about them, planning the good times they'd have when she found them!"

So the Selingers were dead. I remembered the sense of futility I had experienced when I had helped to procure affidavits for the two of them. Intuitively, I had feared it was far too late. That fear had been justified.

Shortly after, we were to learn of the fate of still another friend. A letter came from Hanna in London. She had much to tell. George, her son, was now stationed somewhere in Europe with the United States Army. She had received a letter from him and he was all right. However, he had requested leave in order to visit his mother and this request, to Hanna's sorrow, had been turned down. At this time, Hanna was always afraid that George would be killed in combat.

"Although," she wrote, "so many of our people are daily dying the most tortured deaths, nothing seems to harden us, to immunize our feelings when a dear one is threatened. So I continue to suffer over George and will do so until the war is over and he has survived it. Just recently, Helena, I ran into a relative of Helka's. She informed me that Helka had perished in the Warsaw ghetto. The news was quite shattering, as Helka was a very vibrant girl when we knew her, with all her problems and lovers, remember?"

As if I could forget! Now, I particularly recalled the scene at my home when Helka came to say goodbye. She was departing for Warsaw in 1938, about to be reunited with her long-absent husband. How cheerful she was, her only regret that of leaving her parents and friends behind. How she had pitied all of us who had no chance to leave Vienna and escape the Nazis then! But it seemed they had caught up with her in Warsaw.

63

Mr. Daff made a second trip to England in January, 1943. And again, Mr. Seidelman dispatched him with the request to fully investigate our daughters' situation as well as the possibility of bringing them to America.

Refugee ships and children's transports continued to make the crossings to the United States. We had not heard of any sinkings for some time now. But we still could not make the decision to give our consent for Ingrid and Gerda. Before Daff left, he told Jim that he would, while in England, reconsider every aspect of helping the girls to come over safely. We simply couldn't get over his interest, his kindness to us. The comprehensiveness of his efforts in England was really clear to us, however, when Seidelman handed over the following letter from Daff to Jim.

From : Mr. Al Daff
London

Mr. J. H. Seidelman
Universal Pictures Company, Inc.
New York, New York
Dear Mr. Seidelman :

Immediately upon arrival in Glasgow, I contacted the guardian of Ingrid Hilsen. Shortly after, I questioned Ingrid very closely before indicating there was the slightest possibility of her going to America by steamer, and I found that she was exceedingly happy and very contented with her present circumstances. She is working in our office and living with Mrs. Cresswell and apparently they are quite devoted to each other. I asked the girl if she wanted to go to America and her reply was 'Yes, after the war.' I then asked her if she would go to America by steamer— providing, of course, such a thing was possible.

She said she did not mind and would go to be with her parents, but her father and mother would not give their consent to either children going by water and the guardians were specifically instructed not to permit them to do so.

I told Ingrid that there might be a possibility of getting them across by ship and that I was sure her parents would agree, but of course had to leave the matter in the air until such time as arrangements could be made. On arrival in London, I contacted Mrs. Exiner of the Refugee Childrens Movement who really has charge of the two children. Mrs. Exiner was emphatic in her statement that it was impossible to arrange an early departure. I spoke to both the Cunard Line and Furness Whithy & Co., the two companies controlling passenger accommodation on steamers, under instructions from the Ministry of War Transport. Neither shipping company could do anything and both referred me to the Ministry of War Transport itself. There I saw a Mr. Habgood who went into the matter fully but would not reach a decision without reference to a higher-up. The higher-up was in the person of Mr. A. I. Anderson, the Chief. I had a long discussion with these gentlemen and they were very definite in the statement that the two children have to take their turn. There is a list of children prepared for transportation to the United States. Since there are only one or two ships permitted to carry children or women, the trickle of passengers under this classification is a very thin one. I undertook to assume responsibility for the children on the voyage back to the United States. This had absolutely no influence on the situation because the same conditions applied, taking their turn on the list and finding accommodation once their turn arrived.

Added to the above are these changed conditions. My experience has left me a little less enthusiastic about risking the lives of these children on an Atlantic crossing. I fully understand the attitude of the parents that the bigger girl, who is 16 (and who is positively gorgeous), needs looking after. She is a beautiful blonde young lady, one of the best mannered and sweetest children I have ever known in my life, and it is quite easy to understand the anxiety of the Hilsens. I am attaching clippings from the English press which will further emphasize my point of view. . . . The children are very happy here and I personally do not recommend that there be in any rush in getting them to the United States if they have to go by surface. Money has absolutely no influence in getting them any kind of priority. The Refugee Childrens Movement is very strict in this respect, and I can assure you that the Hilsen children are up towards the top of the list and even under ordinary circumstances it should not be very many more months before their turn would come. By that time, the situation in the Atlantic will possibly be much improved.

Believe me, bringing the children to America would have been a pleasant and very desirable job if the risks involved had not been so great and the circumstances controlling their departure such that, at this time, I can see no way of overcoming them. Please tell Hilsen not to be unduly disappointed and not to worry.

The children are fine, extremely happy, and express at all times their great love and affection for their parents. The people who are looking after them are not stealing their affections away. The children are at all times anxious to be with their parents but are resigned to the fact that they must wait until the opportune moment. Knowing Hilsen, I am sure they don't want to involve the girls in any risks and I know what I am talking about when I say they should not press the matter at this time.

The American consulate here assures me that their visa can be applied for and obtained as soon as the Refugee Childrens Movement advise that the two girls are ready for departure. There are no problems involved in this matter, since, at any time after the preliminary six months, they can present themselves at the consulate and, within a few days, get their visas.

Yours sincerely,
A. Daff

Jim and I re-read the letter several times to get all the details absolutely straight. Perhaps the most exciting line had been " . . . even under ordinary circumstances, it should not be very many months before their turn would come." That line made my heart contract, brought visions of Ingrid and Gerda at the pier. It would not be long; soon, it might be safer! In any case, Jim and I had a job to do. We had to work at once toward getting them visas, in case their turn came up when we could consent to their crossing. Their visas had to be ready and waiting for them.

Since America was at war, the government had released new regulations concerning visas to foreigners, in order to screen dangerous individuals. At this time, everybody had to apply for a hearing at the State Department in Washington.

Jim and I soon received a summons to appear there and made arrangements to go.

Visiting the nation's capital was terribly exciting in itself. But I was so preoccupied and a little frightened about the business at hand that I carried away from the great city only blurred visions of the White House and a vast image that was the Lincoln Memorial.

In the waiting room of the State Department, Jim and I sat nervously before we were called to appear separately. When I entered the courtroom, I was directed to a stand which was placed before three judges. The proceedings began, and one of the judges asked me to tell my story.

Trembling, I heard the sound of my voice in the large and awesome court. It sounded strange, hardly my own, yet it rang out and continued. I told the judges how we had sent our children to England in 1939 to save them from the Nazis, not knowing what our own fate, in Vienna, would be. With good fortune, we had later been able to come to the United States, in 1940. Now, we hadn't seen our daughters for four and a half years and we were longing to have them again. Spontaneously, I drew out pictures of Ingrid and Gerda — children, as we had left them in 1939 — and handed them to the judge nearest me. Then I drew out another set of pictures, taken just recently in England. These I gave to the same man, who observed them closely, then handed them to his colleagues. Several moments of silence ensued, and I clearly saw some emotion color the faces of the three judges who measured our loss by the change in photographed faces.

In the end, it was generally conceded that the two girls posed no threat to the security of the United States. The American consulate in London was advised to grant visas to Ingrid and Gerda Hilsen.

I was glad to get home again. The Washington experience had been too exciting for me. I was in no shape to give performances in vast official halls. These days I seemed at home only with the comfortable, the familiar.

Several days after our return, Jim and I received a surprise visitor. A good looking young man in a khaki uniform stood at our door.

"Bernatz!" I shouted.

"Look at him!" Jim murmured admiringly as my brother stepped into the room.

He did indeed look the picture of a young hero. His face, the uniform, his stance all formed a brilliant picture of the eager soldier.

"I came to say goodbye. I'm going overseas," he told us.

My heart sank briefly, while I calmly told him to sit down. While Jim began to ask questions, I turned away briefly to prepare some coffee. I needed to cry but was determined not to do so.

The two men were talking while I listened. Bernatz was in good spirits, no doubt about it. He would be able to fight back now, and he liked the idea. And there wasn't a thread of fear evident in his consideration of going to the front. Bernatz had been at the front before, but he reminded us, as an absurdly trapped civilian, forced to conceal his identity. Now the fight would be out in the open! Oh, I had to admire his zeal. But I felt sorry for Bernatz. It didn't seem right to me. After escaping death so many times, it did not seem fair that he should jeopardize himself again. If only now he could have had a chance to lead a normal existence, to settle here in New York and raise a family, know contentment for once!

"I don't suppose," I ventured suddenly, "you'll be getting married before you leave?"

Bernatz grimaced and shook his head at me.

"No, Helena. How could I do that? It might mean leaving a widow—possibly an orphan, too. No, my status as a live man is far too uncertain right now."

"An expedient thought!" I teased, poking him in the ribs. Our laughter broke the sobriety of the moment, but each of us knew the fears the others had.

"Well, Bernatz, I think that is a poor reason and I'll tell you why. You are destined to live long. How many times in the past did it seem you were not alive? Yet I never believed you were dead. There is something about you that suggests survival. And now, I am equally convinced that you will come back from the war well and sound."

So Bernatz left, and we did not hear from him again for a while.

About a month later, I received a letter from Hanna, who wrote: "I was doing some housework one day when the doorbell rang. When I opened the door, an American soldier was standing before me. At first I almost screamed because I thought it was George—I hadn't heard from him in a long time. But there was Bernatz. Can you imagine my joy and surprise, Helena? He came inside. We talked and talked. We hadn't seen each other for so long, there was so much to tell! Well, this happened just before Passover, so I quickly wrote to Olga telling her to come from Birmingham and to bring Helga and Gerda. I wrote to Ingrid in Glasgow, inviting her, and then I wrote to Robert. I contacted Esther and her husband. And oh, what a *seder,* what a reunion we had! It was the most marvelous thing. You should have seen Olga's face when she first saw Bernatz! And your two daughters were hardly less thrilled—especially Ingrid, who was very impressed with her handsome uncle. It was a joyful time, Helena, marred only by the absence of George and the uncertainty of his whereabouts."

I thought my heart would overflow at the picture in my mind of that London reunion. I saw the *Pesach* table set in Hanna's modest room, the face of each dear one, the glowing expression of my two big girls.

Hanna's letter came like a gift to us that spring. Jim and I shared a wonderment that so many of my family had been spared, had come together in Hanna's London place to celebrate the Passover, a holy day commemorating the deliverance of our people from bondage.

64

By the beginning of 1943, Hitler's luck had turned. He suffered defeat in Russia and his army retreated into Polish territory. On this route, the German army did not forget about the Jews who remained in Polish extermination camps, their turns not having come up yet for various gas chambers or crematoria. The retreating Nazis made it their business to destroy as many of these survivors as they possibly could. But since they were on the run, it was not possible to continue using extermination-camp facilities. So the Nazis gathered together all the live Jews in every camp they could reach and ordered them to march at gun point in a line behind the retreating army. The fates of this group were various. Many marching in those lines were so starved and ill that they simply dropped into the Polish snow and died. Others, without outer clothing, froze. The Nazis shot as many as they could without slowing up their retreat or attracting the attention of Russian soldiers who might be nearing. A segment of the marching Jews escaped, taking almost insane chances, slipping out of line during chaotic hours, hiding in barns and woods, and occasionally in the homes of Poles courageous enough to take them in.

The important point is that the Nazis had suffered a reversal and it began to be seen in other areas. On the sea, the Allies had gained an upper hand over German U-boats and were sinking many submarines. Now too, the German cities suffered severe damage from the United States Air Force and the British R.A.F. The only thing that appeared unchanged was Hitler's attitude. From all reports, the American public could easily see that he was by no means ready to relinquish his dream of world mastery or the theory of his super-power. Therefore, no one could foresee how long the war would continue.

As the danger on the Atlantic diminished, more ships arrived with refugees from England. Soon we received a letter from the National Refugee Service on Center Street, New York. They, who were in contact with the Childrens' Refugee Committee in London, asked if we would now give our consent, for Ingrid and Gerda's turn had come; they were on a list for a transport to America.

We were more inclined to say yes this time, and we seriously considered giving our consent.

"Do we really dare to refuse it?" Jim asked. "It's taken so long for their turn to come. If we turn down this chance, there may be endless delays and complications when we finally feel the situation is perfectly safe!"

"I have thought of that," I said, nodding.

"Just imagine," Jim added, "the enormous list of refugees and children which is forming and re-forming with every change in the war. When on earth would they get this chance again?"

"I agree with all that you say, but, Jim . . . "

"Yes?"

"Let us hold our decision for yet another day."

By the next evening I was extremely tense. The moment in which I must utter decisive words was approaching. I had arrived home before Jim and I sat in a chair fidgeting. Time dragged so badly for me that I went to the clock, irritably, feeling annoyed with Jim, only to find that only ten minutes had passed since I had come through the door.

When Jim came in a few minutes later, he approached me with quick nervous steps. Poor man, he was as harassed as I!

"Helena, you're so pale," he said, touching my cheek.

"Oh, I'm just tired. I rushed home, Jim. I'd been home all day, mentally, anyhow. When five o'clock came I couldn't wait to get here, because it's in this room that we'll have to work it out. . . ."

Jim took off his coat, then sat down beside me.

"Helena, I had a long talk with Mr. Seidelman today."

I looked up. "And?"

"Well, you know how concerned he has been all along about the girls. I've never gotten over it. That he should care so much! Well, I told him about the letter, how we were faced again with the decision, and I asked for his advice."

"What does he think?" I asked, feeling my tension mount.

"He feels it would be advisable for us to give our consent now. He says all the news of ocean crossings has been good recently."

I was silent for a moment, then murmured, "I see. And what did you answer him?"

Jim laughed a little. "You really want to know? All right, I'll tell you. I said, 'Mr. Seidelman, I frankly believe my wife would have a nervous breakdown if she knew the children were en route on a ship'."

I smiled a little. "How did he take that remark?" I asked.

"He said, 'Couldn't you give consent without your wife's knowledge'?"

"Oh, no!" I interrupted, jumping to my feet. "Never do it, Jim! The girls are yours and mine and we have to share the responsibility for them, as well as the joy of being reunited. No, we must share the consequences should anything happen to them."

Jim rose and put his arm around my shoulders. "Don't worry, Helena. That's exactly what I told Seidelman. I had the same thoughts and when I pointed them out, he admitted they were quite right."

"So how did you conclude it?" I asked, sitting down again.

"We did not conclude a decision in his office. That will have to be done—as you said—in this room. But we did speak of other things. He asked me how much I was making now. I told him and he shook his head. 'Hilsen,' he said, 'that's not enough to take care of your girls.' And he's arranging for me to have a salary increase."

"Jim! How wonderful for you, for all of us. And Mr. Seidelman! His generosity to us has been a crutch at almost every crucial point!"

After this part of our conversation had been uttered, a strange thing happened. We both began to think and to speak as if the decision *had* been made. It seemed implicit somehow for us both. Within a short time both of us understood that we had clearly agreed to give our consent for the girls' passage.

What Jim had not told me, I was to learn much later, was that both he and Seidelman had agreed that I should not be told the actual date of the girls' embarking upon their voyage.

The day after our conversation, Jim and I gave our consent. Shortly after that, a letter came from Ingrid and Gerda, now in London. They told us that they had already received a notice from the American consulate to come there for their visas to the United States. The letter was full of joy at the prospect of seeing us soon. Then followed a description of their new life in London.

"We are staying, of course, with Auntie Hanna now. Yes, there are bombings here, as before, but she takes us to the nearest shelter when the sirens announce that the *Luftwaffe* is close. Don't worry, please! The shelters are so safe, deep inside subways. And the people are marvelous, always joking and laughing just when you'd think they'd all be frightened. When occasionally a house is hit, the wardens are right on the spot, working to remove the wounded and guide the others. It's all so well organized, it's almost become a routine."

At the bottom, Hanna added a few lines: "Helena, Jim, you know perfectly well I never went to the shelters before. But I don't want to risk your daughters and so I take them there without fail at the first warning. Don't worry, either of you. I am like a mother hen to them and am praying, of course, that the four of you will soon be embracing each other."

Days and weeks passed quickly. I was still immersed, physically at least, in my life at the factory. But the monotony of the work left me free to think, to wait. When would we get some definite word?

I noticed Jim becoming nervous, almost a little irritable. When I questioned him about it, he always had an excuse ready.

"You want to hear, too," I sighed. "You want to know when they are coming."

"We will be notified when Ingrid and Gerda leave England," he said. "They told us so."

"True," I conceded, never dreaming that Ingrid and Gerda were already on a ship bound for New York.

So I continued to work in this state of nerves. It is a wonder I managed to produce anything in the factory during those days. Every moment I was imagining the girls, the way they would look, the strangeness they would feel, yet the eagerness, the wild and marvelous joy we all would feel.

One morning in November, my boss approached me as I sat working.

"Helena, would you come into my office for a moment. I'd like to speak with you."

I glanced up at the man apprehensively. Was he going to fire me?

Seeing my confused expression, he blurted suddenly, "Your children have arrived from England."

I jumped up from my chair and screamed. Then I nearly fainted. My boss guided me into his office, where Jim was waiting for me. I threw myself into his arms and we both began to cry without restraint for once.

"How?" I managed to utter through my sobs, "where?"

Jim took me by the arm and gave me his handkerchief.

"Come, Helena. They are at the Hias Building on Lafayette Street."

We went out into the street and caught a taxi. We sat close together, watching the streets between us and our children peel away.

"Now tell me," I whispered fiercely. I was shaking uncontrollably.

Jim laughed. "It was simply wonderful. I was just entering my office this morning when the phone rang. Then I heard a voice saying, "Daddy, we are here!"

"Ingrid?" I asked.

Jim nodded. "That young woman of the world had simply got my number from information! I was so stunned to hear her, it was all I could manage to ask, 'Where are you?' She asked if we hadn't received a cable from Hias and I told her no. Well, Ingrid says they cabled and that she and Gerda were looking for us at the pier."

"Oh, no!" I protested.

"Helena, now don't be silly. What does it matter? They are here. Naturally they were disappointed when we weren't there, but they realized something must have kept us from knowing. They were taken with a number of other children to the Hias Building and they slept there last night. Before they went to sleep, however, they waited quite a while there. They had been told that we were cabled to pick them up at Hias."

"And to think we never received it!" I said.

"Well, finally, they were advised to go to sleep, something would be done in the morning."

"Ingrid told you all this?"

"All? Yes, *all*. Because just at that point, another voice called into the phone, 'Daddy, Ingrid and I couldn't sleep all night. We couldn't wait till the morning would come! Come soon, Daddy, and bring Mummy along.' And for the second time, I was trembling so, Helena, from the sound of a voice. It was all I could do to get over to the factory. . . .'"

Now the taxi was pulling up in front of the Hias Building. As Jim paid the driver, I glanced to think this place had housed my daughters overnight—for the past fifteen hours—while I have not even known they were accessible, right here in the city!

Jim and I entered the hall. There were a number of girls and boys walking around. Jim and I looked around, frightened because the moment had finally come, our eyes seeking Ingrid and Gerda in the group. Suddenly, two tall girls ran toward us, screaming,

"Mummy, Daddy!" They threw themselves into our arms.

I could no longer control myself at all and began to cry out loud. Jim, too, was for once unable to keep his tears back and wept with me. In a moment, all of us were crying. Through my tears of joy I kept looking at my daughters' faces, changed yet familiar, as if I had intuitively known, beyond photographs, precisely how they now looked.

Slowly, the four of us collected ourselves and walked outside together. The five years of separation in which we had lived in terror of losing our children were over. They were here now, ours again.

November 30, 1943, was, without doubt, the happiest day of my life.

Lwow

Epilogue

THIS EPILOGUE IS DEDICATED TO THE MEMORY OF SALA BRAND, her son, Addie, Jim's family, and all the martyrs of Lwow. All that remains of these people are recollections of their agony by a few survivors. Not one possesses a grave to mark his death. The information I am about to disclose was related to me by two relatives of that city who survived: Karla Brand, Sala's sister, and Fred Hilsen, Jim's brother.

Karla was Sala's youngest sister. She was a child when Sala and I were already young women, for their family, like mine, contained nine children comprising two generations. She was not part of my story because she was not of my generation. Yet someone had to survive Lwow—a handful at least. And Karla is one who did survive, who had to remain alive to describe the sufferings which the dead ones had undergone, to bear witness to the anachronism of barbarism in the twentieth century.

When the Nazis took over the city of Lwow they began to establish a ghetto. After the ghetto was formed, they took Jews out of it, singly and in groups, and designated a variety of tortures and deaths for them.

Karla lived in the ghetto of Lwow for fifteen months and knew the fate of each of her dear ones. Her initiation to that life had been severe: even in the first days of Nazi occupation, in July, 1941, the Gestapo had rounded up 1500 Jews, announcing that they needed them for labor. But Karla, who was sus-

489

picious, followed one of her relatives to the end of his walk and was witness to one of the first atrocities in Lwow. On the outskirts of Lwow, the Nazis halted abruptly by a field. They ordered one shift to lie down on the ground and the other shift was forced to jump and trample upon them until they perished. This accomplished, a second "layer" of bodies was formed, and so on until all that remained of those particular victims was a mass of flesh, blood, and dust ground into the earth of the field. This incident characterized the beginning of the Nazi occupation; thereafter, each day brought fresh agonies to the Jewish population of Lwow. Not a single family in the city was untouched.

According to Karla's account, her eldest sister was first to die among the Brands, but this sister was lucky to have a natural death. She had a heart attack when the Nazis carried her husband away. Pepa, my old confidante and co-chaperone, died with her family in the gas chamber of Belsec, an extermination camp in Galicia, north of Lwow. Another sister wanted to save her eleven-year-old son from being dragged off to "labor"; she was shot on the spot. Two Brand brothers died of starvation in the ghetto. The other two brothers and their wives and the remaining children perished in several different extermination camps.

Karla's survival in the face of the situation must be considered no less than miraculous. She saved herself and her three little children by a daring step to escape from the Lwow ghetto at night. It was September of 1942. She managed to board a train with them and rode to a little town in East Galicia. There she lived under the guise of a Polish gentile, in constant terror that her identity as a Jewess would be detected. Her husband, advised of her whereabouts, followed her soon. He, in turn, was hidden behind an old-fashioned wardrobe, and there he remained for the better part of eighteen months.

Later, the Russians were moving rapidly west and neared this town. The Nazis evacuated the civilians, and Karla, in order to maintain her false identity, was forced to take her children and go with them, leaving her husband behind. Two days before the Russians liberated this town, the man was caught when he left his wardrobe hiding place, and was shot on the spot.

After the Nazis withdrew from Galicia, Karla and her children moved to Cracow. There, in June, 1944, she was stunned to encounter Fred Hilsen, Jim's youngest brother. He, too, had escaped from Lwow. Fred knew Jim's New York address and wrote to us. That was the first we knew of the fate of Jim's family. His mother was deported to the extermination camp in Belzec. His father, with another transport, went to the Janowska extermination camp. Jim's brother Lonek was shot in the street. Wilhelm, the actor who had played at the Lwow City Theater, was sent to a prison with other Jews waiting to be shot. The wives and children of these men perished in various gas chambers, except for one of Lonek's sons, who escaped to Russia. Fred and his wife fled the ghetto and hid in the woods of Galicia, living like animals on any edible vegetation that grew there. That they did not die of starvation, cold, and sickness is another miracle.

Last of all is Sala's story. My beloved sister-in-law, fragile even in youth, did not live long enough for the Nazis to get to her personally. In the ghetto, which was rife with want and disease, she caught typhoid and began to waste away with fever. During the height of this fever, she suffered hallucinations that Addie, her long absent son, was standing by her bed. Delirious, she imagined their reunion, clawing at the air to embrace him.

In reality, Addie was not far away from her, for about this time—December, 1942—as Sala Brand's life ended, Addie was passing the city of Lwow with a transport of other Jews, who, like cattle, were carried away in packed wagons to the slaughterhouse in Belzec.

Poor, yet lucky Sala! You didn't live long enough to know the fate of your—of our—beloved Addie.